The Story of the
NORTHERN CENTRAL RAILWAY

From Baltimore to Lake Ontario

By Robert L. Gunnarsson

Greenberg Publishing Company, Inc.
Sykesville, Maryland 21784

Dedicated to my Mother and the memory of my Father

Greenberg Publishing Company, Inc.
7566 Main Street
Sykesville, Maryland 21784
(410) 795-7447

First Edition
First Printing

Manufactured in the United States of America

ISBN 0-89778-157-0

Library of Congress Cataloging-in-Publication Data

Gunnarsson, Robert L.
The story of the Northern Central Railway : from Baltimore to Lake Ontario / by Robert L. Gunnarsson. — 1st ed.
p. cm.
Includes bibliographical references (p.).
ISBN 0-89778-157-0 : $39.95
1. Northern Central Railway Company History. 2. Railroads--Middle Atlantic States—History. I. Title.
HE2791.N8333G86 1991
385'.06'574—dc20 91-36238
CIP

TABLE OF CONTENTS

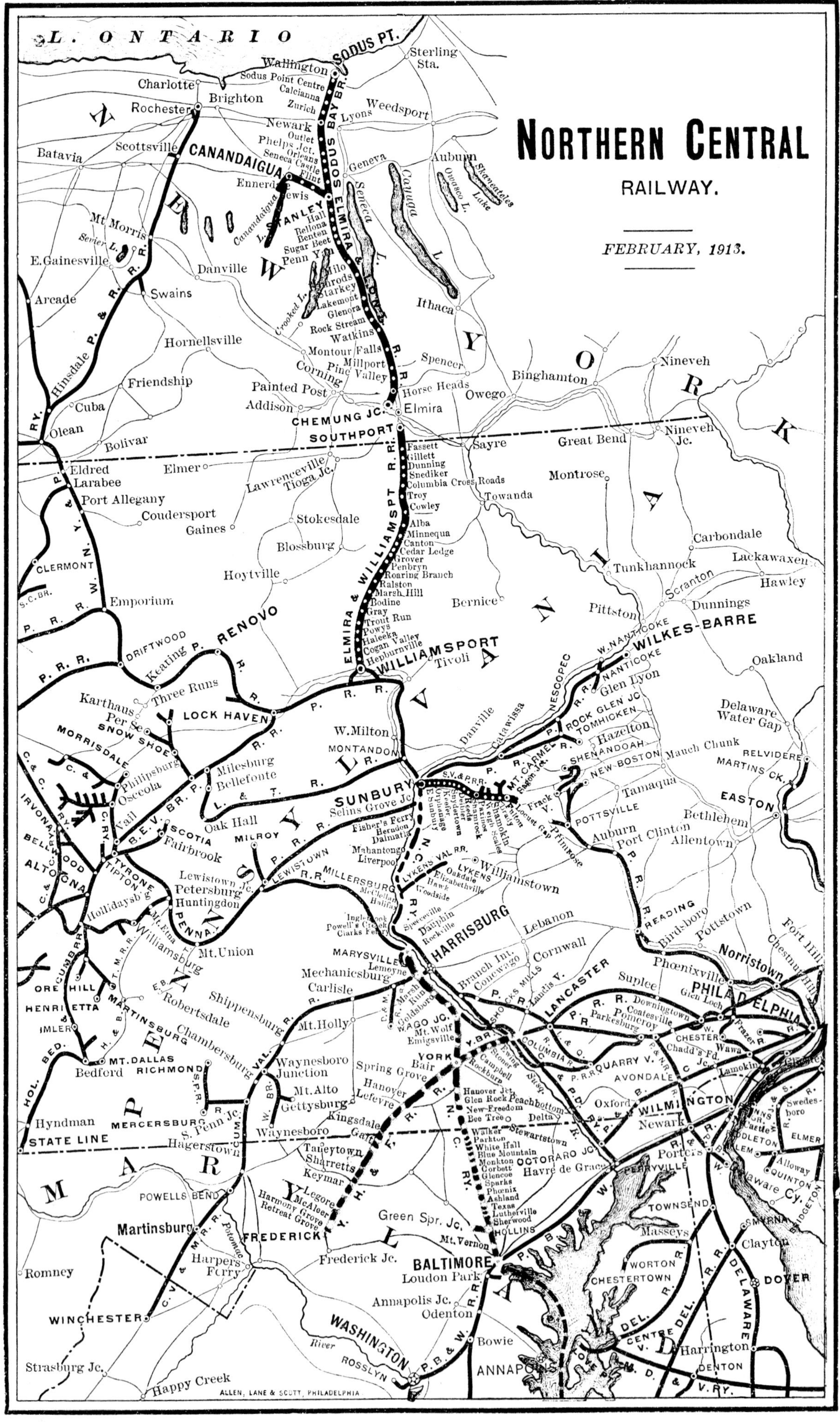

Source: Annual Report of the Northern Central Railway, 1913.

PREFACE

Recording the history of any major transportation enterprise is necessarily a complex undertaking. On one hand, it is the story of a specific business corporation, embracing all the financial, technical, marketing, and operational history of that company. But on the other hand, the subject is far wider; it includes the economic and social effects on the communities and regions which the enterprise served — and, in turn, the ways that those communities affected the fortunes of the carrier.

The story of the Northern Central Railway is typical, but it is also the story of the revolution in the character of 19th Century American life. Now mostly forgotten, the Northern Central was one of America's pioneering railroads. Its roots go back to 1828, just as the Industrial Revolution began taking hold in America. It, like all early railroads, had a significant impact on the economic and social fabric of the area it served. The small towns and industries along the line grew and prospered with the railroad's increasing abilities, achievements, and power. A century later, when trucks and automobiles began to supplant the railroads, the towns, people, and industries shifted their dependence from rail line to highway. The story is all too familiar. The railroads began to wither and die. As transportation modes and corridors shifted, so did the nature of the old "railroad towns." Industries relocated or closed; people employed by the railroads and local businesses moved away or found other work; in some cases the towns themselves began to vanish. When a railroad died, that part of American life went with it. This is a story of that process.

Researching and writing the history of the Northern Central Railway has been a challenging and arduous task. Over the years, many corporate records were lost, destroyed, or dispersed; human memories have dimmed. The records, photographs, and lithographs of the original Baltimore and Susquehanna Railroad are particularly rare and difficult to locate. Early fires took their toll; subsequent corporate mergers, office relocations, and periodic "housecleanings" purged much material and scattered the rest to private collections — some of which are accessible, some not. Enough does exist, however, to put together an accurate history of the Northern Central Railway.

The present book represents a condensation of that work. The original work, considerably more detailed and incorporating footnoted reference sources, is on file and may be made available for future research.

In conducting the research, I am indebted to many individuals, institutions, and their staffs. The personnel at the National Archives, the Library of Congress, the Enoch Pratt Library, the Maryland Historical Society, and the Smithsonian Institution's National Museum of American History were all helpful in getting me access to available records and photographs. Mr. William Gordon of Rochester, New York was instrumental in supplying photographs of the upstate portions of the railroad. Benjamin Kline, Jr. of the Railroad Museum of Pennsylvania opened up both the museum's holdings and his personal collection.

In addition, several specialists reviewed the manuscript and offered many helpful comments, corrections, and supplementary material. Christopher T. Baer of the Hagley Library in Wilmington, Delaware was generous in sharing his incomparable knowledge of canal and railroad history in the East, and particularly in the anthracite region; his help was invaluable. John McGrain contributed his expertise in Baltimore County history, particularly the area's early industries. Other experts included William D. Edson, Charles Boas, Ralph Barger, Rick Barton, and Herbert Harwood, Jr. Mr. Harwood also helped to edit the manuscript.

Many other historical societies and depositories throughout Pennsylvania and New York supplied photographs, timetables, and data. To these organizations and individuals, I remain grateful. Without their help this work would not have been possible. Their contributions are noted in the text.

As a separate operating entity, the Northern Central ceased to exist with its 1914 lease to the Pennsylvania Railroad, and this book concentrates on the period before that date. The final chapter, however, brings major parts of the story up to date. This later material is somewhat less detailed, partly because an enormous amount of material dealing with the Pennsylvania has been published elsewhere, and further research in this period would have been redundant. Also, this work is as much a history of the towns along the line as it is a purely railroad history. After the first two decades of the twentieth century the railroad's influence on these towns steadily diminished. The last chapter chronicles some of that decline.

I have striven to be as accurate as the available data permits. Dates have been checked and verified in at least three primary sources. Newspaper accounts have been carefully scrutinized. Maps and photographs are from the originals and the source is listed with the illustration. Any error or omission is my responsibility alone.

A bibliography appears at the end of the text which details primary sources and their location. In addition, several appendices of technical material pertinent to the text are included at the end of the manuscript.

Robert L. Gunnarsson
Hampstead, Maryland
1991

Publishers Note:

The route to publish a book such as ***The Story of the Northern Central Railway*** *was sometimes circuitous, but always challenging; as participants in the saga, we were impressed with Bob's research and the social significance of the story being told.*

With great appreciation to Herb Harwood for his insightful editing; to paste-up artist Wendy Burgio; and to staff artist Maureen Crum for her overall advice and design of the cover. In addition Terri Glaser, Carole Norbeck, and Donna Price provided very helpful assistance.

Linda Greenberg
Publisher

To many older railroaders and residents of the Northern Central's south end, this scene sums up the railroad: Doubleheaded Pennsylvania RR K-4 Pacifics wrestling the heavy Chicago-bound Liberty Limited through constant curves and over steady grades. The location is Lutherville, Maryland, in 1940. E. L. Thompson photograph.

INTRODUCTION

The Northern Central and the Railroad Revolution

As a distinct operating entity, the Northern Central Railway served the city of Baltimore and the states of Pennsylvania and New York for almost a century; under other names — and now in greatly diminished form — it continues to serve into the 1990s. Its history is a story of dedicated people who believed in new technology and what this technology could do for industry, commerce, the towns, and townspeople. It is the story of speculators, promoters, and scheming politicians. It is the story of industrial revolution, evolution, and modernization. It is also the story of people and the dependence that they developed on the railway. Finally, it is the story of the revolution in the shape and character of 19th Century American life. Then in the 20th Century came decline, decay, and, ultimately, a renaissance denied.

The social history of the United States from the late 1830s through the Gilded Age, and until the development of the internal combustion engine, was strongly shaped by the railroad. Its advent and the introduction of the steam locomotive brought a new standard of efficiency to transportation. No longer would commerce be crippled or slowed by the vagaries of the weather, the blockage of ice, or the muck of spring thaws. Nor would it be limited to the capacity and speed of animal power.

Americans welcomed the railroad with enthusiasm. They invested their savings, supported the promoters, and donated land for the right of way and stations. The spirit of a pioneering people, trying new technology in an undeveloped country, became contagious.

Many groups, however, remained hostile. Farmers feared the loss of a market for their horses and hay; they foresaw an increase in their insurance rates from the dangers of fire. Tavern owners protested the loss of customers. Stage lines and wagon drivers opposed any change in the status quo. Many people feared moral decay as their cloistered existence was shattered. Legislators enacted rate restrictions designed to protect the huge investments made in the canals.

In spite of these difficulties, economic demand rapidly overcame the objections. The seaport cities, in search of more distant markets, pushed the railroad further into the interior.

The railroad was an economic multiplier, and it produced enormous indirect benefits. Farmers, manufacturers, and mine owners received higher prices and expanded their market; consumers got more for their money; real estate values escalated; and the merchant, middleman, and banker increased their profits. Although there were dislocations, the entire community gained, prospered and grew.

In addition, railroads of the 1800s and the first half of the 1900s were labor-intensive. Many people were needed to operate the trains, maintain equipment and track, staff the stations and control towers, handle freight and express shipments, as well as for scores of other occupations. Not only did the rail lines bring commerce and communication to their territories, but employment as well. For example, the railroads created jobs at their own local facilities and operations, plus employment for outside freight handlers, hotel clerks, restaurant owners, and numerous service businesses and activities. Indeed, the prosperity of many communities came to depend on their railroad-related employment.

Needless to say, most communities courted the railroad companies with promises of stock subscriptions, bond purchases, grants of rights of way, and sometimes direct financial aid. When other factors were more or less equal, often it was the community that offered the most attractive financial package that received the rail service.

So as railroad fever swept the country in the second half of the 19th Century, railroad executives became substantial power brokers. They determined which community would be served, and thereby flourish; or which would be bypassed and sentenced to economic deprivation.

Two of the most important factors in those decisions were commercial goals and geography. Commercial goals determined where the railroads ultimately headed; geographic and geological characteristics determined how they got there. The Northern Central's earliest predecessor, for example, was built with the goal of linking Baltimore with the Susquehanna River valley. Once that goal was set, its route — and the choice of communities it would touch along the way — were heavily dictated by the need to find the easiest (and yet most commercially productive) path through rugged Piedmont topography.

Although the railroad brought growth and prosperity to its territory, the same, unfortunately, was not always true for its early investors. Railroading was, and still is, a highly capital-intensive industry, requiring enormous investment to buy land, build a line, and equip it with locomotives, cars, and facilities. Yet in many cases the railroads took years to reach their intended markets and, once there, more time to build enough traffic to cover these costs. Typically, too, the early railroads aggravated their problems by underestimating their construction costs and the time it would take to get into full operation. What profits they did earn had to be quickly reinvested to keep construction moving and provide more equipment for the growing business.

Thus there was little or no quick return for the investors, and some became discouraged and refused further participation — causing a capital shortage when it was most needed. Many companies had to appeal for public funds, but this sometimes turned out to be a mixed blessing, too. Governments, originally supportive, became equally disenchanted when the railroads could not meet their obligations; often they had to take civil action to recover their investments.

Undercapitalized, and with their costs exceeding their revenues, many of the small pioneering lines either went into receivership or sought stronger partners, and the long process of reorganization and consolidation began. The Northern Central's history was typical of this pattern. The company itself was created in 1855 to consolidate four small, financially-troubled lines. In turn, it was eventually controlled by the large and powerful Pennsylvania Railroad; gradually it lost its identity and became simply a segment of that system. And as the Pennsylvania's fortunes declined in the mid-20th Century, it too disappeared into the infamous Penn Central and then into Conrail. The process may not yet be complete.

This was what lay ahead as the Northern Central's first ancestor, the Baltimore & Susquehanna Railroad, began struggling northward from Baltimore into Pennsylvania. While other early seaport railroads would seek their manifest destiny building west, the Baltimore & Susquehanna would breach tradition and commence constructing a major route north. The ramifications of opening that trade artery with Pennsylvania would have both substantial and unintended consequences. The complex web of social, political, and economic pressures exerted influence on the railroad and affected the people and towns along the line.

The study of the Northern Central Railway allows a graphic and detailed look into the establishment, growth, and transition of the towns along its route. It shows how the technology of the railroad became an agent of improvement and advancement for the rural towns — and then what happened when that service declined and the institution itself withered and died.

CHAPTER 1

Background: Baltimore Seeks the Susquehanna

In the early 1820s there were only twelve cities in America with populations larger than 10,000. Not coincidentally, all of them were ports strung out along the East Coast — ports which reflected what George R. Taylor called the "extractive-commercial" character of the American economy. These ports acted as the focus for trade. Raw materials were brought there from inland points for processing and distribution to both domestic and overseas markets; finished goods and certain other raw materials came in by ship for processing and distribution in this country. The ports thus quickly became a combination of manufacturing, distribution, warehousing, banking, and service centers. The factories and shops provided both employment opportunities for the arriving immigrant and a market for the products from the nearby river town mills. These small water-powered mills began producing more consumer goods which were fed into the seaport markets. (Many of these mid-Atlantic ports were located at or near the "Fall Line," the point where the coastal plain and tidewater meets the hillier upland regions, and where navigable waterways turn into more turbulent rivers and streams.) Textiles, grains, paper, and iron products were produced at almost any location where a mill could be constructed on a stream bank.

These seaports grew and changed dramatically. In the first twenty years of United States history, Philadelphia and New York became, in that order, the country's two largest cities. Baltimore was growing, but still far behind the two leaders. By the end of the second twenty years, New York had captured first place and Baltimore was challenging Philadelphia for second place. Unlike some of their smaller brethren along the Atlantic coast, Baltimore, Philadelphia, and New York came to view themselves as something more than merely local ports. Beyond their exclusive hinterlands, they competed with one another for raw material sources and markets over broad, undefined areas of what was then the entire country, particularly the growing territories west of the Alleghenies and around the Great Lakes system.

Each port handled a somewhat different mixture of manufactured goods and raw materials. At Baltimore, for example, grain was processed into flour for export, and small iron and copper manufacturing industries developed, using locally mined ores. Tobacco grown in the region also was exported. In the early 1800s a textile industry developed, based on cotton shipped in from the South. Coffee and sugar were among Baltimore's major imports.

Whatever their individual characteristics, all the ports depended on transportation for their success. Transportation determined how cheaply the goods could be moved to and from the ports, how quickly, how reliably, and in what quantities. But in the early 1820s there were only two forms of inland transportation: roads and waterways.

Both suffered from severe limitations. Road travel — which at that time meant mostly private or publicly built toll roads, called "turnpikes" — involved a jarring ride over unpredictable surfaces, at the mercy of snow, ice, rain, and thaws. And always, it was limited by the speed and stamina of dray animals. All these impediments, added to high turnpike tolls, produced prohibitive costs to move goods over any distance. For example, in 1809 the cost of wagon transportation for 75 miles of toll road travel was more than twice the amount charged for carriage of a similar commodity across the Atlantic Ocean. Similarly, an 1816 United States Senate Committee Report noted that "a coal mine may not exist more than ten miles from a canal...as the cost of land carriage is too great."

More cargo usually could be carried on the water, with less effort. But at this time, most rivers were unimproved and thus difficult to navigate. Behind the Fall Line, rapids, waterfalls, and other obstructions often stood between origin and destination, and varying water levels was a constant problem. By the early 1800s short canals had been built around some of the worst obstructions, such as Conewago Falls on the Susquehanna and Great Falls on the Potomac, but they were of limited help.

Baltimore's success as a seaport was based on two factors. First, the city was situated further west than its two principal rivals; thus the distance to inland points was shorter, significantly lessening the cost of overland transport. Second, Baltimore had a superior road system, particularly to the west. A string of well-built private turnpikes connected the city with Cumberland, Maryland. In 1818 the government-built National Road was opened across the Alleghenies from Cumberland to the Ohio River at Wheeling, Virginia (now West Virginia). Certainly the most extensive public work of its time, the National Road was hard-surfaced and built to the highest standards. Shorter private toll roads — notably the York and the Hanover turnpikes — allowed Baltimore to tap southern Pennsylvania and take some of Philadelphia's "natural" trade.

Although the city had no navigable waterway to the west, it could draw from central Pennsylvania via the Susquehanna River. The Susquehanna, its branches, and such tributaries as the Juniata, drained a vast area of Pennsylvania; it reached into New York State as well. Perversely, however, the river refused to acknowledge state boundaries, and instead of feeding Philadelphia (which then could only reach it over land), it flowed southeast into the Chesapeake Bay at Havre de Grace, Maryland. Thus its natural course led it out of Pennsylvania and into Maryland, making it a bone of contention between the two states and their rival port cities.

The Susquehanna had developed early as a trade route. Along its borders were vast quantities of timber, grain, coal and ores. Various types of river "arks" had transported these commodities down river since the early days of the Republic. Although the rapids at Conewago (below Middletown, Pennsylvania) impeded movement to the Chesapeake Bay, boats moved extensively throughout the upper regions of the river. For example, in 1790 150,000 bushels of wheat came into Middletown, Pennsylvania. In 1814 a resident of Harrisburg saw 86 rafts, 16 arks, and 12 flatboats pass down river in one day; and the pace continued for more than twenty days. From Milton, on the West Branch, 70,000 bushels of wheat descended the river during the harvest season of 1821.

Baltimore made every effort to tap this business. Beginning in 1800 arks were sent over the dangerous rapids at Conewago to tidewater. These rudimentary boats were limited in both capacity and speed, but could carry 40 to 50 tons, and could recover part of their cost when sold as scrap lumber on their arrival at the downriver markets. Not surprisingly, moving freight over this route was a major undertaking. The journey was laborious, and time consuming. Perils and problems awaited every load. The boats frequently wrecked on the rapids, spoiled or damaged the goods on board, and were continuously plagued by theft — but they managed to forward a large volume of commerce into the port of Baltimore. In 1825 a Baltimore resident described the trade of the city from the Susquehanna River as 445,000 barrels of flour, 200,000 bushels of grain, and 10 million feet of lumber. It was, of course, essentially a one-way trade, since moving back up the river was considerably more difficult and usually not attempted. However, problems or not, the Susquehanna valley meant a large market for Baltimore. Anthracite coal in eastern Pennsylvania, then largely unexploited, added to the valley's promise.

Philadelphia was hardly idle. In addition to its own overland road, the Lancaster Turnpike, the city promoted a canal to connect the Susquehanna with the Schuylkill River. Begun in 1822 and opened in 1827, the Union Canal extended from Middletown, Pennsylvania — above the Conewago Falls — to Reading, where it connected with the Schuylkill Navigation Company's canal to Philadelphia. Unfortunately, the Union Canal was shortsightedly designed with narrow 8½-foot locks, limiting its capacity and requiring transloading for many shipments.

Another Philadelphia-inspired project was the Chesapeake & Delaware Canal, first planned in 1799 to allow Susquehanna River traffic to reach the Delaware River via the Chesapeake Bay. The C & D, still a viable and busy entity today (although completely rebuilt), was finally begun in 1824 and opened in 1829. Maryland legislators had to approve its charter and finally did so — but only after assurances that the Pennsylvania legislators would reciprocate and approve the planned Susquehanna & Tidewater Canal, a two-state project planned to improve the lower part of the river and make it more accessible for Baltimore. The Susquehanna & Tidewater was subsequently delayed by political pressures, financial problems, and construction difficulties; it was not opened until 1840.

Unfortunately for both Baltimore and Philadelphia, the year 1825 saw a momentous event which would change the competitive relationships of those two ports and their chief rival — New York. Additionally, it would change everyone's thinking about transportation strategy.

Italy and France had pioneered the building of long-distance canals, and Great Britain had an extensive canal system by the early 1800s. But the United States was slower to adopt this type of transportation. Before the 1820s, canals had been sporadically built in America to overcome the problems of open river navigation. Invariably, however, they were short, special-purpose affairs, usually designed to bypass falls or rapids, or to connect two watersheds. Theoretically, however, a full-length canal could allow far cheaper and more reliable transportation than roads or most of the eastern river systems. There were some drawbacks: the construction cost was high, and the topographic conditions had to be right.

New York decided to take the risk. In 1817 it began building the 349-mile-long Erie Canal, connecting the Hudson River with Buffalo. Governor DeWitt Clinton pushed the project through the legislature with strong New York City backing and an immense bond issue. Some sections of the waterway were opened in 1819, and were profitable even before the full length of the canal was completed in 1825. In a few years, tolls had paid off the debt and were financing improvements. More importantly, the Erie Canal gave New York a decisive advantage in trade with the west. Combined with the wide and placid Hudson River, the canal provided a smooth, almost gradeless, high-capacity route to the Great Lakes. Although the point is debatable, many historians date New York's subsequent supremacy among American ports to the Erie Canal's opening.

The Erie Canal's success immediately put Baltimore and Philadelphia on the defensive. Unfortunately, neither city had anything resembling New York's favorable topographic conditions, and both ports floundered about attempting to find some transportation method which would keep them competitive.

Baltimore's dilemma was the worst. With its road system now made obsolete but with no practical water route west, its merchants and bankers finally were forced to reject the idea of a westward canal altogether; instead they decided to tie their hopes to a new, promising, but almost wholly untried type of carrier: the railroad. In February 1827 they created the Baltimore & Ohio Railroad to link Baltimore with the Ohio River, albeit with little idea of exactly how it would do so. Construction of the B & O began July 4, 1828; the first short segment to Ellicott City, Maryland opened in May 1831. The railroad, of course, quickly proved to be the superior means of transportation in almost all ways — although the problem-plagued B & O did not finally reach the Ohio River until the end of 1852, over 25 years after its founding.

After much argument, Pennsylvania cast its lot with canals — as best it could. In the period between 1826 and 1835, the state planned and built an extensive canal network, and several privately financed canals also were completed. Its "Main Line" canal was designed to accomplish what the Erie Canal did for New York and the B & O was meant to do for Baltimore — to link Philadelphia with the west, in this case Pittsburgh. But to overcome the topographic problems, it was forced to adopt a mongrel succession of canals, inclined planes, and "portage" railroads. Except for the unsatisfactory Union Canal, no direct water route existed between Philadelphia and the Susquehanna River at Columbia, Pennsylvania, and it was decided to build a railroad over this segment. (The railroad also required two inclined planes.) Between Columbia and the base of the Alleghenies at Hollidaysburg a conventional canal was constructed, following sections of the Susquehanna and Juniata Rivers. To hurdle the mountains, a hideously unwieldy portage railroad was designed, utilizing a series of ten inclined planes connected to one another by short, level sections of railroad. Finally, another canal completed the line between Johnstown and Pittsburgh.

Matched against either the existing Erie Canal or the theoretical advantages of a railroad such as the B & O, the "Main Line" canal system was doomed to failure. The system took seven years to build (it fully opened in April 1834) and cost a staggering $12 million. Within four years of completion, efforts to replace it with a railroad had begun. In 1846 Pennsylvania finally chartered a Harrisburg-Pittsburgh railroad to replace the outdated and cumbersome canal. Its great canal project not only lost money but had also set back Philadelphia's western market penetration.

The infamous "Main Line" was not the state's only canal project. As a result of local pressures, branches eventually were built along much of the Susquehanna River system. The "Susquehanna Division," connecting the "Main Line" with Sunbury and Northumberland, Pennsylvania, was opened in 1830. Extensions were then built from Northumberland along both the North and the West branches of the river, and by 1831 such major shipping points as Muncy, Williamsport, Lock Haven, Berwick, and the area below Wilkes-Barre were linked to the system.

Thus, for better or worse, virtually the entire Susquehanna basin now was covered by canals feeding into an eastern terminal at Columbia, Pennsylvania. At Columbia, Philadelphians hoped the traffic would be transferred to the state-owned Philadelphia & Columbia Railroad, the overland link to their port. Upriver at Middletown, Pennsylvania, the earlier Union Canal also existed as a somewhat awkward alternative.

Baltimore's Search for a Susquehanna Canal

Although Baltimore, like its two rivals, was focusing most of its efforts and resources on a western transportation trunk line, it could not ignore the Susquehanna system to its north. But with Pennsylvania devising ways to channel the Susquehanna trade to Philadelphia and generally obstructing Baltimore's efforts to open a better waterway to the Chesapeake Bay, the Maryland city looked for other ways of reaching the river. One early and important attempt to secure a direct canal route into Pennsylvania was made in 1822.

In the spring of that year, the Maryland Legislature appointed George Winchester along with John Patterson and Theodorick Bland as commissioners to survey and establish a route for a canal directly south from the Conewago Falls to Baltimore. (Winchester, whose name will appear soon again, also helped plan and survey the Chesapeake & Ohio Canal.) Frustrated by delays in building the projected Susquehanna & Tidewater Canal directly along the Susquehanna to the Chesapeake Bay, the Legislature was receptive to an alternate canal route between Baltimore and that river. The commissioners first approached the owners of the Susquehanna Canal, located on the east side of the river, in an effort to use that as part of the route to tidewater. The Susquehanna Canal, completed in 1803, was a short eight and one-half-mile waterway extending west from Port Deposit, Maryland. However, the owners of that canal made financial demands that the commissioners rejected as too onerous. When they then surveyed a route directly south overland, the Susquehanna Canal's owners "pressured the Legislators" sufficiently to block the proposed new canal. The Susquehanna Canal had hoped that its waterway would eventually become the prime route into the Chesapeake — but in the end it was bypassed and only earned a small income from local traffic.

The proposed Baltimore-to-Susquehanna canal thus came to nothing, but a seed was planted. Several years later the individuals involved in the canal project — notably George Winchester — would plan, organize, and build the Baltimore & Susquehanna Railroad as a method of accomplishing the same goals.

A Railroad is Born

In 1827, long before the completion of the Susquehanna & Tidewater Canal, several of the turnpike company owners in York County had become disenchanted with the cumbersome movement of commerce into Baltimore over what they considered inadequate facilities. In addition, many Pennsylvanians thought that the trade rivalry between Philadelphia and Baltimore created "restrictive trade routes ... and enriched Philadelphia's merchants at the expense of the farmers of the interior."

As a result an earnest search was undertaken to develop a more efficient transportation alternative to the toll roads. Canals were not always the answer. Although cheap and efficient to use where the conditions were right, they had many inherent drawbacks. They were slow, seasonal (most had to be closed during the winter), and since their routes generally followed waterways, they were limited in the geographic areas they could serve. The alternative had to be more flexible than canals, but able to carry heavy loads, reasonably quickly, and over long distances. The group decided to study the feasibility of establishing a railroad between Baltimore and the Susquehanna River.

Railroads were a new but not entirely unknown technology. For several years American businessmen had been studying the development of the railway in England. Crude mine tramways had existed in the 1700s and the first (but not too successful) steam locomotive had been operated in 1804. But it was not until 1825 that the first true full-length locomotive-powered public railway — the 25-mile Stockton & Darlington — was opened. Although technologically not much more than a mine tramway itself, the Stockton & Darlington proved the practicality of rail transportation. It had been the direct inspiration for the Baltimore & Ohio, organized and chartered in February 1827.

At that time, however, not only was the technology itself in its infancy, but it was uncertain whether the English techniques could be translated to American physical and financial conditions. The Baltimore & Ohio itself would not begin building until July 1828, and even then would be forced to develop its own construction techniques, motive power, and rolling stock by trial and error.

So it was with considerable foresight that, in August 1827, the York Haven Company, along with other local toll road owners, appointed a group of Baltimore businessmen to report on the possibility of constructing a railway from York Haven, Pennsylvania, directly south to the port of Baltimore.

York Haven was a small Susquehanna River town located about 14 miles downstream from Harrisburg and 11 miles directly north of the inland manufacturing city of York, and was one of the best situated points for transshipping Baltimore-bound river traffic. The survey group, supported by the Maryland Legislature, consisted of George Winchester, Shepperd C. Leakin, and John Kelso. It made a reconnaissance of the proposed line with civil engineer William F. Small of Baltimore and General Joseph G. Swift from the United States Army Corps of Engineers. The delegation arrived at York Haven on August 15, 1827. After meeting with local officials and merchants it returned to Baltimore and made a report to the Maryland Legislature. The committee announced that no insurmountable obstacles existed to prevent the construction of a Baltimore to Susquehanna railroad. It then promptly applied for a charter, which the Maryland Legislature granted on February 13, 1828. The new Baltimore & Susquehanna Railroad was born almost precisely one year after the Baltimore & Ohio's incorporation, making it one of the country's earliest railroad companies.

The charter authorized the new company to construct a railroad from Baltimore to York Haven, and it was planned to pass through York en route. York Haven was chosen as the terminus partly because of its proximity to the projected main line of the Pennsylvania Canal, to be built along the opposite side of the river. The directors of the company in its First Annual Report were listed as Charles Carnan Ridgely (Governor of Maryland 1815-1818), George Winchester, Robert Purviance, Thomas Wilson, James Smith, James L. Hawkins, James B. Stansbury, Shepperd C. Leakin, Justice Hoppe, John Patterson, and Theodoric Bland. Messrs. Winchester, Patterson, and Bland will be remembered from the abortive 1822 Baltimore-Susquehanna canal project.

Their first meeting was held May 5, 1828 and George Winchester was elected president of the new company. The charter authorized 20,000 shares at $40 a share, with 6,000 of these shares to be reserved for the City of Baltimore, the State of Maryland, and the State of Pennsylvania. The stock subscription books were opened at the Franklin Bank in Baltimore, and in the first few days of sales the stock was oversubscribed — an example of the railroad fever that swept over the country during the early 1800s. Some early investors expected a quick, profitable return on their investment (which did not happen); many others were more interested in the benefits that a railroad would bring to their businesses or communities.

The Baltimore & Susquehanna Railroad's board of directors submitted the new charter to the State of Pennsylvania to authorize construction of that section of the planned route through the state to the York Haven terminal. The Pennsylvania legislators, however, promptly refused to adopt the proposed charter.

Seaport rivalry and local boosterism were the two primary culprits. First, the "Philadelphia faction" present in the Pennsylvania Legislature obviously did not want Baltimore to flourish at Philadelphia's expense — and the planned railroad clearly would help Baltimore tap the entire Susquehanna River region. Second, many of the Pennsylvania legislators wanted the railroads located within the state's borders to be owned and chartered exclusively by Pennsylvania businessmen and officials. Expected profits would be put to use in Pennsylvania.

Thus the plans for one great railroad north out of Baltimore were quickly stymied. However, George Winchester was not only a shrewd businessman, but an astute politician. The compromise he submitted to the Pennsylvania Legislature in 1829, allowing majority financial participation by Pennsylvania people, would set the stage for the company's future strategy as an interstate carrier. There was still hope.

CHAPTER 2

Beginnings: The Baltimore & Susquehanna Railroad

Armed with its 1828 Maryland charter the new Baltimore & Susquehanna was ready to build north to the river at York Haven — but its founders faced an immediate quandary.

The proposed construction of a "Baltimore-financed" railroad into Pennsylvania precipitated a political furor in the Pennsylvania Legislature. There were both supporters and detractors of the project on each side of the Maryland-Pennsylvania border and while these forces struggled for supremacy, the Baltimore & Susquehanna was, in effect, left with no clear way of reaching its goal.

The Philadelphia members of the Pennsylvania Legislature opposed the new railroad and declared that "the right [to build] will prove a funeral knell to our city." They knew it would be "difficult to bring back" trade and commerce once it was lost to Baltimore.

On the other hand, the city of Baltimore and the state of Maryland aggressively supported the enterprise. Maryland officials believed that trade should "follow a natural avenue" and have "a choice of markets." They knew that the competition between Baltimore and Philadelphia for western trade commenced at Middletown on the Pennsylvania Canal. The officials from Baltimore frequently argued that denial only continued to injure the farmers and merchants who would use the service of the proposed new railroad.

The net result of this political tangle was that, for the moment at least, the railroad lacked the Pennsylvania charter essential to complete its planned route to the Susquehanna. Yet it would need some immediate sources of revenue to help finance its construction costs. It also would need an alternative goal if the Pennsylvania Legislature proved to be too recalcitrant.

The Route Out of Baltimore

Nonetheless, the Baltimore & Susquehanna bravely began building northward. Soon after its incorporation the company arranged for Joseph G. Swift, chief of the United States Army Corps of Engineers, and William F. Small, Charles Ward, James Collins, Jr., and Joseph G. Partridge, civil engineers from Baltimore, to make surveys and select the most appropriate route out of Baltimore to the Pennsylvania state line.

There was no easy route. As present-day drivers on Interstate 83 or the old York Road well know, the area between Baltimore and York, Pennsylvania is a constant succession of hills, cut up by small twisting streams flowing into either the Chesapeake Bay or the Susquehanna. Finding a low-grade path through this choppy country was possible, but required many curves, bridges, and occasional grades to cross from one watershed to another.

As a start, the B & S engineers chose the Jones Falls valley as their exit from Baltimore. (The "Falls" name in such small rivers such as Jones Falls and Gunpowder Falls was a local term referring to an entire fast-running stream, not merely a waterfall.) The stream could be followed for at least six miles, as far as the area now occupied by Lake Roland. (Lake Roland was a later creation, built between 1857 and 1861 as a city reservoir.)

In the summer of 1829, while the city of Baltimore was celebrating its centennial anniversary, the Baltimore & Susquehanna Railroad celebrated its beginning on August 8th by laying a cornerstone at the boundary of Baltimore City, some sixty feet from the present-day North Avenue bridge. As was done with the Baltimore & Ohio a year earlier, there was a grand civic celebration with a parade

The B & S's cornerstone as it appeared in 1931, over 100 years after it had been first placed at track-side near present-day North Avenue in Baltimore. It was moved from its original site in 1870 during the construction of the Pennsylvania Railroad tunnels, and used in a wall at Calvert Station. In 1891 it was rediscovered and placed in the wall of the Northern Central's office building at Calvert and Centre Streets, its location in this photograph. When this building was razed, it subsequently went to the Maryland Historical Society. Smithsonian Institution Collection; C. B. Chaney photograph.

from the center of the city to the site of the installation of the "first stone." There, amid the usual prayers and oratory, the stone was laid in a Masonic ceremony and the new railroad was on its way.

The first section of roadbed was constructed along the west bank of Jones Falls. Construction crews worked throughout 1829 and 1830 building the line toward Relay.

It was a fitful start. In many places construction proceeded slowly. Engineers and directors argued about both the route and means. Railroad location and construction was a new science in America; indeed, much of it was an art. There were differences of opinion about construction standards, materials, and techniques. These differences resulted in personality conflicts emerging and organizational weaknesses soon surfaced.

The only experienced engineers were from the United States Army Topographical Engineers. Lt. Col. Stephen H. Long and Captain William G. McNeill (both veterans of the Baltimore & Ohio project) pushed for quick, cheap construction methods to allow the company to get into business and begin producing revenues quickly; rebuilding to higher standards could come later when traffic demanded it and revenue allowed it. It was agreed that heavy engineering and construction work was a luxury that the fledgling railroad could not afford. Bridges were to be built of wood, and track consisted of strips of iron laid on wood stringers, which in turn were mounted on wood ties. (The B & O, on the other hand, had made the financially disastrous mistake of building both its early bridges and its track structure with stone.) To minimize grading costs, the line followed the twists of Jones Falls as closely as practical.

Irish immigrants from Baltimore built the initial section of the line. The construction hands lived in camps along the line and their consumption of intoxicants at raging campfires became the target of community scorn. Many workers were banned from local communities and residents were urged to avoid them. Nonetheless, the construction crews worked from 1829 until early in 1831 building the line. The work was slow and costly and it was frequently interrupted by inclement weather.

The trackbed and iron "strap" rails were crude but could be installed quickly. The strap iron was manufactured in England and was considered a quality product. The iron was ⅝ inch thick and was cut to fifteen-foot lengths; it was then nailed onto wooden stringers, and these wooden rails were attached to wood sills approximately six inches square. The sills were laid on crossties placed six feet apart. The gauge was four feet eight and one-half inches, already the standard gauge in Britain and for many new American lines such as the B & O. Initially, horse power was to be used, and the space between the rails was raised and graded smooth for the comfort of the horses.

The line was completed as far as the present Lake Roland early in 1831. (A station was built there in 1832 and named Relay, since it became a relay point for fresh horses. In early days the station name was often confused with the Relay on the Baltimore & Ohio's line west of Baltimore, so named for the same reason. In 1874 it was renamed Hollins.) Horse-drawn carriages began operating out of Baltimore's newly established Belvedere Station on July 4, 1831. The event was reported in area newspapers, attended by local dignitaries, and was accompanied with a gala celebration, including a free trip to the temporary terminal at Relay, where holiday celebrations continued all day.

When the Baltimore & Susquehanna reached Relay, the State of Pennsylvania still had not granted a charter. The railroad's officers hoped for a compromise and eventual settlement with Pennsylvania on the originally planned route into the state. However, in 1830 and 1831 no favorable decision had been forthcoming despite the personal appearances and speeches by President Winchester to the Pennsylvania legislators in 1829 and again in 1830.

A strategic decision could be delayed no longer. Although the B & S's engineers had located a proposed route to York, and although the company would continue some construction north on this route within Maryland, the immediate prospects were not encouraging. In his Fourth Annual Report, George Winchester labeled as "bleak" the prospects of terminating the railroad at the barren summit of the Maryland line on the original route.

During the three-year struggle from 1829 until 1832, while President Winchester attempted to gain entrance into Pennsylvania, he also pursued other viable route alternatives.

The B & S's first "terminal" was at Relay House, located near what is now the south shore of Lake Roland. No early pictures of the location exist, but it looked like this in about 1880. The camera looks northwest. The Green Spring Branch curves to the left while the main line is in the foreground. The station shown here (named Hollins at that time) dates to 1876 and was closed in 1926. It burned down in 1933. Photograph courtesy of Baltimore Sun.

Anticipating a possible route change, a supplemental Maryland charter passed on February 7, 1830 had authorized the railroad to build to "the headwaters of the Monocacy River in the vicinity of Westminster." In 1831 it was decided to veer westward from the Relay station and build through the Green Spring Valley, heading for Owings Mills, Westminster, and, eventually, the Allegheny mountains.

This new direction was dictated in part by the need to generate revenue to begin to make the company a solvent entity and help pay for its construction costs. Owings Mills represented an immediate revenue source. The mills of the Gwynns Falls were highly productive and millwrights and merchants of the area were actively seeking rail service. At this time in Baltimore County's history, many merchants and farmers were dissatisfied with the troublesome turnpikes and what they thought were excessive tolls, and they were pressing for cheaper, more dependable shipping alternatives.

President Winchester's decision to build to Owings Mills and toward Westminster was also no doubt influenced by his personal relationship with people of that area. His grandfather had surveyed and laid out the town of Westminster (formerly Winchestertown). The elder Winchester had considerable financial and political interests in the area and the support was used to benefit the rail line. In addition, George Winchester's first wife was Ann Owings of Owings Mills, and the Owings family no doubt was actively courting their son-in-law's rail line.

The Green Spring Line

The new Green Spring line — now considered the company's main line — was put under contract in 1831 and construction continued throughout the year. Its initial section started at Relay House and followed Jones Falls westward through the Green Spring Valley; from there it was projected to run northwest to Reisterstown, passing Owings Mills en route. Reisterstown was chosen as the tentative terminal point because of its trade potential with both the Reisterstown Turnpike and merchandise and coach lines going north to Hanover, Pennsylvania.

During construction the railroad company frequently made arrangements with local property owners to use available resources. The original charter authorized the railroad to use any "earth, timber, gravel or stone, situated on the land." The abundance of timber led to its extensive use in early railroad construction. The bridge over the Jones Falls near the Bellona Powder Works, designed by Colonel Stephen H. Long, was a 67-foot structure made of Susquehanna white pine.

Property owners also often donated land. For example, property for the Owings Mills depot was given to the railroad by Dr. John Cromwell and Mr. Pinkerton Codd. At that time, Codd owned what was known as the Owings Middle Mill, a grist mill near the station.

On June 14, 1832 the Green Spring Branch was opened for business. At this time the line went as far as the newly-built Green Spring Hotel, at Green Spring Valley Road and Moales Lane (later called Chattolanee station) — seven miles from Relay. Horse-drawn carriages left the Belvedere Street depot in Baltimore at 9 a.m., 2:30 p.m., and 5:30 p.m. These early trains went to Relay House where the horses were changed (and thus the name Relay), then continued out the Green Spring line to the hotel. As before, the line had been laid with strap iron rail on wood stringers.

One of the first stops on the newly opened Green Spring Branch was probably the Brooklandville House, still standing today and known as the Valley Inn. This establishment, operated by John R. Gwynn, no doubt capitalized on the location of the railroad's junction with the Falls Turnpike (now Falls Road). It served as a tavern as well as an overnight inn.

The second major stop was at the large Green Spring Hotel at Chattolanee, constructed by the railroad primarily to attract resort business to the beautiful Green Spring Valley and help build railroad passenger traffic. It was opened for business August 11, 1832.

The remaining two miles of the Green Spring line into Owings Mills was constructed during the summer of 1832 and was opened for business on August 20, 1832. The route crossed the Reisterstown Turnpike at Garrison, just north of Green Spring Valley Road, then turned north and crossed the Reisterstown Turnpike again at Gwynns Falls where the Owings Mills terminal was located. Passengers made connections with various stagecoach lines on the Reisterstown Turnpike at the depot.

Passengers paid 51 cents for the trip from Baltimore, a total distance of seventeen miles. Freight was three cents per ton per mile. The Chambersburg Stage Line and the railroad made arrangements to carry the mail over the Green Spring Branch to Owings Mills and then north by stage.

Now the railroad could begin drawing on a variety of sources of freight traffic. Along the Jones Falls valley between Baltimore and Relay were several industries — notably the ore mines at Bare Hill, the textile mill at Mt. Washington, the Bellona (or Beatty) Powder Mill, and several flour mills. Soon afterward, textile milling expanded along the inner part of the valley, profiting from the proximity to the port of Baltimore and the railroad service.

The Green Spring Hotel and station, shown here in an 1857 print, was located where the rail line crossed Green Spring Valley Road at Chattolanee. By the time this picture was made, the hotel had been doubled in size. The original section is at the right. The large wooden building burned down in 1860.

Freight traffic on the Green Spring line was more limited. The three grist mills originally established by the Owings family, located in the vicinity of the Reisterstown Turnpike, became early and important customers. The Rockland Mills, in operation since 1831, and Richard Caton's lime kilns at Brooklandville also used the new railroad. With the later extension of the main line beyond Cockeysville and the establishment of the Ashland furnace (north of Cockeysville) in 1844, the ore banks at Stevenson shipped iron ore to Ashland.

Early train travel on the horse-drawn railroad, while new and exciting, was uncomfortable and sometimes dangerous. The original passenger cars were carriages comparable to stage coaches. The coaches were cramped and passengers were often thrown from the top where they were forced to ride when trains were overbooked. Their speed was slow, usually ten or twelve miles per hour when the train was pulled by two horses. The railroad's two passenger trains were subject to derailment and damage. Track conditions were poor and train capacities were limited to what the horses could haul.

The early "stringer" rails were constructed for the ease of the horses which had to pull two- and three-car trains. The iron strap rails required constant repair and attention. Sometimes they came loose and curled up under the cars, and would break through the floorboards, injuring passengers and damaging freight. However, crews could construct and repair them quickly.

The First Locomotive

During 1830 and 1831 the railroad's executives had begun considering steam power to replace its horses. In one form or another, steam locomotives were in service on the Stockton & Darlington, the Baltimore & Ohio, and the Camden & Amboy railroads, and it was thought that steam might be feasible on the B & S. To test the new form of power, the executive board ordered a 14-ton locomotive from the now-world famous builder, Robert Stephenson of England, in 1831. It arrived in the fall of 1832 aboard the freighter *Herald,* and the railroad promptly named their new locomotive the *Herald* in its honor. Some mechanical alterations were necessary because its wheelbase turned out to be too long for the road's sharp curves. Originally built as a 0-4-0, the *Herald* was rebuilt as a 4-2-0 with an oddly designed swivel leading truck. The alteration proved successful, and it was put on the road immediately after modification. Although the locomotive reportedly attained speeds of 50 miles per hour during test runs, actual operating speeds averaged about 20 miles per hour. The locomotive so impressed the owners that after October 6, 1832, the *Herald* pulled a train on two daily trips from the Belvedere Street depot to Green Spring and Owings Mills.

The new engine cost $4,000 and was accompanied by John Lawson, an engineer from England. He ran the locomotive for several months while it was being modified and tested. Rebuilt again in 1846 as a six-wheel geared engine, the *Herald* remained on the road for an amazing 23 years and would be included in an inventory for the consolidated Northern Central Railway on January 1, 1855. It was finally scrapped in York in 1859.

Despite the *Herald's* success, the railroad did not immediately buy more steam locomotives; its limited mileage, traffic, and finances probably dictated prudence. But between 1837 and 1839, a total of eleven engines were delivered, including two more Stephenson products from England (named *Samson* and *Chieftain*) and eight from the Locks and Canals Company at Lowell, Massachusetts.

Northward Again

Just as the Green Spring line was being completed to Owings Mills, the Pennsylvania charter problem was finally resolved. During 1831 Pennsylvania's Governor Wolf made a personal request to his state legislators to approve the Baltimore & Susquehanna charter, reasoning that trade should be initiated with Baltimore. The deadlock in the Pennsylvania Legislature was broken with a two-prong compromise: First, the state of Maryland would allow the completion of the Tidewater Canal, which would form part of a through canal route allowing access to the lower Susquehanna River and to the Chesapeake & Delaware Canal; second, the new railroad line within Pennsylvania would be entirely owned and financed as a corporate entity of the state of Pennsylvania. Statutes, however, would remain "silent" on operating privileges — that is, on what company might actually operate the Pennsylvania portion of the rail line.

Governor Wolf, in order to get legislative approval for the Baltimore & Susquehanna Railroad to establish a route through York County, agreed only to grant the Maryland

The B & S's first steam locomotive was the Herald, built in Great Britain in 1832. This later model shows the Herald in its original form, before it was rebuilt to cope with the railroad's sharp curves. Smithsonian Institution Collection.

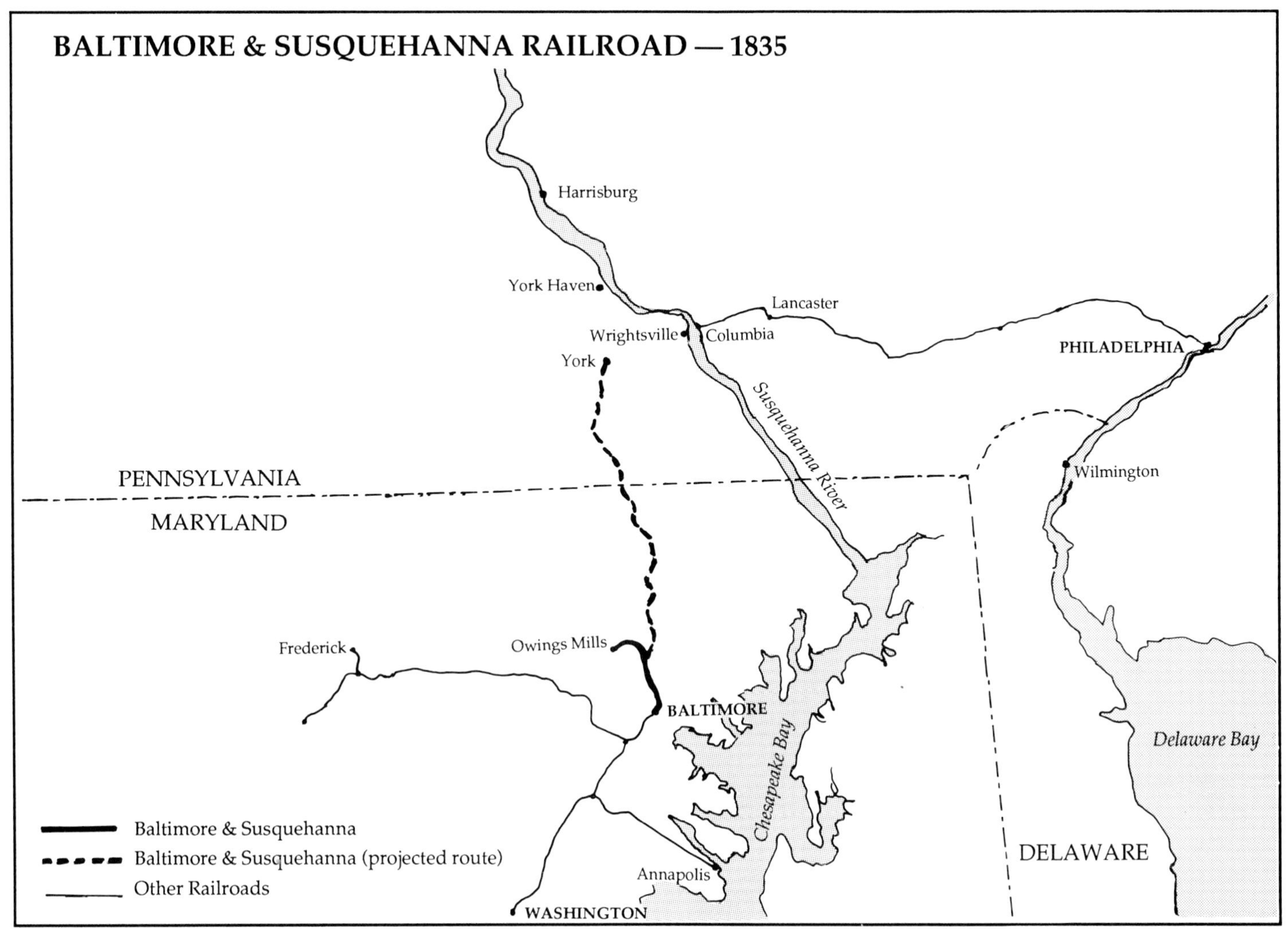

firm "limited" authority in Pennsylvania. The political ramifications of that limited authority resulted in the formation of a separate Pennsylvania corporation — to be named the York & Maryland Line Railroad Company.

This turn of events re-directed the Baltimore & Susquehanna to its original goal. Construction of the line north from Relay — which had been carried on to a limited extent during the early 1830s — was accelerated beginning in 1832. At the same time the York & Maryland Line was incorporated in Pennsylvania to continue the route within the state as far as York — although financial problems delayed the start of actual construction until 1837. With the company's meager financial resources diverted back to the route into Pennsylvania, the Green Spring line was left at its "temporary" Owings Mills terminal. The change in strategy led the company's new president, Alexander Nisbet (1777-1857), to abandon the route to Westminster "until business and population...shall render it more necessary." In truth, the Green Spring line — now relegated to branch line status — had been unprofitable since its 1832 opening, and its primarily rural territory offered little immediate hope of heavy traffic.

The railroad resumed building north from Relay toward Cockeysville, following a Jones Falls tributary now called Roland Run as far as Timonium. Unfortunately, construction costs far exceeded the expectations of both the owners and engineers. Work went on intermittently throughout the years of 1832 to 1836. In 1832 the line had been completed to Timonium and was opened for business on October 16, 1832. The railroad reached the limestone and marble quarries at Texas and Cockeysville in late 1834 and early 1835 respectively.

At Cockeysville the Baltimore & Susquehanna crossed the York Turnpike, entered the Gunpowder Falls valley north of the town, then followed that stream and two tributaries, Little Falls and Bee Tree Run, toward the Pennsylvania border. The right of way was surveyed and constructed by the Baltimore firm of William Gibbs McNeill, engineers. Construction crews worked all year during 1837 building the line, but the need for multiple bridges to cross the twisting Gunpowder and its tributaries — as well as rock cuts and earth fills — slowed the process and increased the costs. Nearing the state line at Freelands, the route left the Gunpowder watershed and climbed a ridge into Pennsylvania at New Freedom. Surmounting this 1.5 % grade — later known to the railroad operating people as "New Freedom Hill" — would be the railroad's major operating challenge in moving trains between Baltimore and York.

Aggressive and rapid construction plans resulted in the Baltimore & Susquehanna applying for financial aid from the state of Maryland and the city of Baltimore. From 1834 to 1839 both the loans and shares sold totaled the following amounts:

Loans:	State of Maryland	$1,884,043
	City of Baltimore	850,000
Shares:	Individuals	250,000
	State of Maryland	100,000
	City of Baltimore	100,000

This financial structure graphically points up the company's basic weakness. Clearly the Baltimore & Susquehanna had to depend heavily on public funds. Apparently the more sophisticated and experienced private investors correctly saw that its territory could not support a railroad out of its own resources and viewed the B & S as a poor risk. Its inability to raise more than $250,000 in individual shares purchased, which the directors thought was a meager response, would eventually combine with other difficulties to force the railroad line into insolvency. Typical of many early lines, the company's construction costs (and thus its debt) were high; still far short of its planned goal, it could not generate adequate revenue, and its meager income had to be plowed back to upgrade the primitive original facilities and make improvements.

Nonetheless, there was at least some potential freight business available. The railroad's route followed the Jones Falls and the Gunpowder Falls, both of them fast-running streams where mills already had been established and more would soon appear.

On the main line out of Baltimore, the railroad did a substantial business with the local, water-powered mills. These establishments were quick to take advantage of lower transportation costs into the seaport. The Druid Mills at Woodberry and the Washington Cotton Mills at Mount Washington had been in operation since 1810 and used the railroad as soon as it opened for business. (Both of these locations are now part of Baltimore City, although then they were in Baltimore County.) The Beaver Dam marble quarries and the lime kilns at Texas also predated the railroad and used the new mode of transportation into the city and port.

In northern Baltimore County, numerous river mills also produced traffic for the railroad. For example, John Weise's White Hall paper mill began operations in 1832 and used rail service as soon as the Baltimore & Susquehanna reached White Hall in 1836. In 1844 the iron furnaces of Christian Geiger's Ashland Iron Works began manufacturing pig iron and provided a rich source of revenue for the railroad. By 1840 traffic from the Beaver Dam marble pits required that the railroad construct a short spur line to that facility from Cockeysville, which provided a substantial amount of freight business over the years.

In the meantime the Green Spring line began to wither. With the Pennsylvania route problem resolved, the branch from Relay to Owings Mills was left in limbo, essentially an appendage without a purpose. The Baltimore & Susquehanna's capital and interests were directed elsewhere, and the Green Spring line fell into neglect and disrepair. By 1840 it could only be used in the summer season, and even then it could only handle horse-drawn carriages. Citizens of both the Green Spring Valley and Westminster, who had been promised an operational railroad, became impatient with the Baltimore & Susquehanna. The company claimed that it would take $20,000 to repair the branch and that the line was not profitable enough to pay for new track.

The Green Spring Line Goes Its Own Way

In 1846 citizens from Baltimore and Carroll counties lobbied the Maryland Legislature sufficiently to obtain an act authorizing the repair of the Green Spring line by the Baltimore and Susquehanna Railroad "or any new company organized to do the work." The group, including many residents of the Green Spring Valley, indicated that they planned to build their own railroad to Westminster.

Eventually this was done. After several false starts and changes of plan, local interests formed the Baltimore, Carroll, and Frederick Railroad in 1852. Renamed the Western Maryland Rail Road a year later, it planned to connect Baltimore with Carroll County, and, eventually, with the Cumberland Valley at Hagerstown. The Baltimore & Susquehanna encouraged and supported the new line, and offered to sell it the Green Spring Branch and allow it to use the B & S's main line into Baltimore.

After exploring several routes the new Western Maryland selected the Green Spring line as its Baltimore entryway, using trackage rights over the Baltimore & Susquehanna from Relay (at the later Lake Roland) into the city. On October 1, 1857 a deed to the branch was signed between the Western Maryland and the Northern Central (which by then was the Baltimore & Susquehanna's successor firm); it stipulated the return of the line to the Northern Central if and when the Western Maryland built its own line or used another route into Baltimore.

The Western Maryland bought the Green Spring line from Relay House to Owings Mills and immediately began to reconstruct the roadbed. The new company finally opened for business between the Northern Central's Calvert Station and Owings Mills on August 5, 1859. It reached Westminster in 1861, Union Bridge in 1862, and Hagerstown in 1872.

That did not quite end the Green Spring Branch story. In 1873 the Western Maryland built its own line into Baltimore as an adjunct to the massive Pennsylvania Railroad-sponsored rebuilding program there. Under the terms of the old deed, most of the now-orphaned Green Spring line reverted to the Northern Central and lapsed back into a light-density rural branch line. (Actually, the western end of the old branch, between Garrison and Owings Mills, was retained by the Western Maryland as part of its main line, so the Northern Central operated the Green Spring line only between Hollins and the WM junction at Garrison.) During the balance of the 19th Century it carried passengers to and from a large summer resort hotel at Chattolanee, but otherwise served a pretty area made up of country estates and farms, but with few people and almost no industry. Although occasionally used as an emergency detour route, it lived out its remaining life in obscurity, its pioneering days long forgotten. It was finally dismantled in 1960.

PROFILE: George Winchester 1787–1840

Typical of Baltimore's early railroad promoters, George Winchester, the first President of the Baltimore & Susquehanna Railroad, combined a variety of business and political interests; in addition he was an experienced engineer. By the time he became associated with the fledgling Baltimore & Susquehanna he was already a wealthy and influential individual.

George Winchester's grandfather, William Winchester I, an accomplished surveyor, immigrated to America in 1729 from Kent, England. William eventually purchased a thousand-acre tract in what is now Carroll County (then part of Frederick County), which he named *White Level,* and there he laid out the village of Winchester Town. Later the name was changed to Westminster, after the family's estate in England.

The Winchester family prospered in the United States. William Winchester II, George Winchester's father, fought in the American Revolution and served as Justice of the Peace in Baltimore between 1778 and 1783. Afterwards he became a wealthy merchant and banker, serving as president of the Union Bank of Baltimore and a director of the Bank of Baltimore. He willed the family farm near Westminster to his sons George and William III.

George Winchester was trained as a lawyer, but apparently disliked law; he entered politics and also became a civil engineer. He was a presidential elector for John Quincy Adams and was elected to the Maryland Senate in 1816. Winchester also became a long-time personal friend of Supreme Court Justice John Marshall.

As an engineer, he helped survey the Chesapeake & Ohio Canal, and in 1822 he surveyed the route of the proposed Susquehanna Canal. And, as related in Chapter 1, Winchester was one of the Commissioners who studied the feasibility of a railroad between Baltimore and the Susquehanna River at York Haven, Pennsylvania.

In addition, Winchester was a director of the Canton Company in Baltimore, which owned substantial waterfront property, and was a large investor in various Canton businesses.

Winchester's marriages demonstrate his close ties with influential Maryland families. He was married first to Ann Owings of the Owings Mills family, and fathered six children. He was remarried in 1827 to Marie Campbell Ridgely, the widow of Charles Ridgely of Hampton. For many years Winchester owned the "Bolton" mansion and estate, where the Fifth Regiment Armory now stands.

When the Baltimore & Susquehanna Railroad was incorporated in 1828 George Winchester became its first president; he was a heavy investor in the company and a major force in its early development. The railroad's 1831 decision to change its route and build to Owings Mills and Westminster undoubtedly was influenced by Winchester's relationship with the Owings family (he had married Ann Owings in 1809) and his own family holdings at Westminster. He also donated part of his "Bolton" estate property for use as the railroad's shops.

Winchester's political experience and influence were primary factors in overcoming the young company's first crisis — the reluctance of Pennsylvania legislators to allow the railroad into that state. He made at least two personal appearances before the legislature and was able to negotiate a political compromise to permit eventual construction to the Susquehanna.

His health failing, George Winchester resigned the Baltimore & Susquehanna's presidency in 1837 and died in 1840 at the young age of 53.

CHAPTER 3

The Baltimore & Susquehanna Expands

North to Pennsylvania: The York & Maryland Line Railroad

In accordance with the requirement that the Baltimore & Susquehanna's extension into Pennsylvania be incorporated in that state, a new company was created. In 1832 the Pennsylvania Legislature approved and incorporated the York & Maryland Line Railroad Company. The new firm was authorized to build a railroad from York, south to "any point on the Maryland side that the executive officers deemed most suitable." This, of course, meant a direct connection with the Baltimore & Susquehanna. Capital stock was fixed at $200,000, divided into 4,000 shares. The company's directors from the borough of York were George Small, Michael Doudle, Daniel Inginfity, Jacob Laumaster, James Shall, Charles Weiser, Peter Ahl, Jacob Bailor, Phineas Davis, George Morris, and Jacob Emmitt. York County officials for the firm were Charles A. Barnity, Henry Snyder, Daniel Raman, Joseph Osborn, John Hellings, John Smith, and William Patterson.

In 1833, after initial surveys had been completed and construction costs had been submitted, additional authority was granted by the Pennsylvania Legislature to increase stock subscription to an amount not to exceed 10,000 shares, or $500,000. However, construction was delayed for several years because the required funds could not be raised. Then, in 1835, additional authority was again granted for the company to borrow money, not to exceed an aggregate of $400,000 to construct the road and purchase cars and motive power.

The railroad finally began construction in 1837 and the tracks reached York in 1838. The line opened for business that year, operated by the Baltimore & Susquehanna. The charter of the original York & Maryland Line Railroad had mandated only that the line be incorporated in, and owned by, Pennsylvania residents; it contained no restrictions on either who could or should operate it.

Politicians from both Maryland and Pennsylvania understood that once the railroad was built, there would be no doubt that the Baltimore & Susquehanna would operate it. In essence this was the compromise that George Winchester had originally worked out with the "Pennsylvania faction" in the winter of 1829. Eventually the Baltimore & Susquehanna gained ownership of the line by buying capital stock in the amount of $199,265 and through the acquisition of stock and bonds amounting to another $344,499, which resulted from construction loans.

The York & Maryland Line was essentially a "paper company," created to satisfy legal requirements; for all practical purposes, it was a part of the Baltimore & Susquehanna and was built to the same construction standards. It was single-tracked and used strap iron rail laid on wood stringers. As before, the engineers wanted to complete the railroad, produce revenue, and rebuild and upgrade it later.

The topography of the Pennsylvania portion of the route to York was no easier than the Maryland section. Fortunately, a single watercourse, the south branch of Codorus Creek, could be followed most of the way between New Freedom, Pennsylvania and York. This section of the line, transversing an agriculturally productive area, crossed the creek and its tributaries several times, requiring extensive and costly bridge work. The Irish construction crews erected seven large wooden trestles and many smaller ones in the area between Glen Rock and York, and the farmers along the line supplemented their income by providing the workers with lumber. (Between Baltimore and York, the railroad had been forced to build no less than 93 bridges, an average of almost two a mile.)

The cost of the line was also increased by the necessity to bore a tunnel north of Gladfelters. Here the Codorus

Typical of the topography faced by the B & S over both the Maryland and Pennsylvania sections of its route was this section near Glen Rock, Pennsylvania, shown here in 1892. C. G. Ehrman Collection.

Creek made a long and tight oxbow curve around a granite wall, and the engineers dug and drilled through 300 feet of rock rather than twist the line around it. The tunnel was opened for traffic in 1838 (although the stone facework was not finished until 1840) and thus was one of the country's earliest railroad tunnels. It was named the "Howard Tunnel" in honor of Colonel John Eager Howard of Baltimore, a Revolutionary War hero, wealthy landowner, and investor in the railroad. (The Baltimore & Susquehanna's original route into downtown Baltimore passed through Howard's estate, "Belvedere," and the company established its first station on what was then the estate property.) Like the rest of the line to York, the Howard Tunnel originally was single tracked, but was enlarged in 1868 as part of the double tracking project carried on during and after the Civil War.

Although the Codorus Creek proved to be a substantial impediment to construction, it was also a viable revenue source. The German farmers who had immigrated to the area were highly productive, and water-powered mills dotted the stream bank.

The clear, cold creek water provided a valuable natural resource for the early nineteenth century American industrial processes. Grist mills, paper mills, tanneries, bark mills, and stone quarries soon populated the area. Some, in operation prior to the arrival of the railway, quickly took advantage of the new mode of transportation and reduced their dependence on the Baltimore Pike (today's York Road).

The little farming hamlets grew quickly under the influence of the railroad. At New Freedom, Smyser's (Seven Valleys), and Hanover Junction, mill owners discov-

Glen Rock was an important agricultural center on the B & S route to York. As can be sensed from the background of this 1900-era photograph, the town developed a thriving industry and commerce after the railroad's arrival. The building in the center was used as the railroad station, although it clearly was a commercial structure oriented to the main street. C. G. Ehrman Collection.

ered that with faster and more reliable transportation service they could expand their markets and thereby increase production. During the 1850s many of these locations became established mill towns. For example, Daniel Diehl's milling operation in Seven Valleys required the construction of eight tenant residences to accommodate workers for the grist mill, bark mill, and tannery. Glen Rock went through a similar transition. Originally named Heathcote Station, it was renamed for the hard rocks at a nearby glen through which the railroad crews had to dig. The paper mills and grist mills of Glen Rock soon expanded both employment and markets to meet the demands brought about, in large part, by the advent of rail service. Hanover Junction milling operations, local in output, became interstate when the railroad arrived.

The York & Maryland Line Railroad was the first railway to reach York, Pennsylvania, then a town of 7,000. Previously, York had been served by turnpikes and, since 1833, by the Codorus Navigation Company, a local canal connecting it with the Susquehanna River. The start of rail service to York in 1838 opened new markets for the area's farmers and merchants, and reduced their dependence on the canal and toll roads. To many Pennsylvanians, including the legislators at Harrisburg, their most pessimistic expectations were now fulfilled. Trade and commerce that should have gone to Philadelphia was now proceeding south on the new railroad to Baltimore.

After reaching York the Baltimore & Susquehanna at last was within reach of one of its major original objectives — the Susquehanna River. At York the company's executives again were faced with a choice in route strategy. They could seek authorization to build north to York Haven, the original goal, or they could build directly east toward Wrightsville, another river town. Wrightsville, 12 miles from York, was directly across the Susquehanna from Columbia, the eastern terminal of the Pennsylvania canal system and also the terminal of the Philadelphia & Columbia Railroad. A long wooden covered bridge connected the two towns. Wrightsville itself was to be the terminal of the planned Susquehanna & Tidewater Canal. The railroad officers decided that Wrightsville was the more strategic spot and offered greater revenue opportunities. They would reach that objective through the construction and financial support of another company — the Wrightsville, York & Gettysburg Railroad.

The Wrightsville, York, & Gettysburg Railroad

The Wrightsville, York, & Gettysburg was chartered by the Pennsylvania Legislature in 1837. Part of the original charter authorization permitted perpetual use of the line by the York and Maryland Line Railroad, providing that similar privileges were granted to the Wrightsville company. Construction began in 1838 and proceeded uninterrupted until the road was completed to Wrightsville in 1840. The railroad was built east from York roughly following the

Typical of many early railroads, the B & S's line was built through city streets at several locations, and in many cases the old street trackage remained into modern times. Such is the case with Pershing Street in York, shown here in July 1966 as train 554, a mid-day Harrisburg-Baltimore passenger train, leaves town. H. H. Harwood, Jr. photograph.

On June 1, 1840 the B & S advertised one connecting passenger train each way between Baltimore and Wrightsville, plus one additional York-Wrightsville round trip. The locomotive Baltimore, shown at what is believed to be the Bolton shop in Baltimore, was built by the Locks and Canals Company at Lowell, Massachusetts, in 1837. Smithsonian Institution Collection.

route of the Lancaster turnpike. At Wrightsville, rails were laid on the wooden bridge across the river to reach Columbia.

The new railroad borrowed a considerable amount of money from the Baltimore & Susquehanna, and its outstanding debt was converted into stock in 1839. Specifically, stock ownership was valued at a par value of $158,650, and bonds amounted to another $95,000. In addition, the Baltimore & Susquehanna provided a construction loan of $19,981.39. The Baltimore & Susquehanna operated the line after 1839.

Again, this extension of a "Baltimore railroad" created considerable opposition in Pennsylvania. While the citizens of York and the surrounding countryside were enthusiastic supporters of the project because they needed and wanted rail service, others, including many prominent businessmen and government officials in Philadelphia, saw it as another attempt to divert trade and commerce away from Philadelphia which the canal system had been built to secure. In fact, it did.

Like the York & Maryland Line Railroad, the Wrightsville, York, & Gettysburg was largely a paper company, organized and chartered solely to give a semblance of control to the state of Pennsylvania in return for their charter rights. But unlike its sister company, the Wrightsville line did own some equipment, including two 1836 Stephenson steam locomotives, the *Harrisburg* and *Wrightsville.*

The early operation of the Wrightsville line was hampered by two obstacles, one financial and one physical.

The financial problem involved rate relationships with the Baltimore & Susquehanna. Customers on the Wrightsville line who shipped to Baltimore, for example, quickly found that the Baltimore & Susquehanna's rates for the portion of the haul between the state line and Baltimore were double those of the Pennsylvania section. The Pennsylvania Legislature finally forced the Baltimore & Susquehanna to equalize its rates by authorizing the Wrightsville, York & Gettysburg Railroad to increase its rates to become compatible with the rates of the York & Maryland Line and the Baltimore & Susquehanna railroads. The threat of legislative action forced the Baltimore & Susquehanna to reduce its rates.

Operationally, the railroad was plagued by inadequate roadbed and bridges. The track consisted of the usual strap iron rail, but the bridges were light, lattice-type structures. The railroad was plagued with bridge fractures, and as a result retained a local engineer to study the problem. A young West Point-trained civil engineer, Herman Haupt, only 23 years old at the time, was hired for the job. He immediately discovered that both the prepared plans and the selected timbers were too light for the anticipated loads, and began calculating the strength of a trussed bridge. He was astonished to learn that no engineers in the United States, with one exception, had calculated the strength of a trussed bridge outside of the triangular system. Working on the Wrightsville line and experimenting with bridge trusses, Haupt calculated the stresses of the counter-brace, developed algebraic formulas for strain sheets and (he later claimed) conic sections, and experimented with models of his own design. He remained on the line, making observations and experiments until 1841 when he published anonymously *Hints on Bridge Construction,* which attracted a large response and some controversy. We will meet this amazing and intelligent individual again as the story progresses.

The connection with both the Susquehanna River and the canal at Wrightsville was a substantial strategic accomplishment for the Baltimore & Susquehanna. It provided the railroad with the first junction capable of siphoning traffic away from waterways and onto the rails. Available evidence shows that the Baltimore & Susquehanna accomplished exactly what the directors had hoped to achieve. Annual reports after 1840 show a large increase in southbound tonnage out of Wrightsville. Typical freight commodities were coal, lumber, and pig iron.

The little town of Wrightsville progressively expanded under the railroad's influence. From a population of 45 in 1840, it grew to over 200 residents and 23 businesses by 1852. Towns such as Wrightsville, once exclusively supporting watercraft operations, rapidly developed into what can be called "canal junction towns." Basically, the canal junction towns prospered with the advent of connecting mode of transportation. Although the canals certainly remained viable for many years, the introduction of railways brought faster service, expanded markets, and additional employment — both in railroad support functions and service businesses. As the railroad built further north into Pennsylvania, the economic and social significance of these canal junction towns will become increasingly important in this history.

For the next eleven years Wrightsville remained the Baltimore & Susquehanna's primary northern terminal. A nationwide depression lasting from 1839 to 1843 helped discourage any immediate expansion. Throughout the 1840s the directors had not forgotten York Haven, the earlier goal which lay on the Susquehanna north of York. More important now was Harrisburg, the state capital, 14½ miles upriver from York Haven. In addition to its location on the river and the Pennsylvania Canal, Harrisburg had been a key railroad junction point since the late 1830s. By 1840 it was the terminal of an all-rail route east to Lancaster and Philadelphia, and also a line to Chambersburg, Pennsylvania in the heart of the Cumberland Valley. And at Chambersburg the Cumberland Valley Railroad connected with another (and rather shaky) railroad to Hagerstown, Maryland.

An even more significant railroad project also was in the offing. In April 1846 the Pennsylvania Railroad was chartered to build a rail line between Harrisburg and Pittsburgh. This was Pennsylvania's long-delayed challenge to Maryland's Baltimore & Ohio and New York's evolving railroad network — and it clearly promised to replace the

Wrightsville as it appeared in 1894. Alongside the Susquehanna River is the terminal of the Susquehanna & Tidewater Canal. The rail line from York can be seen entering town at the left center of this print and following Front Street along the river. The station and connecting bridge to Columbia are in the center foreground. Historical Society of Pennsylvania Collection.

B & S trains entered Harrisburg over the Cumberland Valley Railroad's wooden bridge, originally built in 1839 and rebuilt after a fire in 1844. This 1874 print looks toward Harrisburg from Bridgeport. Smithsonian Institution Collection.

state's unwieldy "Main Line" canal system. Linked with the existing railroads east of Harrisburg, the new Pennsylvania Railroad would form an all-rail route between Philadelphia and Pittsburgh. Once it did so, the importance of the Columbia-Wrightsville rail/canal terminals obviously would lessen.

Harrisburg thus promised to be the future focus for Pennsylvania's rail lines. More immediately the Cumberland Valley Railroad already offered the opportunity to link the valley to Baltimore by rail — admittedly a somewhat roundabout routing, but clearly an improvement over the hilly wagon route between Baltimore and Chambersburg. Recognizing all this, in the mid-1840s the Baltimore & Susquehanna's executives began planning an extension from York to Harrisburg under the name of still another separate company — the York & Cumberland Railroad.

The York & Cumberland Railroad

The York & Cumberland Railroad was incorporated on April 21, 1846 with the authority to build from York, north to a junction with the Cumberland Valley Railroad at some point between Mechanicsburg and the west bank of the Susquehanna River. The capital stock was fixed at $1.5 million, divided in 60,000 shares of $25 each. The law provided that if the funding was not sufficient to construct the road, then the directors could borrow a sum not to exceed the stock amount. Difficulties in raising the required construction funds delayed the project. Letters of Patent were not issued until September 1848. Then in 1849, after the firm failed to raise adequate funding from Pennsylvania, stock offerings were placed on the open market. Baltimore financial brokers purchased $530,000 in stock and another $200,000 of bonds of the new railroad. The Baltimore & Susquehanna quietly purchased most of the investment offering.

The original incorporation of the York & Cumberland Railroad produced Articles of Agreement between it and the Baltimore & Susquehanna for operating rights. Thus once again the Baltimore & Susquehanna made itself the actual operator of a Pennsylvania-chartered company. The Articles were signed and dated January 21, 1850.

The formation of another "Baltimore enterprise" produced the usual response from the Philadelphia legislators. However, the merchants, farmers, and industry owners along the route supported the new railroad and let the legislators know it. Approval was granted.

Finally, in 1850, construction began. The route followed the Codorus Creek basin north from York, crossed a summit into Mount Wolf, then dropped into the Susquehanna valley east of York Haven. From York Haven, it followed the west shore of the Susquehanna to Bridgeport (now called Lemoyne), across the river from Harrisburg. At Bridgeport it was to connect the Cumberland Valley Railroad and use the Cumberland Valley's bridge over the Susquehanna River into Harrisburg. The single-track line was completed to Bridgeport in 1851.

York Haven became the second canal junction town supplying freight to the Baltimore & Susquehanna. Numerous mills and furnaces along the west bank of the Susquehanna immediately began using the railroad. From 1852 until the 1880s the town prospered. Population, industry, and commercial activity all increased steadily under the railroad's influence. The town's grist mills, like those of the P. A. Small family in York, sent flour to Baltimore to be exported to Brazil. Iron products were sent over the line to both domestic and international markets.

Although now a relatively large regional system, the Baltimore & Susquehanna and its various satellite lines were financially marginal. The burden of construction costs combined with insufficient revenues (partly the result of allowing freight customers to use their own equipment at low rates) continued to cripple the lines' earning power. Added to these problems was now the necessity of paying high bridge tolls to the Cumberland Valley in order to reach Harrisburg.

So in 1851 the directors of the Baltimore & Susquehanna looked farther north — to the rapidly developing anthracite fields of south central Pennsylvania. The railroad saw coal revenues as the panacea to its financial problems, and began planning an extension northward along the river from Harrisburg to Sunbury, Pennsylvania. En route, it was to connect with several feeder lines which already were carrying coal from the inland mines to the Susquehanna. To build the new line, the Baltimore & Susquehanna interests created another subsidiary, the Susquehanna Railroad Company.

The Susquehanna Railroad

The Susquehanna Railroad was chartered on April 24, 1851 with authority to construct a railroad connecting with either the York & Cumberland Railroad, or with the Pennsylvania Railroad, on any side of the Susquehanna River; it was then to proceed through Halifax and Millersburg in Dauphin County, and build into Sunbury and Williamsport. Capital stock was fixed at 30,000 shares in $50 denominations.

But, of course, the expected political objections resurfaced in Harrisburg. The proposal to build yet another "Baltimore-financed scheme" brought forth considerable opposition in the Pennsylvania Legislature. The entrance of the rail line into the Pennsylvania coal fields certainly would boost Baltimore at Philadelphia's expense. In addition, the legislators objected to creating a railroad that would parallel the canal in which the state had invested enormous amounts of capital. They hypothesized that the planned railroad would siphon traffic off the canal and benefit "foreign owners" more than the state of Pennsylvania.

The Susquehanna Railroad was surveyed late in 1851. The route was planned to run north from Bridgeport on the west bank of the Susquehanna River through Marysville, then would cross the Susquehanna on a long bridge to Dauphin and follow the east bank of the river through Millersburg, Trevorton Junction (now Herndon), and into Sunbury. The reason for the expensive bridge at Dauphin is somewhat mysterious, since two railroad bridges over the Susquehanna already existed nearby — the Cumberland Valley's Harrisburg bridge and the new Pennsylvania Railroad crossing at Rockville. It is believed, however, that the company wanted to avoid high bridge tolls and dependency on another railroad.

Stock subscription for the planned railroad had not been as enthusiastic as the company had hoped. Merchants and businessmen were reluctant to invest large sums of money in a railroad which would basically parallel the already existing canal. However, the farmers, industry owners, and town officials along the projected route were anxious to obtain rail service. As early as May 20, 1851 a delegation of both investors and boosters from Baltimore went to Sunbury to discuss the benefits of the planned railroad to the area's businessmen and merchants, and attempted to seek financial support. The committee chairman, the notable Baltimorean John Pendleton Kennedy, extolled the advantages of a "natural thoroughfare to a large region" leading to "Baltimore as the nearest seaport, and the increased trade that would result."

Some support resulted. The Lykens Valley Railroad, one of the coal feeder lines operating to the river, was "eagerly awaiting" rail service, and the president of the Dauphin and Susquehanna Coal Company promised "to pour mineral resources from Dauphin into the lap of Baltimore." In the final presentation at Sunbury the committee told an audience of some 300 people that the "citizens of Baltimore City would be expected to support the railway." It went on to say that the railroad expected to forward 100,000 tons of coal per year into the seaport, and would reduce shipping rates three and one-half cents below the tariff charged by the canal and river transporters.

Noble in intent, the delegation accomplished little in purpose. Without strong local financial backing, the Susquehanna Railroad had to borrow a considerable amount of capital from other sources just to begin construction. Much of this came from the Baltimore & Susquehanna and the York & Cumberland railroads in exchange for stock issued in its own name to the creditor railroads. Legislative acts passed in 1852 and 1853 permitted the Baltimore & Susquehanna's three Pennsylvania affliates — the York & Maryland Line, the York & Cumberland, and the Wrightsville, York & Gettysburg — either separately or collectively, to loan or to subscribe to $500,000 in the stock of the Susquehanna Railroad. The York & Cumberland had the best credit of the three railroads and obtained $500,000 for the project by issuing bonds, guaranteed by the city of Baltimore, and lent the amount to the Susquehanna Railroad. But that was insufficient to construct the line, and it appeared that the firm would go bankrupt. However, in 1853 additional authority was granted to increase the stock to any amount needed to complete the line, and Baltimore City financially supported the project.

The construction contractors for the Susquehanna Railroad — Philip Dougherty, George Lauman, William Travers, and Zenus Barnum — were put under contract as early as November 24, 1851. Actual construction began early in 1853 and continued until 1854. By then 26 miles, from Bridgeport to Millersburg, were completed to the point where this section was ready for rail. The bridge over the Susquehanna River between Marysville and Dauphin, however, was still under way. In fact, it was not until May 24, 1853 that the McCallum Bridge Company was hired to begin work on it. Grading was done for the remaining 28 miles between Millersburg and Sunbury, but was not complete enough for track laying.

Work on the line was frustratingly slow. All along the planned route inland mine operators were loading coal onto canal and river boats, and a potentially rich revenue source was within reach. But the railroad was continually hampered by construction difficulties, financial problems, and labor shortages.

Difficulties in raising capital plagued the project, causing stop-and-start construction work. Chief Engineer Anthony B. Warford reported in the company's first (and only) annual report that the lack of funds had delayed both the bridge work over the Susquehanna River and the completion of the roadbed to Sunbury. Labor shortages in the 1853-1854 period compounded the problem. Workers on the line found that they could make better wages in the nearby coal mines than in railroad building.

In this same annual report, President Simon Cameron described its financial problems as "minor," even though by the time the report was published the railroad was entering into receivership. The firm's secretary, Robert S. Hollins, and the President of the Board of Directors, William F. Packer, reported that as of January 1854 the total investment in the line was $1.3 million. Most of this capital was borrowed from the Baltimore & Susquehanna and the York & Cumberland railroads, and the debt had been converted into Susquehanna Railroad stock and bonds held by the two railroad companies.

Simon Cameron, incidentally, deserves a special note here. Cameron was far more than merely the president of the struggling Susquehanna Railroad. A wealthy businessman and rising political power in Pennsylvania, he was especially interested in promoting and developing the Susquehanna valley. Among other interests, Cameron owned the construction companies that were building the line and, in fact, had helped finance and build most of the Baltimore & Susquehanna's affiliate lines in Pennsylvania. Scheming, avaricious, and unscrupulous, Cameron went on to greater political and financial successes, and remained a major figure in the railroad's affairs. We will become increasingly familiar with him as the story progresses.

In 1854 the Susquehanna Railroad's financial problems worsened. It had expended all of its funds for construction and could not obtain further credit. Stock subscriptions had come to an end. In the fall of that year, construction work was suspended when funds and credit were exhausted. Eight hundred thousand dollars had been spent, and the contractors accepted $300,000 in bonds in lieu of payment for their services. By accepting these bonds, Simon Cameron, George Lauman, and Zenus Barnum became major creditors; this status eventually gave them direct access to the Board of Directors of the Susquehanna Railroad's successor, the Northern Central Railway.

By that time too, a new complication had appeared. Although the Susquehanna Railroad originally had vague hopes of extending beyond Sunbury to Williamsport (and also perhaps to the Wyoming Valley near Wilkes-Barre), another railroad project had appeared in this territory. Called the Sunbury & Erie, it planned to build northwest from Sunbury, through Williamsport, and on through the wilderness to Lake Erie at Erie, Pennsylvania. The project actually dated back to 1837, but had been long dormant. In early 1852, however, it came to life — strongly backed by Philadelphia interests, which obviously were not particularly friendly to the "Baltimore" railroad which was building toward Sunbury.

The "new" Sunbury & Erie was legitimized by an act of the Pennsylvania Legislature in March 1852. Among other things the act gave the Sunbury & Erie the right to build down the Susquehanna from Sunbury to Harrisburg if the Susquehanna Railroad did not complete its line by 1855. Although it had scarcely begun building north of Sunbury, the Sunbury & Erie almost immediately began surveying its own route south to Harrisburg. The Susquehanna Railroad's two top officers — Simon Cameron and William Fisher Packer (who became Governor of Pennsylvania in 1858) — also were political powers in the state and quickly managed to stop the Sunbury & Erie from poaching on their territory. With much more to occupy itself, the S & E gave up the fight. Eventually the two lines worked closely together, but through the mid-1850s they remained antagonists.

Rebuilding and Development

During the 1840s and early 1850s, while the Baltimore & Susquehanna was struggling northward toward its various goals in Pennsylvania, it was simultaneously forced to improve its original Maryland section. Much of this had been built cheaply and expediently, and sections had been in operation for almost 20 years. Steam power had long since replaced horses, and both locomotives and cars were becoming progressively heavier and capable of handling greater loads. Yet the line was still using strap iron rail, and was plagued with sharp curves and inadequate bridges. Train derailments and customer complaints were frequent.

Similarly, the towns along the line were also evolving and changing. The agricultural milling locations rapidly developed into "mill towns." Water-powered industries moved adjacent to the right of way to take advantage of lower transportation costs. The result was increasing demands for more service and better facilities.

Furthermore, the railroad's early Baltimore terminals were stopgap affairs and needed improvement. The 1831 Belvedere Depot could no longer handle the increase in business. The firm's route through Baltimore City to the harbor had developed as a disjointed collection of lines laid mostly on city streets. Local ordinances prohibited steam power on these streets, necessitating the use of horses. Movement was slow, capacity was limited, and the port facilities themselves were becoming obsolete.

Its capital already severely stretched and faced with multiple rebuilding needs, the company had to decide where to put the money first. It decided to try to solve its Baltimore problems, then rebuild the roadbed.

Baltimore Terminal Facilities, 1831-1854

In its earliest years the Baltimore & Susquehanna did not even own a line to the Baltimore harbor. As best as can be determined now, the railroad's original terminal, known as Belvedere Depot, was located in the vicinity of Eager and North streets. (North Street, not to be confused with present-day North Avenue, is now Guilford Avenue.) It was from this point that passenger service was operated in 1832, and it was from here that the body of President William Henry Harrison was taken on its westward journey on June 28, 1841.

Almost nothing is known about this early station other than its general location. The maps of Baltimore City from the early 19th century are somewhat ambiguous on its precise location. The Fielding Lucas, Jr. map from 1836 places the structure at the southeast corner of Eager and North streets. However, the Lucas map of 1841 positions the structure at the northwest corner of the same intersection. Nor does anyone now know what it looked like. Extensive research has failed to uncover either a description, drawing, or lithograph of the station. It is possible that the railroad merely used some existing structure, perhaps simply space in a local hotel — a common expediency in the earliest years of railroad construction. What is known is that the station was on the property of John Eager Howard's estate "Belvedere" and was within sight of his residence. Although the Belvedere Depot was located in the Jones Falls valley a relatively short distance from the harbor, the company made no immediate move to build its own line to the waterfront.

In late 1832 the railroad did begin development of what became its primary yard, shop, and locomotive terminal at a newly acquired facility known as Bolton Yard. Bolton Yard was located on about five acres of high ground in the area bounded by Cathedral Street on the east, Preston Street on the south, Foster Alley (later Brevard Street) on the west, and Dolphin Street on the north. Much of this same area is now occupied by the Baltimore & Ohio's 1896 Mt. Royal Station, now owned by the Maryland Institute College of Art. Bolton's name came from the "Bolton" estate, owned by George Winchester. (The "Bolton" mansion itself was located where the Fifth Regiment Armory now stands.) Over the next several years the railroad built a machine shop, roundhouse, and operating offices here. A two-story frame passenger station and office was located on the east side of the property on Cathedral Street, near Preston.

Bolton became the starting point for the Baltimore & Susquehanna's first route to the harbor. In 1832 the Baltimore & Susquehanna and the Baltimore & Ohio jointly built a single-track line south on Howard Street from Bolton to the B & O's main line on Pratt Street. Each railroad owned a 50 percent interest in the line, which was used mainly for interchanging freight traffic. By using the B & O Pratt Street line, the Baltimore & Susquehanna could reach the various Pratt Street piers and the City Dock, located on the east side of the harbor.

This original route to the waterfront was not a particularly congenial arrangement. Since the track was laid in city streets, animal power had to be used. In addition, the Baltimore & Susquehanna used B & O terminal facilities, and was thus at the B & O's mercy — and relationships between the two companies were always tenuous. In 1840 the Baltimore & Susquehanna finally began building its own line to the waterfront, following a route through the eastern part of the city. This line started at the Bolton Yard, went past the Belvedere Depot, east on Oliver (John) Street, south on North Street (Guilford Avenue) to Monument Street; it then followed Monument Street east to Canal Street (now Central Avenue). At Canal Street, it went due south to the City Dock. This line also was laid mostly on city streets, again meaning horse power, but at least the company had full control of its own route to the dock. In 1847 the portion of this line between Oliver Street and Monument Street was realigned off of the city streets; a new branch also was built directly south on North Street from Monument, which was to reach a planned new passenger and freight terminal south of Centre Street.

In 1847 the Baltimore & Susquehanna directors began planning an imposing new Baltimore passenger and freight terminal building, which also would house all the offices of

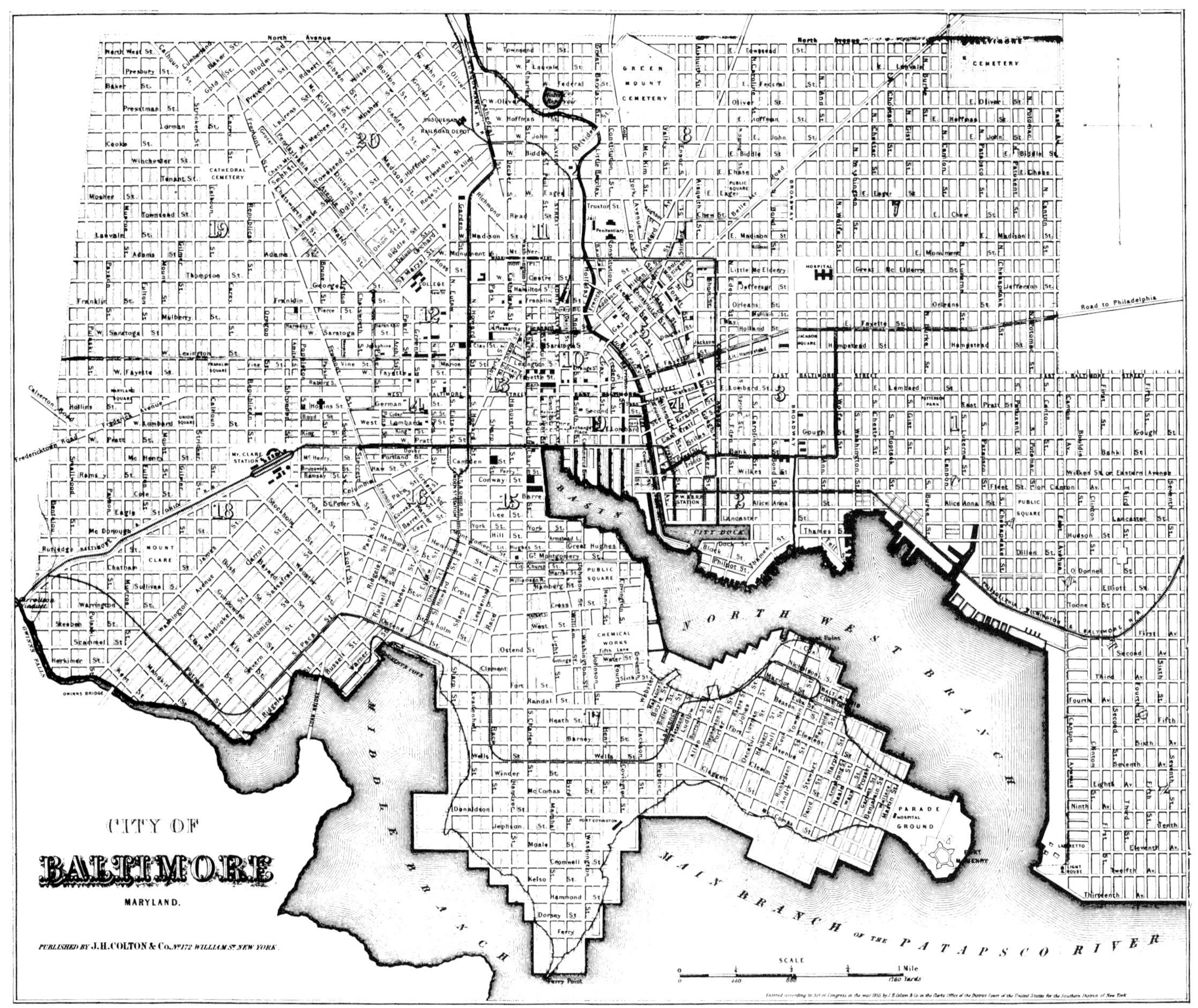

Baltimore in 1855. The B & S line enters the city from the north at the top center; the Bolton depot is immediately south of this point near Cathedral Street. A branch extends south on Howard Street to meet the B & O at Pratt Street, while the B & S "main line" may be seen in the map's upper center, terminating at Calvert Station at Franklin Street. A B & S freight branch turns east from this line and follows Monument Street and Central Avenue to the waterfront at the City Dock. University of Maryland Library Collection.

the company. The railroad hired the prestigious architectural firm of Niernsee and Neilson to design the new structure. Work on what became known as the Calvert Station began in 1848; it opened in early 1850 amid elaborate ceremonies. In the words of its architects:

> *the depot will consist of a car house 315 feet long, 112 feet wide, occupying the ground owned by the Company at Calvert Street...and terminating in a large building with a front of 112 feet in the Italian style, two stories in height, containing the passenger entrance, the ticket office, the transportation office and the necessary rooms for the President and Directors... The roof of the car shed will be of sheet iron, sustained by wrought iron trusses... The pillars are of cut granite. The space contains two passenger tracks and platforms with three tonnage (i.e., freight) tracks.*

The completed station was an impressive structure indeed. Designed in the Italianate style, it had arched windows and doors, with twin three-story towers at each end of the main building. The waiting rooms as well as the offices were heated exclusively by large fireplaces capped off with black marble mantles. The building was finished with a stucco texture, tinted light brown, with matching trim colors. It was justifiably considered one of the finest facilities in the nation, sometimes referred to as "the elegant

All of Baltimore's early railroads were cursed with the necessity to use animal power on much of their downtown street trackage. "String teams" such as this moved freight cars of the B & S and its various successors well into the 20th Century. This scene, near the old City Dock, dates to 1917, but was essentially the same 60 years earlier. F. A. Wrabel Collection; J. W. Wolf photograph.

depot of the Baltimore and Susquehanna Railroad." After the construction of a new freight house in 1865 it was used exclusively as a passenger terminal. Sadly, in later years it fell into disrepair and became dirty and neglected. It was finally demolished in 1948 to make room for the present Sunpapers building.

(Interestingly, in 1862 the B & S's successor, the Northern Central, considered razing Calvert Station and relocating its Baltimore passenger terminal several blocks south. Calvert apparently suffered from what was then considered an "uptown" location, and the company felt that a facility closer to the city's center would help capture more passenger traffic by avoiding the cumbersome transfer procedures most Baltimore travelers had to endure.)

The freight route to the City Dock was later extended to Jackson's Wharf, at the foot of Bond Street in Fells Point (see Chapter 4), giving the company access to additional dock and warehouse facilities. But the necessity of using horses to haul cars over city streets created a slow, awkward, and expensive operation. The area surrounding the harbor was heavily built-up, severely limiting the space available for more piers, freight handling facilities, or trackage. As a result the company attempted to build an entirely new line to a proposed marine terminal located on the vast open waterfront at Canton, on the far east side of Baltimore Harbor. In 1850, the same year that Calvert Station opened, the Baltimore & Susquehanna's directors authorized the company to begin land acquisition for what became known as the "Canton Extension."

"Canton" was a large and relatively undeveloped area of waterfront on the southeast side of Baltimore's harbor. Although the main line of the Philadelphia, Wilmington & Baltimore Railroad passed through its northern extremities, most of Canton had no rail facilities. Yet its large acreage and excellent deepwater pier sites made it an ideal solution for the Baltimore & Susquehanna's port dilemma. Thus the 1850 planning for a Canton line began a long difficult effort to reach the facility, an effort which was not to bear fruit for another 23 years.

Most of the Canton land, along with some other Baltimore waterfront property, was owned by the Canton Company, which had been incorporated in December 1828. Its original directors had included George Winchester, William Patterson, Fraiser Price, Columbus O'Donnell, Sheppard C. Leakin, James Ramsey, and the New York entrepreneur and philanthropist Peter Cooper. Eventually the company acquired not only the Canton property but other harbor sites at Fell's Point and Sollers Point, including Jackson Wharf and Susquehanna Wharf. Without direct rail connections, however, Canton itself had largely languished, with a few waterfront industries established along with some hotels, taverns, and breweries.

Between 1850 and 1853 the Baltimore & Susquehanna obtained several plots of land for the construction of its planned Canton branch. By 1854 grading and tracklaying had been completed on a portion of the new route east from Gay Street (Belair Road) to the Canton property. The single-track line was to be located off the streets on a private

The magnificent Calvert Station in Baltimore belied the B & S's chronically precarious financial state. Opened in 1850, it originally combined passenger and freight facilities as well as the company's headquarters offices. Courtesy of Baltimore Sun.

right of way and would be capable of handling heavy trainloads.

However, legal difficulties soon arose. In late 1854 several merchants, residents, and then the city government obtained injunctions against the railroad, and effectively stopped it from procuring a complete right of way and finishing the project.

Although local citizens had initiated the legal proceedings, railroad competition played a major part in delaying the project. At the center of the controversy was the Baltimore & Ohio, which had convinced city officials to support the injunction. A high-capacity Canton facility would have siphoned the traffic off the B & O's Pratt Street line and its newly opened (in 1849) Locust Point marine terminal on the south side of the harbor.

The completed section of the Canton extension remained dormant for several years. Eventually the line was abandoned, its completed sections scrapped, and the property sold. As noted in the next chapter, it was briefly brought back to life in 1858 using a different route, but was again stopped by legal action. It was not until after the Civil War that the project took on a different form and finally was completed.

Rehabilitating the Main Line

Beginning in 1852 the Baltimore & Susquehanna Railroad rebuilt its worn-out original trackbed in both Baltimore and York Counties. By this time coal had begun to trickle down the route into Baltimore; heavier loads were wearing out the strap iron rail and the sharp curves of the Jones Falls Valley were interfering with train movements.

The work was slow and expensive. Large amounts of capital were used to purchase rolled iron rail from England, and the realignment of the Jones Falls right of way cost more than the directors had anticipated. Virtually all bridges needed to be replaced, a process which stretched into the early 1860s. (The 1861 bridge data shown in an appendix

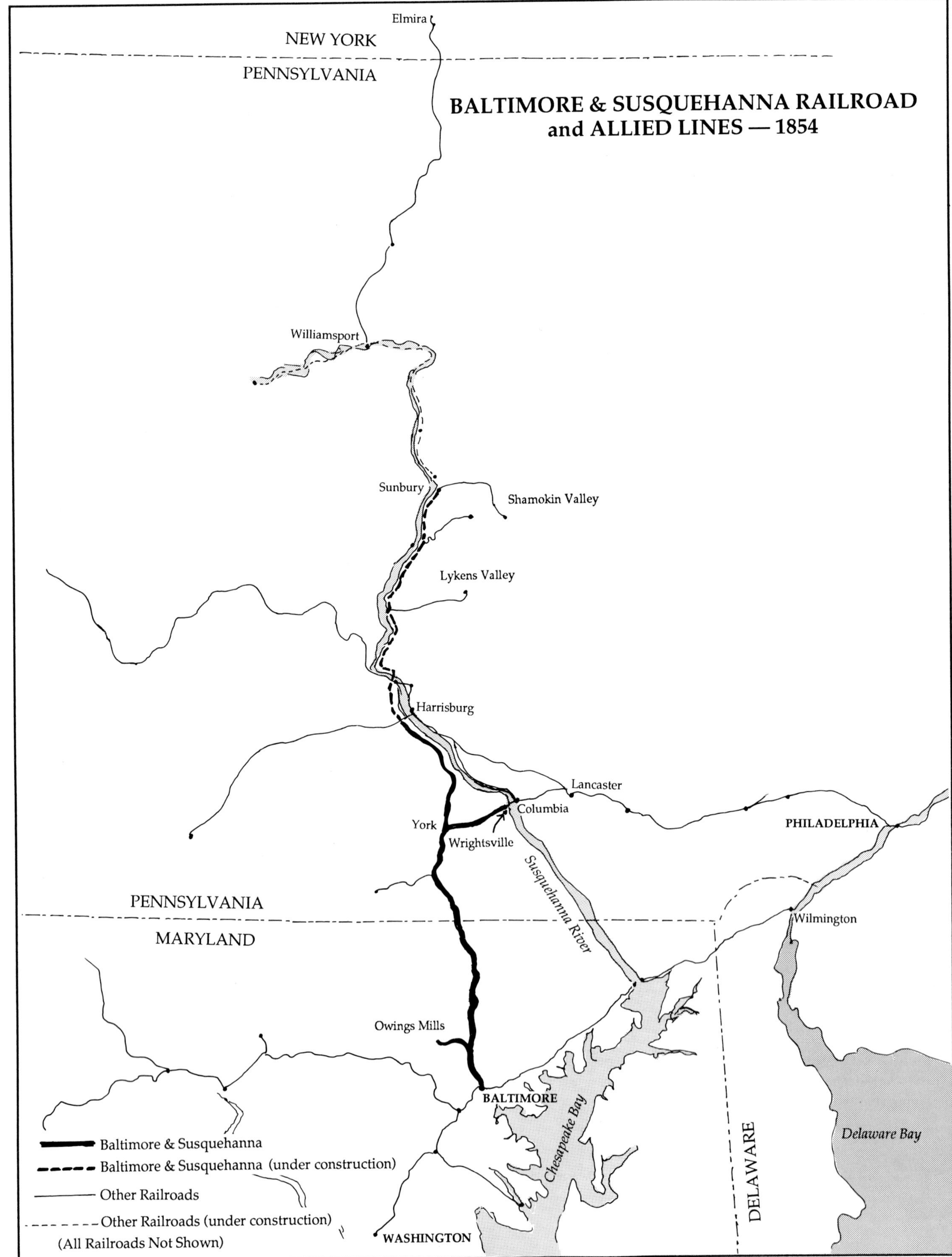
BALTIMORE & SUSQUEHANNA RAILROAD
and ALLIED LINES — 1854
Elmira
NEW YORK
PENNSYLVANIA
Williamsport
Sunbury
Shamokin Valley
Lykens Valley
Harrisburg
Lancaster
Columbia
York
Wrightsville
PHILADELPHIA
Susquehanna River
PENNSYLVANIA
MARYLAND
Wilmington
Owings Mills
BALTIMORE
Chesapeake Bay
DELAWARE
Delaware Bay
WASHINGTON
Baltimore & Susquehanna
Baltimore & Susquehanna (under construction)
Other Railroads
Other Railroads (under construction)
(All Railroads Not Shown)

gives a graphic picture of the work that was done.) Loans from the State of Maryland along with a bond issue helped to defray the expense, and by 1854 the most pressing parts of the reconstruction project had been completed.

Heavier motive power also was acquired. Beginning in 1851 and running through 1858, the B & S and its successor, the Northern Central, bought a total of nineteen ponderous but powerful 0-8-0 "Camels" from Ross Winans, the inventive but unconventional Baltimore locomotive builder.

Thus by 1854 the Baltimore & Susquehanna had a single-tracked railway from Baltimore to Bridgeport (Lemoyne), Pennsylvania, with trackage rights into Harrisburg over the Cumberland Valley. From Bridgeport an uncompleted right of way straggled north to Sunbury. The company also operated the branch from York to Wrightsville, connecting with Columbia via the long covered bridge over the Susquehanna. (The bridge trackage was owned by a separate company, the Columbia Bridge Company.) And finally there was the stepchild Green Spring branch, from Relay to Owings Mills — which later would be turned over to the Western Maryland. The operating main line was now reasonably straight and equipped with new rolled "T" rail.

Also, at that time the Baltimore & Susquehanna was operating the Hanover Branch Railroad under an agreement. This independently built short line extended west from a spot on the Baltimore & Susquehanna called Hanover Junction (a mile south of Seven Valleys) to Hanover, Pennsylvania. It had been chartered on May 1, 1847, constructed in 1851, and opened to Hanover on October 22, 1852. For the first two and one-half years of its life, it was operated under contract by the Baltimore & Susquehanna; after April 1, 1855 it took over its own management and afterwards remained independent under various names. In 1858 another independent company, the Gettysburg Railroad, built an extension of the route from Hanover to Gettysburg; the two companies eventually merged to form a through route from Hanover Junction to Gettysburg, and later built farther west.

The Hanover Branch Railroad was of minor importance when first opened, but gradually grew into an important feeder for the Baltimore & Susquehanna and a strategically vital line during the Gettysburg campaign in the Civil War. It was, among other things, the route Lincoln took on his legendary trip to Gettysburg. The little line was finally absorbed by the Western Maryland Railway in 1886; afterwards, much of its traffic was diverted to Western Maryland routes, and Hanover Junction declined as an interchange point. The section west of Hanover Junction was abandoned in the late 1920s, although the original Hanover Junction station miraculously still stands.

Prices to ship commodities over the 71 miles from Bridgeport to Baltimore were, per mile, quite cheap by the standards of the time. Per ton, the rates were: coal $1.38, iron $1.35, grain $2.20, and salt $2.00. Through horses were $3.75 and passengers paid $2.12 or three cents per mile. Under its original charter the Baltimore & Susquehanna also was hauling privately-owned four-wheeled freight cars, which at that time paid only $3.37 for the trip. In effect the company was undercutting itself, allowing private operators to haul freight over its lines at lower rates than the railroad itself charged, but paying only a minimal amount to the railroad. This practice was a major factor in the Baltimore & Susquehanna's marginal financial performance.

The Railroad's Effect on its Communities

By the early 1850s the railroad was well established, and the on-line territory was developing rapidly. Residents and businesses rushed to use it; industries expanded to meet increased demand; employment escalated and the rural towns began to grow and prosper.

For example, both the Mt. Vernon (Baltimore) and Phoenix textile mills in Maryland started operations in 1847 and began using the railroad the following year. The Oregon iron furnace near Cockeysville, Maryland, became operational in 1849 and chrome was shipped from the Bare Hill mines after 1855. These industries prospered, in large measure because the railway provided lower transportation costs for their products to reach the seaport.

Residents were equally as eager to use and support the railroad. Many enterprising individuals built hotels and restaurants along the right of way. For example, Charles W. Bentley not only built the resort hotel "Glen House" in Bentley Springs, Maryland (north of Parkton) but also donated the land for the community's railway station. Other prominent citizens in many of the towns made similar gifts. Amon Bosley donated the land for the Timonium station and Henry T. Burns donated a plot of land for the Grey Stone depot, between White Hall and Parkton.

On the other hand, some towns were much less fortunate. York Haven was one. When the Baltimore & Susquehanna began using the point as a canal junction in 1851, it was a small river transshipping point and farming community. From the 1850s until the 1870s York Haven progressively prospered and expanded, based on its strategic location as a railroad and river terminal. Mills, manufacturing concerns, and mercantile establishments soon proliferated throughout the town. Tradesmen and day laborers moved to the area to take advantage of the increased opportunity. Taverns and hotels provided service to the traveler while blacksmiths and mechanics found employment with either the railroad or canal. Then, when the railroad located more northern terminal facilities and the canal became obsolete, the town began to disintegrate. By 1880 York Haven had deteriorated to the point where the historian J. T. Scharf lamented that the traveler "would scarcely recognize the metropolis it once was."

Crisis and Disaster

With its imposing new Calvert Station, its rebuilt right of way, and its expanding territory, the Baltimore & Susquehanna superficially seemed to be prosperous and growing. But it was an illusion. Indeed, finances were rapidly becoming a critical problem as the company tried to cope with its rehabilitation needs and also complete the Susquehanna Railroad from Harrisburg to Sunbury.

In fact, by 1854 the Baltimore & Susquehanna was insolvent. It had used its credit and large sums of cash to build both the York & Maryland Line and the Wrightsville, York, & Gettysburg railroads, and for all intents and purposes owned them all. The earnings of all three firms, although rich in traffic and potential, were insufficient to meet the interest on obligations.

Of all the companies, only the York & Cumberland was showing any earning power, and it had been in operation for just eighteen short months. Although operated by the Baltimore & Susquehanna, this line was a separate corporation which received substantial lease payments from the Baltimore & Susquehanna. In addition, the growing interchange business with the Cumberland Valley Railroad kept its earning capability rather high when compared to the Baltimore & Susquehanna and its other affiliates.

The road from Baltimore to York and Wrightsville represented a total investment of $4,364,000, divided as follows:

Stock		$ 450,000
State of Maryland loans	1,884,000	
City of Baltimore loans	850,000	
Collateral loan	150,000	2,884,000
Debt of interest, funded by Maryland for 15 years without interest		1,036,000
Debt on interest not funded		400,000
Total		4,770,000
Less investment in branch lines		460,000
		$4,364,000

For the years 1844-1854 the Baltimore & Susquehanna had paid the State of Maryland an average of $40,000 per year on the interest obligations of $113,000. It paid the City of Baltimore nothing. The city fathers agreed to a suspension of interest payments.

Throughout the early 1850s both the states of Maryland and Pennsylvania, along with the directors of all the affected railroads, had been discussing reorganization and refinancing. To resolve the financial crisis, it was proposed to consolidate all the railroads and revise some of the debt commitments. It was a delicate task because each of the affiliated railroads had outside security holders, in addition to obligations to governmental agencies.

To make the consolidation attractive to the York & Cumberland Railroad, the State of Maryland agreed to settle its claim against the Baltimore & Susquehanna for $90,000 a year. That annuity would be secured by a mortgage of the line from Baltimore to York (subject to the first mortgage of $150,000), and junior liens on the remainder of the property. It was stipulated that the annuity could be canceled and the mortgage released with a payment of $1,500,000 to the state of Maryland within a ten-year period. The City of Baltimore, which consented to fund its claim without interest payments, agreed to relinquish that debt entirely on the condition that the line to Sunbury be completed and that the terminal line to the Canton wharves be built. (The original Canton extension was still tied up in litigation, but a new line was planned over a different route.) The City of Baltimore demonstrated great restraint in releasing part of its debt. However, it should be remembered that the objective was commerce. Trade was the city's lifeblood, and Baltimore was willing to make sacrifices to push itself ahead of Philadelphia.

Then, on July 4, 1854 tragedy abruptly intervened to accelerate the reorganization process.

Independence Day 1854 was a typical summer day — sunny, hot, and humid. All day long Baltimore residents had been leaving Calvert Station for Rider's Grove, where Fourth of July celebrations had become a tradition. By late afternoon, four to five thousand excursionists were at Rider's Switch station (now Riderwood) ready to return home.

At 3:30 that afternoon, Conductor William Scott gave the proceed signal for his northbound train to leave the station. As the train chugged along Jones Falls, everyone on board knew that they soon would be stopping at Relay, the Green Spring branch junction point. There, the regular daily procedure was to pull onto the Green Spring branch far enough to let southbound trains clear the junction on the single-track line — and this is what Scott's train did. The train normally left the junction at 4:15 on its way to York, but today there were extra excursion trains on the line to move the crowds south from Rider's Switch. Scott was supposed to wait until 5:30.

Standard operating procedure, in those days before the company adopted the telegraph, was for the crew of the southbound train to tell Scott if the track ahead was clear. But this day the southbound crew gave Scott no message. The stage was set for disaster: there were still two excursion trains at Rider's Switch, one of which had just left the station on its way south.

Apparently unaware, Scott backed his train onto the main line at the junction and continued on north. At 4:25 he was three-quarters of a mile north of the junction when the crew of the southbound excursion train, John Struby and Jacob Waltmeyer, saw the northbound heading toward them. Struby reversed, jumped, and survived the wreck; engineer Waltmeyer stayed with his locomotive and, although scalded, survived. Many others were not so lucky.

The locomotives collided in an explosion of fire and steam. The wooden passenger cars telescoped together, mangling many people. Benjamin Merryman, baggage master on the York train, was killed instantly. The wife of Martin Boyd watched horror-stricken as her husband burned to death while trapped on the firebox of one of the locomotives. Many children were injured and two small youngsters were burned beyond recognition in front of a dazed crowd of spectators who had begun gathering at the scene.

Some of the first to arrive were nearby residents. Doctors Thomas Dorsey, A. V. Cherbonnie, and Jacob H. Jones, along with Vincent Heaton and Grafton M. Bosley, began treating the injured. Their account, reported in the *Baltimore American and Commercial Advertiser* on July 6th graphically described the mangled wreckage and victims. One woman's body was literally torn apart as her remains were extracted from the debris.

Rescue trains from Baltimore reached the scene at 8:00 p.m., bringing additional doctors, nurses, and medical supplies. They found survivors stunned and milling around the area. Some of those who had escaped injury were walking down Falls Road back to Baltimore.

At an inquiry the next day, Coroners Goldsmith and Stevens found "carelessness" in Conductor Scott's performance of his duties. Scott was taken into custody after the hearing and released on parole on July 6th.

Twenty-eight people were killed in the disaster, and seven died later from their injuries. Over 100 others were injured, some of them seriously. The wreck cost the railroad $28,359 in property damages and $53,882 in settlement costs.

The hapless Scott was dismissed from the company; he died at the young age of 49, still plagued with memories of Independence Day 1854.

The disaster helped push the Baltimore & Susquehanna into bankruptcy. Out of the ashes, both literally and figuratively, emerged a new charter, a new corporation, and a new name — the Northern Central.

PROFILE: Philip Albright Small 1791–1875

Philip A. Small of York, Pennsylvania was an outstanding example of the manufacturers and businessmen who helped promote the Baltimore & Susquehanna and the Northern Central as a means of developing their own enterprises.

The Small family was a diverse group of entrepreneurs living in York who maintained a variety of business interests. They held considerable land in the city, owned numerous dry goods stores, and operated several nearby flour mills. In addition, the Small family managed one of the most extensive short horn cattle herds located on the east coast.

Philip Small and his brother, Samuel (1799-1885), were among the original incorporators of the Baltimore & Susquehanna Railroad and were active advocates of the Baltimore-York line. It was estimated that enterprises belonging to the Small family provided one-sixth of the freight that the railroad carried to Baltimore during its early years of operation.

Philip's son, George (1825-1891), moved to Baltimore in 1850 to oversee the family flour export business with special concentration on the Brazilian market. The later grain exporting piers at Canton were largely an outgrowth of the early export business established by Philip and George Small.

In 1844 Philip Small, Samuel Smith, and Christian Geiger, along with their respective wives, chartered and opened the Ashland Iron Works near Cockeysville, Maryland. The industry and the town that was constructed for the labor force were purposely placed along the rail line that the Small family helped establish. Ashland grew steadily from 1844 until the 1870s, absorbing the nearby Oregon furnace in 1852. The Northern Central brought iron ore, lime, and anthracite to the furnaces and transported a high quality pig iron out of the facility to Baltimore's seaport.

The Ashland Iron Works managed to survive until the 1880s. Newer technology, however, cut deeply into Ashland's product line and President George Small announced closure in 1884. He died in 1891, only one year before the plant at Ashland was dismantled and taken to Sparrows Point as scrap.

CHAPTER 4

The Northern Central Emerges

Less than six months after the Independence Day disaster, the Baltimore & Susquehanna and most of its Pennsylvania affiliates had vanished. Taking their place was a consolidated company carrying one of the more memorable and romantic names in railroading: the Northern Central Railway.

As noted earlier, the reorganization process was financially complex and politically sensitive. The State of Maryland and City of Baltimore had heavy financial involvement in the lines, as well as an obvious commercial stake; powerful political forces in Pennsylvania, such as Simon Cameron, also had an interest in it. Neither state wanted the insolvent enterprise sold at public auction and risk it falling into unknown (and possibly hostile) hands.

Complicating the process was the need for large amounts of new capital. The Bridgeport-Sunbury line lay unfinished, and further rehabilitation had to be done on the existing lines. Finally, the July 4th wreck had brutally dramatized the shortcomings of a single-track railroad with steadily increasing business.

Unification

Concurrent actions by the Maryland and Pennsylvania legislatures chartered the Northern Central Railway, which was authorized to absorb four of the old companies: the Maryland-chartered Baltimore & Susquehanna, and the Pennsylvania-chartered York & Maryland Line, the York & Cumberland, and the Susquehanna Railroad. The consolidated company thus owned the complete main line between Baltimore and Bridgeport/Harrisburg, plus the still-incomplete extension to Sunbury.

Not included in the merger was the Wrightsville, York & Gettysburg, which owned the line between York and Wrightsville/Columbia. The reasons for this omission are unknown, and somewhat mysterious, considering that the old Baltimore & Susquehanna had invested over $250,000 in building the line. By this time Wrightsville and Columbia had become secondary terminals, and it is possible that the new company's directors wanted to maintain the option of selling this branch to help finance their primary goals. Whatever the reasons, the Northern Central continued to operate the Wrightsville line until 1870, when it was sold directly to the Pennsylvania Railroad — which by then also controlled the Northern Central.

The first meeting of the directors and officials of the new firm was held at the Calvert Station late in 1854; John Pendleton Kennedy was elected its first president. Articles of Union were dated December 4, 1854 and filed in both Maryland and Pennsylvania within a week. The Northern Central officially took over its properties January 1, 1855.

All of the existing debts of the consolidated railroads were carried forward to the Northern Central, and its capital stock was fixed at $8 million. Authority was granted to issue stocks and bonds, and to borrow money from the states of Maryland and Pennsylvania in order to complete the line to Sunbury, obtain adequate rolling stock, and to double-track the main line. As a result of the state and city financing, the Northern Central was also mandated to build a line from the Calvert Station in Baltimore to Canton and to construct docks and piers there. This was the second attempt at a Canton extension; as noted earlier, it was to use a different route than the original line.

To put the new company on a firmer financial footing, its directors had insisted on a charter provision prohibiting the old practice of allowing private parties to place their own equipment on the line at a lower than normal rate. Afterwards, the Northern Central's revenues improved steadily. A new $2.5 million six percent bond issue was floated to complete the line to Sunbury, as well as the branch to the planned Canton marine terminal.

The Maryland Legislature, recognizing the importance of the Sunbury extension (and particularly the Pennsylvania anthracite traffic) to Baltimore's trade, promptly executed a mortgage to the state of Maryland requiring annual payments of $90,000. Provisions were created to extinguish that annuity within ten years upon payment of the full debt of $1.5 million, which included previous loans. However, the Northern Central needed the money to finish the line.

In contrast, the Pennsylvania Legislature was careful to try to protect Philadelphia. The Northern Central's reorganization statutes stipulated that if the old companies and their officials could not agree on a charter, then the Susquehanna Railroad would consolidate with the Sunbury & Erie Railroad, and that the portion of the unfinished roadbed south of Dauphin would be conveyed to the York & Cumberland Railroad. In effect, this would have given the Philadelphia-backed Sunbury & Erie the route from Sunbury to Harrisburg, with the implication that its traffic would be channeled to Philadelphia rather than Baltimore. However, the companies themselves and the state legislators did agree on the consolidation plan, and nothing became of the Sunbury & Erie alternative.

The Northern Central Starts Operations

The new Northern Central took over the Baltimore-Bridgeport main line on schedule in January of 1855. It also continued to operate the Wrightsville branch, as well as the independently owned branch between Hanover Junction and Hanover, Pennsylvania. (This latter operation was brief; the Hanover line was turned over to its owners on April 1, 1855.)

All the old problems remained, however. The Sunbury line had to be completed as quickly as possible. The Northern Central's property was still in poor condition and needed additional renovation — not to mention the company's charter obligation to double-track its main line. And much of its equipment was obsolete and limited in capacity. At the time of consolidation, the Northern Central rostered 26 locomotives, including the 1832 *Herald.* Slightly less than half of this fleet was built in the 1851-1853 period and thus was relatively new, but several others dated to the late 1830s. Much of the freight and passenger equipment was still crude; most freight cars were little more than a wooden box on four wheels. Clearly, a large sum of money would have to be raised, and earnings plowed back into the facilities.

The company's strategy in 1855 was to make only the most necessary improvements to its track and facilities while putting most of its financial resources into the Sunbury line. There were, indeed, persuasive reasons for completing the project.

Establishing a Great Lakes terminal was one. Since the Erie Canal's opening in 1825, it had become increasingly evident that the Great Lakes would become a main artery for commerce between East and West. By the early 1850s other railroads — notably the Erie Railroad and a string of connecting lines across New York state — were linking the East Coast with the Great Lakes system. The Sunbury & Erie, which opened its first 40 miles between Sunbury and Williamsport on January 7, 1856, promised eventually to provide a connecting route between the Northern Central and Lake Erie. (It would take time, however; the Sunbury & Erie — renamed the Philadelphia & Erie in 1861 — would not reach Erie until 1864.) Another potential Great Lakes connection, the Elmira & Williamsport, was projected, and partly constructed, toward Elmira, New York; at Elmira it would connect with the Erie Railroad into Buffalo. The completion of these lines would make the Northern Central the shortest route between Baltimore and the Great Lakes.

An even greater traffic potential was more immediate and closer at hand. The coal mine owners at both Lykens and the Shamokin area wanted a rail line opened to the Baltimore markets. So did the Schuylkill coal field; although primarily oriented to Philadelphia, the Schuylkill field mines also used the Schuylkill & Susquehanna line into Dauphin. The Sunbury extension along the east bank of the Susquehanna would put these mines closer to Baltimore than Philadelphia.

Sunbury at Last

Late in 1855 the Northern Central issued the contracts for the work on the Sunbury line. The road work was given to Daugherty, Lauman and Company while the bridge work was given to the McCallum Bridge Company for $750,000. At the time, the line was in operation only as far north as Marysville, at the south end of the Susquehanna River bridge; the bridge itself had yet to be constructed.

Work on the roadbed began soon after the contracts were let. Four different groups of workers labored several years building the line, which was finished in its center before either end. The section between Millersburg and Trevorton Junction (later Herndon) was completed first and opened in April of 1856. The next section, between Dauphin and Millersburg, was opened in January 1857. At that time, the Northern Central established an interchange with the Lykens Valley Railroad and began coal shipments to Baltimore, using the Pennsylvania Railroad's Rockville bridge as a stopgap route to cross the Susquehanna.

The last remaining superstructure of the fourteen-span covered bridge over the Susquehanna River at Dauphin was completed in July 1858. Finally, the north end of the line from Trevorton Junction to the Sunbury city limits

The Susquehanna River bridge between Marysville and Dauphin was the Sunbury extension's primary engineering and cost hurdle. Originally all of its fourteen spans were wood, but some were later replaced with iron trusses as a result of fires and floods. This 1874 view shows both types. R. Bosley Collection.

was completed and opened in August 1858, despite financial depressions and contractor labor problems during 1857. The Northern Central inaugurated rail service from Baltimore to Sunbury on August 18, 1858.

The event was accompanied with a gala celebration. Supporters and boosters of the project, along with railroad officials, chartered a special train from Harrisburg to Sunbury and then on to the Trevorton Hotel. There, dinner and parties continued into the early hours of the morning.

Actually, the railroad barely reached the town of Sunbury. Approaching Sunbury along the river from the southeast, it was stopped at the city limits by recalcitrant local officials. The city politicians were supporters of the "Philadelphia faction" in the Pennsylvania Legislature and did not want trade diverted to Baltimore that could be sent over other routes which would benefit the home port of Philadelphia. They viewed the Northern Central as an "encroaching enemy."

The Sunbury & Erie Railroad, which had arrived in Sunbury from Williamsport in late 1855, also was initially hostile. Both it and the then-building Lackawanna & Bloomsburg Railroad — which was finally completed be-

A Northern Central passenger train at Sunbury during the 1860s. The high-wheeled 4-4-0, No. 64, was turned out by Rogers in 1854. Railroad Museum of Pennsylvania Collection.

This rare engraving was made for Egle's History of Pennsylvania in 1875. The view looks north from Sunbury toward Northumberland, Pennsylvania, as it was in 1855. To the right, the Sunbury & Erie Railroad crosses the North Branch of the Susquehanna on two sets of wooden covered bridges. The Northern Central used this line to reach Williamsport.

tween Scranton and Northumberland in mid-1860 — viewed the Northern Central's encroachment into the area as an attempt to divert Pennsylvania resources to a "foreign" seaport.

As a result, the Northern Central was temporarily stymied. Freight had to be manually transferred to wagons, and passengers took horse-drawn coaches between the Northern Central and the Sunbury & Erie terminal in the center of town at Market Square and Third Street. Eventually, the two railroads used the S & E station at Third Street, which was frequently referred to as the "Central Hotel." This in turn was replaced in June of 1872 by the "new" Sunbury station, a large two-story brick combination depot and office, which cost $35,000. It still stands in the center of Sunbury today.

When the Northern Central arrived in Sunbury in mid-1858, it and the Sunbury & Erie negotiated an operating agreement. The struggling, underfinanced Sunbury & Erie, still trying to build westward from Williamsport, could not afford to build new trackage and to operate its existing line at the same time. Previously it had contracted with the Catawissa, Williamsport & Erie (later to become the Catawissa Railroad and eventually a Reading branch) to operate part of its line. Once the Northern Central had made its connection in Sunbury, the NC took over operation of the Sunbury & Erie as far as Williamsport, and in 1859 extended service west to Lock Haven. This arrangement lasted until 1860, when the Sunbury & Erie gradually acquired enough equipment to run its own trains — although Northern Central cars were used for some time afterwards.

The two companies also agreed to a mutual trackage rights contract, allowing the Northern Central to use the Sunbury & Erie's line to Williamsport, while the Sunbury & Erie could use the Northern Central's line south of Sunbury into Harrisburg. The two firms thus established an early cooperative relationship; in 1858, however, the Northern Central was still denied the use of the Sunbury & Erie's station in Williamsport, for reasons unknown.

As a result of its financial problems, in 1861 the Sunbury & Erie applied to the Pennsylvania Legislature for refinancing and rechartering. The company changed its name to the Philadelphia & Erie Railroad, and the Pennsylvania Railroad purchased a controlling amount of its stock. By then the Pennsylvania also had an interest in the Northern Central, and one result was the Northern Central's use of the P & E stations at Sunbury and Williamsport.

Incidentally, the 45-mile section of railroad between Dauphin and Sunbury was the only line built new by the Northern Central Railway. Although the company considerably expanded its system in later years — particularly its strategic extensions toward the Great Lakes and into the coal fields — all subsequent expansion would involve acquisitions of facilities previously built by other companies.

Business Begins to Boom

In 1857, after the Northern Central connected with the Lykens Valley at Millersburg and the Schuylkill & Susquehanna at Dauphin, President Kennedy made plans to ship a 50-car train south to Baltimore each day for 300 days

Along the Sunbury line was this rail-canal coal transfer facility at Millersburg, Pennsylvania, shown in the 1860s. The canal is a spur from the Wiconisco Canal, which connected the Pennsylvania state canal system. B. F. G. Kline collection.

a year. He reported that this would put 70,000 tons of coal in Baltimore each year.

The following year, when the Northern Central reached Sunbury and completed its Susquehanna bridge, the estimate was increased threefold. The railroad planned to forward a million tons of coal to Baltimore each year beginning in 1860.

The business of the Northern Central increased steadily in every year from 1856 until 1860. Despite crop failure and business depressions during some of these years, the total business during the period grew over 80 percent. That increase required the railroad to not only expand its facilities but to buy more and heavier equipment.

Sadly, the 1855 consolidation had not particularly strengthened the enterprise, either financially or physically. Financially, the earlier debts and interest costs were added to the cost of completing the line, resulting in a heavy burden. Moreover, the directors were amazed to find that the liabilities were greater and assets were less than they expected. Physically, the four predecessor railroads had been built on meager credit, and the physical condition of the system and its equipment still left much to be desired. Caught between the company's needs and its resources, the Northern Central's new president and directors decided in 1855 to do their best to continue former President Wright's 1852 program to renovate the south end of the railroad.

Improvements in the Late 1850s

One of the first projects undertaken was another attempt to resolve the Baltimore port facilities problem. During the 1840s and 1850s, the old inner harbor (then usually called the "Basin") became congested with coal and lumber, and this part of the harbor proved too shallow to accommodate larger ocean craft. In 1858, when the Northern Central completed its line to Sunbury, the increase in coal traffic soon overloaded the City Dock area. As a result, the railway revived the stillborn Canton extension project of several years earlier. Canton, it will be remembered, was a large and mostly undeveloped waterfront area on the east side of the harbor, as yet untapped by any railroad. Before 1918 it was outside the city limits.

This reincarnation was no luckier than its predecessor. Work on the "new" Canton extension began in 1858 by the Pleasanto Construction Company, but ceased in 1859 shortly after it started. Difficulties in securing necessary rights of way along with more legal action by private property owners stopped the project. The Northern Central did manage to construct a branch from its City Dock line to Jackson's Wharf in Fells Point to handle escalating coal shipments, but the facility was limited in capacity and, of course, animal power was necessary. The Canton project, while not forgotten, was dead for the time being.

Meanwhile, the company continued its main line renovation. During 1858 all the remaining strap iron rails were replaced with rolled iron from England. The iron was expensive and the work took several years to complete. Strap iron remained in sidings and yard facilities for many years, however.

In addition, the Northern Central installed telegraph lines along its route during 1858-1859. By April 1, 1859 the telegraph line had been completed from Baltimore to Sunbury, and by the end of that year telegraph operators were working at all the major stations.

Finally, operations were improved and tightened. Freight trains were given schedules, which were adhered to as closely as possible. Speeds of both passenger and freight traffic were increased; freight running time between Sunbury and Baltimore was reduced to 24 hours. Delays and transfers were reduced. In 1859 it was possible for passengers from Baltimore to take an "express" train from Calvert Station to Sunbury without changing trains at York or Harrisburg. Passenger traffic grew simultaneously. In 1859 the Northern Central carried 25,000 passengers, and business increased every year thereafter.

Numerous other facilities were built. The bridge replacement program continued; at least 77 new bridges were built on the main line between Baltimore and Marysville, Pennsylvania in the 1855-1859 period, most of them iron girder spans. Turntables were installed at both Hanover Junction and York in 1858, and stations were constructed at Mt. Washington, Bridgeport, and Trevorton Junction in the same year. Local residents were employed as watchmen for the bridges and water stations to help prevent loss from fire.

During the years immediately after the Northern Central's formation, the firm purchased a large amount of equipment. Newer, more efficient locomotives were acquired, larger and more comfortable passenger cars were put on the line, and the freight fleet was greatly expanded.

The Northern Central purchased large amounts of rolling stock and locomotives during 1858. The need for more powerful locomotives led the railroad to the Lancaster Manufacturing Company, William Swinburne's Locomotive Works, and Ross Winans; a total of nine new engines were bought that year, including the last group of Winans 0-8-0s. The equipment was expensive, and to help defray the expense the Northern Central disposed of several "useless" locomotives — including some of its earliest steam power. The *Herald, Samson, Wrightsville, Pennsylvania, Howard*, and *Susquehanna*, relics of the 1830s, were all taken to the yards at York and dismantled in the 1859-1860 period.

By 1859 the Northern Central listed the following equipment on the property for its tax records:

Equipment	No. of wheels	Quantity
Locomotives		41
Passenger Cars	8	31
Baggage	8	8
Freight	8	265
Gondola	8	146
Stock	6	5
Freight	6	4
Lumber	6	61
Wood	6	13
Lime	6	45
Stone	6	9
Freight	4	57
Lumber	4	156
Lime	4	140
Wood	4	18
Powder	4	2
Coal	4	785
Dump	4	10
Ore	4	32
	Total	1828

The large number of coal cars reflected what was becoming the company's major business — hauling coal to Baltimore from the eastern Pennsylvania anthracite mines, especially the Lykens and Shamokin fields. Once the Sunbury extension fully opened, freight business increased dramatically and the railroad found itself short of cars in 1859. However, its financial condition at the time prevented all but the most necessary purchases.

The high cost of renovation and rehabilitation meant that not much of the increase in revenues could be converted into required interest payments. By 1860 debt and interest charges had increased substantially because of the bonds that had been issued for construction, along with the considerable amount of money spent on new equipment and facilities. On December 31, 1860 funded debt had increased $2.4 million, and floating debt by $450,000. Income available for interest charges in 1860 was a meager $283,000 — not enough to pay the firm's debt.

So in late 1860 the railroad was back in financial trouble. It had hoped that the State of Maryland would postpone collecting its $90,000 annuity. The state, however, which had been so supportive during the early years, filed a foreclosure suit in November 1860.

The company was rescued by a $120,000 loan from John S. Gittings and Company. Mr. Gittings was then the president of the Northern Central and his personal credit, as well as that of his firm, was used to acquire the needed funds for payment of the annuity. The suit was again litigated in 1861 but the foreclosure proceedings were canceled when war revenues allowed the Northern Central to begin payments. The debt to the State of Maryland was liquidated in 1862.

Whatever its immediate problems, the Northern Central had begun to show considerable promise. Its property and equipment were gradually improving, and its Calvert Station in Baltimore was a national showpiece. Its commercial position was strengthening dramatically, as traffic flowed from Pennsylvania to the port of Baltimore.

For one thing, the railroad had active junctions with the Susquehanna River and Pennsylvania's canal system at many points along its route. These early "canal junction towns" were important revenue sources while the railroad was completing its lines through Pennsylvania. Historically, the canal junction towns were the first strategic objec-

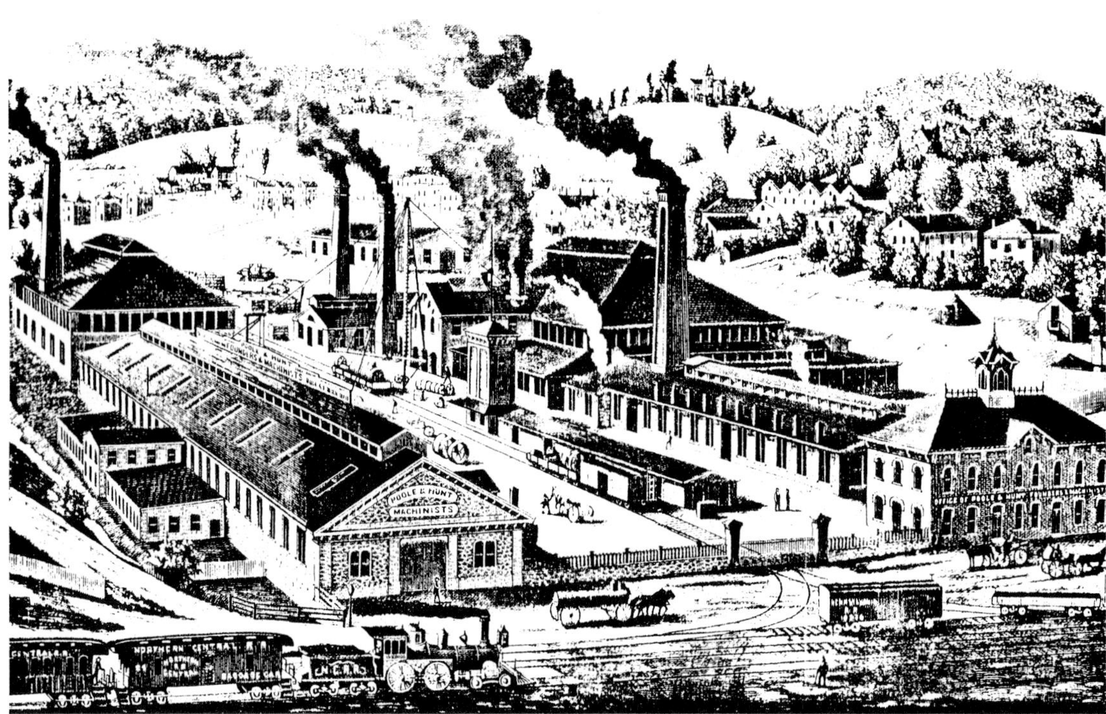

Typical of the industry which developed along the Northern Central was the Poole & Hunt foundry and machine works at Woodberry, in what is now Baltimore City. This complex was first developed in 1853, and became a major manufacturer of industrial machinery. The company also cast the iron columns and brackets supporting the U.S. Capitol dome. This lithograph, done for J. Thomas Scharf's The History of Baltimore City and County, dates to the early 1880s. Poole and Hunt ceased operations in the 1920s, but many buildings remain.

This impressive post-Civil War-era station and division office building at Sunbury served both the NC and Philadelphia & Erie. The photo dates to the 1890s. Paul Thomas Studio Collection.

tives of the owners. Revenues from traffic received from the canals for the railroad, in large measure, were used to build the line further north.

In all, five major canal junction facilities were progressively established as the railroad expanded: Wrightsville (1840), York Haven (1852), Dauphin (1858), Millersburg (1857), and Trevorton Junction (Herndon) (1858).

The completion of the railroad to Sunbury was unquestionably the Northern Central's most commercially significant strategic accomplishment to date. The hard-fought and expensive extension gave it direct access to the rich coal fields of central Pennsylvania, plus the agricultural and forest products from the upper Susquehanna River system — which now flowed to the railroad via the canals and new railroad connections.

Reaching Sunbury also gave the Northern Central access to the Great Lakes — after a fashion. From Sunbury to Williamsport, Pennsylvania, business moved over the Sunbury & Erie. At Williamsport, a transfer was made to the Williamsport & Elmira Railroad, which ran north to Elmira where it connected with the broad-gauge Erie Railroad; the Erie completed the route to Buffalo.

By 1859 the Erie signed a formal agreement allowing the Northern Central to forward business over its line on a pro-rate basis.

In 1858 the opening of the Buffalo route was considered a substantial accomplishment in Baltimore. The event was given ample coverage in the newspapers; the Northern Central advertised itself as forming "the shortest route between Baltimore and the Great Lakes," and exalted the "increased benefits." But in reality, the route was slow, disjointed, and required several transfers. A passenger trip between Baltimore and Buffalo took the better part of three days. The Williamsport & Elmira (which later would become a part of the Northern Central) had been built on a shoestring budget, and, although completed only four years earlier, already was dilapidated. Rail and ballast were poor; weather and floods also had taken their toll of the roadbed. In fact, several documents of the time referred to the railroad as one laid on "quick sand." It would be some years before it would become a true main line route.

The most important aspect of the Sunbury extension, however, was coal. This grew to be the lifeblood of the Northern Central. Pennsylvania anthracite was now becoming a staple in the Northeast, and the railroad's location allowed it to draw from large producing areas in the hills and mountains east of the Susquehanna.

So, by 1861 the Northern Central was beginning to mature and show impressive potential — albeit still with a worrisome financial structure. Then two momentous events changed both the railroad's immediate life and its future. Almost simultaneously came the Civil War and the Pennsylvania Railroad.

PROFILE: John Pendleton Kennedy 1795–1870

First President of the Northern Central, John Pendleton Kennedy was a unique blend of creative writer, politician, civic booster, and businessman. An early and strong proponent of rail transportation for Baltimore (in 1834 he wrote "Baltimore must imitate the spider and spread out her lines in all directions"), he was a heavy investor in the Baltimore & Susquehanna and also participated in numerous political, educational, and civic organizations.

Kennedy was born in Baltimore October 25, 1795, the son of John Kennedy, an immigrant from Northern Ireland. After graduating from Baltimore College in 1812 he immediately joined the American forces in the War of 1812. Following the war Kennedy studied law and was admitted to the Maryland bar in 1816.

He apparently found the law tedious and confining; he changed careers to a combination of writing and politics, and distinguished himself in both.

In 1820 Kennedy became Speaker of the Maryland House of Delegates, and was a supporter and elector for John Quincy Adams. In 1838, as a Whig, he was elected to fill a vacancy in the House of Representatives, where he served on the Commerce Committee and the legation to Chile. In 1852 he was appointed Secretary of the Navy by president Millard Filmore, but afterwards withdrew from active politics.

Kennedy's literary career was equally notable. In 1826 he was appointed a professor of history at the University of Maryland and eventually became provost for the university. He wrote and published several novels including the famous *Swallow Barn*, a story of life on a Virginia plantation, as well as biographical and other works. Other authors benefited from his help and support, including the struggling Edgar Allen Poe. Kennedy also combined his literary and political interests as an inveterate and effective editorialist, writing numerous tracts, articles, and letters on civic and political issues in Baltimore.

As a civic booster during the early days of Baltimore's railroad development, Kennedy vigorously argued for the rapid completion of the Baltimore & Ohio Railroad during the mid-1830s (a dream that was 20 years too soon); in 1844 he persuaded the Maryland legislature to appropriate money for Samuel F. B. Morse's demonstration telegraph line along the B & O's Baltimore-Washington route.

While serving in the Maryland House of Representatives, he met George Winchester. The two men shared similar political views along with a vision of the benefits of a north-south railroad from Baltimore into the Susquehanna valley. He became a significant investor in the line and, as noted in the previous chapter, actively boosted the Sunbury extension in the communities along the route. When the Baltimore & Susquehanna was reorganized as the Northern Central Railway in 1855, Kennedy was named the new company's first president.

At the onset of the Civil War Kennedy actively opposed Maryland's secession, and his writings helped influence the state to remain in the Union. After the war, however, he became involved in a bitter conflict over the course of Reconstruction and left Maryland. He died in Newport, Rhode Island on August 18, 1870.

CHAPTER 5

The Pennsylvania Railroad Enters the Picture

During the decade of the 1860s the Northern Central entered a wider, more complex, and, for several years, more turbulent world. Almost simultaneously the railroad went through a change in corporate control, a financial turnabout, its most extensive rebuilding thus far, plus expansion into several major new markets — and all of this against the background of a brutal and devastating war. This and the next three chapters cover specific aspects of this convulsive period, neatly arranged by subject as only the historian's hindsight can allow.

The first and by far the most significant event occurred quietly in April 1861, when the promising but financially shaky Northern Central got a new parent — the Pennsylvania Railroad.

At the time, the Pennsylvania was the dominant railroad in its home state. Starting with its original Harrisburg-Pittsburgh rail route, it had absorbed the "main line" of the old state-owned canal and railroad system as well as several independent railroads. By 1861 it spanned the State of Pennsylvania from Philadelphia to Pittsburgh and con-

Harrisburg, Pennsylvania, was the junction point between the Northern Central's north-south route and Pennsylvania Railroad's east-west main line. The PRR's grandiose "Union Station" served trains of the PRR, NC, Cumberland Valley (another PRR affiliate), and the Lebanon Valley (later a part of the Philadelphia & Reading). Appropriately, a PRR train dominates this scene at the center while a Northern Central train waits less conspicuously at the right. Library of Congress Collection.

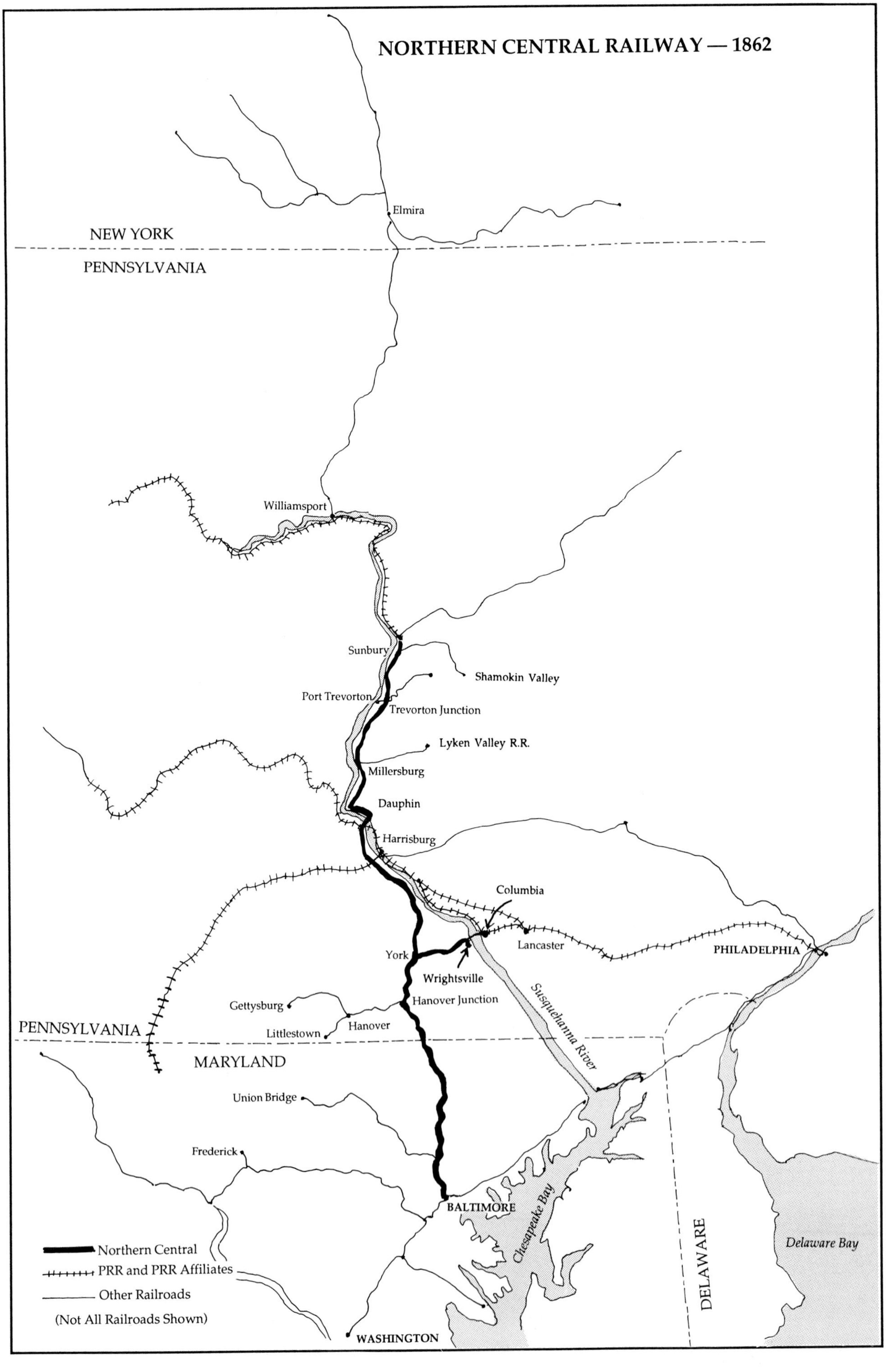

NORTHERN CENTRAL RAILWAY — 1862

Elmira
NEW YORK
PENNSYLVANIA
Williamsport
Sunbury
Shamokin Valley
Port Trevorton
Trevorton Junction
Lyken Valley R.R.
Millersburg
Dauphin
Harrisburg
Columbia
Lancaster
PHILADELPHIA
York
Wrightsville
Hanover Junction
Gettysburg
Hanover
Littlestown
PENNSYLVANIA
MARYLAND
Susquehanna River
Union Bridge
Frederick
BALTIMORE
Chesapeake Bay
DELAWARE
Delaware Bay
WASHINGTON

Northern Central
PRR and PRR Affiliates
Other Railroads
(Not All Railroads Shown)

trolled the Cumberland Valley Railroad, giving it a branch to Chambersburg with a leased extension to Hagerstown, Maryland.

The Pennsylvania was more than merely a large regional railroad, however. Through independent connections at Pittsburgh, it formed an east-west trunk line reaching Chicago and Cincinnati. In addition, its two top managers were among the most capable and ambitious in the business and represented a unique pairing of personalities which, when working together, could conceive bold but sound strategies and outmaneuver any opposition. President J. Edgar Thomson, a brilliant but introverted civil engineer, was usually described as sober, thoughtful, and thorough. Thomas A. Scott, his ranking vice president appointed in 1860, was outgoing, expansive, politically adroit, and a plunger. "In harness," noted one observer, Thomson and Scott "were a lethal combination."

It was not until after the Civil War, however, that the Pennsylvania would begin the breath-taking expansion that made it the country's largest and most powerful railroad. By 1874 the PRR owned or controlled lines to Chicago, St. Louis, Cincinnati, New York, Washington, and several Great Lakes ports.

The Pennsylvania's appearance on the Northern Central scene started at a time of national uncertainty, and also at the dawn of territorial railroad power politics. Nationally, the crisis of secession had created severe doubts about the federal government's ability to hold the nation together. The election of Lincoln as president seemed to strengthen fears of national division and an inevitable confrontation. Astute investors realized that in the developing conflict the railroads would be strategically important, and undoubtedly the first targets. Many people, including political, social, and corporate leaders, began to divest themselves of their holdings in the stocks of railroads located along the border states.

Northern Central stockholders had additional worries; already in 1860 the State of Maryland had instituted its foreclosure suit, threatening the loss of their investment.

At that time one major Northern Central stockholder was none other than John W. Garrett, president of the Baltimore & Ohio. The Philadelphia & Reading Railroad also owned a large block of Northern Central stock. Garrett had been quietly acquiring the stock since the Northern Central's early days as a company. His reasons are not known precisely, since original documents and later literature give conflicting interpretations. It appears likely, however, that he had become aware of the Northern Central's future potential as both a benefit to the B & O and a threat. The B & O and NC, of course, were both Baltimore-based and originally had been created to serve that city — although each had been designed to reach a different market territory. But as the national railroad system grew, and each of them established new connections and reached new markets, they had begun to turn into competitors.

For one thing, the Northern Central now connected with the Pennsylvania Railroad at Harrisburg, and through that route it competed with the B & O in the same western markets. Also, the B & O was a heavy bituminous coal carrier; the Northern Central had begun to tap the rich Pennsylvania anthracite fields and could deliver that coal to Baltimore more cheaply than the B & O's Cumberland-area bituminous. The Reading operated from Philadelphia to Harrisburg and was also a PRR competitor.

Whatever the reasons for Garrett's heavy investment in the Northern Central, he changed his mind and threw his holdings onto the open market early in 1861 during a brief financial panic in Baltimore caused by Lincoln's election in November 1860. His stock was purchased personally by Pennsylvania president J. Edgar Thomson; Thomson initially bought a block of 12,775 shares, or 28.26 percent of the 43,614 outstanding shares that, at the time, were available for sale. The Pennsylvania, in its own name, purchased the remainder of the available stock and placed it in a sinking fund. Later in the year Thomson's stock was also transferred to the Pennsylvania Railroad after the State Legislature, on April 23, 1861, approved the exchange.

Almost two years later, on January 14, 1863, the Pennsylvania purchased another 2,500 shares of Northern Central stock which were offered for sale on the London market, thereby increasing its total Northern Central stock ownership to 33.79 percent.

Although the Pennsylvania owned less than a majority of the Northern Central's stock (and, in fact, would not directly own over 50 percent until 1900), it was now the largest single stockholder, and in a position to exercise working control over the company.

In part, the Pennsylvania's working control was based on a close community of interest with Simon Cameron, one of the Northern Central's large stockholders. (His financial interest in the railroad originally came out of his involvement in several of the NC's Pennsylvania subsidiaries, including his role as contractor for the Sunbury extension.) Cameron, as noted earlier, had many business interests in Pennsylvania and was a major political power in the state, serving at various times as a United States Senator. Perhaps not surprisingly, he was on close terms with the politically active Tom Scott. Evidence exists that, indeed, it was Cameron who had originally persuaded J. Edgar Thomson to buy into the railroad. According to historian James A. Ward's reconstruction of the events, Cameron approached Thomson and Scott in June 1860 with a plan to jointly capture control of the Northern Central. At the time the Pennsylvania's managers needed Cameron's political help on a state tax problem; for this reason or perhaps their own, they agreed. Allied with Cameron's holdings, the Pennsyl-

The hilly territory along the Gunpowder Falls north of Baltimore was dotted with summer resorts, country estates, and small "tank town" communities. Glencoe, Maryland was a typical example, shown in this early 1880s engraving made for Scharf's The History of Baltimore City and County. The NC station in the lower center survived in 1991 as a residence.

vania eventually could command more than a stock majority.

The Northern Central remained at arm's length for several years afterwards; it had its own independent president until 1874 and a separate local operating management until 1914. But a significant shift had taken place. Between the Pennsylvania Railroad and the Cameron family's interests, the company was now clearly dominated by people from the state of Pennsylvania, rather than from Maryland. And although the Pennsylvania Railroad had no direct role in the Northern Central's management until 1874, both the railroad world and the financial world viewed the two companies as part of one "family." After 1864 the Northern Central board of directors was dominated by Pennsylvania officers and others associated with the larger railroad.

Nonetheless, Thomson and Scott were taking a risk. By the Pennsylvania's financial standards of the time, the total cost was high and the Northern Central's own financial outlook was questionable. Large improvement expenditures were needed, and the oncoming Civil War would cause considerable damage and disruption. Fortuitously for the railroad — if not for the public good — Simon Cameron was in a position to help, and did. That story will be told in the next chapter.

Whether or not the Pennsylvania executives consciously planned it, however, the Northern Central gave them several strategic advantages. Most obvious, and perhaps most appealing, it linked Baltimore with the Pennsylvania's east-west main line at Harrisburg. Besides being a lucrative market in its own right — and a new outlet for Pennsylvania coal — Baltimore was the stronghold of the B & O, one of the Pennsylvania's chief rivals. Undoubtedly, Thomson and Scott savored the idea of being able to camp on the doorstep of the hated John W. Garrett. And in the future, Baltimore would become the jumping-off point for one of Tom Scott's special dreams — the expansion of the Pennsylvania into the South.

The Northern Central also gave the Pennsylvania an entry to the anthracite fields where, thus far, it had no direct routes of its own. By then other PRR competitors — notably the Philadelphia & Reading — were entrenched in the anthracite region and moving large tonnages to Philadelphia and the New York area. As told in Chapter 7, the Pennsylvania would work with the Northern Central in acquiring coal branches and developing coal properties in the Middle and Southern Fields; in 1872 it also would directly acquire a line connecting the Northern Central at Sunbury with the heart of the Northern Field at Wilkes-Barre, Pennsylvania.

Finally, the Northern Central would be a key link for PRR expansion into northwestern Pennsylvania and upstate New York. As the next step in that direction, on January 1, 1862 the Pennsylvania leased the now-destitute Philadelphia & Erie (the one-time Sunbury & Erie), and by 1864 had helped it complete its line to Erie.

But in April 1861 all that lay ahead. First came the cataclysm.

PROFILE: Simon Cameron 1799–1889

Surely one of the most colorful and controversial characters in the Northern Central's history, Simon Cameron was a symbol of both the good and evil of the 19th Century businessman-politician. For the Northern Central, he was a beneficial force, substantially aiding the railroad through a critical time in its existence. But nationally he became notorious for his blatant blending of public office with private gain.

Cameron was born in Lancaster County, Pennsylvania on March 8, 1799, the son of Charles and Martha (Pfoutz) Cameron. Early in his life he was apprenticed in the printer's trade, and entered the newspaper business. In 1821 he was editor of the *Bucks County Messenger* at Doylestown, Pennsylvania; a year later he went to Harrisburg as a partner in the management of the *Pennsylvania Intelligencer.* Cameron purchased the Harrisburg *Republican* in 1824, and shortly afterward was awarded the position of State printer. He married Margaret Brua in 1822; five of their children were to grow to maturity. A son, J. Donald Cameron, inherited many of his father's business and political interests including the Northern Central's presidency.

Early in his career, Cameron became involved in state politics, and was commissioned as adjutant general of Pennsylvania in 1828. He also developed a wide range of business interests, including banking, insurance, ironmaking, and canal construction. In 1832 he established the Bank of Middletown (Pennsylvania). After being appointed commissioner for the settling of Winnebago Indian claims in 1838, he was accused of bilking large sums of money by issuing certificates to third parties without requiring bond. Afterwards enemies gave him the derisive title of "The Great Winnebago Chief."

Through his banking interests and construction companies, Cameron also became directly involved in railroad building, notably the various Pennsylvania extensions of the Baltimore & Susquehanna. By the mid-1840s, Cameron's political activities intensified. In 1845, with the support of a coalition of parties, he won the U. S. Senate seat which had been vacated by the election of James Buchanan. He lost the seat in the 1849 election, however, and also failed in a 1855 bid.

Simon Camerson, as he looked in 1862. National Archives Collection.

In 1856 Cameron joined the new Republican Party, a political allegiance he would hold for the rest of his life. With Republican backing he entered the 1857 election as a candidate for the U. S. Senate and this time won. He became a leader of the Pennsylvania Republican Party, and would remain so for the next two decades.

Cameron became a serious candidate for the Republican presidential nomination in 1860 and gathered considerable support. But the promise of a cabinet post from Lincoln's managers persuaded him to swing the Pennsylvania delegation's votes to Lincoln. Although Lincoln balked at the bargain, Cameron was appointed Secretary of War, and resigned his Senate seat.

Characteristically, Cameron carried his personal business interests and morality over to his new position. As soon as he took office, he dispensed War Department contracts to friends with impunity. He gave military traffic to the Northern Central (in which he still held a large interest) which would greatly enhance the railroad's profits.

Following the "Pratt Street riot" in Baltimore and the subsequent destruction of the Northern Central's bridges in April 1861 — and upon learning that the Union forces moving to Washington either were halted or were returning to Pennsylvania — Cameron gave the inflammatory order: "Send them on...prepared to fight their way through...." Lincoln immediately countermanded his Secretary.

This proved to be only the beginning. Cameron's behavior as Secretary of War became the subject of an investigation by the Committee on Government Contracts. This group reported flagrant fraud in military shipment contracts with the railroads to serve his personal interests and those of his friends — notably the Pennsylvania Railroad's managers. (Indeed, he had appointed the Pennsylvania's Tom Scott as Assistant Secretary of War in August 1861.) The report suggested criminal sanctions. The scandal embarrassed Lincoln, who arranged to have him sent out of the country in January 1862 as ambassador to Russia, and appointed Edwin M. Stanton to head the War Department.

Cameron did not stay long in Russia; he returned to the United States that September and resigned the Russian post the following February. In 1867 he was again elected to his old Senate seat, where he continued to be faithful to his business interests and friends. As related in Chapter 8, he was instrumental in helping the Pennsylvania Railroad obtain rights to the Potomac River bridge at Washington in order to expand into the South, and was a partner with the PRR group in its southern railroad investments.

During the 1860s and 1870s Cameron consolidated his political power in Pennsylvania, creating a party machine which dominated the state's government. In 1871 he became chairman of the Senate Foreign Relations Committee. During the Grant administration he controlled his state's federal patronage, and in 1876 he had the satisfaction of seeing his son, J. Donald Cameron (1833-1918), appointed Secretary of War.

President Rutherford Hayes, however, refused to extend the younger Cameron's appointment. Simon Cameron resigned as U. S. Senator in 1877, and eight days later the Pennsylvania Legislature elected the son to succeed him. The 78-year-old Cameron thus closed his political career, but his Republican organization in Pennsylvania remained a power for more than 40 years.

He retired to his 1200-acre estate, "Donegal," near Mount Joy in Lancaster County, which he had purchased in 1872. (The buildings still existed in 1991.) He also owned the former John Harris mansion in Harrisburg, bought in 1863; this building now houses the Dauphin County Historical Society, which also owes many of Cameron's personal papers.

Simon Cameron died June 26, 1889 at the age of 91, and was buried in the family plot in Harrisburg.

CHAPTER 6

Civil War: Trial By Fire and Blood

Mention of the Civil War evokes visions of gallant young boys leaving their farms, factories, and homesteads to fight a rebellion that, at the time, promised to be only a short insurrection — fighting in a conflict that they had thought little about and understood even less.

The Civil War also summons images of divided families, conflicting political ideologies, and opposing social environments: an agricultural and aristocratic South versus an industrialized North.

Less romantically, perhaps, the Civil War was the first "modern" war, a war where industrial power made the difference — and also the first war where railroads played a pivotal role. Balloon-stack eight-wheelers hauled troops by the thousands, tons of supplies, armaments, food, and rebuilding materials, all of it quickly and flexibly. To no small degree, the more unified and better-developed railroad network of the North gave it a decisive advantage. The North, in fact, had a two-to-one numerical superiority in rail mileage and equipment, as well as the majority of plants which produced rail, locomotives, and cars.

For better or worse, the Northern Central was one of the key routes. As it turned out, it was indeed both better and worse. The railroad's strategic location between the northern cities and industries and the southern battlegrounds brought heavy traffic and high revenues — a position enhanced by the influence of its "friends" in the federal government, notably the soon-to-be infamous Simon Cameron. This bonanza helped strengthen its anemic finances and gave it the wherewithall to expand its lines and complete its much-needed rebuilding program.

On the other hand, the Northern Central's southern section was a bit too strategically located. Running through an unstable border state and, at times, an area of active combat, it was periodically exposed to destruction and disruption.

In one form or another, the Northern Central was involved for the full length of the drama — and longer. Long before active hostilities, its location across the Mason-Dixon Line had made it a reluctant link in the Underground Railroad; it was also the supposed scene of the famous "assassination plot," to be carried out during Lincoln's trip to Washington for his inauguration. And, sadly, it was part of the war's tragic postscript, helping to take the martyred president on his last ride home.

The Underground Railroad

Rooted in the slaveholding state of Maryland, the Northern Central and its predecessor, the Baltimore & Susquehanna, mirrored the difficulties of trying to juggle the law, customs, and popular feelings. The Fugitive Slave Act of 1850, an ill-fated attempt to resolve the issue, had only served to further solidify sectionalism and create divisiveness. Many Baltimore County slaveholders "lost" their servants to the Underground Railroad, and with increasing frequency the Northern Central route was used as one of the many preferred routes of escape across the Mason-Dixon line.

There is evidence to suggest that while the Baltimore & Susquehanna maintained an official policy of providing facilities for the return of fugitive slaves, unofficially many individuals along the route provided help to fleeing slaves. Thus the company ended up being both a protector and a pursuer.

For example, in July 1850 several runaway slaves belonging to R. M. Dorsey and Dr. S. Rogers of Howard

County were captured by Baltimore & Susquehanna workmen who were doing trackwork near Parkton, Maryland. The bounty was $300 which the seven workmen divided among themselves. At Freeland, the first station south of the Mason-Dixon Line — and certainly an ironic name in this case — the railroad maintained both holding pens and boxcars, and upon request, would provide transportation for the bounty hunter and his captive.

By 1851, the year of the nationally publicized "Christina Riot," the situation had reached a point where both officials and bounty hunters were regularly watching the line of the Baltimore and Susquehanna Railroad along with the York Turnpike.

There are many oral legends which claim various stations of the Baltimore & Susquehanna and Northern Central as links in the Underground Railroad. The mill at Monkton, the stations at Parkton and Cockeysville, along with the rail facility at White Hall, were some of the more frequently cited "depots." Although such accounts undoubtedly were based on fact, it was difficult then (and is much more so now) to differentiate truth from fiction. Many of the stories were fabrications, created by abolitionists in hopes of making slavery appear doomed.

By 1859, if the Underground Railroad had not demonstrated that railroads in general would become an integral part in the sectional crisis, John Brown's attack on the Baltimore & Ohio at Harper's Ferry made the point painfully evident. Then, in early 1861, events in and around Baltimore brought the Northern Central to the very center of the hostilities.

Lincoln's Inaugural Journey to Washington

In November 1860 Abraham Lincoln was elected president, and was immediately thrust into the job of preserving order in a country where order was disintegrating. Lincoln had continuously been the subject of assassination plots during his campaign, and now his trip to Washington for his inauguration produced similar threats of violence.

Lincoln's train from the west arrived in Harrisburg on the night of February 21, 1861. The original plan had been to use the Northern Central route directly from there into Baltimore, and the line had been surveyed and was under guard. However, word from Allan Pinkerton had reached Judge David Davis and Colonel Ephraim E. Ellsworth, Lincoln's security advisors, that a conspiracy to assassinate the President-elect had been uncovered in Baltimore. The security men traveling with Lincoln then decided to abandon the Northern Central routing and continue to Philadelphia. There they would use the other rail route to Baltimore, the Philadelphia, Wilmington & Baltimore Railroad. The change would frustrate any attempt to attack Lincoln along the well-publicized Northern Central route. Pinkerton had the President's train blacked out, had the new route guarded by security officers, and all telegraph wires between the two cities cut. Lincoln's train arrived, unmolested, at the PW & B's President Street station in Baltimore at three o'clock on the morning of February 22, 1861. The transfer to Camden Station and the trip to Washington were made without incident.

To this day the existence of the conspiracy remains questionable. Original documents report conflicting views. However, they do name, as alleged conspirators, such Baltimore notables as the United States Marshal of Police, George P. Kane, and the city's mayor, George William Brown. Marshal Kane, upon learning of the accusation, published a denial of the existence of any assassination plot in the *Baltimore American* on February 25, 1861. In a letter to the editor, he pledged support to the Union and to the president-elect. Local newspapers decried the "escapade" and editorialized on the President-elect's ability to avoid the public and "sneak" through Baltimore.

Whatever the truth, the incident gave a foretaste of the role the railroads in and around Baltimore and Washington would play in the developing confrontation. Unhappily, they were the indirect cause of the next step, too. Little did anyone realize that events in Baltimore would produce the first casualties of the "War of the Rebellion" and also directly result in the first of many depredations perpetrated against the Northern Central.

Bloodshed in Baltimore: April 19, 1861

The war began on April 12, 1861 when Confederate forces shelled Fort Sumter, but inflicted no casualties. President Lincoln immediately called for 75,000 volunteers. Troops from the northern states were immediately ordered to proceed to Washington to protect the capital. Militia units from Massachusetts and Pennsylvania began arriving in Baltimore on April 18th, the same day that Virginia troops attacked a second target, Harper's Ferry.

The situation in Baltimore could not have been more precarious. Not only did Baltimore contain a large pro-Confederacy population, but it was the key — and weakest — link in the through rail routes between North and South. Two main routes from the north entered the city — the Northern Central from Harrisburg, and the Philadelphia, Wilmington & Baltimore from Philadelphia. There they met the Baltimore & Ohio, which operated the only line between Baltimore and Washington. The only direct connections between any of the three railroads were over city streets in the downtown area. A city ordinance required animal power over the streets, meaning that trains had to be broken up at their terminal stations and each car slowly hauled by horses from one railroad to another. Widely known as the "Baltimore Bottleneck," the city was an Achilles Heel in the Union's transportation system. (Philadelphia was even worse, with a complete break in rail routes through the city, but was not quite as strategically sensitive.)

The infamous "Baltimore Riot" or "Pratt Street Riot" of April 19, 1861, scene of the Civil War's first casualties, was a direct result of Baltimore's awkward and unwieldy railroad connections. Maryland Historical Society Collection.

For example, the Philadelphia, Wilmington & Baltimore had to transfer any Washington-bound traffic from its President Street Station over the Baltimore & Ohio's Pratt Street line to reach the B & O's Camden Station. Similarly, the Northern Central had to send southbound cars down a horse-powered line along Howard Street to the Pratt Street line. In fact, the Northern Central maintained stables near the Bolton Yards for over a hundred horses used in the transfer process.

Baltimore's pro-Confederate population was quick to take advantage of the vulnerable layout and began to vent its hostilities on the slow-moving passengers and equipment.

As the first Union troops arrived on April 18th, crowds of Southern sympathizers jeered and taunted the soldiers as they proceeded along Pratt Street. Nonetheless, they managed to reach Camden Station and Washington without incident. The next day, however, the news of the attack on Harper's Ferry reached Baltimore and the situation became volatile. The resulting confrontation, known as the infamous "Baltimore Riot," or "Pratt Street Riot," was the site of the first casualties of the Civil War.

In the early morning hours of April 19, 1861 the Sixth Massachusetts Volunteer Regiment arrived in Baltimore at the PW & B's President Street Station, and readied itself for the laborious transfer across Pratt Street to Camden Station. Policemen had been posted along the route in an effort to avoid the problems of the previous day. However, an angry crowd of Southern sympathizers began to jeer and taunt the soldiers; each man was issued six rounds of ammunition in anticipation of trouble.

It came. At 11:30 that morning the railroad cars carrying the troops began the one-mile trip to Camden Station. The crowd continued to grow in both size and degree of hostility. Nine cars reached the station safely, but the tenth was stoned. Word spread throughout the mob not to allow any further movement of troops along the route. At Gay Street some track and several gutter bridges were torn up, and a sand cart and ship's anchor were thrown onto the track amid cheers from the mob. Facing such obstacles, the soldiers returned to the President Street Station.

Calm temporarily settled over the rioters as word spread that the troops would return to Philadelphia on the next northbound train. But, at the station the troops were actually planning a foot march across town. When the mob learned of this it attacked the formation with bricks and stones as the soldiers began a double-time march along Pratt Street.

At the Jones Falls crossing Mayor Brown accompanied the troops, believing his presence would help to quell the disorder. He begged restraint.

At Commerce Street a large segment of the crowd again stoned the soldiers and obstructed their path. Blocked on all sides, the commanding officer, Captain Albert S. Follansbee, gave the order to open fire. In the melee that followed several soldiers, citizens, and bystanders were killed.

Temporarily stunned, the mob retreated; but the troops continued west on Pratt Street at a run. At the intersection of Light Street Marshal Kane assisted in protecting the militiamen until they arrived at Camden Station. As the troops were boarding their train at the depot, the mob attempted to tear up the track in front of the engine. It was a futile effort. The train departed for Washington and as it pulled out of the station the soldiers fired random shots from the coach windows, wounding more innocent bystanders.

A total of eight rioters, two soldiers, and one bystander were killed. One soldier, whose musket misfired, had it taken from him and was bayoneted with it. He died later from his wounds. A contingent of the Philadelphia Volunteer Regiment which had remained at the President Street Station throughout the episode returned to their home state. The war's first blood had flowed — ironically, in a battle between soldiers and civilians.

The Destruction of the Railroads

After the attack on the Massachusetts soldiers rumors spread throughout Baltimore that Union forces would retaliate and seek retribution for the "heinous" crime. The incident prompted city officials to call several meetings during the day. During the evening hours of April 19, 1861 a meeting of the city political leadership was quickly organized at Monument Square to plan Baltimore's defense from federal intervention. Attending were Mayor Brown, Marshal Kane, and ex-Governor E. Louis Lowe, all of whom had consulted with Maryland Governor Thomas H. Hicks. When it was reported to the committee that additional troops were proceeding from Harrisburg to Baltimore over the Northern Central, the officials present ordered the rail lines leading into the city from the north severed.

At about 12:30 a.m. on April 20th Mayor Brown, "by the authority of the Governor of Maryland," ordered two groups of local militia out to "break down the bridges" of both the Northern Central and the Philadelphia, Wilmington & Baltimore.

An hour and a half later the two militia parties left Baltimore — one heading for the Philadelphia, Wilmington & Baltimore, the other for the Northern Central line.

The first group, commanded by Colonel Isaac R. Trimble and consisting of police and a company of Baltimore City Guards, set out for the PW & B's President Street Station. There the militia took a Philadelphia train east and burned the long trestles over the Bush and Gunpowder rivers.

The Northern Central group, under Captain J. G. Johannes and containing elements of a company of Baltimore City Guards along with Marshal Kane and a contingent of policemen, proceeded north from Calvert Station to Melvale (near present Cold Spring Lane in Baltimore), where it burned a wooden trestle. At Relay House an iron bridge was dismantled, and several wooden bridges were burned near Cockeysville. Telegraph lines all along the route were cut and the poles were chopped down. Just after daylight the vigilantes returned to Baltimore, their mission a success.

Meanwhile, 2,500 Pennsylvania troops from Harrisburg camped on the farm of Peter Cockey in Cockeysville because their train had been halted by the burned bridge over Beaver Dam Run. In Baltimore local officials feared that the Pennsylvania militiamen would march into town, but they succeeded in convincing President Lincoln to withdraw the troops north of the Mason-Dixon line. After frantic Maryland officials received word that the soldiers would return to Pennsylvania, the commanding officer of the Baltimore County Horse Guard, Captain Charles Ridgely, was instructed to burn the bridges of the Northern Central all the way to the state line.

Major General George H. Stewart, the commander of the state militia in Baltimore, instructed Ridgely "not to commit or permit any hostile act against the retreating troops...even if they started for Baltimore." Captain Ridgely assigned the task of burning the bridges to Lieutenant John Merryman, who happened to be a prominent Baltimore County landowner and slave owner.

About 25 men were detailed to Merryman's home at "Hayfields" to carry out the destruction. ("Hayfields," incidentally, still stands north of Shawan Road at Interstate 83.) According to official documents, the bridges at Mile Branch, Owl Brook, Bee Tree, and the Little Gunpowder (now Little Falls) were "put to the torch." Witnesses at a later investigation testified that Merryman, apparently on several occasions, drew his sword in front of a gathered crowd of on-lookers and declared that "we'll stop them from...stealing our slaves." The bridge burning which began on April 21st was completed by April 24, 1861. In addition to the bridges, many telegraph poles and lines were destroyed.

Merryman's activities eventually led to his arrest and incarceration at Fort McHenry for espionage. The resulting appeals brought about the celebrated Supreme Court case "Ex-Parte Merryman" in which the suspension of the writ of habeas corpus was ruled unconstitutional.

In the days that immediately followed the riot and the destruction of the railroads, rage swept across the northern states. Reports circulated around Baltimore of "laying the city to ashes" and of "blasting a way through Baltimore with cannon." Although many period documents discount the validity of this threat, it appears to have some basis in fact. It was Simon Cameron — now in a new role as Lincoln's first Secretary of War — who, upon learning of the attack on the Massachusetts soldiers, gave the order for federal troops to proceed to Washington and if necessary, be "prepared to shoot their way through Baltimore." When Lincoln heard about Cameron's communication he became furious, countermanded the order, and made arrangements to send the Union troops around Baltimore rather

This print depicts "Camp Small" at "Melville, Maryland" in 1861 (actually Melvale, in the Jones Falls valley at what is now Cold Spring Lane in Baltimore), typical of the encampments set up to protect the Northern Central's line out of Baltimore. It was manned by the Ellsworth Zouaves from York, Pennsylvania, named for Colonel Elmer Ellsworth, a Chicago patent attorney and promoter of the Zuoave drill system. The camp itself was named for the property owner, Charles W. Small. Maryland Historical Society Collection.

than through the city. (They were sent down the Chesapeake Bay and landed at Annapolis.) Cameron, for mishandling this incident as well as other major infractions, eventually was replaced and sent out of the country.

Meanwhile, Baltimore's militia forces were making other arrangements for the planned federal "invasion." Militiamen took possession of the Calvert Station and disrupted business to such an extent that the Northern Central's president, Anthony B. Warford, moved the company offices to the Harrisburg station for the remainder of 1861. (Warford, incidentally, was the brother-in-law of Simon Cameron, and reflected the shift in the Northern Central's center of power from Baltimore to the State of Pennsylvania.)

In addition, the citizens in and around Baltimore began to rapidly enlist in local Guard companies. Many residents began arming themselves for the "invasion," while others, who preferred to leave, could be observed moving north along the York Turnpike in caravans of wagons.

By Sunday, April 28, 1861, the situation in Baltimore had become so unstable that President Lincoln, who had summoned Mayor Brown and Governor Hicks to Washington for two previous conferences in an effort to prevent further violence, agreed not to send any additional troops through Baltimore. Social order was finally restored when Mayor Brown issued a proclamation to the city's populace, advising them of the President's action.

Nonetheless, the combination of Baltimore's instability and its strategically vital position helped influence Lincoln to order General Butler to occupy the city in May 1861.

In retrospect, Baltimore had brought its troubles on itself. The Pratt Street riot and the destruction of the two rail lines were given substantial national coverage, helping to divide the nation further. The city's political and social leaders had misunderstood the situation, misjudged Lincoln's resolve to keep Maryland in the Union, and, indeed, had seriously endangered the Union.

The city leaders had ordered the railroads destroyed just at the point when they would be needed the most. The action left Baltimore precariously close to invasion by the Confederacy. Moreover, the destruction cost the city a substantial amount of money. The Northern Central and the Philadelphia, Wilmington & Baltimore railroads submitted charges to the city not only for direct damages but for lost business as well. The Northern Central was disabled for a full month, until May 21, 1861, and the cost of repairs alone amounted to $117,609.63. (Thanks to Cameron's influence, however, the Northern Central was restored before the Philadelphia, Wilmington & Baltimore. In the meantime, troops were sent south over a route via the Central Railroad of New Jersey and the Philadelphia &

Reading to Harrisburg, then the Northern Central to Baltimore.)

Union forces slowly moved into Baltimore and its surroundings to protect and preserve the railroad network. On May 5, 1861 Major General Benjamin F. Butler took over the Annapolis & Elk Ridge Railroad and the junction of the Baltimore & Ohio's main line and Washington Branch at Relay. Soon, all rail lines were under sentry protection and General Butler himself marched into Baltimore and ordered occupation. This situation existed for the extent of the conflict.

Prosperity and Temporary Peace for the Northern Central: May 1861 to June 1863

After the depredations of April 1861 relative calm settled on the railroad for more than two years. With the war being fought elsewhere, the Northern Central was given a breather and could concentrate on hauling the heavy wartime traffic and earning money. Sporadic attacks by small groups of Southern sympathizers in both Baltimore and York counties caused some minor damage, but for the most part the railroad not only could operate without obstructions, but could begin a serious rebuilding of its property.

As already noted, Lincoln's first Secretary of War — the person most responsible for giving out wartime contracts — was none other than Simon Cameron. A leading power in the Republican Party at the time, Cameron had negotiated the job with Lincoln's managers in exchange for his support at the 1860 Republican convention. Characterized by one historian as "a man who always stood ready to combine his personal business with the public's," Cameron proceeded to dispense contracts for both men and material with impunity. Needless to say, the Northern Central was a major beneficiary — although, in fairness, the railroad was strategically situated as a north-south route and stood to handle a large amount of traffic in any event. The resulting revenue began to have an impressive effect on the railroad's profits. (Cameron's conduct caused a scandal, and Lincoln eased him out in January 1862, sending him as Minister to Russia.)

When war began the Northern Central's President, Anthony Warford, and Vice-President J. D. Cameron were faced with a debt of $617,507. As noted earlier the State of Maryland had instituted suit to recover payment on earlier loans. Warford and Cameron had complained bitterly of the railroad's "deplorable financial condition" stating that the firm "spent too much...bought too much" and generally "contributed to its own poor financial position." However, by late 1862 the situation had changed entirely. War traffic had increased tonnage 63 percent.

The combination of wartime traffic and inflation produced a dramatic climb in the company's income; by 1865 total revenue had swelled a spectacular 186 percent above the 1861 level. The year-by-year figures were:

Year	Revenue
1861	$1,418,000
1862	1,921,000
1863	2,122,000
1864	3,051,000
1865	4,050,000

Source: Annual Reports of the Northern Central Railway, exclusive of leased lines from 1860.

Not all of that increase in income came from war traffic; by the 1860s the company had begun to expand its lines into the anthracite region and upstate New York, and its general business level grew. But even in 1865, with the war ending that April, its direct war traffic revenue amounted to $336,835.

The new wealth was put to good use. The main line was upgraded to handle the now-growing coal business, and the deferred double-tracking project finally began in 1861. And, with the backing of its new parent, the Pennsylvania Railroad, the Northern Central started an active program of market expansion. In early 1863 it directly entered the anthracite mining country for the first time, by leasing the Shamokin Valley & Pottsville Railroad; several months later it headed in another direction by leasing the ailing Elmira & Williamsport.

All of these projects will be covered separately in subsequent chapters, but suffice it to say that throughout this period of expansion the war was still raging. It returned to Northern Central territory with a fury in mid-1863, in the form of the Gettysburg campaign.

Prelude to Gettysburg

The Army of Northern Virginia began its move north on June 3, 1863, when Lee's troops crossed the Potomac and entered Union territory. When reports of the invasion reached Baltimore, the city felt directly threatened. The *Official Records of the War of the Rebellion* report that the "panic north of the Potomac was intense" and *Harpers Magazine* reported "the most intense apprehension." Worried Northern Central officials suspended business south of Harrisburg on June 15th. On June 25th all shipments over the road were halted.

Everyone knew that a battle was imminent; the obvious question was, where? A partial answer was dramatically delivered on Friday, June 26th, when the Confederate cavalry severed the telegraph lines at Hanover, Pennsylvania.

The standard strategy of an invading army during the Civil War was to send out advance cavalry forces to disable communication and transportation routes. These rapidly moving mounted forces severed rail and telegraph lines, and also gathered intelligence about the strength of defending forces. The purpose was to minimize resistance by preventing the defenders from reinforcing or supplying themselves quickly. Both sides used the strategy throughout the war, and became quite proficient at it. The flamboyant and colorful Confederate cavalry became famous and feared for its daring raids, and for its habit of extorting "contributions" from the towns that it invaded.

This time the Confederate cavalry had picked the Northern Central's main line and the rail link to Hanover and Gettysburg as its primary targets. Specific objectives were the rail facilities at Hanover, Pennsylvania (on The Hanover Branch Railroad), Hanover Junction, York, Wrightsville, and York Haven. As it turned out, these advance raids made little difference in the Gettysburg campaign. First, the Union army was already in pursuit of Lee and second, there were other lines besides the Northern Central available as supply routes. Nonetheless, the Confederate advance forces were partially successful.

Several Confederate units were involved in the attack on the Northern Central — General J. E. B. "Jeb" Stuart's cavalry, General Jubal Early's soldiers, General Gordon's Corps, and troops of the celebrated "Comanche" division under the command of Colonel Elijah V. White (so named for its "rebel yell" in battle, which was thought similar to the American Indians). Fire was their most effective weapon.

Generals Stuart and Early arrived in Hanover on Friday, June 26, 1863. While Stuart's forces occupied Hanover, Early was dispatched north to York and Colonel White was sent south to Hanover Junction. They left Hanover on June 27th and fanned out over York County with specific instructions to "destroy railroad connections" and "skirmish with the boys in blue" who were guarding the rail lines.

Colonel White's battalion, some one hundred strong, followed the Hanover Branch Railroad from Hanover to Hanover Junction, where it joined the Northern Central main line. It burned three major wooden trestles along the Hanover Branch line and arrived at Hanover Junction early in the afternoon of the 27th. After arriving at the Hanover Junction station, the cavalry immediately "put the torch to the first bridge north of the rail junction." Next, the soldiers cut down the telegraph wires and poles, and smashed the telegraph equipment in the depot office. They remained in the town for about one hour, but before leaving they "destroyed" the turntable behind the station — probably by burning it.

After leaving Hanover Junction the Comanches followed the Northern Central line north to York. Along the way they destroyed two other bridges, the so-called Fishel and Black structures, burning one and blowing up the other with explosives.

The bridges had been guarded by the 20th Pennsylvania Militia commanded by Lt. Col. William A. Sickels. The responsibility for protecting the Northern Central line in Pennsylvania was assigned to the 20th Pennsylvania Volunteer Militia, and according to the war records, their response to the attacking Confederate cavalry was less than admirable. Although the documents report a skirmish where shots were exchanged, the record goes on to say that the Union defenders "threw down their pieces and hastily retreated."

The contingent of Pennsylvania volunteers contained 44 officers and 927 soldiers. They were spread out along the line of the Northern Central road from Harrisburg to the Maryland line. The sight of the Comanches advancing on the town of Hanover Junction was apparently enough to convince the Union troopers to exercise the better part of valor. They retreated east to the Wrightsville-Columbia bridge, where they were given a part in the preparations for defense of that structure. A special investigation after the war chastised the commanding officer for so rapidly evacuating his troops.

Meanwhile, General Early's cavalry had been in York, destroying Northern Central facilities north and south of town. His soldiers burned several bridges near the city, cut telegraph lines, and ripped up rail at several locations. They also "burned and crippled cars at both Gettysburg and York." The cavalry remained in York until June 30, 1863, the day that evacuation of both York and Carlisle began.

The Wrightsville line suffered similar devastation. Colonel White's battalion eventually joined with Major General John B. Gordon's Corps and accompanied them on the march to the Susquehanna at Wrightsville. En route, the Confederate forces severely damaged the branch between York and Wrightsville. The line had numerous small wooden bridges, and the soldiers "burned every one." As the invading forces approached Wrightsville, the citizens of Columbia — directly across the river — along with the forces of the 20th Pennsylvania Militia, who had been humiliated at Hanover Junction, burned the railroad bridge connecting Wrightsville to Columbia in order to prevent the enemy from crossing. The date was June 30, 1863, the same day that portions of Lee's army were at the Susquehanna River opposite Harrisburg.

The Army of Northern Virginia advanced as far north as the west bank of the Susquehanna River at Bridgeport

Hanover Junction, in a famous Matthew Brady view. The camera looks north. The NC main line to York curves to the far right; the independently operated line to Hanover and Gettysburg is at the center and left. The brick building at the left is a hotel serving both railroad passengers and travelers on the adjacent road. Amazingly, both structures still stood in 1991. National Archives Collection.

(Lemoyne), opposite Harrisburg, but then pulled back. Lee's original plan had been to cross the river and move into Lancaster County. Many later histories have stated that Lee's army was deceived into retreat from Harrisburg by the representation of 15,000 raw recruits appearing as an army of over 60,000. This was not so. Lee was looking for a fight, and the original records reveal that his change in direction was a deliberate move to concentrate his somewhat fractionalized forces.

Lee had received intelligence reports on June 29th and 30th of the location of the segments of Meade's army; its commander, Hooker, had just been relieved, and the Confederate general knew the enemy needed time to adjust to the change. Lee felt that he could consolidate his own troops, and overwhelm the segmented Union forces piece by piece. The intelligence reports were enough to turn both his plan and his army around.

The following telegraph, dispatched by Herman Haupt (then in charge of construction and repairs for the Union's military railroads) at Harrisburg, summarizes the plan and movement of the Confederate Army.

Harrisburg, Pa., June 30, 1863.

Major-General Halleck, General-in-Chief:

Lee is falling back suddenly from the vicinity of Harrisburg, and concentrating all his forces. York has been evacuated. Carlisle is being evacuated. The concentration appears to be at or near Chambersburg. The object, apparently, a sudden movement against Meade, of which he should be advised by courier immediately. A courier might reach Frederick by way of Western Maryland Railroad to Westminster. This information comes from T. A. Scott, and I think it reliable.

H. HAUPT
Brigadier-General

The "T. A. Scott" referred to by Haupt was Tom Scott of the Pennsylvania Railroad, who had been intermittently involved in managing the military railroad movements in the area.

Although the site of the eventual confrontation at Gettysburg turned out to be somewhat accidental, the Confederate army had done an efficient job of destroying the Northern Central's lines in the general area. In all, 33 bridges in the area had been destroyed, rail had been ripped up and twisted at numerous locations, and major sections of telegraph wire had been removed. On the section between Hanover Junction and Harrisburg, nineteen bridges were gone, some of them substantial structures. On the independently owned line into Gettysburg, a large bridge over the Conewago Creek near Oxford, Pennsylvania had been completely destroyed, and a smaller bridge was "severely damaged" on another independent rural branch between Hanover and Littlestown, Pennsylvania.

The Wrightsville line had been totally destroyed. All of the wooden trestles had been burned, track was destroyed, and telegraph lines were demolished. The Wrightsville bridge over the Susquehanna River had been burned, not by the Confederate forces but by local authorities to prevent the enemy from crossing.

Although the Confederate cavalry, under the command of J. E. B. Stuart and Jubal Early, had killed and maimed many soldiers; had destroyed property and rail-

This photograph shows the NC's bridge at Hanover Junction after it had been rebuilt by the U. S. Military Railroads' construction crew in 1863. The track in the foreground is the line to Hanover and Gettysburg. Library of Congress Collection.

roads with impunity; had raided the residents for supplies, there were moments of compassion and diplomacy. General Early, for example, issued this proclamation to the citizens of York:

York, Pa. June 30, 1863.

To the Citizens of York:

I have abstained from burning the railroad buildings and car shops in your town because, after examination, I am satisfied the safety of the town would be endangered, and acting in the spirit of humanity, which has ever characterized my government and its military authorities, I do not desire to involve the innocent in the same punishment with the guilty. Had I applied the torch, without regard to consequences, I would have pursued a course that would have been fully vindicated as an act of just retaliation for the authorized acts of barbarity perpetrated by your own army on our soil, but we do not war upon women and children and I trust that the treatment you have met with at the hands of my soldiers will open your eyes to the monstrous inequity of the war waged by your Government upon the people of the Confederate States, and that you will make an effort to shake off the revolting tyranny under which it is apparent to all you are yourselves groaning.

J. A. Early
Major-General C. S. Army.

Although the telegram is an obvious "political" declaration, it does illustrate the strength and depth of the social forces that prevailed during the Civil War. General Early, in addition to being an excellent cavalry officer, was an astute politician. He knew that a large segment of the local population was pro-Confederate; he took every opportunity to build sympathy for his cause, and to let the Northerners know that the southern states had suffered the most damage in the rebellion.

Repairing the Northern Central

News of the cavalry raid on the Northern Central was sent swiftly to Washington by couriers, reaching there June 29, 1863. Although primarily concerned with repelling the invasion, the Union army recognized the Northern Central's importance as a potential supply line for the Army of the Potomac. Plans were made to repair the damage immediately.

General D. C. McCallum, the commanding officer of the Transportation Division, issued orders to the United States Military Railroads Corps to proceed from their headquarters at Alexandria, Virginia to Hanover Junction, and to repair the Northern Central for possible use in supplying Union forces at Gettysburg. McCallum gave the project to the capable and energetic General Herman Haupt — the same Haupt who, as a civil engineer, had surveyed the Wrightsville branch bridges years earlier. Now the Chief of Construction for the United States Military Railroads, Haupt proceeded to Harrisburg via Philadelphia on June 30th to evaluate the situation. He arrived late in the evening and after obtaining information from Pennsylvania Governor Curtin and Thomas A. Scott, left Harrisburg for Baltimore on July 1, 1863.

Haupt arrived back in Baltimore later that day and began planning the repair of the Northern Central. There he telegraphed his information to Washington from the Eutaw House, then started for Westminster, Maryland over the Northern Central and Western Maryland railways. Westminster, about 35 miles northwest of Baltimore, was still 24 miles by road from Gettysburg, but the Northern

Central-Western Maryland rail route to that point was undamaged. It thus was an alternative way to reach the battlefield.

At this point in its history the Western Maryland Railway had only built as far west as Union Bridge, 12 miles beyond Westminster, and it had no water or telegraph stations. Haupt estimated it could only accommodate four trains a day; he needed 30 trains each day to supply the Union Army. Improvement work that would normally take several months would have to be done immediately.

Consequently, he simultaneously started repairs on the damaged section of the Northern Central (which could directly reach Gettysburg via Hanover Junction) and upgrading of the Western Maryland into Westminster. Complicating his task even more, the superintendent of the Northern Central, J. N. DuBarry, requested that he "be relieved because of the firm's inability to handle military operations." Haupt requisitioned Adna Anderson from Alexandria, along with his force of 400 United States Military Railroads workers. They brought "a train of split wood, lanterns, buckets and assorted hardware" to Baltimore for the two projects. (Alexandria, it might be noted, was immediately south of Washington; the military railroad organization used the facilities of the Orange & Alexandria Railroad — now part of the Southern Railway — as one of its major depots.)

The military railroad forces worked day and night in repairing the Northern Central and upgrading the Western Maryland. The Assistant Engineer, J. R. Clough, made a reconnaissance of the Northern Central as far north as Harrisburg and located the nineteen main line bridges that had been destroyed. In addition, he located three bridges on the Hanover Junction and Gettysburg Railroad that had been damaged. He put the majority of his construction crew to work on these bridges and ordered "all available portable truss bridges" from Alexandria to be used in their repair.

By July 2nd, while the battle of Gettysburg raged on, Haupt and Anderson had managed to forward fifteen convoys of trains carrying material into Westminster to supply the Union Army. The trains took supplies and munitions in, and the wounded out. Haupt left Anderson in charge of the Western Maryland; he proceeded to Hanover Junction to survey and repair the damage to the Hanover Branch Railroad in order to open the direct rail route into Gettysburg.

While a somber nation learned of the carnage at Gettysburg, Haupt kept supplies moving there as best he could. From the Eutaw House in Baltimore he dispatched numerous convoys of five and six trains out of Baltimore through the Green Spring Valley into Westminster over the Northern Central-Western Maryland route. ("Convoys" in this case meant a group of trains dispatched together as a single unit, one closely following another.) To prevent sabotage he ordered the trains, bridges, and right of way guarded with Union soldiers. He instructed the troops at Westminster to "unload supplies and return the trains" as soon as humanly possible in order to "prevent congestion" on the single-track Western Maryland.

In addition Haupt hired the Adams Express Company, under the directorship of S. M. Shoemaker, to supply Westminster with additional ambulances. Adams Express was instrumental in removing approximately 15,000 wounded soldiers, both Union and Confederate, from the battlefield to the railhead at Westminster. The company also provided wagon transportation for doctors and nurses traveling from Westminster into Gettysburg. The feat won Shoemaker considerable praise and recognition after the campaign.

Although the Western Maryland Railway line at Westminster was relatively close to Gettysburg, there still remained the 24-mile road trip to reach the town. The joint route of the Northern Central, the Hanover Branch, and the Gettysburg railroads provided direct access to the battlefield — but these lines were unusable until repairs were made. Haupt also had to see to this repair as soon as possible.

He designated two crews to repair the Northern Central. One, under the command of E. C. Smeed, worked south from Harrisburg. The second crew, directed by George W. Nagle, worked north toward it from Hanover Junction. A division of the second crew, commanded by Haupt himself, worked to reopen the branch line from Hanover Junction to Gettysburg.

The construction crew assigned to the Northern Central main line replaced the bridge at Hanover Junction on July 4, 1863. The following telegraph message summarizes the progress of the construction crews that day.

Hanover Junction, July 4, 1863

Major-General Halleck, General-in-Chief:

All the supplies offered for transportation on Westminster Branch have been sent forward, and sidings at Relay are clear. Our arrangements work well.

Our men rebuilt entirely the bridge at this junction, three spans about forty feet, this morning. They expect to reach York to-morrow night.

I will endeavor to secure for you, when I reach Hanover, more rapid communication by telegraph with Gettysburg.

H. Haupt
Brigadier-General

Haupt's own crew, working on the Hanover Branch and the Gettysburg railroads, found the "large bridge over the Conewago Creek at Oxford, Pennsylvania completely destroyed." Replacing this structure, just seven miles east of Gettysburg, would take several hours, and delayed the route's anticipated opening. A "train load of hardware, railroad ties, and portable trusses" managed to reach the site by sunset on July 5, 1863. The construction crew worked by "lantern light" to restore the structure and finally reestablish rail service into Gettysburg itself.

Herman Haupt returned to Baltimore Sunday night to begin planning train movements over the Hanover Junction line. Meanwhile, construction crews continued working on the Northern Central line toward York. It took two additional days to reopen the main line to that city.

Most of the work on the Northern Central and the Hanover Branch and Gettysburg lines had been done while the battle was in progress; by the time they were opened, it was too late to affect the outcome. But their repair aided tremendously in the evacuation of both Union and Confederate wounded into area hospitals. Haupt had insisted that returning supply trains transport the wounded, "regardless of uniform," to hospitals in York, Hanover, and Baltimore — an accomplishment which, after the war, won him considerable praise from peers, citizens, and former adversaries.

On July 14, 1863 the United States Military Railroads work crews completed repairing the Northern Central to Bridgeport, and left this area for the Cumberland Valley. They had restored the Northern Central, the Hanover Branch, and the Gettysburg railroads in just over two weeks. The Corps had dispatched over 1500 tons of supplies daily into the war zone and ferried out the wounded. Thirty-three bridges were repaired or replaced, along with thousands of crossties and large quantities of rail. Telegraph lines were repaired and placed back in operation. The military's work, fortunately, saved the Northern Central the major cost of rehabilitating itself.

There was more to be done, however. It took several months to clear away the charred remains of buildings, bridges, and cars. Repairs to the trackbed and supporting rail structure took another two months. All this, borne by the railroad, amounted to $234,000. The estimates of lost business during the Gettysburg campaign came to another $108,793. Then, in addition to the war damage, heavy rains from July 12th until July 14th washed away several bridges between the Maryland line and York, including the one just replaced at Hanover Junction. It took the Northern Central another five days to repair the line and open it for business. In compensation, perhaps, the patched-up Northern Central and Hanover Branch route participated in another piece of history; the following November, it carried Lincoln to Gettysburg for his dedication address.

The Gettysburg Campaign was not the last invasion that the Northern Central would have to endure, however. One more was still to come.

Herman Haupt, the bearded, derby-hatted figure on the bank at the right, supervises one of his construction crews. (Note that the USMRR locomotive carries the name "General Haupt.") Although this photograph was taken on the Orange & Alexandria Railroad in Virginia, it typifies Haupt's work on the Northern Central. National Archives Collection.

The Confederate Raid of 1864

The final Confederate raid on the Northern Central came during the July 1864 campaign. This particular invasion, frequently called the "Johnson and Gilmor Raid," was the last and least destructive of all the assaults directed against the railroad.

It was part of an operation designed by General Jubal Early to both threaten Washington and to rescue Confederate prisoners held in Maryland. Although the raid failed to accomplish its major objective, the cavalry

These two scenes illustrate Herman Haupt's devices to keep the damaged railroads running. ***Top Photo:*** *This prefabricated wooden "shad-belly" truss bridge could be carried quickly to the site of a destroyed bridge.* ***Bottom Photo:*** *Twisted rails were straightened by crews like this, some of them made up of slaves who had fled the South. Both photographs, National Archives Collection.*

did manage to temporarily cripple several railroads around Baltimore. The Northern Central's main line was attacked in the vicinity of Cockeysville.

The Confederate forces, under the command of both General Bradley T. Johnson and Major Harry Gilmor, had been assigned the task of cutting rail and communication lines between Maryland and Washington. Gilmor's units were assigned as Johnson's point column. Included on their list of objectives were the Northern Central facilities at Cockeysville, and the Ashland Iron Works just north of Cockeysville.

General Early planned to maneuver directly toward Washington, and Johnson's cavalry was to strike the Confederate prisoner of war camp near Point Lookout in St. Mary's County, free the prisoners, and return them home. Noble in purpose, the plan was strategically deficient and accomplished very little. The Confederate forces were too near the numerically superior Union regiments.

Nonetheless, Gilmor's force arrived at Cockeysville on July 9, 1864 and immediately burned the first railroad bridge over the Gunpowder River north of town. General Johnson's force joined Gilmor at Cockeysville later that day and established headquarters at "Hayfields," the residence of John Merryman. While there Johnson also ordered other Northern Central bridges "put to the torch," and also let it be known that he planned to destroy the Ashland Iron Works. However, Merryman, a Confederate sympathizer himself, interceded on the behalf of James C. Clark, the manager of the Ashland company, and convinced Johnson to countermand his orders and save the facility. The order read as follows.

Hdqt., Johnson's Cavalry
Brigade
July 10, 1864

Protection will be given the person and property of Mr. James C. Clark by all Confederate soldiers. To violate a safeguard is death.(sic)

Bradley T. Johnson
Brigadier-General

The original documents do not discuss the reasoning behind the change in orders, but it is believed that Merryman traded the planned destruction of Ashland for intelligence information. Speculation notwithstanding, the order saved the Ashland railroad station and the iron works.

On July 10th General Johnson separated his forces and Major Gilmor proceeded south toward Towson while Johnson eventually moved into the Green Spring Valley. By July 11th Johnson's cavalry was in Owings Mills (on the Western Maryland Railway), ripping up rail and cutting telegraph lines. The soldiers burned the bridge at Eccleston on the Green Spring Valley line, which was then owned by the Western Maryland. Gilmor's troops, on the other prong of the invasion, were moving toward Towsontown (now Towson), burning bridges on the Northern Central's main line.

In all, the soldiers burned four large wooden trestles and six small bridges south of Cockeysville. Telegraph lines were cut and poles were chopped down at several locations. The raid managed to halt rail operations between Baltimore and York for about a week.

Although the Confederate invasion was swift and virtually unopposed, it was a failure. The objective of freeing prisoners was never realized. Mustering Union forces from both Washington and Baltimore prevented the planned assault on the prison camp. The Confederate cavalry was forced to retreat south rapidly. The raid did, however, sever the railroads leading into Baltimore from the north and west, and thereby isolated Washington and Baltimore from the remainder of the nation for five days.

The United States Military Railroad Corps, which would have normally repaired such damage, was occupied in other theaters of action and could not work on the Northern Central. The railroad itself repaired the damage at a cost of over $34,000.

It was the last full-scale Confederate invasion in the North, the last raid on the Northern Central's property, and the last full year of war for a weary nation.

Double-Tracking and Other Wartime Improvements

Concurrent with its wartime traumas and traffic loads, the railroad carried on an extensive rebuilding program. Improvements to the main line had been needed since early in 1859. The increasing volume of coal shipments had begun wearing out the rails, and beginning in 1861 the war traffic had saturated the system beyond its capacity. The railroad's soaring income now finally provided the wherewithall to do the job.

In 1861 money was allocated and work began on double-tracking the main line from Baltimore to Harrisburg. The grading and track work went fairly quickly, but the numerous bridges along the route slowed progress past the planned completion date. Double-tracking was completed to Relay House (Hollins, at Lake Roland) in 1862, to Cockeysville in 1863, and York in 1865. Work on the balance of the main line from York to Sunbury stretched through the late 1860s and early 1870s.

With the takeover of the rundown Shamokin Valley & Pottsville and the Elmira & Williamsport in 1863, money immediately was put into rebuilding those lines, too. The coal-hauling Shamokin line was refurbished with new rail, additional ballast, and improved passenger facilities. The

As part of the double-tracking program, the NC's only tunnel, Howard Tunnel (south of York), was rebuilt. This 1870 view looks south. R. Bosley Collection.

Elmira & Williamsport, locally derided as a "snake path," was surveyed in late 1864 by the Northern Central's then-president, J. Donald Cameron, along with superintendent J. N. DuBarry. At an impromptu executive meeting during a tour of the line, it was decided to upgrade the 78-mile route as the projected future main line toward the Great Lakes.

Work also resumed on the perennially delayed Canton extension project in Baltimore. More property was purchased for the hoped-for new harbor terminal branch during the early 1860s. By then the horse-operated street trackage and confined freight facilities at Fells Point and the City Dock were inundated; but unhappily, the Canton line remained bogged down in right-of-way litigation, as well as management uncertainty about the length and course of the war. Final resolution would not come until after the war, and trains would not actually operate into Canton until 1873.

More positively, the railroad's Baltimore terminal complex was dramatically expanded. The 1850 Calvert Station, originally built as both a passenger and freight terminal, had become overwhelmed with business. As the war was ending in 1865, the railroad opened a commodious new block-long brick freight depot fronting on Centre Street immediately north of the old station. Afterwards Calvert Station handled passenger trains exclusively, serving until 1948. The 1865 freight depot, noted by the *Baltimore American* as "the largest and probably best railway depot building in the United States," proved far more durable. In somewhat altered form, it stands today as the Downtown Athletic Club.

Elsewhere on the line, new passenger stations were built at Cockeysville (completed 1866) and at York. The new York depot replaced the original structure; in turn, it was replaced in the late 1800s with a large and substantial brick building which still stands. The wooden Cockeysville station survived a slight relocation in 1930, and stood over 100 years before it was demolished in 1974.

Particularly significant to Baltimore County residents during the early 1860s was the initiation of the locally-famous "Parkton Local." This train, scheduled for commuter traffic to and from Baltimore, started on November 23, 1861; later expanded, the service lasted for almost 100 years. An 1868 schedule for the Parkton local shows it leaving Parkton at 6:39 a.m. and arriving at Calvert Station in Baltimore at 8:20; returning in the afternoon, it left Baltimore at 5:30, pulling into its Parkton terminal at 7:12. At the same time a similar commuter service was offered from York to Harrisburg.

The equipment roster also was renovated. Large numbers of coal and freight cars were purchased. Beginning in 1862 the railroad adapted the 4-6-0 type for heavy freight service, gradually replacing the now-obsolete Winans Camels. That year Baldwin delivered nine such Ten Wheelers; over the next eleven years, 43 4-6-0s had been acquired from Baldwin, the New Jersey Locomotive and Machine Works, and the NC's own Bolton shop.

During 1863 the Northern Central underwent a significant executive change. President Warford had become increasingly ill and as a result he turned over leadership of the railroad to James Donald Cameron, who had been the company's vice president. Donald Cameron was Simon Cameron's son, and was becoming a stand-in for his father in several of his business and political activities; eventually, in fact, he succeeded Simon Cameron in the United States Senate and inherited his powerful Pennsylvania political machine. Cameron got an immediate baptism of fire, taking over the Northern Central presidency at the time of the

Typical of the NC's upgraded locomotive roster was No. 78, a heavy Ten-Wheeler built by the New Jersey Locomotive & Machine Works in 1864. It was retired in 1883. Smithsonian Institution Collection.

113. NORTHERN CENTRAL RAILWAY LINE.

J. D. CAMERON, Pres., Harrisburg, Pa. C. G. MILLER, Vice Pres., New York. JOHN S. LEIB, Treas., Baltimore, Md.
STEPHEN LITTLE, Auditor. ROBERT S. HOLLINS, Secretary, Baltimore, Md.
J. N. DUBARRY, Gen. Superintendent, Harrisburg, Pa. J. A. REDFIELD, Asst. Gen. Supt., Elmira, N.Y.
Edwin S. YOUNG, General Ticket Agent. J. M. DRILL, General Eastern Freight Agent, Baltimore, Md.
E. L. DUBARRY, Assist. Supt., Harrisburg, Pa. S. S. BLAIR, Supt., Baltimore Division, Baltimore, Md.
E. S. BOWEN, Division Superintendent, Elmira, N.Y. A. R. FISKE, Supt., Shamokin Div., Shamokin, Pa.
HUGH PITCAIRN, Superintendent, Susquehana Division, Harrisburg, Pa. H. S. GOODWIN, Chief Engineer.
ISAAC M. SCHERMERHORN, General Western Freight Agent, Buffalo, N.Y.

Trains Leave. May 10, 1868. **Trains Arrive.**

Acc.	Acc.	Acc.	Acc.	Exs.	Fast	Mail	Mls	STATIONS.	Mls	Mail.	Exs.	Fast	Acc.	Acc.	Acc.	Acc.
P. M.	P. M.	A. M.	P. M.	P. M.	A. M.	A. M				P. M.	A. M.	P. M.	A. M.	A. M.	A. M.	P. M.
4 30				8 45	8 00			.....Washington......		9 50	9 50					
				P. M.	A. M.	P. M.										
				11 05	11 50	7 50	0	.....Philadelphia. ...	423	4 50	6 40					
				P. M.	P. M.	A. M		*Phila. W. & Bal.*		P. M.	A. M.					
7 00	3 30		5 30	10 50	12 10	8 30	98	....**Baltimore** 1. ...	325	5 20	6 45	10 15	8 20			
7 06	3 36		5 36	10 56	12 16	8 36	1	........Bolton.........	324	5 14	----	10 09	8 14			
7 29	3 59		6 00	— —	— —	8 58	7	........Relay 2........	318	4 53	— —	9 46	7 50			
7 45	4 15		6 18	— —	— —	9 13	11	...... Timonium	314	4 37	— —	9 31	7 32			
7 57	4 25		6 30	— —	12 50	9 23	15	....Cockeysville......	310	4 25	— —	9 20	7 20			
8 14	4 42		6 45	— —	— —	9 37	19	........Sparks........	306	4 10	— —	9 05	7 05			
8 25	4 52		6 55	— —	— —	9 47	23	.... Monkton	302	3 59	— —	8 54	6 56			
8 45	5 13		7 12	12 00	1 23	10 06	28	........Parkton........	297	3 41	5 25	8 35	6 39			
9 03	5 30		P. M.	— —	— —	10 23	34	.......Freelands.......	291	3 22	— —	8 17	A. M.			
9 25	5 52			— —	— —	10 45	42	........Glenrock........	283	2 58	— —	7 53				
9 40	6 06			12 46	2 05	10 58	46	...Hanover Junction 3...	279	2 43	4 39	7 37				
9 48	6 15	A. M.		— —	— —	11 05	49	.......Glatfelters.	276	2 35	— —	7 28				P. M.
10 15	6 40	6 20		1 20	2 39	11 35	57	.... York 4	268	2 05	4 09	7 00				7 00
10 56		7 11		1 51	3 15	12 12	72	.......Goldsboro'	253	1 20	3 31	A. M.				6 00
— —		7 50		3 45	3 45	1 30	83	......Bridgeport 5	242	12 50	3 05				9 35	5 15
11 45		8 05		3 30	4 20	1 20	85	.... .**Harrisburg** 6.....	240	12 30	2 40				9 50	5 00
				— —	: :	1 39	85	.......Fairview........	240	— —	— —				9 28	
				4 02	: :	1 55	91	...... Marysville.......	234	— —	— —				9 15	
				4 10	4 45	2 05	92	.......Dauphin 7......	233	11 50	1 55				9 05	
				— —	5 00	2 22	98	.....Clark's Ferry	227	11 35	1 40				8 50	
				4 41	5 17	2 42	105	........Halifax	220	11 19	1 23				8 30	
				4 56	5 31	2 58	111	.....**Millersburg** 8	214	11 04	1 07				8 12	
				— —	— —	3 12	117	..... Mahontongo.......	208	10 53	— —				7 58	
				5 20	5 57	3 25	121	......Georgetown.......	204	10 40	12 43				7 45	
				5 32	6 08	3 40	126	....Trevorton Junc. 9...	199	10 29	12 30				7 30	
				5 47	6 23	3 57	133	..... Selin's Grove	192	10 15	12 15				7 15	
				— —	6 40	4 15	138	... .**Sunbury** 10....	187	10 02	12 03				7 00	
				8 15	8 25	6 55	178	..**Williamsport** 11..	147	8 15	10 15					
				— —	P. M.	— —	185	....Cogan Valley.......	138	— —	— —					
				— —		— —	191	...... Trout Run.	133	— —	— —					
				— —		— —	197	........Bodine's.	127	— —	— —					
				— —		— —	202	.......Ralston.........	122	— —	— —					
				— —		— —	206	....Roaring Branch....	118	— —	— —					
				— —		— —	211	.....Carpenter's	113	— —	— —					
				— —		— —	217	........Canton.........	107	— —	— —					
				— —		— —	325	.... West Granville.....	100	— —	— —					
				— —		— —	221	.... .Troy.........	94	— —	— —					
				— —		— —	236	...Columbia X Roads...	89	— —	— —					
			Acc.	— —	Acc.	— —	244	.......Gillet's........	81	— —	— —	Acc.	Acc.			
			P. M.	— —	A. M.	— —	247	......State Line.	77	— —	— —	A. M.	P. M.			
			6 40	12 10	6 50	11 05	256	......**Elmira** 12.....	69	5 00	5 35	11 00	11 15			
			7 05	— —	7 05		262	......Horse Heads	63		— —	10 42	10 55			
			7 18	— —	7 18		266	......Pine Valley......	59		— —	10 28	10 43			
			7 43	— —	7 47		275	........Havana........	50		— —	9 58	10 15			
			7 52	— —	7 55		278	...... .Watkins.......	47		— —	9 50	10 05			
			8 25	— —	8 30		289	........Starkey........	36		— —	9 15	9 33			
			9 00	— —	9 03		301	.......Penn Yan	24		— —	8 38	9 00			
			9 37	— —	9 44		314	.... Gorham.	11		— —	8 01	8 22			
			9 51	— —	9 58		319	...... .Hopewell.......	6		— —	7 47	8 07			
			10 10	— —	10 15		325	.**Canandaigua** 13.	0		1 50	7 35	7 50			
								N. Y. Central R. R.								
			12 15	5 00	12 00		354	...... Rochester			12 30	6 00	6 02			
P. M.	P. M.	A. M.	A. M	P. M.	P. M.	P. M.		ARRIVE] [LEAVE		A. M	P. M.	P. M.	A. M.	A. M.	A. M.	P. M.

Northern Central passenger services in May, 1868. Note the "Parkton Local" schedule, an early example of suburban commuter service in and out of Baltimore.

Gettysburg campaign. Not only did he survive it, but he remained in the job for eleven years more, overseeing the Northern Central's wartime and postwar expansion programs. The younger Cameron was to be the Northern Central's last "independent" president; afterwards the position always was held by the president of the Pennsylvania Railroad. His departure would end an era for the railroad.

Financially, the railroad used its wartime earnings to stabilize its debt position. The money was used to liquidate and eliminate both outstanding bonds and indentures which were held by private investors as well as the State of Maryland. Many of these debt instruments had been inherited from the precursor companies and had plagued the Northern Central with high interest payments since the company was formed.

The war years had been perilous and turbulent times. The railroad's facilities had been invaded, burned, and destroyed. Its executives, unsure of the outcome of the war, had to surrender the rail operations to military authorities and were forced to postpone important projects. On the other hand, war traffic probably had rescued the railroad from another financial collapse and had helped start it on its way to becoming a first-class facility. In any event, the trial by fire and blood was over.

The Last Act

Although the war had ended, the Northern Central played one final, tragic military role. Its last military train was hauled slowly over the line on April 21, 1865, draped in black crepe, carrying Abraham Lincoln's body back home to Illinois.

The funeral journey was made under the auspices of the United States Military Railroads organization as its final assignment before being disbanded. The trip from Washington to Springfield, Illinois was intentionally roundabout to allow the casket to be displayed at major cities and state capitals along the way. The B & O took the train from Washington to Baltimore; from Baltimore it followed the Northern Central to Harrisburg, then the Pennsylvania Railroad to Philadelphia. From Philadelphia, it was routed to New York City, and afterwards traveled through Albany, Rochester, Buffalo, Cleveland, Columbus, and Chicago.

The special left Washington on the morning of April 21st for an uneventful trip to Baltimore, arriving at Camden Station at 10:00 a.m. In Baltimore the assassinated President's body lay in state beneath the rotunda of the Exchange Building, and thousands of citizens turned out to pay their respects. Black mourning flags were draped from every building. Government and business offices closed, factories shut down. This time Baltimore's citizens displayed a vastly different attitude toward Lincoln than in 1861, when his inauguration train was forced to "sneak" through the city.

The funeral train left Baltimore for Harrisburg late that afternoon, and stopped at York to take on fuel and water. While there, a group of young ladies placed a wreath of red and white roses on the coffin.

All along the Maryland and Pennsylvania countryside between Baltimore and Harrisburg, where country roads crossed the tracks, people assembled to pay their respects to the man that they had come to admire. Citizens and merchants, farmers and children, with saddened faces and bowed heads, watched the train until it vanished over the horizon. Thousands of people had flocked to the rail line to pay their respects to the gentle and compassionate man who had saved the Union.

PROFILE: Herman Haupt 1817–1905

A major figure in American railway engineering history — and in the history of the Civil War — Herman Haupt was involved in bridging a Northern Central predecessor early in his long career. And, during his service as Chief of Construction for the U. S. Military Railroads during the war, he returned to rebuild portions of the damaged Northern Central.

Haupt was born in Gettysburg, Pennsylvania in 1817 and graduated from West Point in 1835. He briefly served as a lieutenant in the 3rd U. S. Infantry, but resigned after only half a year of service to pursue a career as a civil engineer.

While the young Haupt was home on furlough in 1835, some of his West Point classmates convinced Henry R. Campbell, a locomotive designer, to interview him for employment. Haupt eventually took a job with Campbell and was assigned to make drawings of locomotives. Although Campbell is generally credited with developing the famed 4-4-0 "American"-type locomotive, the universal wheel arrangement of the mid-19th Century, some sources state that Haupt was actually responsible.

In late 1835 Haupt worked as a transitman surveying a rail line between Norristown and Allentown, Pennsylvania. Then, late in that year, Campbell suggested that Haupt work on another new line to run from Gettysburg to Hagerstown, Maryland. While in Gettysburg he met Anna Cecilia Keller, and the two were married August 30, 1838. He built his home, "Oakridge," on several acres of what would become the famed Seminary Ridge in Gettysburg. While not surveying railroads, Haupt taught civil engineering at Pennsylvania College, now called Gettysburg College.

It was between 1839 and 1847 that Haupt became interested in bridge design. He patented a simple timber truss in 1839, and the following year became principal assistant to Samuel Mifflin rebuilding bridges on the York — Wrightsville line.

In the winter of 1840-1841, while surveying along the Susquehanna River, he contracted the "ague," a common affliction of the day. His doctor recommended a change in climate, so Haupt tried farming on Maryland's Eastern Shore. He disliked it immediately and returned to Gettysburg.

Between 1842 and 1847 he completed the bridge work along the Wrightsville line. It was during this period that he wrote his *Hints on Bridge Construction*, published anonymously in 1842. Shortly afterwards Haupt returned to Pennsylvania College at Gettysburg as a professor of mathematics and engineering. Between 1844 and 1846 he wrote his *General Theory of Bridge Construction*, which was published in 1851. His success at solving problems associated with bridging major obstructions gave him a national reputation in the profession, and even today his books are revered as pioneering manuals in railroad engineering.

In 1847 Haupt began what was to become an off-and-on career with the Pennsylvania Railroad, which in that year was beginning construction under J. Edgar Thomson, its chief engineer. He was promoted to Thomson's assistant in 1848 and by 1849 he was superintending the work on the long Susquehanna River bridge at Rockville, Pennsylvania. It is also believed that during this period Haupt was responsible for designing a standardized iron truss bridge which was extensively used on the Pennsylvania's lines in the 1851-1861 period.

Beginning in 1856 Haupt became involved in a project he would quickly come to regret: the awesome task of drilling a 24,700- foot-long tunnel under Hoosac Mountain in Massachusetts for the Troy & Greenfield Railroad. A heavy investor in the project as well as contractor, Haupt was financially ruined by it; beset by political, financial, and engineering problems, he was forced to abandon the job. (The Hoosac Tunnel finally was finished by others in 1875.) By then, however, Haupt was on his way to war.

Secretary of War Edwin Stanton called Haupt to Washington in early 1862 and put him in charge of rebuilding and operating damaged railroads in the various war zones. As Chief of Construction for the U. S. Military Railroads he organized its construction corps and developed a variety of methods to destroy enemy railroads and quickly rebuild his own. Among other things he designed a portable truss bridge (nicknamed "shad-belly") which could be shipped from the U. S. M. R. R. base at Alexandria, Virginia, and installed to replace damaged spans.

Historians have often stated that the Civil War was the first war in which railroads played a decisive role, and Haupt's skills contributed heavily to the Union's eventual victory by keeping the railroads operational. He was also a demanding and idiosyncratic person, who usually refused to wear a military uniform and often quarreled with army commanders. His refusal to accept a commission as Brigadier General led to a conflict with Secretary Stanton, who relieved him of command on September 12, 1863.

Back in civilian life Haupt's career continued to be marked by engineering innovations and financial disasters. He lost considerable funds in legal confrontations with the state of Massachusetts over the Hoosac Tunnel project. In 1870 he bought the Old Dominion Granite Company and steadily lost money operating it. During the 1870s he returned to the Pennsylvania Railroad, and in 1876 he designed and built the country's first long-distance oil pipeline in northwestern Pennsylvania. In the 1880s he served as managing engineer of the Northern Pacific Railroad. During the later years of his long life he worked as an independent engineering consultant with a prestigious reputation.

Haupt died in 1905 at the age of 88, four years after writing his memoirs. Although in many cases he was denied the financial reward he rightfully deserved, Herman Haupt is still recognized as an engineering genius who not only helped win the Civil War, but contributed substantially to the form of 19th Century railroading and industrialization.

CHAPTER 7

Key to Success: The Pennsylvania Coal Fields

As the newly-formed Northern Central was struggling northward along the east bank of the Susquehanna in the late 1850s, it was also pushing itself into a new world of anthracite coal mining. It was a world of black earth, man-made mountains of mine refuse, gritty "company towns", and helmeted, hard-working soot-covered miners.

Anthracite: Now an almost-negligible part of the country's economy, it was once a dominant fuel. A hard coal with a carbon content of over 86 percent, it burns slowly, uniformly, and relatively smokelessly. In an era before the widespread use of oil, natural gas, and electricity, it was the preferred home heating and cooking fuel; it also provided energy for many industrial uses. Almost the entire United States anthracite reserve was buried in mountainous eastern Pennsylvania, in three somewhat arbitrarily grouped fields. The Susquehanna River formed the far western boundary; from there the coal fields stretched east, through the upper Schuylkill valley to the Lehigh River, and northeastward through the Lackawanna and Wyoming valleys.

Serious commercial mining began about 1820. At first the coal was carried out of the hills in wagons from the little mining camps to the rivers of the region — the Schuylkill, Susquehanna, Lehigh, and Delaware — and floated east and south to the markets. By the early 1830s, canals had been completed along all of these waterways, and primitive animal-operated mine tramways were being built or planned to replace the agonizing inland part of the haul. Main line steam railroads came afterward and the anthracite region grew spectacularly. The mines had produced 864,000 tons in 1840; by 1860 total output had risen to an amazing 8,513,000 tons. Coal was carried out in trainloads by railroads such as the Philadelphia & Reading, the Delaware, Lackawanna & Western, the Lehigh Valley, and the Delaware & Hudson. The mountains and valleys became honeycombed with mines, served by an ever more complex network of rail feeder lines — some of them built or owned by the main line railroads, some by the mine operators or owners themselves.

Anthracite was the primary reason that the directors of the Northern Central had been so adamant about completing the Susquehanna Railroad to Sunbury in 1855. Clearly it would be a major traffic source for the railroad and a benefit to the port of Baltimore. Although the railway's route up the Susquehanna did not directly tap any of the coal fields itself, it would intersect with several of the already-existing independent feeder lines built to carry the coal to the river and the canals. In the next few years after Northern Central rails finally reached Sunbury in 1858, other feeders were opened. For almost three decades afterward, the Northern Central and its new (in 1861) parent, the Pennsylvania, would develop this territory; and like other railroads in the region, they would gradually take over specific feeder lines and coal lands as a way of controlling routing and marketing. The Northern Central was never one of the largest anthracite coal carriers, but it grew to be one of the most significant to the Lykens, Trevorton, Shamokin, and Nanticoke coal fields.

The First Coal Feeder Junctions

When the Northern Central started service along the Susquehanna, four independent rail lines already were bringing coal to the river from the mountains to the east. Two of them — the two which the Northern Central eventually took over — were among the earliest railroads in

New coal tonnage demanded heavier locomotives. Ten Wheeler No. 22 was an 1867 product of the NC's Bolton Shop. Smithsonian Institution Collection.

the anthracite region, and had complex and sometimes confusing histories of their own. All four lines had been built by mine operators to move coal to the canals along the Susquehanna, and, like many such operations, reflected their owners' concerns with minimum cost and expediency; they were, in short, rugged lines in a rugged topography.

These four coal feeders joined the Northern Central main line at Dauphin, Millersburg, Trevorton Junction (later Herndon), and Sunbury itself. At Dauphin was the Schuylkill & Susquehanna Railroad, which connected with another line reaching mines at Lorberry. (The Schuylkill & Susquehanna also connected with the Pennsylvania Railroad at Rockville, two and one-half miles downriver.) The Lykens Valley Railroad & Coal Company line from Short Mountain interchanged at Millersburg, and the Trevorton Coal & Railroad Company connection at Trevorton Junction delivered coal from the Trevorton area. At Sunbury the Shamokin Valley & Pottsville Railroad delivered coal from the numerous mines at Shamokin and Mount Carmel. The first two lines also transferred their traffic to the Wiconisco Canal, which linked Millersburg with the state's "Main Line" canal; the latter two connected directly with the Susquehanna Division canal.

Typical of NC passenger power as the railroad began expanding was 4-4-0 No. 111, a handsome 1868 product of the Pittsburgh Works. Author's collection.

The earliest lines had started out as horse-drawn tramways, and in a few cases had incorporated inclined planes to avoid heavy grading and extra mileage. However, the lines had been progressively improved over the years and by the time the Northern Central built along the river, they were capable of managing steam train operations to the mines. The mine railroads immediately constructed junction facilities with the Northern Central, and began using the rail route directly south to the port of Baltimore. Once the Northern Central arrived at the junctions, the mine owners found that they could cut over 160 miles and four days of travel time from their shipping schedules. Based on this far faster and cheaper transportation, the railroad estimated it would handle a 200 percent increase in coal tonnage from the mines into Baltimore.

Two other connections appeared after the Northern Central's Sunbury line opened: In June 1860 the Lackawanna & Bloomsburg completed its line down the North Branch of the Susquehanna between Scranton, Kingston (opposite Wilkes-Barre), and Northumberland, immediately north of Sunbury. This company, sponsored by the Delaware, Lackawanna & Western Railroad, was never planned as a Northern Central feeder; it existed primarily to carry coal from mines in the Nanticoke-Kingston area to Scranton, where the D L & W forwarded it east and north. It also served on-line iron furnaces and ore resources. It did, however, connect the Northern Central and the Philadelphia & Erie with mines and other railroads in the Wyoming Valley region.

The second connection appeared in 1871, when a company originally called the Danville, Hazleton & Wilkes-Barre Railroad opened a line from Sunbury up the North Branch of the Susquehanna to Catawissa. At Catawissa its route turned inland, running eastward through the mountains to Tomhicken, Pennsylvania (near Hazleton), where it served some mines and connected with the Lehigh Valley Railroad. Although originally independent, this line later was taken over by the Pennsylvania Railroad and was made part of a new PRR route from Sunbury to Wilkes Barre; as such, it became a key adjunct to the Northern Central.

Acquisitions Begin

While all these connections originally were independent lines operating primarily as arms of specific mining or land companies, the entire complexion of the coal business began changing after the Civil War. As more mines and railways opened, competition became intense for the same markets. Factors such as transportation costs, pricing, labor supply, and labor relations became critical — and increasingly unpredictable. Inevitably, railroads and mine operators moved to protect their markets by consolidating and controlling the entire process of production, pricing, transportation, and selling. Gradually, each of the major anthracite-hauling railroads acquired their own fully-controlled collections of coal properties and feeder lines. At the same time, some large mining companies bought or built their own railroads. When the process was finally over in the late 19th Century, the region's production and transportation facilities had been concentrated into a relatively small group of highly competitive, more-or-less integrated companies.

Thus the Northern Central's territory changed too, both positively and negatively. By the 1880s either the

Early mining operations in the Shamokin area. In the upper center, horses haul tiny loaded cars out of the mine to the breaker at the left. Below, lines of wooden Northern Central gondola cars wait to be loaded. Author's collection.

Coal Breaker, Lykens, Pa. Pub. by Frank Wynn

SHORT MOUNTAIN SLOPE, LYKENS, PA.

NO. 2 SHAFT, WILLIAMSTOWN, PA. 7367

Three later scenes of anthracite mining operations and facilities in the Northern Central's Lykens field. The postcard scenes date to the early 1900s. Author's collection.

Northern Central or the Pennsylvania controlled three of the six Northern Central feeders mentioned above; the competitive Philadelphia & Reading had taken two others, and still another rival, the Delaware, Lackawanna & Western, formally absorbed the sixth. Traffic flows changed accordingly.

The Northern Central directly leased two of the feeders — the Shamokin Valley & Pottsville Railroad in 1863, and the Lykens Valley Railroad & Coal Company in 1880. The third line, the Danville, Hazleton & Wilkes Barre, was taken over by the Pennsylvania in 1872 for use as a Northern Central feeder. Through these branches, the NC channeled large coal tonnages to the Atlantic ports at Baltimore and Philadelphia, and, after 1884, to Lake Ontario at Sodus Point, New York — as well as many inland markets. Well into the 1890s some of its coal business was transferred to the canals for delivery.

The first acquisition, the 27-mile Shamokin Valley & Pottsville, came in the midst of the Civil War, financed in part by Simon Cameron's generous war contracts. Oddly, it was a railroad even older than the original Baltimore & Susquehanna.

The Shamokin Valley & Pottsville Railroad

Leased by the Northern Central on February 27, 1863, the Shamokin Valley & Pottsville started at Sunbury and wound its way uphill along Shamokin Creek to collieries around Shamokin and Mount Carmel, Pennsylvania. Its antecedent company had been one of the first railroad firms chartered in the United States. Originally called the Danville & Pottsville Railroad, it had been organized in 1826 with the ambitious purpose of connecting the Schuykill River at Pottsville with the Susquehanna River. In effect it was to be a portage railroad between the two rivers, replacing the old Centre Turnpike.

The company was promoted primarily by the Philadelphia capitalist Stephen Girard and Daniel Montgomery. Girard owned about 30,000 acres of undeveloped coal land along the planned route; he hoped that the railroad would permit coal to be shipped from his land to the Schuylkill Canal. Montgomery was interested in getting the road to terminate at Danville, on the North Branch of the Susquehanna.

The Danville & Pottsville Railroad Company was incorporated in Pennsylvania on April 8, 1826. The Act provided that the Letters of Patent would be issued when $50,000 of stock had been subscribed to and $5,000 actually paid into the firm. The Act further provided that construction of the line should begin by 1829 and be completed by 1833.

The railroad's initial route was planned to connect the inland mines with both the Schuylkill Canal (at Pottsville) and Danville, above Sunbury. However, authority was later granted to make Sunbury the terminal of the new railroad.

The line was surveyed in 1828 by Moncure Robinson, the civil engineer who later laid out and built the Philadelphia & Reading, then went on to control and manage railroads in Virginia. But the underfunded Danville & Pottsville was regarded as one of Robinson's few failures; the country was rough and mountainous, and, in accordance with the practice of the time, he was forced to incorporate a series of inclined planes to carry the line down out of the mountains to the Schuylkill.

It was not until 1831 that the paid-in subscriptions were enough to secure the Letters of Patent for the corporation, which were issued on February 18th of that year. Construction work began in the spring of 1831, but proceeded slowly through the difficult terrain. The first section to be opened was at the eastern end of the line, nine miles between Wadesville (where it connected with the Mount Carbon Railroad to Pottsville) to Girardville, east of Ashland. Completed in 1834, it was a primitive horse-powered line, built with wood stringer rail and included six inclined planes.

Construction west of Girardville was suspended and crews were transferred to the western end of the line at Sunbury to speed up completion of the Sunbury-Shamokin section — apparently because it promised to be the most immediately productive. On November 26, 1835, this line opened between Sunbury and Paxinos, 13.5 miles from Sunbury and about 5.5 miles from Shamokin. Finally, on August 15, 1838, it was completed into Shamokin. Like its eastern counterpart, the Sunbury-Shamokin line was built with wood stringer rail and used horse power. Its route followed the Shamokin Creek valley through what today is known as Uniontown, Paxinos, and Snydertown, and entered Sunbury on the east side of town.

At this point the Danville & Pottsville had two ends but no middle. At its east end it was in operation between Wadesville and Girardville, feeding coal to Pottsville; on the west it ran down Shamokin Creek from Shamokin to Sunbury. In the center, between Shamokin and Girardville, was still an 18-mile gap. This was never closed; the isolated "eastern" section, with its difficult inclined planes, carried very little coal compared to other lines in the Pottsville area; it ceased operating about 1838. In the early 1860s a different company, the Mahanoy & Broad Mountain, succeeded in building a line from Pottsville to Shamokin over a similar but somewhat different route.

In the hope of replacing its horse power, the railroad ordered two small 4-2-0 steam locomotives, the *North Star* and *Mountaineer*, from the Philadelphia builder Garrett & Eastwick in 1837. Delivered in 1838-1839, they were put in service on the Shamokin division. The *North Star* was recorded as delivering 40 cars of coal, totaling 100 tons, from Shamokin to Sunbury on August 15, 1838. However, the steamers turned out to be too heavy for the stringer-rail track structure and continuously broke the rails, derailing the engine and cars, and damaging the equipment and cargo. The horses were brought back and used until 1852, when the primitive track structure was replaced with iron rails mounted on standard crossties.

With its "main line" unconnected and its construction and operating expenses unexpectedly high, the Danville & Pottsville entered bankruptcy in 1849. It was sold at foreclosure in 1850, and in 1851 was conveyed to a new company called the Philadelphia & Sunbury Railroad. (The Philadelphia & Sunbury should not be confused with the Sunbury & Erie or the Philadelphia & Erie — companies we have introduced earlier as the Northern Central's main-line connection running northwest from Sunbury to Williamsport.)

When the Philadelphia & Sunbury took over the line, one of its first objectives was to extend the Sunbury-Shamokin line eastward from Shamokin to open new coal lands. This was accomplished during 1854 and 1855 with an eight-mile extension to Mount Carmel. In addition, the firm spent a large amount of capital rebuilding the Shamokin-Sunbury section. New iron rail and crossties were installed, and the roadbed ballast was upgraded to handle the ever-increasing loads.

The new Philadelphia & Sunbury turned out to be no more successful than its predecessor. It continued to be an expensive operation, and its financial problems were aggravated by the cost of the Sunbury-Shamokin rebuilding work between 1852 and 1854. The firm entered bankruptcy proceedings in 1857.

Afterwards the property was separated into two sections — the moribund "eastern division" and the active Sunbury-Shamokin-Mount Carmel line. The Sunbury-Mount Carmel portion was sold to E. S. Whelen on November 5, 1857; Whelen then transferred ownership in the property to the newly created Shamokin Valley & Pottsville Railroad Company on April 9, 1858.

The long-disused eastern section, from Wadesville to Girardville, was transferred to W. R. Lejee on November 27, 1858 as trustee for the previous owner. In 1862 it was sold to the Philadelphia & Reading Railroad, which acquired the property merely to protect the right of way of the Mahanoy & Broad Mountain line and never operated it.

In March of 1858 the Pennsylvania Legislature finally approved the proposed reorganization of the Sunbury-Shamokin-Mount Carmel property. The Shamokin Valley & Pottsville Railroad took over ownership of the line on April 9, 1858, along with ownership of hundreds of acres of coal property. When the new company was established, the Northern Central's executives purchased shares in both the railroad and the numerous coal lands it held in its own name. This investment, which was a factor in the Northern Central's failure to meet its financial obligations in 1860, was the beginning of the railroad's strategy to control the coal supplies.

The interests now controlling the Shamokin Valley & Pottsville showed up clearly in its list of directors. For example, J. N. DuBarry of Baltimore, J. D. Cameron of Harrisburg, along with Thomas A. Scott of Philadelphia were all prominent Shamokin Valley & Pottsville directors as well as directors of the Northern Central. DuBarry was the Northern Central's superintendent; Cameron, of course, represented the Simon Cameron interests, and Scott was the aggressive Pennsylvania Railroad vice president. In addition, E. C. Biddle, Wistar Morris, Edmund Smith, and Jacob P. Jones, all of Philadelphia, were investors in the Shamokin Valley & Pottsville.

On February 27, 1863 the Northern Central took over direct operation of the Shamokin Valley & Pottsville by leasing it for 999 years. The lease required a payment of six percent on the par value of the firm's $869,450 worth of capital stock; it also required the payment of seven percent interest on a bonded indebtedness of $700,000. In all, the lease cost the Northern Central $122,167 per year.

With this lease came approximately 3,000 acres of anthracite coal land which had been accumulated by the old Philadelphia & Sunbury and the Shamokin Valley & Pottsville. At the time the property was worked by five collieries with a daily capacity of 1800 tons. To improve its control over the coal operations (which traditionally had been leased to various partnerships on a royalty basis), the Northern Central formed a new subsidiary, the Mineral Railroad & Mining Company, to operate the mines. The MRR & M was incorporated on May 4, 1864, owned two-thirds by the Northern Central and one-third by outside investors, many of which were associated with the Northern Central or Pennsylvania Railroad. (The Pennsylvania bought up this one-third interest in 1875.) The Mineral Railroad & Mining Company later expanded its operations by taking over other operating leases and buying additional coal land; it was the only operator of Northern Central/PRR mines in the Shamokin area.

In short, acquisition of the Shamokin Valley & Pottsville gave the Northern Central a major coal feeder branch from Sunbury to Shamokin and Mount Carmel, plus extensive coal lands and mining properties. The Shamokin Valley & Pottsville itself remained a separate corporate entity, although the Northern Central and Pennsylvania together gradually acquired all its stock. Between March 31 and November 14, 1871 the Northern Central purchased 12,034 shares, exchanging an equal number of shares in its own stock. By the end of the 1870s the Northern Central had increased its Shamokin Valley & Pottsville stock ownership

This 20th Century view of mine operations near Shamokin illustrates the full range of typical structures, machinery, and topography of the area. Paul Thomas Studio photograph.

to two-thirds of the existing 50,000 shares; the Pennsylvania Railroad held the remaining one-third. But like many components of large railroad systems, the old Shamokin Valley & Pottsville continued its separate corporate existence through the Northern Central and Pennsylvania Railroad eras; it finally was merged into the Penn Central Corporation on December 31, 1979.

On July 1, 1871 the Shamokin Valley & Pottsville executed a mortgage, with the consent of the Northern Central, for $2 million. Of that amount, $700,000 was applied to the payment of the bonds maturing upon the previous mortgage of $833,000. The balance was used to purchase coal lands near Shamokin. These valuable tracts amounted to 833 acres of anthracite property with a mine and breakers in full operation since 1870.

An additional plot of land was purchased on Green Mountain. A total of $425,000 was used to acquire the coal property of the Green Mountain Coal Company. These lands consisted of 2,066 acres but there were no operations being conducted on the property at the time.

The Northern Central progressively upgraded the Shamokin line after the takeover. Iron T-rail was installed and other improvements brought the line up to Northern Central standards. By the end of the 1860s the Northern Central had invested $115,635 in the line for improvements in both roadbed and supporting coal properties.

Additional coal branches were gradually built around the Shamokin area. The short Montelius Branch at Mount Carmel was built in 1862, before the Northern Central assumed operations. Later spurs included the Richards Colliery Branch (1893) and Scott Branch (1894), the Fagely Branch (built between October 1901 and December 1903), the Green Ridge Branch (which dated back to 1855), and East Sunbury (circa 1855) branches. Typically, these were merely spurs into individual mines and were seldom more than two miles long.

By 1864 the traffic of the Shamokin line had been increased from 300,000 tons per year to 557,000 tons per year. After the renovations were done to the property, the tonnage increased every year. By the end of 1872 total traffic amounted to over 683,000 tons. In that year, earnings for the Shamokin Division were $309,361, of which 91 percent came from freight (primarily coal) — although passengers did contribute $25,019. It should be noted, however, that a large proportion of the NC's Shamokin-area coal moved east onto the Reading for forwarding to the densely populated countryside in eastern Pennsylvania, New York, New Jersey, and southern New England. Much of the coal hauled south by the NC went to supply the iron works of the lower Susquehanna Valley and to towns such as York, Lancaster, and Harrisburg.

In future years the anthracite traffic from the Shamokin-Mount Carmel area would become one of the Northern Central's largest profit-producers, and would allow the company to expand in other areas and make numerous physical improvements.

Over seventeen years passed before the Northern Central leased its second and last coal feeder line — the 20-mile Lykens Valley. And again, it picked up a pioneering railroad in the process.

The Lykens Valley Railroad & Coal Company

Like the early Shamokin line, the Lykens Valley Railroad & Coal Company was one of the Northern Central's original connections — at Millersburg, Pennsylvania — when the Baltimore company built north along the Susquehanna in the late 1850s. It had been there, in fact, since 1834.

The coal from the Northern Central's Shamokin-Mount Carmel mines, although of excellent quality for industrial uses, was inferior to the coal found in the Lykenstown area (known today as Lykens), some distance to the south. Lykens Valley "red ash coal," discovered near Short Mountain in 1825, became highly valued for domestic heating and cooking because it kindled easier and produced less dusty ashes. Actual mining began about 1832.

To move the coal out of Short Mountain and down to the Susquehanna Canal, the Lykens Valley Railroad was chartered under a special act of the Pennsylvania Legislature on April 7, 1830. The firm was granted the right to construct and operate a railroad between Millersburg and Short Mountain near Lykenstown, completely within Dauphin County, Pennsylvania; it was Dauphin County's first railroad. Letters of Patent were issued on December 18, 1830 and the firm was organized on January 19, 1831. At the time, no canal existed on the east side of the Susquehanna, and the new company had to move the coal across the river from Millersburg to the newly-built Susquehanna Division canal which followed the river's west bank.

As originally built the "railroad" (actually, closer to a tramroad) was 14.6 miles long and roughly followed Wiconisco Creek to the Susquehanna, via Elizabethville. Surveyed by William Hanlin, C. E., it included an inclined plane at the mine mouth. The line was finished October 21, 1833. Like the Danville & Pottsville to the north, it was a single-track line built with strap iron rails, and used horse power. At Millersburg the coal was loaded onto "flatboats" (some sources say a crude carferry), and floated across the river to a point called Mount Patrick on the Susquehanna Division canal.

Operation of the rail line was turned over to various Short Mountain mine owners. Their cost was calculated on

Two views of the rail-canal coal transfer at Millersburg, Pennsylvania. Anthracite from the Lykens Valley line was interchanged to the Northern Central or to boats on the Wiconisco Canal. Millersburg Historical Society Collection.

both Baltimore and Philadelphia. In 1846 the first steam engine, the "Lykens Valley," arrived.

By the late 1840s the long-delayed Wiconisco Canal was completed along the east side of the Susquehanna from Millersburg down to Clark's Ferry, where it connected with the state's "Main Line" canal to Harrisburg and Columbia. Afterwards the Lykens Valley was at least spared the awkward cross-river transfer at Millersburg, but the mine operators felt limited by the capacity, speed, and seasonality of the canal system. As early as 1850 they began soliciting the Baltimore & Susquehanna to push the Susquehanna Division to completion.

When that connection was finally established in 1857 the owners of the Lykens Valley and Short Mountain coal mines promised an output of 700 to 800 tons of coal each day to the railroad. For the future, the Northern Central's executives hoped to carry a million tons of Lykens coal per year to Baltimore. But the perennially delayed Canton extension frustrated their plans. As of 1862, the railroad owned three locomotives and a minimal rolling stock roster — one sole passenger car, one baggage car, and a single freight car. All other cars were supplied by the coal mine operators.

On January 31, 1865 the Lykens Valley Railroad entered bankruptcy; it was purchased February 1, 1865 by Josiah Caldwell, a prominent Pennsylvanian, who operated it in his own interests for a year. He extended the east end of the line 4.7 miles from Lykenstown to Williamstown in 1865, donating land for the right of way in exchange for his ownership of the railroad.

Caldwell operated the property until January 31, 1866. A financial reorganization on February 1, 1866 created the Summit Branch Railroad, which leased the Lykens Valley Railroad in the interests of the various coal mining companies in the area. The Summit Branch Railroad and its accompanying coal properties were owned primarily by New York City investors. After the takeover, the company offices were moved from Philadelphia to Secretary F. A. Platt's offices at 13 William Street in New York.

a pro-rata scale according to each firm's use of the facility and the amount of their initial investment in the project. The railroad was operated in this fashion from the time it opened until 1845, when operations were suspended for reconstruction.

By then the increasing number and weight of the coal cars had worn out the fragile roadbed. The company had to rebuild and regrade the property completely, using 50-pound iron rails and crossties. The line was not reopened until October 31, 1848. However, the expense of the renovation was soon offset by the demand for Lykens coal in

During the fourteen years that the Summit Branch Railroad operated the Lykens Valley property it made considerable improvements to the roadbed. The track was relaid again with iron rail, the inclined planes were removed, and wooden bridges were replaced with either stone or iron structures. In 1866, the year the Summit Branch Railroad began operating the property, it had cost a total of $117,871 to build, reconstruct, and place equipment on the railroad. Another $262,000 in short term notes and credits were issued by the Summit Branch Railroad for improvements.

The investment soon paid handsome dividends. At both Lykens and Wiconisco were several highly productive coal mines. Together the Summit Branch Coal Company, the Lykens Valley Coal Company, and the Short Mountain Coal Company mined and forwarded several hundred thousand tons of coal each year to the junction at Millersburg. This high-grade anthracite went exclusively for domestic use and was in great demand in Baltimore and other eastern seaboard cities.

This poor quality photograph is the only known view of a locomotive lettered for the Summit Branch Railroad. While the 4-6-0 cannot be identified, this line had three such engines built new by Baldwin in the 1871-1873 period, plus two former PRR Ten Wheelers. B. F. G. Kline Collection.

Ownership of the railroad property brought with it vast holdings in coal lands in the Lykens area. The Lykens Valley Railroad coal property grew to include 9,200 acres of coal land and 3,000 acres of farming real estate. Ownership of these tracts was vested in the Summit Branch Railroad, which owned 7,319 shares out of the 9,883 total stock amount of the Lykens Valley Railroad.

As with the Shamokin-Mount Carmel fields, the Northern Central and the Pennsylvania Railroad gradually moved to control the Lykens mining area. By 1874 the Pennsylvania Railroad had bought up over 50 percent of the Summit Branch's stock. Then on July 1, 1880 the Northern Central leased the Lykens Valley Railroad. Along with the lease were the rights to the Summit Branch Railroad and rights to operate several thousand acres of coal lands in the Lykens area. The cost of the lease for the Northern Central was $62,500 per year. By then, the Canton branch in Baltimore finally had been completed (in 1873) and the railroad could handle heavy coal volumes through the port.

Sunbury-Wilkes-Barre-Tomhicken Lines

As the Northern Central became more deeply involved in the Pennsylvania anthracite region, so did its parent, the Pennsylvania. Indeed, the interests of the two railroads became increasingly intermingled and fed one another. In the decade between 1872 and 1882 the PRR acquired two lines in the Susquehanna region which, when eventually put together as one unit, effectively extended the Northern Central from Sunbury to Wilkes-Barre and to another anthracite field near Hazleton, Pennsylvania. In later years the Wilkes-Barre route outgrew its dependence on anthracite. Long after the collapse of that industry in the mid-20th Century, it helped sustain sections of the one-time Northern Central with heavy movements of merchandise freight and bituminous coal.

An independent line called the Wilkes-Barre & Pittston Railroad originally had been incorporated April 15, 1859 to build south along the North Branch of the Susquehanna from Pittston (north of Wilkes-Barre) to either Danville or Sunbury. The company remained dormant until April 10, 1867, when it woke up, reorganized itself as the Danville, Hazleton & Wilkes-Barre Railroad, and began construction. Starting at a joint connection with the Northern Central and the Philadelphia & Erie at Sunbury, it reached Catawissa on the North Branch in 1869.

After a pause there it changed its immediate goal. In 1871 it obtained authority to turn inland into the mountains from Catawissa and head for Hazleton to tap the anthracite fields of that area.

When finally completed in 1871, the railroad extended 45 miles from Sunbury to Tomhicken, Pennsylvania, a mining community nine miles west of Hazleton. At Tomhicken it connected with a Lehigh Valley Railroad branch from Hazleton and served several coal properties in the area.

Interested in entering the Hazleton fields, the Pennsylvania leased the Danville, Hazleton & Wilkes-Barre in March 1872 and proceeded to purchase 2119 acres of coal lands around Tomhicken. In an 1878 reorganization, the Danville, Hazleton & Wilkes-Barre reemerged as the Sunbury, Hazleton & Wilkes-Barre — which again was leased to the PRR. Coal from the Tomhicken mines flowed to the Northern Central at Sunbury for forwarding to Baltimore, Philadelphia, and other PRR points. After 1887 the Pennsylvania also reached Tomhicken from the east, via its new line between Philadelphia and Pottsville plus some Lehigh Valley trackage rights.

While the original Danville, Hazleton & Wilkes-Barre never got to Wilkes-Barre, another company appeared in 1871 to try to complete the route. The North & West Branch Railroad had been incorporated on May 13th of that year with a plan of building from Wilkes-Barre down the east bank of the Susquehanna's North Branch, then turning west to reach Williamsport. The company struggled for about ten years without much being accomplished; all the while, the Pennsylvania patiently but unsuccessfully tried to buy it in order to link it with the Danville, Hazleton &

Wilkes-Barre line at Catawissa to create a direct route between Sunbury and Wilkes-Barre.

By this time the PRR had acquired almost 6,000 acres of coal lands in the Wyoming Valley around Nanticoke, and was forced to depend on the Lackawanna & Bloomsburg Railroad and the canal to move the output to the Northern Central at Sunbury. While the Pennsylvania owned the Wyoming Canal Company, the Lackawanna & Bloomsburg was controlled by the competitive Delaware, Lackawanna & Western; its formal sale to the DL & W in June 1873 only weakened the Pennsylvania's position and intensified its desire to control its own rail route to Wilkes-Barre. Happily for the Pennsylvania, the North & West Branch's promoters were forced to give up in 1881. Wasting no time, the Pennsylvania took control, reorganized the company in July 1881, and completed the 43 miles between Catawissa and Wilkes-Barre by November 1882.

Afterwards the Northern Central had another strong coal feeder and a direct link to other railroads in the Wilkes-Barre area — particularly the Delaware & Hudson and the Lehigh Valley. Joint routes developed with these railroads to reach markets beyond the anthracite region. By the mid-20th Century the coal flow ironically would be reversed, with the Pennsylvania feeding bituminous coal up from Sunbury to the Delaware & Hudson for distribution to New England and Canada.

Top Photo: *Northern Central power poses along the Susquehanna division in the 1890s. 4-4-0 No. 15 is at McClennan, Pennsylvania (near Halifax). Railroad Museum of Pennsylvania Collection.* ***Bottom Photo:*** *No. 100, a D3 class 4-4-0 (shown at an unknown location), came secondhand from the Pennsylvania in 1881 and originally was built by the PRR's Altoona shop in 1873. B. F. G. Kline*

Independent Coal Feeders

The NC's Shamokin and Lykens Valley branches, along with

the PRR's Wilkes-Barre and Tomhicken lines, formed the backbone of the Northern Central's anthracite business. But three other feeders also contributed coal tonnage in varying amounts over the years. These, too, had begun as independently promoted mining railroads, and were early and valuable Northern Central connections. Gradually, however, they were gathered up by rivals of the Northern Central and PRR, and eventually much of their traffic went to market over competitive routes.

Nonetheless, these three lines remained Northern Central connections for many years, and the junction towns themselves developed in part because of the interchange activity. At Dauphin, the Schuylkill & Susquehanna Railroad extended inland, connecting to mines in the Lorberry Creek area. A second line, the one-time Trevorton Railroad, interchanged with the Northern Central at Trevorton Junction (later called Herndon), 34 miles upriver from Dauphin. And finally, the Lackawanna & Bloomsburg's line down the North Branch from Scranton and Kingston terminated at Northumberland, just north of Sunbury. Technically this line joined the Philadelphia & Erie rather than the Northern Central, but most of its interchange traffic at this point went south from Sunbury over the Northern Central.

Both the Schuylkill & Susquehanna and the Trevorton line slightly predated the Northern Central's Susquehanna main line. The more extensive and complex of the two, the Schuylkill & Susquehanna had its genesis in the Dauphin & Susquehanna Coal Company, originally formed in 1826. The first segment of this railroad, a 20-mile line from Rausch's Gap to the Pennsylvania "Main Line" canal at Dauphin, was begun in 1849 and opened in 1851. Like most of its brethren, its route included at least one inclined plane, located on a mine spur at Yellow Springs.

The Dauphin & Susquehanna turned out to be a disaster for its promoters. It had been built to carry coal to Dauphin from mines at its eastern end, where the company and its promoters had bought large quantities of coal land. As it turned out, the coal was either nonexistent or uneconomical to mine. Left with little on-line traffic, the company then tried to transform itself into a rail shortcut between Allentown, Pennsylvania and the Pennsylvania Railroad's main line at Rockville, 2.6 miles south of Dauphin. The idea was to create a new through route between New York and the west. To accomplish this, it built a short extension from Dauphin to Rockville (completed about 1852), and in 1854 it extended its eastern end 31 miles to the Schuylkill River at Auburn, where it could connect with the Philadelphia & Reading. From Auburn it intended to build farther east to Allentown.

Mercifully, it never did. Bankruptcy came in 1858, and in 1859 it emerged as the Schuylkill & Susquehanna. Within two years of that the Philadelphia & Reading had bought stock control, primarily to protect itself against potential competition. The Reading finally merged the line in June 1872 and integrated it into its system. Coal from the Pine Grove-Lorberry area mines was largely routed to the Reading main line through Auburn rather than to the Northern Central at Dauphin. Never a particularly heavy business-producer, the branch was finally dismantled in the early 1940s.

The Trevorton line's story was much the same. Created in the early 1850s to carry coal out of the Trevorton area (about seven miles west of Shamokin), it had included Simon Cameron as one of its early backers. (Trevorton, incidentally, had been named for John B. Trevor of New York, another major backer.) The railroad was originally incorporated as the Trevorton, Mahanoy & Susquehanna in March 1850; true to its name, it was to build from Trevorton down Mahanoy Creek to the Susquehanna — a total of 15.3 miles.

At the time, the Northern Central's predecessor, the Susquehanna Railroad, was only in the planning stage, and a direct rail connection was still uncertain. Unhappily, there was no direct canal connection either; the Susquehanna Division of the state canal was across the river on the west bank. Thus the company planned a 3600-foot bridge over the river (crossing at White Island), to be built by a sister corporation, the Susquehanna & Union Bridge Company. Work started in 1850, but suffered a two-year interruption; afterwards the entire project was consolidated in 1854 as the Trevorton & Susquehanna and was finally finished January 1, 1855. Its canal terminal on the west side of the river, Port Trevorton, consisted of a 12-foot-high trestle with three tracks and chutes on each side, capable of loading 40 canal boats a day. The long river bridge included eight 150-foot spans across the east channel, a 1400-foot trestle across the island (later filled), and fifteen 150-foot spans over the west channel. In addition to the single railroad track it carried a road and footpath. Unfortunately, the bridge's $120,000 cost buried the little railroad in debt, and in 1856 it went through the first of a series of reorganizations and sales, becoming the Trevorton Coal & Railroad Company.

As the newly-formed Northern Central hurried to finish its Sunbury line in the late 1850s, it managed to open an unconnected section along the river between Millersburg and a junction with the Trevorton line in April 1856. According to some sources the Northern Central used the Port Trevorton bridge to transfer its traffic to the canal while its own Susquehanna bridge was being completed downstream between Dauphin and Marysville.

Once the Northern Central's main line was fully opened in 1858, increasing tonnages of Trevorton coal came to the railroad at what was then called Trevorton Junction. The company's 1863 annual report, for example, noted that all the line's traffic, more than 30,000 tons of coal per year, was forwarded from the feeder line to the Northern Central interchange at Trevorton Junction.

Despite a fair coal business and a stimulating economic effect on both Port Trevorton and Trevorton Junction, the feeder railroad suffered through a succession of financial problems and reorganizations, culminating in the bitter region-wide miners' strikes during July and August of 1868. Again bankrupt, it had become the Zerbe Valley Railroad in April 1868, and an attempt was made to sell it to the Northern Central. But before this could be consummated Franklin Gowen, the Philadelphia & Reading's expansionist president, purchased it and assumed control July 1, 1868. At the time the line had no connection with the Reading, but the new owner promptly built a new branch to Trevorton from its terminal at Shamokin. This was completed in 1870, and afterwards most Trevorton coal flowed east over the Reading rather than west to the Northern Central. The impressive Susquehanna bridge to Port Trevorton was abandoned in 1870. Diminished in importance, the Herndon (Trevorton Junction) rail interchange remained until the Reading abandoned that section of its branch in the early 1950s.

The Northern Central's final "independent" coal feeder was the 80-mile Lackawanna & Bloomsburg Railroad, extending from Northumberland to Kingston and Scranton. This company originally dated to 1852, and slowly pushed its line down the Lackawanna Valley and the North Branch of the Susquehanna during the late 1850s; it finally arrived in Northumberland in June 1860. The line's northernmost 25 miles passed through a continuous anthracite field, and in the area between Bloomsburg and Danville it also served an iron ore region. The company was backed by the Delaware, Lackawanna & Western Railroad, a major anthracite carrier rooted in the Scranton area; thus most of the Lackawanna & Bloomsburg's business moved to and from its DL & W connection at Scranton. But some of its coal flowed through Northumberland to the numerous furnaces along the Susquehanna River from Harrisburg to Columbia, and for domestic fuel in Baltimore. In addition the ore was used in the iron furnaces at Ashland, Maryland, north of Cockeysville.

In the earlier years the Lackawanna & Bloomsburg also served as an outlet for coal owned by the Pennsylvania Railroad which originated in L & B territory. As noted earlier, the PRR had purchased over 5800 acres of coal lands in the Nanticoke area near the Lackawanna & Bloomsburg line, and originally used the L & B (along with its own canal) to feed the coal to the Northern Central and Philadelphia & Erie at Northumberland.

Never truly independent, the Lackawanna & Bloomsburg was merged into the DL & W on June 16, 1873. After the Pennsylvania put together its own route from Sunbury into the Wilkes-Barre area in 1882, most Northern Central and PRR traffic moved over that route rather than the old L & B.

Coal Traffic Booms

Almost immediately after completing its Sunbury extension, the Northern Central became a heavy coal hauler to Baltimore and, in later years, to Philadelphia and other eastern points. By 1861 the railroad was carrying almost 160,000 tons a year, fed to it by the following lines:

Feeder Line	**Tonnage (tons)**
Lykens Valley	55,058
Shamokin Valley	42,332
Trevorton	28,332
Schuylkill & Susquehanna	22,667
Lackawanna & Bloomsburg	10,665
	159,054

Coal volume grew with breath-taking speed afterwards; within ten years the line was handling an almost three-fold increase in tonnage. In 1870 it totaled 360,000 tons, broken down as follows:

Feeder Line	**Tonnage (tons)**
Lykens Valley	109,055
Shamokin Valley	104,555
Trevorton	55,665
Schuylkill & Susquehanna	60,245
Lackawanna & Bloomsburg	30,222
	359,742

Although the Northern Central would not reach its peak performance until the 1880s, coal traffic over the line during the 1860s and 1870s improved solidly.

Lumber Traffic

While coal came to dominate the Northern Central's business, other commodities also grew in importance. Lumber was one of the largest and most important. The line's Sunbury extension had not only tapped the Pennsylvania anthracite fields, but had also put the railroad in a position to handle the vast amounts of lumber produced in the Williamsport area.

Wood products had been shipped out of the Pennsylvania mountains since the early days of the Republic. A small and technologically limited industry, lumbering managed to meet the demand for the preindustrial revolution markets. But with increased immigration, expansion of the western frontier, and the rapid industrialization of the east coast port cities, the lumber industry of 19th Century America rapidly expanded. The business grew, in large measure, because the expanding coal and railroad industry during the 1850s required massive increases in the output of lumber and related products. Within the Northern Central's territory, the wood was used in Pennsylvania coal mine operations, railroad construction and rolling stock, Baltimore shipbuilding, and many other uses.

Lumber traffic became significant to the Northern Central as soon as it reached Sunbury in 1858, and it continued to be so until about 1911. The railroad line paralleled the Susquehanna River, which was both an early and a major water route for the timber rafts coming out of the West Branch Valley. Logs were milled at Williamsport and sent out by either the railroads of the area or by canal boat down the Susquehanna River.

The Northern Central, as the shortest route between Williamsport and Baltimore, received a large portion of the finished lumber trade to the seaport. In addition, the numerous canal junctions that the Northern Central maintained with the Susquehanna Canal throughout the lower reaches of the river did a thriving lumber business in the products from the Williamsport mills.

In the early 1800s, timber rafts were floated down the West Branch of the Susquehanna to the mills at Williamsport. Later, around the late 1860s, logging railroads were constructed throughout the vast forest region of south-central Pennsylvania to ferry the logs to the river branches of the Susquehanna where the products were again floated to the mills in Williamsport.

Frequently, farmers and land owners could supplement their meager income by engaging what became known as the "prop-merchant" trade. The work was exceedingly hard and the people who worked in the woods had to endure the hardships of both severe weather and primitive accommodations. However, in the 1860s the lumber industry was dramatically expanding, and many individuals made fortunes in the business.

Some of the largest mills at Williamsport, although changing names over the years, became world famous for the high quality of their products. For example, the Central Pennsylvania Lumber Company became known for the quality of its building lumber. The Dent Lumber Company and the Herdic and Company products were prized for ship construction. Each of these firms, along with several others, operated for many years in Williamsport and their total output exceeded ten million feet annually.

Exact statistics on the amount of lumber that went to Baltimore are not known. What is known, however, is that the majority of the finished lumber went to the port for clipper ship construction. The by-products of the milling operation, such as bark, slab wood, and other usable residues, went to local tanneries and stave mill operators. The wood that was of lesser quality and could not be used to produce board lumber went to the coal mines for prop timber and similar uses. The Northern Central's 1865 annual report listed the firm as transporting 75,000 tons of lumber over its line. By 1880 that figure had risen to over 120,000 tons.

Carrying coal and lumber to Baltimore was a prime objective of the Northern Central's line from Sunbury, but there was still another: the establishment of the first direct rail route between Baltimore and the Great Lakes. So as the company expanded into the coal fields, it was simultaneously working its way north into New York State toward Lake Ontario.

PROFILE: Daniel Miller 1750–1828

In 1807 Daniel Miller, a school teacher and lay preacher by occupation, founded the town on the Susquehanna River which today carries his name. In 1790, following a previous trip up the Susquehanna which had impressed him with the natural beauty of the area, he purchased 979.25 acres of land at the confluence of the Susquehanna and Wiconisco Creek from William Von Phul of Philadelphia. He paid 1,700 pounds sterling for the property. In 1805 he brought his wife, Elizabeth, and two children to the location and constructed a residence. In 1807 Miller had Peter Williamson survey the property into lots and for $33 apiece he disposed of a large segment of the property in a lottery.

The discovery of coal at Lykens in 1825 and the subsequent building of both the canal and railroads into Millersburg brought economic activity and prosperity to the hamlet. Daniel Miller died in 1828, unaware of the phenomenal growth that those new arteries would bring to his town.

CHAPTER 8

Completing the System: Upstate New York Lines and New Baltimore Terminals

Sunbury meant more than coal to the Northern Central when it arrived there in 1858. As noted in Chapter 4, the railroad could now also advertise an all-rail route between Baltimore and the Great Lakes at Buffalo, New York. The glamour of a Great Lakes line captured Baltimore's popular imagination perhaps more than the grubby (albeit much more profitable) coal business, but the reality was something else. Like many early "through" railroad routes, it was somewhat disjointed, involving three other railroads, one of which was a different gauge and another of which was in poor condition.

With the Northern Central now terminating at Sunbury, its "Great Lakes" traffic moved north from there over the Sunbury & Erie between Sunbury and Williamsport, then over the Williamsport & Elmira Railroad to Elmira, New York. At Elmira, the Williamsport & Elmira connected with the Erie Railroad's main line to Buffalo. The Erie and several of its feeder lines had been built to six-foot gauge, over a foot wider than the "standard gauge" used by the Northern Central and most other eastern railroads. Thus cars could not be moved through; passengers had to transfer and freight had to be transferred manually from one car to another. The Williamsport & Elmira Railroad was at least standard gauge, but that was its sole advantage. Originally built on a meager budget and plagued by blizzards and washouts, it was in poor physical condition and financially shaky.

Also connecting at Elmira was another railroad line extending northward to Canandaigua, New York. This route actually consisted of two interconnecting companies: the Chemung Railroad owned a line from Elmira to Jefferson, later called Watkins, at the south end of Seneca Lake. From Jefferson, the Elmira, Jefferson & Canandaigua continued the route to Canandaigua. Although they were incorporated as independent companies, in the 1850s and early 1860s both of these railroads were, in effect, Erie lines; they had been built to the Erie's six-foot gauge and were leased to the Erie.

At Canandaigua a connection was made with the New York Central Railroad, which extended east and west across New York State, reaching such cities as Albany, Syracuse, Rochester, and Buffalo. And both the Erie and New York Central routes to Buffalo connected with the Buffalo & Erie, which in turn formed part of a chain of railroads reaching westward to Cleveland, Toledo, and Chicago. (These lines later were consolidated as the Lake Shore & Michigan Southern, which eventually was folded into Cornelius Vanderbilt's New York Central system.)

Thus, working through traffic-handling agreements with the Sunbury & Erie, the Williamsport & Elmira, and the Erie Railroad, the Northern Central potentially could solicit business to and from Buffalo and Canandaigua. It was hardly an ideal arrangement, however. Even without the gauge difference between the Erie and the other lines, there were difficulties. Since all of the "cooperating" railroads were independent and controlled their own operations, they often did not mesh tightly together, and in some cases the traffic agreements were not particularly profitable to one company or another. The Northern Central's executives could only "hope they worked satisfactorily." Much to their chagrin, they often did not.

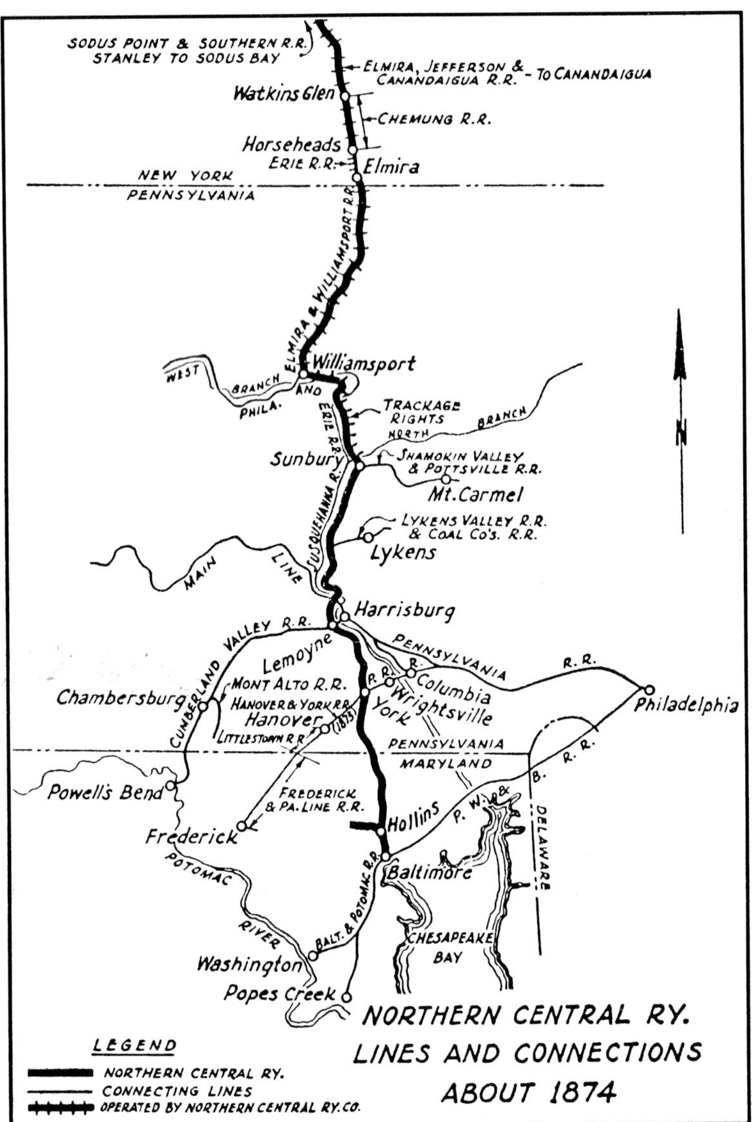

Pennsylvania Railroad Collection.

For example, depending on specific origins and destinations, "through" passengers had to change trains at York, Harrisburg, Sunbury, Williamsport, Elmira, and Canandaigua. In addition, travelers and shippers frequently complained of delays, damaged equipment or freight, and lost freight and luggage.

Nonetheless, by the early 1860s a relatively substantial amount of through traffic developed between the NC and upstate New York points. Inter-railroad relationships improved, and on May 1, 1863 the Erie and Northern Central entered into a joint traffic contract which, among other things, gave the Northern Central use of the Erie's routes into Buffalo and into Canandaigua.

More important, however, the Northern Central took the first step in a strategy to control its own line into upstate New York and, ultimately, to Lake Ontario. On April 15, 1863 it formally directly leased the Elmira & Williamsport Railroad (the Williamsport & Elmira's 1860 corporate successor).

North to Elmira: The Elmira & Williamsport Railroad

The Elmira & Williamsport lease effectively gave the Northern Central operating control of a line between Baltimore and Elmira, New York — 256 miles in all. Technically, it was a broken line; the 39 miles of track between Sunbury and Williamsport was owned by the Philadelphia & Erie, the Sunbury & Erie's corporate successor. But by then the P & E was also part of the Pennsylvania Railroad "family" and a close working partner.

The Elmira & Williamsport was another very early American railroad, and suffered through many of the same problems and frustrations as the original Baltimore & Susquehanna. Incorporated in June 1832 to connect Williamsport, Pennsylvania with Elmira, it was a pioneering venture indeed. At the time it was conceived there were no rail lines anywhere in its territory; the railroad was primarily designed as a portage between two parts of the Susquehanna River system and to open the coal and iron resources in the intermediate territory. Its south end connected with the West Branch Canal, a part of the state's Susquehanna canal system; at Elmira it met the then-building Chemung Canal extending north to Jefferson (Watkins).

Construction began in the spring of 1834, and followed the narrow, rugged but beautiful Lycoming Creek Valley northward. This valley, rich in the history of numerous tragic encounters between the Indians and pioneers, required the railroad engineers to build several river crossings along the valley floor, slowing the work. Harsh winter weather also created delays, but the line was opened on January 12, 1837 as far north as Ralston, Pennsylvania, 24.5 miles from Williamsport. Like the Baltimore & Susquehanna, the Williamsport & Elmira was built with iron strap rail laid on wood stringers, and used horses as its motive power.

During its early years the line carried mainly lumber, forest, and agricultural products into Williamsport, then an important lumber center on the Susquehanna River. There were no industries or towns of much note along the line. Typically, its early years were trying. The crude track structure frequently broke, and the trains careened off the line causing damage and delay. Customers, reluctant to use the accident-prone railroad, became skeptical of its potential and many returned to wagon transport. The infant railroad also shared another of the Baltimore & Susquehanna's early weaknesses: the early state laws considered railroads as public highways and allowed shippers to put their own cars on the line, and thereby undercut tariff charges.

Although that practice substantially reduced profitability, the state did manage to muster some token relief for the company. In April 1832 the legislature required that "no car or carriage shall use said road until numbered and registered with the company" and the law provided for a registration fee. Another law required "cars having a tendency to run from the track...or injure the road" to be "immediately removed." In 1836 much needed financial support was given the railroad from the United States Bank of Pennsylvania when the enabling charter of that institution required that the bank subscribe to $200,000 of the railroad's capital stock.

Typical of construction standards on the Elmira line was this wooden truss bridge at Field, Pennsylvania, 17 miles north of Williamsport, shown in 1874. R. Bosley Collection.

This early aid, however, was not sufficient to prevent bankruptcy. Like many early railroads, the Williamsport & Elmira cost more to build than had been anticipated. Cost overruns, excessive stock premiums, and the practice of granting rebates led to low revenues, a negative cash flow, and ultimately an inability to pay fixed charges on its bonds. On April 5, 1849 the line was sold at foreclosure to William Chester, a local investor who represented the lien holders. The property was reorganized under the same name; Mr. Chester became president of the new company and began an aggressive program of expansion and renovation.

At this time Ralston, Pennsylvania was still the little line's northern terminal; it remained 50 miles short of its goal at Elmira. Among its other problems, the railroad shared another unhappy similarity with the Baltimore & Susquehanna: As a Pennsylvania company it had difficulties crossing the state line into New York and, presumably, diverting New York trade southward into a "foreign" state. Chester made several trips to the New York Legislature and cultivated many politicians to support the railroad's entry into Elmira. He "boosted" the benefits of both additional revenues and employment that the railroad would bring to the State of New York. His approach, much like that of George Winchester's appeal to the Pennsylvania Legislature for the Baltimore & Susquehanna entry into that state, was designed to demonstrate that trade to any port benefited the people and towns of the interior. He argued that a rail line to any

NC No. 79 poses at Ralston, Pennsylvania, some time in the 1880s. The inclined plane to McIntyre terminated out of the picture in the front of the locomotive. Railroad Museum of Pennsylvania Collection.

seaport would benefit all participants and that "...trade, like water, would seek a natural level."

Chester was apparently successful, for on April 9, 1850 the New York Assembly capitulated and approved a special act to allow the Williamsport & Elmira to build across the state line and into Elmira. He not only constructed the line into Elmira, but rebuilt the original section with iron rail and purchased the firm's first steam locomotive. Chester spent a considerable amount of money on the line and, unfortunately, also added to its debt.

Elmira was at last reached in September 1854, giving the railroad a total length of 75 miles. By then the Erie Railroad had passed through the city and, although there was the inevitable gauge difference, the line at least had a railroad connection. But its meager earnings from the iron ore, lumber, and agricultural business could not support the debt, and it was again sold at foreclosure on April 18, 1860. One Edward S. Whelan purchased the property, which was reorganized as the Elmira & Williamsport Railroad, simply reversing the name of its predecessor.

The Elmira & Williamsport was equally unprofitable, and almost as soon as it was chartered its owners began searching for a buyer or operator.

At the same time the Northern Central was flush from its Civil War earnings, and the Pennsylvania Railroad was now its principal stockholder. The Elmira & Williamsport fitted into the ambitions of both, since it provided entree to upstate New York and the potential springboard for further expansion into that territory.

In early 1863 Northern Central executives approached the Elmira & Williamsport's owners and, after two months of negotiations, leased the line for 999 years effective April 15, 1863. At the time of the takeover the company represented an investment of $2.1 million. The total annual of rental fee was fixed at $154,000. Along with the property, the Northern Central inherited 16 locomotives, 58 gondola cars, and 521 coal cars.

At the time, the Elmira & Williamsport had only limited on-line coal traffic, and it is thought that the large fleet of coal cars may have been used to carry anthracite from the Northern Central's Shamokin and Lykens mines north for distribution in New York State via the Finger Lakes and the canal system.

Although the lease was effective from May 1, 1863, it would take several years of work by the Northern Central construction crews to renovate the line to its standards. Once the lease was effective the company began replacing rail, ballasting the line, and replacing the dilapidated wooden trestles with new bridges. New way stations were constructed at Canton, Minnequa, and Troy.

This harrowing inclined plane brought coal from the McIntyre mines to the railroad depot at Ralston. The view dates to the early 1870s and shows the plane's original appearance. R. Bosley Collection.

The opening of Northern Central rail service to this area of Pennsylvania and New York had a stimulating effect on the area's economy. Period newspapers throughout the area reported that the citizens and the merchants were "pleased with the improved level of service" and overall, that users and industry profited from the increased demand for Pennsylvania's resources to the port of Baltimore.

The town of Ralston was an excellent example. Named for Matthew C. Ralston, this was an important iron center beginning in 1831 and actively solicited rail service once the economic advantages of railroads were recognized. Both Matthew and Robert Ralston, owners of the iron furnaces at Ralston, were quick to admit that the "railroad brought prosperity to the little cities." They were both advocates of rail service to the town and significant investors in the project; once the railroad arrived in Ralston, they connected their mine trams to the line. Afterwards, ore output and employment began to escalate dramatically. Building statistics tripled in four years.

Then, in 1870 coal mining at Ralston was expanded and the town entered a boom period. The McIntyre mines constructed an inclined plane to the Northern Central line, built the town of McIntyre at the top of the mountain, and employed over 1500 workers. Ralston not only was the rail shipping point for this coal, but it also provided a variety of service businesses such as hotels, taverns, and restaurants. By the 1880s the McIntyre mines were forwarding over 200,000 tons of coal each year.

During the years following the lease the Northern Central continued to improve the Elmira & Williamsport property. Besides the bituminous coal from Ralston, anthracite was flowing north from Northern Central mines into New York State in ever-increasing amounts, and traffic in forest and agricultural products along the Williamsport to Elmira section also grew.

Much less could be said for the operations north of Elmira. The Northern Central's line from Williamsport actually ended at the south end of the city, a point called Southport, and depended on the Erie Railroad to get into town and to connect with the line to Canandaigua. (The Elmira-Canadaigua trackage actually began at Chemung Junction in Horseheads, about four miles from the center of Elmira.) The Erie was still broad gauge (it was not rebuilt to standard until the late 1870s), as were the two railroads making up the branch to Canandaigua — both of which had been leased to the Erie. Thus the Northern Central faced both physical and corporate traffic barriers at Elmira. Traffic beyond here had to be handled by the Erie under contract and, of course, required a physical transfer.

But still working towards full and permanent control of its own Great Lakes route, the Northern Central next negotiated a lease of the two railroads which together linked Elmira with Canandaigua, New York. On January 19, 1866 it purchased the Erie's unexpired leases of both the Chemung Railroad and the Elmira, Jefferson & Canandaigua Railroad, which had another thirteen years to run. The arrangement turned out to be a turbulent one, with touches of comedy, but now the Northern Central could operate directly to Canandaigua.

The Route to Canandaigua

The contract with the Erie which granted the Northern Central the unexpired leases of the two railroads was technically a sub-lease; since the Erie actually held the lease, it still was to pay the rental to the owners of the two railroads — an arrangement which soon caused trouble. The lease, in effect, made Canandaigua the Northern Central's primary interchange point and eliminated its use of the Erie line into Buffalo. In return, the NC was to handle Erie freight to Williamsport and Harrisburg.

The contract was doomed from the start. Neither firm actually wanted to negotiate with the other. In a broad sense they were both competitors (particularly considering that the Northern Central was a Pennsylvania Railroad affiliate), and they represented competitive states. In the agreement each company wanted concessions from the other that would benefit the lessor, and also would prevent the out-of-state firm from siphoning off commerce into a rival seaport.

Several contracts were written, but only lasted for a short duration. Then hostilities would arise and new arrangements would have to be hammered out.

When the Northern Central obtained the lease of the Chemung and the Elmira, Jefferson & Canandaigua railroads it immediately installed a third rail over the route to handle standard gauge equipment. The costly work was completed in 1868; when it was, the Northern Central had a 325-mile all-standard gauge line from Baltimore to the junction with the New York Central at Canandaigua. There, freight and passengers could be forwarded on a pro-rata scale to all points in upstate New York and west along the Great Lakes. (As already noted, however, the NC used trackage rights on two portions of the route — the Philadelphia & Erie between Sunbury and Williamsport, and the Erie through Elmira.)

The Northern Central's working relationship with the New York Central Railroad appeared to be harmonious — more than can be said of its association with the Erie.

In 1869 legal difficulties arose between the Erie and Northern Central over the lease contract of 1866. The Northern Central had been attempting to obtain a more secure control of its connections north of Elmira by buying stock of the Canandaigua line; when the Erie discovered this a confrontation ensued. The Erie (then under the con-

Along with its new upstate New York acquisitions, the NC inherited heavy winter weather problems. In this 1895 scene at Watkins, six locomotives were needed to bring the first train through town after a blizzard. Chemung Historical Society Collection.

trol of the notorious Jay Gould-Jim Fisk-Daniel Drew trio) responded by claiming encroachment from a rival firm, and attempted to break the Northern Central's hold on the route by declining to pay the rental on the Chemung line. The rental fee was required under the lease of 1866, and non-payment would have resulted in forfeiture of the Northern Central's operating privileges. In order to prevent that occurrence and to protect its investment, the Northern Central paid the rent itself. Force was frequently threatened, and in one particular instance it was used. A gang of

At Elmira, the NC used Erie trackage and the Erie passenger station, shown in the 1890s. Author's collection.

Erie railroaders ripped up the track north of Elmira, which forced the situation into the courts. The Northern Central obtained an injunction against the Erie to prevent similar obstructions, and began planning for a permanent settlement to the rivalry.

After legal resolution and renegotiation, the Northern Central retained the sublease of both the Chemung and the Elmira, Jefferson & Canandaigua railroads, and was also allowed to proceed with the stock purchase of both lines. The process of gaining ownership began almost immediately.

On December 29, 1871 the Board of Directors of the Northern Central authorized the issuance of income bonds which were used for the purchase of the majority of the stock in both the Chemung and Canandaigua rail lines. These bonds and a cash payment enabled the Northern Central to obtain a total of 14,094 shares (64 percent) of the Chemung Railroad and 14,706 shares (58 percent) of the Elmira, Jefferson & Canandaigua Railroad. By May 9, 1872 the purchase of the stock was completed. For all intents and purposes, the Northern Central owned both lines.

The purchase forced all other railroads in central New York to recognize the Northern Central's physical presence in the territory and its determination to reach the Great Lakes. It also forced the Erie Railroad back to the negotiating table. The Erie, it will be remembered, also owned the trackage through Elmira which gave the Northern Central access to the city and linked the two disconnected segments of its Williamsport-Canandaigua route.

On the day after the purchases had been completed, the Northern Central and Erie signed a new agreement allowing the Northern Central the use of the Erie's bridge over the Chemung River into Elmira as well as a right of way through the city and the use of station facilities. In addition the new contract annulled the January 1, 1859 agreement, but it preserved the payment of a yearly rental fee of $25,000 to the Erie for the unexpired term of the January 19, 1866 lease, which was valid until December 31, 1878. It was the last step in cementing the Northern Central's control over the entire route and eliminating any dependence on the Erie. At Canandaigua it had a harmonious interline relationship with the New York Central — and also was now close to completing its own route to a Great Lakes port.

While a lake port was always a Northern Central goal, up to now the specific point had been undefined. But after the acquisition of the Chemung and Canandaigua routes the protected harbor at Sodus Point on Lake Ontario, roughly 35 miles north of Canandaigua, became the objective. This final step would not be taken for another decade, however.

According to the Pennsylvania Railroad's official historians, George Burgess and Miles Kennedy, in the earlier years the Chemung and Canandaigua lines were of more value to the Pennsylvania than the Northern Central. Because the PRR handled a considerable amount of New York State traffic through its Northern Central junction at Harrisburg, Pennsylvania it agreed to pay half the costs of the leases of those lines.

The Chemung Railroad and the Canandaigua Line

The two railroads which made up the Elmira-Canandaigua route corporately dated to 1845, but were physically finished in the 1850-1851 period. Always intended as interconnecting lines — which in turn would connect with the newly-built Erie Railroad at Elmira — both were originally built to the Erie's odd six-foot gauge. Like many early independently built short lines, they had suffered from construction overruns, poor revenue producing capabilities, and bankruptcy. The company owning the Watkins-Canandaigua section, in fact, went through no less than four name changes in fourteen years.

The Chemung Railroad's 17-mile line actually started four miles outside the center of Elmira at a spot called Chemung Junction, near the town of Horseheads, New York. From there it followed the Catherine Creek valley through Montour Falls, ending at Jefferson (later Watkins) at the south end of Seneca Lake.

Planned to parallel and supplement the Chemung Canal, the railroad was intended to link Elmira with the busy waterborne traffic of Seneca Lake. The company was organized on May 14, 1845, but it took several years to plan the route and raise the required funds. Construction crews began work in the spring of 1849; the road was completed in mid-December 1849 and opened January 15, 1850. The cost of the original construction was $380,000.

The Chemung Railroad was a "paper railroad," with no equipment of its own, and no employees other than its directors. From its opening on January 15, 1850 until May 9, 1872 it was leased to the Erie Railroad. It was this lease which the Northern Central sub-leased in 1866, and which became the center of the maneuverings mentioned earlier here.

The railroad became a channel for coal originating at the Blossburg, Pennsylvania fields, destined for transfer to the lake at Jefferson. This traffic came from both the Fall Brook and Morris Run Coal Company and the Blossburg Coal Company, and moved out of the coal fields to Corning, New York, where the Erie brought it east to the Chemung line. During the 1870s each of these coal companies maintained its own piers at Jefferson for loading coal onto vessels bound for lake ports or points on the Erie

Canal. These coal operators, incidentally, had been some of the original backers of the railroad.

Aside from its coal transshipment facilities, Jefferson became a traffic source in its own right. In 1849 salt was discovered there, and was shipped out by both rail and water. Also, Seneca Lake itself attracted large numbers of tourists to the area, and became a magnet for resort traffic.

The Chemung Railroad was one part of the planned route between Elmira and Canandaigua, a total of about 65 miles. The second and final section of the route, operated under various names during the 1840s and 1850s, became the Elmira, Jefferson & Canandaigua Railroad. It was built partly to serve the agriculturally productive plateau regions between Seneca, Keuka, and Canandaigua Lakes, and partly to reach another railroad connection — the New York Central, which had assembled an east-west line across New York State from Albany to Buffalo.

The company originally was incorporated as the Canandaigua & Corning on May 14, 1845, started construction in August 1850, and opened its 47-mile line from Jefferson (Watkins) to Canandaigua in September 1851. The railroad's route followed along part of the west shore of Lake Seneca, then passed through Pen Yan on Keuka (Crooked) Lake and Stanley, New York before terminating at Canandaigua. Like its connection to the south, the Chemung Railroad, the Canandaigua line was built to the Erie's six-foot gauge; since the New York Central was standard gauge, there could be no direct interchange of cars. (Another company, the Canandaigua & Niagara Falls, had extended the six-foot-gauge route to the Suspension Bridge gateway in 1854; in 1858, however, the New York Central bought control, changed the gauge, and broke the connection.)

At Canandaigua the NC connected with the New York Central's "Auburn Road." Here an NYC train waits at the Central's station; the NC used facilities in the hotel at the rear. W. R. Gordon Collection.

The NC's Canandaigua freight house and roundhouse, seen in the 1880s. Chemung County Historical Society Collection.

Canandaigua Lake steamers also interchanged freight and passengers with the NC at this pier, which still existed in 1991. The NC's pier station is at the far right. Author's collection.

Costly to build, but with apparently thin traffic, the company proceeded to suffer a series of name changes, foreclosures, and sales: the Canandaigua & Corning became the Canandaigua & Elmira in September 1852, then the Elmira, Canandaigua & Niagara Falls (May 1857), and finally, on February 18, 1859, the Elmira, Jefferson & Canandaigua. This was the company which the Northern Central sub-leased from the Erie in 1866 and eventually purchased.

The Northern Central Influence on the Elmira Line

After taking over the Williamsport-Elmira-Canandaigua lines, the Northern Central invested some capital in the route, but not a major amount. Most of the money went toward projects on the southern end of the line. Initially the Chemung and the Canandaigua lines remained financially weak, and President Cameron wanted to wait for their potential to improve before upgrading the route.

After bituminous coal was discovered at Ralston in 1870, traffic over the Canandaigua division steadily improved. The coal was marketed exclusively to customers north of Ralston, including New York State and Canada. In addition, the Northern Central used McIntyre coal in its locomotives operating north of Williamsport. The coal business meant that the line north of Williamsport would begin to show a "return on its investment" and improvements could be made on the rather crude facilities.

In 1869 the line employed 250 people and was moving 200,000 tons of freight each year. Furthermore, it did a substantial tourist trade to Niagara Falls and the Finger Lakes. The line was becoming famous for its rugged beauty and majestic scenery — a theme that the company would capitalize on during the 1880s and 1890s.

By 1873 the revenue produced from the line was $527,021.80 and the expenses were $435,602.41. The yearly lease fee was $12,500; therefore, the Northern Central profited almost $80,000 from the railroad. That amount, considered good at the time, would become trivial when compared to large coal revenues of later years.

The Northern Central in the Early 1870s

By the late 1860s the company was showing impressively high gross revenues, although not spectacular growth. Revenues between 1867 and 1874 were:

Year	Gross Revenue
1867	$3.5 million
1868	4.1 million
1869	4.2 million
1870	4.3 million
1871	4.4 million
1872	4.6 million
1873	3.0 million (financial panic of 1873)
1874	4.6 million

During the period the main line double-tracking project was finally completed. The line from Dauphin to Millersburg was double-tracked in 1869, while the section between Sunbury and Millersburg was finished in 1874.

Breaking the Baltimore Bottleneck

In the years immediately after the Civil War the railroad world rapidly expanded and, at the same time, began to coalesce into large territorial systems. One by one the older locally-promoted railroads were absorbed or controlled by powerful, growing trunk-line systems such as the Pennsylvania, Cornelius Vanderbilt's New York Central & Hudson River, and the Baltimore & Ohio. And as these systems expanded they also became more directly and aggressively competitive with one another. Where once each company largely had its territory to itself, now the large systems were invading one anothers' markets and trying to carve out new markets before someone else got there.

The Pennsylvania's J. Edgar Thomson and Tom Scott unquestionably were the most aggressive and effective — although, after a late start, Vanderbilt was closing the gap. When Thomson died in office in May 1874 the Pennsylvania was a sprawling 6,000-mile system, the country's largest and most economically powerful.

As an early member of the Pennsylvania family, the Northern Central found itself both the tool and the beneficiary of the Pennsylvania's power politics. Its expansion into the Pennsylvania anthracite territory and upstate New York had been done with the Pennsylvania's encouragement and support. And, at nearly the same time, its chronic Baltimore terminal problems would be solved through one of the Pennsylvania's boldest and most famous strategic coups.

At the Civil War's end, the Northern Central's terminal situation in Baltimore was little different from what it was in 1850. Its port facilities were still limited to the City Dock and Fells Point. Both were confined, congested, and, of course, still bogged down by horse operations over the streets. Its interchange connections with the Baltimore & Ohio and the Philadelphia, Wilmington & Baltimore were handled the same way. As noted earlier, the Baltimore & Susquehanna and Northern Central had been struggling to build an extension to a new port terminal at Canton since 1853, but had been frustrated by right of way acquisition difficulties and litigation. The B & O had developed extensive terminal facilities of its own at Locust Point and Camden Station, but it was hardly interested in sharing them with the Northern Central, which it properly viewed as a Pennsylvania Railroad vassal. In fact, the B & O periodically would refuse to book through passenger and freight traffic between Washington and Northern Central/PRR points.

By this time too, however, the Pennsylvania's own expansive ambitions and its increasing rivalry with the Baltimore & Ohio were prodding it to take some bold action in Baltimore — action which would coincide with solving the Northern Central's terminal problems. At this point the Northern Central, although corporately separate, linked the Pennsylvania's east-west main line with Baltimore and effectively was the PRR's Baltimore entry. Through the Northern Central, the Pennsylvania could directly compete in the B & O's home city and reach many of the B & O's western markets.

Also, the Pennsylvania and B & O found themselves maneuvering for the New York-Philadelphia-Baltimore-Washington markets, the area known today as the "northeast corridor." In 1865 neither company owned a through New York-Washington route and, in fact, the Pennsylvania was barely even a presence along the "corridor." The B & O owned the rail line between Baltimore and Washington, which was Washington's sole rail link with the north; indeed, it had a state-guaranteed monopoly on the route. The remainder of the "corridor" line, from Baltimore to Philadelphia and New York, was operated by a group of independent railroads. The PRR, however, began to recognize the strategic importance of the route, and its managers — particularly Tom Scott — also developed ambitions of reaching into the Deep South through the Washington gateway.

Once the war ended the Pennsylvania moved — subtly and inconspicuously at first, but firmly and aggressively. In essence, the Pennsylvania's J. Edgar Thomson and Tom Scott joined forces with the Northern Central's J. Donald Cameron to resolve their mutual problems and outmaneuver the Baltimore & Ohio. All too aware of the B & O's political power in Maryland and its own status as an unwelcome "foreigner," the PRR made effective use of Maryland-chartered companies, including the Northern Central and two locally promoted, originally independent corporations — the Baltimore & Potomac Railroad and the Union Railroad. The Baltimore & Potomac would give it a line between Baltimore and Washington, which would cleverly (but legally) break the B & O's state-guaranteed monopoly of the route. The Union Railroad would provide the Northern Central's long-sought access to Canton and also connect the PRR-affiliated lines with the Philadelphia, Wilmington & Baltimore Railroad's main line between Baltimore and Philadelphia. Still independent at that time, the PW & B was a key link in the New York-Washington rail route.

Building these lines — and particularly tying them all together in Baltimore — would not be easy. Generally, the problems in locating a private railroad right of way through Baltimore were only becoming worse. The original street trackage had been necessary because, even in the 1830s, the city was tightly built up, and there were no separate rights of way available without resorting to extremely expensive and controversial property condemnations. By the mid-1860s the city was expanding outward, aggravating the problem. Added to this was Baltimore's hilly topography, which by itself made any new rail line through the city difficult and expensive. Carrying out the project would require extensive tunneling.

It was through the Northern Central that much of what is traditionally identified as the Pennsylvania's invasion of Baltimore was accomplished. The Northern Central acquired most of the land for the Union Railroad, and helped push the Baltimore & Potomac line to completion. In addition, its route into Baltimore was realigned to provide the connecting link between the Baltimore & Potomac and the Union and the access to what would become the joint passenger station for the various lines.

Route to Washington: The Baltimore & Potomac Railroad

The first and worst problem faced by the Pennsylvania Railroad group was how to get from Baltimore to Washington. Back in 1833 the State of Maryland had substantially aided in the original financing of the Baltimore & Ohio's Washington Branch, and took a portion of the line's passenger revenues. To protect itself and the B & O, the state would not allow any new railroad to be chartered between the two cities.

A way was found, however. On May 6, 1853 an obscure company called the Baltimore & Potomac Railroad had been chartered by the Maryland Legislature. A locally promoted agricultural railroad, this project was designed to connect Baltimore with the tobacco-growing region in southern Maryland; its route was to run from Baltimore to an unspecified port on the Potomac River in Charles County. Five years later the company settled on Pope's Creek, about 75 miles directly south of Baltimore, as its southern terminal. At Pope's Creek it hoped to operate a carferry across the river to the Richmond, Fredericksburg & Potomac Railroad's terminal at Aquia Creek, Virginia and establish a connection to Richmond.

Essentially, the Baltimore & Potomac was to connect the farms with the city markets and the river port. Its original charter also allowed the company to build "lateral" or branch lines "not to exceed 20 miles in length" to reach various towns near its main line. This type of provision was frequently included in charters of the time as a means of placating the rural towns who had supported a railroad, but then were bypassed by its main line.

The company remained dormant for many years. In December of 1858 the corporate officers were elected and a Board of Directors was formed. Surveys of the proposed line were made in 1859, but investment capital remained insufficient, and construction had to be delayed.

In 1861 Oden Bowie, a prominent Maryland politician and the patriarch of the famed Bowie family of tobacco growers in southern Maryland, was elected as president of the company. Shortly thereafter, Bowie approached John W. Garrett, president of the Baltimore & Ohio, in an effort to secure additional funding for the Baltimore & Potomac. Unsuccessful with Garrett, he also contacted the executive officers of the Northern Central and the Pennsylvania. Bowie knew that the two companies were unhappy with the Baltimore situation, and that they were also looking for approaches to southern markets.

In 1861 a modest amount of construction was completed in the vicinity of Upper Marlboro, Maryland, but the company still lacked sufficient financial resources. The outbreak of the Civil War served to delay the project further.

But soon after the war, mysterious events began to take place. In 1866 the Baltimore & Potomac was purchased by one George W. Cass. By a peculiar coincidence, Cass had been a director of the Pennsylvania Railroad between 1859 and 1865, and was also president of the Pittsburgh, Fort Wayne & Chicago Railway, one of the Pennsylvania's key (but still independent) connections at Pittsburgh. Cass was not a direct member of the Pennsylvania's ruling hierarchy, but was heavily involved in the PRR's western connections and in the "fast freight" shipping lines operating between eastern and western points. In addition he participated in many joint ventures with J. Edgar Thomson and Tom Scott.

Then the veil dropped. In 1867 the Pennsylvania's J. Edgar Thomson and Northern Central president J. Donald Cameron each purchased $400,000 in the Baltimore & Potomac's securities for their respective companies, giving it enough to begin serious construction.

At the time, Oden Bowie was serving in the Maryland legislature, and in 1869 was elected governor of the state. Still president of the Baltimore & Potomac, Bowie was effective in pushing the project through the legislature, including securing amendments allowing construction. (Bowie remained the titular president of the Baltimore & Potomac until he died in 1904.)

The real point of all this activity, however, was not to build a rural farm-to-market railroad through southern Maryland — although that had to be done. It was the provision in the company's charter allowing "lateral" branches up to 20 miles long. The Pennsylvania's astute management realized that the Baltimore & Potomac's line could be routed through Bowie, Maryland; from there a

The PRR was determined to have a dominant presence in Washington, and its 1873 passenger terminal certainly accomplished that aim. The building faced Pennsylvania Avenue at the site now occupied by the National Gallery. In the background is the Mall, crossed by PRR tracks. Author's collection.

"branch" could be built to Washington under the original state-approved charter. Both the state and the B & O had been outmaneuvered.

Construction of the revitalized Baltimore & Potomac began in earnest during the spring of 1868. It was reported that the contractor had 35 miles of line graded by the end of the year. The Washington line, however, was delayed by political problems. The District of Columbia had previously approved the Baltimore & Potomac's "branch" line into the city; however, the United States Congress wavered on allowing the line entry because it could not agree on the location of proper station facilities. Working through their political ally in Congress, Senator Simon Cameron, the Pennsylvania-Northern Central group was able to obtain the legislation that allowed them both to build the Baltimore & Potomac into Washington, D.C. and to build its terminal station. As an indication of the railroads' political power, the Baltimore & Potomac's line was built directly across the center of the Mall so that it could terminate close to Pennsylvania Avenue. Its impressive passenger terminal was located at 6th and B Streets, now the site of the National Gallery of Art; designed by the Philadelphia architect Joseph Wilson (who later designed the Pennsylvania's Broad Street Station in Philadelphia), it was an ostentatious Victorian Gothic structure built of brick and stone, with a large corner clock tower terminating in a spire. Demolished in 1908, the station still is remembered as the place where President James Garfield was assassinated in 1881.

A Baltimore & Potomac train from Baltimore has just arrived at the Washington terminal in 1887. H. H. Harwood, Jr. Collection.

At the same time, the Pennsylvania-Northern Central-Simon Cameron combination accomplished another key strategic objective: direct and exclusive access to the southern rail lines at Washington. The "Long-Bridge" over the Potomac River, built by the government during the Civil War, was the sole all-rail link into Virginia east of Harper's Ferry. At the time, it was being operated by the Baltimore & Ohio, which had its own ambitions for extending into the South. Congressional legislation in June 1870 evicted the B & O from the Long Bridge and turned it over to the Pennsylvania Railroad.

It was a startling defeat for the Baltimore & Ohio and a stunning victory for the Pennsylvania. The extent of political pressure on Congress is not revealed in the literature; however, it would have had to have been immense. The railroads had lobbyists working the halls of Congress — not the least of whom was the charming Tom Scott — and Cameron himself was a powerful politician who no doubt was heavily responsible for the success of the plan. In 1871 the "Pennsylvania group" — which included Thomson, Scott, Simon and Donald Cameron, and George W. Cass — formed the Southern Railway Securities Company, an early holding company designed to acquire control of key southern lines.

The Washington "branch" finally was completed on July 2, 1872 and began operations immediately. But the tunnel entry to Baltimore was still far from finished, and the railroad was forced to start Baltimore-Washington service from the isolated temporary Fayette Station in West Baltimore. The full length of the line to Pope's Creek was officially opened January 1, 1873.

The Baltimore & Potomac Tunnels and New Station Facilities

In Baltimore the Pennsylvania and Northern Central had to solve three problems simultaneously: the Baltimore & Potomac had to be linked with the Northern Central's main line; it also had to be connected with the Philadelphia, Wilmington & Baltimore Railroad in order to provide a through route between Washington, Philadelphia, and New York. And finally, as part of a separate project, the Northern Central was to be extended southeast through the city to reach the Canton waterfront. To accomplish all of this, two separate sets of long tunnels were planned across the city's north side. A western set of three closely-spaced tunnels, collectively called the "B & P Tunnel," would bring the Baltimore & Potomac line into the city center to join the Northern Central. To the east the so-called "Union Tunnel," built by the separately incorporated Union Railroad (about which more will be said soon), continued the line eastward to the PW & B and to Canton. Between the two tunnels a "union" passenger station, serving the B & P, Northern Central, PW & B, and Western Maryland would be built where the line crossed Charles Street.

The "B & P Tunnel" was the longest and most difficult of the two. Work on it began in June 1871, after numerous political disputes with the city council about property acquisition; it was finally completed in 1873. Taken as a single tunnel, it was 7,499 feet portal to portal, but had two intermediate openings, each about a block long. Most of the tunnel's length, 5889 feet, was built using the "cut-and-cover" technique — that is, by digging out an open cut, then building the tunnel structure and filling in the top with earth to restore the original ground level. The engineers elected to use the "drift" method for the remaining 1064 feet to avoid razing existing buildings and rebuilding street intersections.

The Baltimore & Potomac tunnel was constructed with five rings of brick and both the portal face and "wing" walls, as they were referred to, were composed of stone shipped to the site from the Cockeysville quarries. The facade was white marble while the wing walls were "blue stone." Over 700 workmen were employed at the project at one time.

The drifted section of the tunnel was the most complicated portion of the project. A hole was dug in the earth and then "crown bars" were set where the top of the tunnel would exist. From that point, the tunnel was actually dug from the top down to the bottom. The roof of the arch was supported by shingle boards to prevent cave-ins while the five rings of masonry work were mortared into place. Special keystones called "skew-backs" were placed in the arch to distribute pressure to points throughout the arch. Then the tunnel was constructed along its length. The supporting timber structure, which in effect became a shell around the arch, was left in place. In all, a total of 102,122 cubic yards of material were removed from the tunnel passage.

The tunnel cost $3 million to build and was financed by "tunnel bonds" underwritten by the Northern Central and the Pennsylvania railroads on a 50-50 basis. In exchange the PRR and Northern Central were issued stocks and bonds of the Baltimore & Potomac, which, in effect, was jointly controlled by the two companies.

The Baltimore & Potomac tunnel's route began on the west at Fulton Avenue, followed underneath Winchester Street and then Wilson Street, and emerged on the east end into the Jones Falls Valley at North Avenue. For much of its length it passed under a developing residential area. At the point where the center portion of the tunnel emerged at Pennsylvania Avenue, a small suburban station was built directly into the tunnel portal. This structure also housed large fans to help clear steam locomotive smoke from the tunnel.

Extensive tunneling was necessary to break the Baltimore bottleneck. This is the eastern portal of the "B & P Tunnel," located immediately beneath North Avenue. The junction in the foreground became known as "B & P Junction," The NC main line from the north approaches at the right; the tracks curving into the tunnel are the B & P line to Washington. Although the surroundings have changed, the tunnel portal and track layout were essentially the same in 1991. Smithsonian Institution Collection.

Immediately east of the North Avenue tunnel portal the Baltimore & Potomac tracks joined the realigned Northern Central main line at a point named "B & P Junction," located alongside Jones Falls where the present-day Howard Street bridge crosses the valley.

Just east of B & P Junction on the relocated Northern Central line the various Pennsylvania-affiliated railroads built a joint passenger station at Charles Street near Oliver. Officially called "Union Station," it was also known as the "Potomac Station," and served all Northern Central trains as well as the newly-established Washington-New York services operated via the PW & B. After stopping at the new Union Station, most Northern Central passenger trains continued on to the old Calvert Station, which was much more convenient to Baltimore's commercial center.

The Baltimore & Potomac tunnel was completed June 26, 1873 and opened for traffic June 29th. Once the Washington route was physically linked to the Northern Central, it became a through connection both for the Northern Central itself and for the Pennsylvania, which had been forwarding trains down the Northern Central line from Harrisburg. (Unfortunately, no photographs of the opening events or even the actual construction of the tunnel have been located.)

Originally the Northern Central's main line into Baltimore had climbed out of the Jones Falls Valley north of North Avenue, passed through the Bolton Depot, turned east and crossed town roughly along the line of Preston Street, then dropped back into the valley at about Chase Street to reach Calvert Station and the waterfront branches. As part of the tunnel and station project the line was relocated to follow Jones Falls all the way into town, passing the new B & P Junction, the new Union Station, and continuing southeast to meet the old line at Guilford Avenue near Chase Street. To nobody's sorrow most of the steeply-graded old line was abandoned, although the western end was retained as a freight spur into the Bolton Depot. The locomotive and car shops at Bolton were relocated to elaborate new facilities at what was called Mt. Vernon Yard, on the old line just north of North Avenue. Afterwards Bolton became a coal delivery yard until it, too, was relocated in 1886 to make way for Mt. Royal Avenue.

As a by-product of the Baltimore & Potomac project the Western Maryland Railway also relocated its Baltimore entryway. By 1872 this company had shaken off its inertia and extended its main line over the Blue Ridge to Hagerstown, Maryland, then continued to the Potomac River at Williamsport, Maryland. In 1873 it built a new line into Baltimore, leaving the one-time Green Spring branch at a spot called Kirk, near Garrison, and extending south through suburban Pikesville and Arlington. The revised Western Maryland route joined the Baltimore & Potomac at Fulton Junction, just west of the B & P tunnels at Fulton Avenue in Baltimore. From there WM trains used B & P and Northern Central trackage into Union Station and to a newly built (in 1876) terminal at Hillen Street in downtown Baltimore. Service over the new route began October 15, 1873; the WM's operation of the old Green Spring line between Garrison and Relay House (renamed Hollins at that time) was discontinued, and this section was turned back to the Northern Central under the original agreement.

Although essentially a Pennsylvania Railroad subsidiary, the Baltimore & Potomac owned its own equipment and operated as a separate organization for many years. In 1873 its roster listed 26 locomotives, 45 passenger cars, 10 baggage cars, and 275 freight cars. Also, of course, it handled through equipment for its "friendly" connections such

The PRR built its new Baltimore "Union Station" at the point where Charles Street crossed the Jones Falls valley. The original 1873 station apparently was a temporary wooden structure about which little is known. This view shows the station as rebuilt in the mid-1880s. It, in turn, was replaced by the present Pennsylvania Station in 1911. Author's collection.

as the Pennsylvania, Northern Central, and PW & B. Other PRR-controlled lines extended south of Washington, and increasingly, the Baltimore & Potomac became a key link in through passenger services between the South and Northeast. By 1874 its business had increased to the point where substantial revenues were being generated. That year the Pennsylvania began concentrating B & P stock in its own hands; by the end of 1874 it had accumulated 36.572 shares and bought out the Northern Central's interest in the line. (On November 1, 1902, the Pennsylvania merged the B & P with the PW & B to form a new subsidiary called the Philadelphia, Baltimore & Washington Railroad.)

The Link to Canton and Philadelphia: The Union Railroad

Concurrently with the Baltimore & Potomac project, the Pennsylvania Railroad interests were working on the connection eastward to the Canton marine terminal and the connection with the Baltimore-Philadelphia rail line. Like the Washington line, this project was built in the name of a separate company, the Union Railroad, although it differed in form and background from the Baltimore & Potomac.

As related in earlier chapters, the Northern Central and its predecessor, the Baltimore & Susquehanna, had been trying vainly to establish a high-capacity Baltimore port terminal at Canton since the early 1850s. This area, located on the east side of Baltimore Harbor, offered a wide expanse of both deep water harbor frontage and inland space for yards and other support facilities. Several attempts were made to build a Canton branch, but legal

As part of the PRR's Baltimore project, the NC's shops were relocated from Bolton to a larger area just north of North Avenue, called Mt. Vernon. This early 1900s view looks north from North Avenue. The NC main line is immediately behind the locomotives. In the distance on the other side of Jones Falls is the Maryland & Pennsylvania Railroad's line. Smithsonian Institution Collection.

problems and other difficulties had continually frustrated the railroad, and none had been completed.

The Baltimore & Susquehanna had acquired some land for its Canton extension and a section of the line was actually built in 1853. However, land acquisition litigation in 1854 and the merger into the Northern Central in 1855 effectively halted the enterprise.

The Northern Central renewed the project after the company began life in 1855. Its charter had provided financial support to the company from the city of Baltimore, providing that the line was extended into both Sunbury and the Canton Company property. The legislative authorization set a time limit on completion of the project. However, as the land acquisition litigation proceeded through the judicial system, the financial panic of 1857 postponed the Canton extension even longer.

During the early 1860s the Civil War mandated priority to other more pressing problems. Moreover, in 1862 the grants offered from the city of Baltimore to support the venture had expired and the city government began to back away from its financial support of the Northern Central.

In a last effort, however, two new legislative authorizations were introduced through the Baltimore City Council: one extended the mandated construction deadline for the Canton line; the other provided for city financial support for the line. Both were quickly vetoed by the mayor. The city's financial interest in the Northern Central had been in dispute, and by 1865 the city sold its holdings in the company for $860,000.

As all this was happening, the Canton Company was undergoing its own travails. As noted in Chapter 3, this company dated to 1828 and was the primary owner and developer of the Canton property. It owned large acreages in Canton, most of which was still undeveloped because of the area's relative remoteness and the delays in building rail connections. In 1850 and again in 1860 it fell prey to stock speculators, then saw the Civil War delay its planned construction and land acquisition projects.

By 1865 the Canton situation had reached a crisis point. Largely as a result of the Northern Central's inability to fulfill its charter obligation to extend its line to the Baltimore waterfront, many railroad executives and prominent Baltimore merchants began suggesting an independent "union" line to Canton, open to all competing railroads. Planning was done on a sporadic basis.

In 1866, after the war's end, the idea of establishing Canton as what the *Baltimore American* called "a converging point for a great railway system" became "clearly established." Partly behind the city's new awareness were the intolerable wartime congestion and delays caused by the "Baltimore bottleneck". That year the Canton Company, in its own name, secured a charter from the State of Maryland authorizing construction of the Union Railroad.

As constituted in 1866, the Union Railroad was to be a privately-financed independent company, open to all railroads willing to invest in it or pay usage fees. William G. Harrison was named as the Union Railroad's first president; major original investors in the line included prominent people with ties to the Canton Company or businesses in Canton. Among them were Horace Abbott, owner of the Abbott Iron Works in Canton; Jesse and Isaac Tyson, who operated the Baltimore Copper Smelting Company there; and Joseph H. Stickney, owner of the Stickney Furnace, located in Canton at Clinton and 11th Streets.

The enabling legislation authorized the Union Railroad to connect with the Northern Central in Baltimore, and with the Philadelphia, Wilmington & Baltimore Railroad at a point near Canton. The company's capital stock was fixed at $600,000; it also was authorized to purchase any land previously bought by the Northern Central for its stillborn Canton extension. Although the Union Railroad subsequently used a route different from the Northern Central's, it acquired some Northern Central property near the terminal points at Canton, Orangeville, and Baltimore.

Describing the project as a "federation of railroads," Harrison sought funds and invited the participation of the Canton Company and all Baltimore railroads, including the Baltimore & Ohio. Probably to nobody's surprise, the B & O emphatically refused to invest or participate in any way. By that time it had its own spacious and well-developed marine terminal at Locust Point. Also, rather shortsightedly, it had no ambitions to extend its operations east of Baltimore — a decision that it would later regret.

Work on the Union Railroad began in 1867, but soon ran out of money. That year the company's charter was amended to allow an increase in its capitalization. Work was suspended in 1868 while new funds were sought; it resumed in 1869, but again stopped.

In 1870 the Union Railroad's charter was again amended to increase its capitalization to a total of $2.1 million. In April of that year the Canton Company's board of directors agreed to support the project directly with the purchase of $200,000 of Union Railroad stock and bonds. The money for this purchase was largely advanced by the Pennsylvania Railroad after the Baltimore City government backed away from any commitment because of conflict of interest allegations. Then, on October 28, 1870 the Canton Company effectively took control of the Union Railroad by buying $590,000 of its stock and endorsing $873,000 of its bonds.

Unlike the Baltimore & Potomac, its companion railroad on the west, the Union Railroad was never meant to be an operating company. Its purpose was strictly to build and own the line; to use the terminology of the time, it was managed as a "toll road," giving trackage rights to other railroads at an initial rate of .05 cents per ton mile. The

Northern Central was a major user, but the Union line also was designed to link the Baltimore & Potomac with the PW & B for New York-Washington traffic.

With heavy backing from the Pennsylvania Railroad and Northern Central, the project restarted in earnest. Contracts were awarded in late March of 1871, and construction resumed May 1st. C. P. Manning was chief engineer for the railroad, assisted by resident engineers J. C. Wrentshall and J. R. Kenly; the construction contractor was Drill, Wiley & Andrews, Inc.

The Union Railroad's route began at a junction with the Northern Central just east of the site of the new Union Station in the Jones Falls Valley. The spot, called Union Junction, was located where present-day Guilford Avenue crosses the valley; like B & P Junction to its west, Union Junction's name remains today, long after the railroad company disappeared. From Union Junction the line climbed out of the valley and angled gently southeastward to Bay View, where it joined the Philadelphia, Wilmington & Baltimore's main line. Slightly west of Bay View, at a point called Canton Junction, the Canton line turned directly south to the waterfront, ending at Ninth and Second streets in Canton. In deference to local industry, the track consisted of 72-pound rail rolled at Abbott's Rolling Mill in Canton. Most of the line was laid at grade level and relatively easy to build — but another long tunnel was required to pierce a hill just east of Union Junction.

The NC reached the port of Canton over the Union Railroad in 1874. This rare lithograph shows its first Canton terminal. Author's collection.

Union Tunnel, as it was called, was shorter (at 3410 feet) than the B & P tunnels through the west side of town and the earth was less rocky. Beginning on the west at Greenmount Avenue it followed beneath Hoffman Street and emerged at Bond Street, west of Broadway. Most of the Union Tunnel was cut-and-cover construction, although a short portion was "driven," using the steam bore method. Its maximum depth was 70 feet, about 20 feet deeper than the B & P bore. Over 300 men worked on the project.

The Union Railroad officially opened July 24, 1873, about a month behind the Baltimore & Potomac tunnel project. Thanks primarily to its tunnel, the line cost over $3 million. But the entire Pennsylvania-Northern Central Baltimore terminal project was now complete, with a high-capacity route across the city free of any street trackage. In all, it had been tremendously costly but ultimately worth it. The Northern Central (and through it, the PRR) at last had its link to Canton — not only a spacious deepwater port, but later a thriving industrial center.

Even more strategically important, particularly for the Pennsylvania, the Baltimore & Potomac and Union Railroad projects created a PRR-controlled route to Washington and the South, plus a direct connection to the Baltimore-Philadelphia railroad. For the future, this was the key move in making the Pennsylvania the dominant carrier over the entire New York-Washington corridor. By the time the new Baltimore facilities were opened in 1873, the PRR also operated the rail line between New York and Philadelphia. Although the Philadelphia, Wilmington & Baltimore was still independent, and neutrally handled both Baltimore & Ohio and Pennsylvania traffic between Baltimore and Philadelphia, the new PRR-controlled route through Baltimore avoided the plodding, unwieldy downtown street transfer which the B & O was still forced to operate.

There was a negative side, though. By 1874 Baltimore newspapers were warning train riders to keep the car windows closed to avoid the "possibility of passengers choking to death from the smoke while passing through the Baltimore tunnels." It was advice well taken. Both the B & P and Union tunnels were built with stiff grades — 1.2 percent eastbound in the Union Tunnel, and a particularly brutal mile-long 1.34 percent westbound climb in the B & P Tunnel. In an era of steam power and steadily increasing traffic the tunnels became the bane of passengers, the surrounding residential neighborhoods, and the railroad itself. The problem was not completely solved until the line was electrified in 1935.

When the Northern Central reached Canton in 1873 there already was traffic waiting there for it. The Canton Company had built a small 100,000-bushel grain elevator, known as "Gardner's Union Elevator," and several manufacturing industries had been established. Almost needless to say, companies owned by some of the Union Railroad's original backers immediately took advantage of rail service — notably Horace Abbott's Canton Rolling Mill, the Baltimore Copper Smelting Company of Jesse and Issac Tyson, and Joseph Stickney's Stickney Furnace. Stickney's iron works was improved in 1872 and added a new furnace in 1882. Also in the area were two distilleries, a saw mill, a car wheel and carriage shop, a coal oil refinery, and oyster and fruit packing houses.

An 1874 *Journal of Commerce* article reported that "the prospects of Baltimore are brilliant as a star" because of the "finest port on the Atlantic." The article also reported that the Northern Central's coal business from the Pennsylvania fields to the port increased 500 percent. Finally, it concluded that because the Northern Central could deliver anthracite to Baltimore at a lower price than competing lines, "the stranglehold that the Baltimore & Ohio held on the port was destroyed."

Soon afterwards railroad-oriented bulk terminals were added. In 1876 the Northern Central built its own 500,000-bushel grain elevator, following it with a slightly larger one in 1879. The Baker-Whitely Coal Company constructed two coal piers, and piers for handling ores and general merchandise were added over the next few years. The complexion of Canton began to change rapidly. Bishop's Racetrack left the area, and the taverns and breweries gave way to an ever-expanding complex of grain elevators, docks, and rail yards. Canton's industry expanded to include oil and kerosene plants in the 1870s, a petroleum pipeline terminal, lard works, and a cotton factory.

In 1880 the Northern Central purchased 20 large lots from the Canton Company for the development of its rail yard. When this yard was fully completed in 1886 it could hold over 2,000 standing cars.

The Pennsylvania Assumes Executive Management

Throughout the early 1870s pressures were building from certain Northern Central stockholders to lease the railroad to the Pennsylvania. The issue had first surfaced in 1863, when a stockholder committee had recommended such a lease. The group was concerned about the cost of rebuilding and improving the NC, and preferred a guaranteed income rather than bearing this financial risk. President J. D. Cameron had pushed for continued separate management and hoped that once the Great Lakes route became established, the company would produce enough revenue to absorb the costs.

A similar stockholders' committee surfaced in 1873, and for similar reasons. The new Canton extension meant large new expenditures for waterfront terminal facilities and another general line upgrading to handle the increased business, and the newly-acquired upstate New York lines needed rebuilding. Financing these expenditures would be costly, and again the committee recommended a lease. This time a greater number of stockholders voted in favor of the lease than in the 1860s, and they succeeded in establishing a group to present an "offer" to the Pennsylvania.

The action produced an executive crisis for the company. On December 8, 1874, President Cameron — apparently tired of fighting the "lease faction" — resigned, along with the entire Board of Directors.

The stockholders' lease committee approached the Pennsylvania's new president, Tom Scott, who had succeeded J. Edgar Thomson in June 1874. Whatever the pros and cons of the proposal may have been, the timing was wrong, and Scott declined to take over the line. The Panic of 1873 had ushered in a depression and the Pennsylvania, faced with its own financial needs, could not make the Northern Central stockholders a satisfactory offer. The naturally expansive Scott, in fact, found himself frustrated not only by hard times, but by his own directors. The heady expansion of the previous ten years had vastly increased the Pennsylvania's capitalization and produced a stockholder backlash. An investigating committee had been established in March 1874, which eventually resulted in reining in the company's growth.

Scott and the Northern Central stockholders were now left in a quandary. The Northern Central had no executive management, and the Pennsylvania was either unable or unwilling to lease the line. After numerous meetings, the various parties agreed that the Northern Central would continue managing its own operations as a separate corporate entity — but that the president of the Pennsylvania would also serve as the Northern Central's president. In essence, the Pennsylvania would directly influence the company's policies and strategies, while the Northern Central ran its railroad with its own operating management.

Cameron thus was the Northern Central's last "independent" president. He had taken the railroad through more than a decade of trying times, including war, expansion, and rebuilding — then, ironically, he left on the eve of its most notable years. It was the end of one era and the beginning of another.

PROFILE: Archibald McIntyre

The town of McIntyre, atop the mountains of Pennsylvania's Lycoming Creek Valley near Ralston, was named for an individual who became a significant booster of the area's natural resources. Archibald McIntyre was a Philadelphia entrepreneur who became an important investor and an absentee owner of numerous enterprises in central Pennsylvania. He was a director and substantial financial supporter of the original Williamsport & Elmira Railroad, envisioning the line as both a trade artery between Williamsport, Pennsylvania and Elmira, New York, and a medium for exploiting the resources of the area. He invested heavily and lost significantly.

During the 1850s McIntyre hired "ore specialists" to attempt to locate coal in the Lycoming Valley mountains adjacent to the railroad he helped to build. The mining experts searched for many years without success. By late 1868, however, a significant deposit of bituminous coal had been discovered just east of Ralston and Archibald McIntyre began exploiting the resource. He incorporated the McIntyre Coal Company in 1869, initiated mining operations in 1870, and began construction of the mining town which would become his namesake. In 1870 the mining company constructed a dual incline plane down the mountain to Ralston's rail facility and began shipping coal over the Northern Central line. Within three years, the McIntyre mines were in full operation and the town of McIntyre grew rapidly. Boarding houses, residences, a general store, a meeting house, and a church were rapidly erected to accommodate the influx of miners. During the decade of the 1880s the town reached a population base of 1500 people.

Tragedy struck the town of McIntyre at least twice during its existence. First, during the 1870s the tow cable on the incline plane broke, coal cars plummeted down the mountain, and several people were killed in the resulting crash. Then, during 1881 to 1883 a severe epidemic of typhoid decimated the town's inhabitants. The gravestones of its victims are still visible on top of the mountain. Nonetheless, the town of McIntyre remained a viable mining center until 1899. After the incline tragedy, a newer and safer "bucket system" designed to bring coal into Ralston was placed in operation. That particular technology remained in service until trucks hauled the coal off the mountain. At the turn of the century, the Rock Run mining center (located on the adjacent mountain) began to eclipse the mines of McIntyre and the town began a long production decline and a descent to oblivion. By the 1930s trucks hauled coal out of the mines on a limited basis. Many of the town's structures were either razed, burned down, or collapsed. In 1950 only three families lived at the location and coal was no longer mined on the mountain. By 1960 only a few stone foundations, various slag piles, and the community graveyard remained to designate the once prosperous mining town named for Archibald McIntyre.

CHAPTER 9

The "Glory Years"

In the 1880s, the Northern Central entered its "glory years," a period which lasted into the early 20th Century. During the early years of this era the Northern Central completed the shape of its system and acquired additional independent feeders. Afterwards, it reached a peak of physical form, traffic density, economic power, and prestige. These were the "glory years" for the Northern Central's on-line communities too, as their industries and commerce grew around the railroad — and were bolstered by the railroad's own large local employment.

Nationally, of course, railroads were then overwhelmingly the dominant form of transportation. These years coincided with the completion of the country's rail network (which peaked in 1916), the establishment of coal as the primary industrial and residential energy source, and the use of steam as the prime power in American industry. And happily for the Northern Central it was allied with the country's most powerful railroad company, and thus could share in the bonanza more than many. During this period the Northern Central became internationally renowned. It was especially recognized for its ability to deliver anthracite at low cost to both the port of Baltimore and to Lake Ontario at Sodus Point. Moreover, it was particularly distinguished for its personalized service, the care of its property, and its scenery. For example, in 1881 J. Thomas Scharf's *History of Baltimore City and County* described the

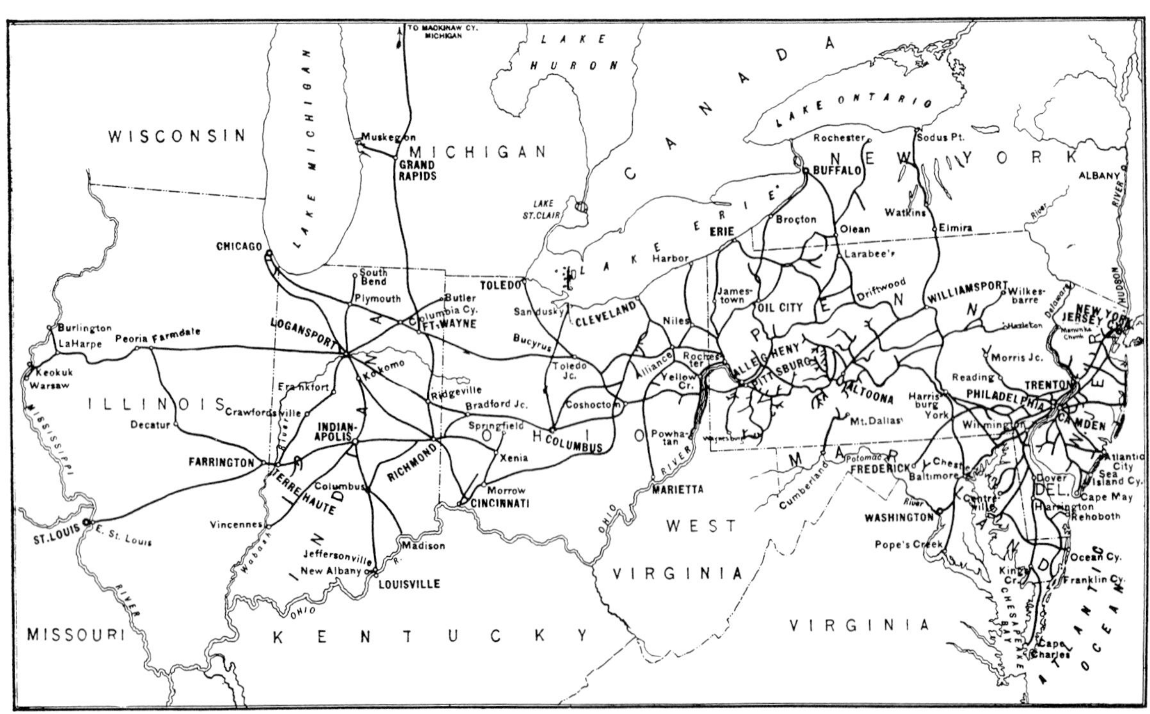

The PRR system in full flower at about 1900. By this time the NC had essentially become an integral part of this vast network.

Northern Central as "...one of the best managed and operated railways in the world." In addition, the *American Railroad Manual* consistently recognized the Northern Central as being "...eminently successful..." and "maintaining a high financial and accommodating reputation."

The anthracite business made much of this possible. Although the Northern Central was not as significant in this trade as several other major railroads, its coal revenues produced a peak of economic and social significance and provided the towns along the line with continued prosperity.

The coal exporting business became a strong market for Northern Central anthracite, and its ports of Baltimore and Sodus Point on Lake Ontario (reached in 1884) shipped heavy tonnages to both overseas and to other domestic ports. Coal use was escalating everywhere. Mill and manufacturing establishments were consuming large amounts, as were the increasingly busy steam-powered railroads. And anthracite, because of its burning characteristics and low smoke, was increasingly becoming the preferred residential fuel. Also, the new Sodus Point facility allowed the Northern Central to extend its reach to coal markets throughout the Great Lakes and into Canada. In addition to its revenues from hauling coal, the company also benefited from direct ownership of the coal lands and mines.

Coal was far from the sole commodity that produced revenue for the Northern Central. Central Pennsylvania lumber was a staple commodity during the 19th Century; grain shipments from the productive agricultural regions of New York, Pennsylvania, and Maryland also provided a good, but seasonal, source of tonnage. Passenger business also grew, of course; besides traffic to and from points on its own lines, the railroad formed a key link in through travel over the extensive Pennsylvania system, particularly between Baltimore, Washington, and cities on the PRR's Pittsburgh-Chicago-St. Louis main lines.

Primarily fueled by its growing bulk freight traffic, the Northern Central's gross revenues grew correspondingly through the period. In the years after the Civil War and through the 1870s total revenues had generally run in the $3-$4 million range, but by the 1880s they rose sharply and dramatically. The combined revenue and traffic trend for selected years from 1880 to 1913, the company's last full "independent" year, is illustrative:

	Income (millions)		**Major Commodities**		
	Revenue	**Profit**	**Coal (millions)**	**Grain (millions)**	**Lumber**
Year			**(tons)**	**(bushels)**	**(tons)**
1880	$ 5.05	$2.00	4.196	19.851	120,000
1881	5.44	1.87	5.076	17.911	
1883	6.08	1.09	3.526	13.602	
1890	5.04	2.019	7.01	10.210	210,000
1894	6.03	1.797	9.374	5.726	
1895	6.50	1.907	7.015	—	240,000
1896	6.28	1.643	6.491	14.662	
1897	6.73	1.934	7.181	24.716	
1899	7.23	1.950	8.324	22.719	
1901	8.26	2.511	8.044	.752	175,000
1911	12.80	1.840	11.738	7.523	
1913	13.56	1.083	11.699	17.531	150,000

Source: Annual Reports of the Northern Central Railway

The coal and other traffic figures above do not include traffic handled by other railroads which operated over Northern Central tracks under trackage rights contracts. At one time or another, railroads such as the Erie, the Susquehanna & New York, the Pennsylvania, and the Philadelphia & Erie used such trackage rights over the NC.

Sodus Point coal pier as it looked in about 1900. At this time it was a simple trestle design, with hopper cars unloading directly into pockets and chutes. Wayne County Historical Society Collection.

A New President and the Last Extensions

The 1880s began for the Pennsylvania and the Northern Central with another executive management change. Exhausted and frustrated from years of dealing with depressed business levels, dissatisfied stockholders, the violent 1877 labor troubles, and problems with his own personal ventures, Tom Scott suffered a stroke. With his health deteriorating, he resigned the Pennsylvania's presidency June 1, 1880 at age 56, and died a year later. Succeeding him as joint president of the Pennsylvania and Northern Central was George B. Roberts, a civil engineer like J. Edgar Thomson. Well-born and well-educated, Roberts was a conscientious, hard worker — but less brilliant and aggressive than the Thomson-Scott team.

To a large degree, however, Roberts reflected a change in the Pennsylvania's corporate climate. Its years of explosive territorial expansion were now mostly behind it; Roberts's seventeen years as president concentrated on internal improvements and rebuilding to cope with the rapidly growing business. A gentleman by temperament, Roberts unfortunately also had to deal as best he could with the peak years of bare-knuckled railroad competition, with their rate wars and territorial invasions by new lines.

The early years of the Roberts regime did include some expansion, and it was during this time that the Northern Central's system was completed. His first move was to fill out the railroad's coal feeder lines. As already noted in Chapter 7, on July 1, 1880 Roberts implemented a new lease of the Lykens Valley Railroad property. The previous lease had only authorized the Northern Central to operate coal trains out of Wisconisco, but other valuable sources of coal were close by. The new lease was made possible by additional stock purchases in the Lykens Valley line; it allowed the Northern Central to operate the entire Lykens Valley Railroad line into Williamstown, Pennsylvania, and also operate the coal properties owned by that firm. In effect, the Northern Central now had exclusive operating rights for all the railroad facilities in Lykens and Wisconisco.

Early the following year Roberts made the greatest single coup of his career. In March 1881, with the prodding and help of vice president A. J. Cassatt, he bought control of the Philadelphia, Wilmington & Baltimore Railroad — deftly outmaneuvering the B & O's John W. Garrett in the process. The move gave the Pennsylvania its own fully-controlled New York-Washington route and, in fact, made it an almost-unbeatable competitor in the cities along this "corridor." The purchase was made outright by the Pennsylvania, since the PW & B had little traffic flow in common with the Northern Central.

In a related move during the same year, however, Roberts arranged for the Northern Central to purchase the entire capital stock of the Union Railroad in Baltimore. The par value of the stock was $600,000, but in actual cash outlay the takeover only cost the company about two-thirds of that amount. Ownership of the Union Railroad gave the Northern Central direct control of the line into the Canton terminal; it also gave the Pennsylvania indirect control of the connecting link between the Baltimore & Potomac Railroad and the Philadelphia, Wilmington & Baltimore for its New York-Washington services.

The NC's tug Cornelia worked the Sodus Point harbor. The PRR keystone on its stack was added after 1914. Wayne County Historical Society Collection.

En route to Sodus Point, the NC crossed the former Rome, Watertown & Odgensburg (later NYC) line at Wallington, New York. The NC train is southbound. W. R. Gordon Collection.

Finally Roberts extended the Northern Central to its long-sought goal: the Great Lakes. In 1884 the company bought a struggling railroad called the Sodus Bay & Southern, which extended north from Stanley, New York (12 miles east of Canandaigua) to Sodus Point on Lake Ontario. The 34-mile line had been opened in 1873, and over its short life had been through two bankruptcies. Its terminal on Great Sodus Bay, however, seemed well situated for transshipping coal to Canadian ports on the lake. After buying the line the Northern Central immediately built a coal trestle at Sodus Point. At this point in the railroad's history, the line's completion to Lake Ontario represented less the realization of the original dreams of its early Baltimore promoters and more simply a segment of the Pennsylvania Railroad's strategy to open coal markets to the north. (The Sodus Bay line, incidentally, was the first railroad venture of E. H. Harriman, who had acquired it in the hope of selling either to the PRR or New York Central.)

Sodus Point traffic was slow to develop at first, but the pier was enlarged in 1894. The renovation resulted in an increased capacity rating of 150,000 tons per year, although at the time it was only operating at about 50 percent of capacity. The demand for anthracite throughout the Great Lakes and Canada soon overburdened the facility. By 1911 the dock was loading five million tons per year, more than the tonnage flowing into Baltimore. Besides anthracite, Sodus Point also increasingly handled bituminous shipments from mines in the PRR's central and western Pennsylvania lines. During the 1920s the coal export business from Sodus Point became so immense that in 1927 the Pennsylvania Railroad, by then the owner of the facility, found it necessary to construct a completely new loading pier there.

On December 31, 1886 Roberts consolidated all of the Northern Central's New York State lines north of Elmira into a single corporation. The Chemung Railroad, the Elmira, Jefferson & Canandaigua, and the Sodus Bay & Southern railroads were merged into a new corporation called the Elmira & Lake Ontario Railroad Company. This company was little more than a streamlining of accounting ledgers. But along with the new corporation came a new stock issue, which was used to finance various construction projects.

Although the Northern Central's geographic expansion had essentially ended in 1884, less than five years later a short but significant spur was built from the Canton terminal to serve the newly-built steel plant at Sparrows Point, at the far southeast side of Baltimore Harbor. In 1887 the Pennsylvania Steel Company bought large acreages at Sparrows Point and began building a mill complex which was to use iron ore brought in by water. The spot was somewhat remote from adequate land transportation; early in 1889, however, the steel company completed its own railroad, the Baltimore & Sparrows Point, between Sparrows Point and the Northern Central line at Colgate Creek, east of Canton. (The Baltimore & Ohio also built a similar branch to Colgate Creek to connect with the Baltimore & Sparrows Point.) The Baltimore & Sparrows Point inaugurated passenger service to the uncompleted mill on February 11th of that year.

The first furnace at Sparrows Point began operating in October 1889, and by 1891 the plant was producing steel rail. Renamed the Maryland Steel Company in 1891, it suffered through some doldrums in the mid-1890s, but then began a steady expansion, which included a large shipyard. In 1916 it was absorbed by Bethlehem Steel, and eventually became the country's largest integrated steelmaking complex — and a major freight shipper and receiver. The Northern Central and the Pennsylvania handled heavy tonnages of inbound coal (much of which came from Bethlehem-owned mines in central Pennsylvania) and outbound steel products of all kinds. In 1913 the Philadelphia, Baltimore & Washington (a Pennsylvania Railroad subsidiary) took over the Baltimore & Sparrows Point Railroad, giving the PRR and Northern Central a direct route to the plant via Dundalk and Turners Station. The Pennsylvania continued operating a passenger service between Baltimore and Sparrows Point until the late 1930s.

Several independent Pennsylvania feeder lines also were built to connect with the Northern Central during the last quarter of the 19th Century and the early 1900s. By 1875 a line linking York with Frederick, Maryland had been completed and was taken over by the Pennsylvania Railroad that year. This 56-mile branch served a mostly rural territory, but reached industries on the west side of York and at Hanover, Pennsylvania. At Frederick it connected with the Baltimore & Ohio. Until 1902, the PRR operated the Frederick line itself, in conjunction with the York-Wrightsville branch (which the NC's parent had managed since 1870); thus although the line was part of the "family," it was not directly affiliated with the NC.

Another connection at York was the one-time Peach Bottom Railway, an independent narrow gauge line which opened between York and Red Lion in 1874 and was completed to Delta, Pennsylvania in 1876. By 1884, as the York & Peach Bottom, it had reached Peach Bottom, Pennsylvania and also connected with another narrow gauge line between Delta and Baltimore. This company's thinly populated route and its gauge difference limited its interchange with the Northern Central, but in 1895 (now as the York Southern) it was standard gauged and a direct track connection established east of the Northern Central's York passenger station. Reorganized as the Maryland & Pennsylvania Railroad (the "Ma & Pa") in 1901, the old Peach Bottom line developed into a modestly active freight feeder; in addition to factories in York itself, the scenic, twisting little railroad served furniture and cigar manufacturing industries at Red Lion and several quarries in the Delta, Pennsylvania-Whiteford, Maryland area.

Another rural feeder was the seven-mile Stewartstown Railroad, opened in September 1885. The Stewartstown was a typical late 19th Century locally promoted "farmers' railroad," built to link the southern York County town of Stewartstown with the Northern Central's main line at New Freedom, Pennsylvania. Bucolic though it was, the Stewartstown Railroad stimulated the establishment of several manufacturing industries at Stewartstown which provided a steady flow of interchange traffic at New Freedom. In 1906 a separately-incorporated company extended the railroad another seven miles east to New Park and Fawn Grove, Pennsylvania.

North of Williamsport, the Susquehanna & New York Railroad was built to the Northern Central's main line at Ralston, Pennsylvania in 1903. This 45-mile line served some of central Pennsylvania's largest lumbering operations. At various times in the early 1900s it interchanged with the Northern Central at Ralston, Marsh Hill, and West Williamsport (Newberry Yard); during the late boom years of Pennsylvania logging it fed large tonnages of lumber plus chemicals and coal to the Northern Central.

All of these feeders are covered more extensively in the following chapter.

One potential feeder which haltingly appeared, disappeared, then reappeared as a competitor was an early 1870s project called the Maryland & Pennsylvania Railroad. The M & P was one of several companies created to build from Baltimore northeast to Bel Air, Maryland, with the idea of eventually forming a new rail route between Baltimore and Philadelphia. The M & P was organized in 1873 and planned to use the Northern Central's line out of Baltimore as far as a junction near Lake Roland; from there its route branched east, following Towson Run to Towsontown (now Towson), and continuing toward Bel Air. Grading was completed along Towson Run from the proposed Northern Central junction to Towsontown, and had progressed about seven miles northeast from Towsontown when the M & P went bankrupt and all work stopped.

In 1876 another company appeared with the mouth-filling name of the Baltimore, Towsontown, Dulaney's Valley & Delta Narrow Gauge Railway. This company planned to run in the same general direction as the defunct Maryland & Pennsylvania, but was planned as a more modest local line connecting Baltimore with Delta, Pennsylvania. Since this project was to be narrow gauge, the idea of connecting with the Northern Central at Lake Roland was abandoned and, eventually, a separate route was built into Baltimore via the Stony Run valley. The company was reorganized as the Baltimore & Delta in 1878; merged with the York & Peach Bottom Railway (noted above) in 1891, it became a theoretical Northern Central competitor between Baltimore and York. But its narrow gauge and its roundabout curve-ridden route hardly presented much of a threat. The line was standard gauged between 1894 and 1900, and in 1901 became the "new" Maryland & Pennsylvania Railroad. (This Maryland & Pennsylvania had no direct relation to the old one, although it did use some of the original grading east of Towson.) An interchange connection was established with the Northern Central near the M & P's Baltimore terminal at North Avenue, but the originally planned route from Lake Roland to Towson was never completed. The abandoned grade can be partly seen today; the present Towsontown Boulevard occupies another part of the uncompleted right of way.

Physical Plant Improvements

The Northern Central's rising gross income allowed it to pay debts and dividends, build new facilities, renovate older ones, and to purchase additional stock in several of the feeder lines that it operated. It was during the 1880s and 1890s that the company undertook the last complete renovation of the property. To the consternation of many Northern Central stockholders, who still preferred that the Pennsylvania lease the line and pay the improvement costs, it was a long and expensive program. But when it was completed in the late 1890s the railroad had emerged as a first-class, heavily built property which would need relatively little additional improvement in the future.

As the Northern Central became more closely affiliated with the Pennsylvania Railroad, its original Susquehanna River bridge between Marysville and Dauphin became redundant. About two and one-half miles downstream was the Pennsylvania's own Rockville bridge, which had been rebuilt in 1877 as a double-track iron structure. The wooden Dauphin bridge had been a constant source of maintenance problems for the Northern Central, so in 1881 George Roberts ordered the Northern Central to be connected with the Pennsylvania at Rockville and the NC's own aging structure abandoned. Between 1881 and 1882 the Northern Central built a new line along the east bank of the Susquehanna between Dauphin and Rockville, along with new connections at each end of the Rockville bridge. Once completed the new routing also eliminated what was known as the "Rockville recross." Previously Northern Central trains between Harrisburg and Sunbury had to cross the Susquehanna twice: at Rockville a Sunbury-bound train crossed from the east bank of the river to the west, proceeded about a mile to Marysville, then crossed back to Dauphin. Using the new Rockville-Dauphin connection these trains simply followed the east bank of the Susquehanna all the way from Harrisburg to Sunbury.

In 1883 President Roberts began an aggressive program of replacing the bridges along the line. Over the next fifteen years, the obsolete iron bridges, along with the remaining wooden trestles, were gradually replaced with stone or heavy steel structures. Many of the original wooden bridges on the Williamsport-Elmira line were replaced between 1885 to 1895. Also, by 1897 most of the main line bridges in Baltimore and York Counties had been rebuilt either in steel or stone, some of them quite impressive. For example, south of Brilhart station in York County a large twin-arch stone span carried the tracks over both Codorus Creek and a road. Many of these sturdy structures still exist today; unfortunately, some others, including several of the unique stone arch bridges spanning Codorus Creek, were victims of Tropical Storm Agnes in 1972.

Station buildings also were replaced during the Roberts administration. Although many (such as White Hall in 1883 and Emigsville in 1890) followed the Northern Central's standardized single-story wood frame designs, several architecturally distinctive masonry structures were built along the line. Most notable was the Baltimore Union Station, completed in 1886, a large combination two-and three-story brick and stone building with an adjacent iron trainshed. (Somewhat oddly, the original 1873 Union Station apparently was a temporary wood structure, about which little is known.) Like its predecessor, Union Station served the Northern Central, the New York-Washington services, and the Western Maryland. It was built at ground

The NC's old Bolton Shop built saddletank switcher No. 25 in 1870. Note the meticulous striping on wheels and counterweights. Clearly, the shop forces were proud of their work. Maryland Historical Society Collection.

NC No. 41, an 1877 Baldwin Consolidation, and its crew at Southport (Elmira, New York) yard about 1900. Note the four-wheeled wooden caboose. Library of Congress Collection.

level in the valley, but had a street-level entrance on Charles Street and a long inclined driveway leading from Charles Street to the waiting rooms and baggage handling facilities. The open-sided trainshed measured 76 feet wide and about 360 feet long; passengers entered and left it from the side, and usually had to cross busy tracks to reach their trains.

Other stations of the late Roberts era included a large brick structure at York (1890), an attractive suburban stop of stone and wood construction at Ruxton, Maryland (1892), an unusual two-story brick building at Millersburg, Pennsylvania (1897), and a simpler but nonetheless distinctive single-story wood station at Monkton, Maryland (also 1897). Happily, all of these but Ruxton still stand.

George Roberts succumbed to a heart attack in January 1897. His successor, the ill-starred Frank Thomson, assumed the presidency during a financial depression and died himself in June 1899 at the age of 58. At best, he only had a chance to complete some of Roberts's programs. Following Thomson, however,

This dramatic scene symbolizes the Northern Central at the turn of the century: heavy freight power, curves, grades, and line-side mills. The northbound freight has just left Mt. Vernon yard in Baltimore and is passing the 1863 Clipper textile mill along the Jones Falls valley in 1901. The mill complex still stood in 1991, although long since converted to other uses. Smithsonian Institution Collection.

came one of the Pennsylvania system's most outstanding presidents: Alexander Johnston Cassatt. The Cassatt era marked the Pennsylvania's last and greatest period of construction, and probably the height of its corporate power.

The Administration of A. J. Cassatt

As a young man, the aggressive and capable Cassatt had risen rapidly in the Pennsylvania's hierachy during the Thomson-Scott years, but then "retired" in 1882, reportedly because of his distaste for George Roberts. Independently wealthy, he pursued his own interests for seventeen years, returning reluctantly to assume the presidency in 1899. Cassatt came to office in a time of crisis for the Pennsylvania and, in fact, for the entire railroad industry. Traffic was growing rapidly and demanding greater handling capacity; yet the free-handed, chaotic competition in the railroad industry depressed earnings and discouraged investment. During the seven short years of his presidency Cassatt worked to stabilize both his own company and the entire industry, and at the same time give the Pennsylvania vastly expanded facilities to move its future business. While the Northern Central was not among his most pressing concerns, Cassatt dramatically affected the appearance and role of the railroad. And also, perhaps unknowingly, he planted the seed of the line's later decay and dismemberment.

One immediate move was a corporate housecleaning. After taking office on June 9, 1899 Cassatt complained bitterly about the Pennsylvania system's "cumbersome corporate structure" and the "legal and tax problems" created by the multiplicity of subsidiary companies. He pushed for consolidation and simplification as an antidote to corporate "sluggishness."

As part of this streamlining, Cassatt authorized the Northern Central to take over operations of the two Pennsylvania-owned secondary lines radiating from York, Pennsylvania — the York-Frederick (Maryland) line and the York-Wrightsville-Columbia branch. Beginning June 1, 1902 both branches were operated by the Northern Central from its York yards. Ironically, the Wrightsville/Columbia line was returning to the Northern Central fold after a 32-year absence. As noted earlier, it had been built as part of the Baltimore & Susquehanna's original main line, but had been taken over by the Pennsylvania in 1870 after the Northern Central lost interest in it. Although neither branch was a major revenue producer, the move streamlined services and management by concentrating all regional operations at the Northern Central's York facilities. Afterwards, for all practical purposes, such points as York, Hanover, Wrightsville, and Frederick were Northern Central territory.

Some local PRR freight operations in Baltimore also were turned over to the Northern Central. On November 1, 1904 the Northern Central began operating the line from Bay View Yard to President Street Station, adjacent to Baltimore's inner harbor. This trackage originally had been the western end of the Philadelphia, Wilmington & Baltimore Railroad's main line, but by this time it was predominantly a freight branch with a modest local passenger service. Much of the line was laid in streets, and was interlaced with the Northern Central's own street trackage in the Fells Point area; it also touched some of the territory served by the Northern Central's Canton branch. Combining the two operations put all of the PRR-affiliated freight and local passenger services in East Baltimore under a single operating control.

A far more memorable and significant accomplishment of the Cassatt administration was the massive program of new facilities to handle the Pennsylvania's enormous and ever-growing freight and passenger business. These included large freight classification yards, a network of entirely new through freight lines to avoid grades and congested areas, and commodious new station buildings.

Harrisburg, Pennsylvania was the hub of the Pennsylvania system's entire eastern network. Here, its routes from New York, Philadelphia, Baltimore/Washington, the upper Susquehanna Valley, and the Cumberland Valley converged to meet the PRR's main line west to Pittsburgh, where it fanned out to Chicago, St. Louis, and many other midwestern points. Heavy and complex flows of freight traffic had to be switched from route to route and train to train. In addition, the Pennsylvania's entire main line passenger train fleet was funneled through the area.

Characteristically, Cassatt conceived a bold and sweeping solution to this bottleneck: Somewhere within this area he would build an enormous freight classification yard, which would be linked to newly built all-freight lines reaching the major East Coast terminals. As much as possible, the freight lines would have minimum grades and would be separate from the congested passenger routes.

The most suitable site for the new central freight classification yard turned out to be on the Northern Central's line along the west bank of the Susquehanna at a tiny "flag" station called Enola, located upriver from Harrisburg between Lemoyne (the old Bridgeport) and Marysville. At one stroke this stretch of Northern Central track became one of the most strategically important sections of the entire Pennsylvania Railroad system. At its west end it would be linked to the PRR's main line west and the Rockville bridge through elaborate separated junctions.

For the primary freight route east from Enola the Northern Central main line would be used as far as York Haven, about 19 miles. At York Haven (actually a point

Before the opening of Enola Yard, the NC operated this small yard at Marysville, a slight distance upriver. Note the octagonal yard office tower, a variation of the NC's distinctive interlocking tower design. Railroad Museum of Pennsylvania Collection.

called Wago Junction) a newly built freight line would continue east along the Susquehanna, crossing the river at Shocks Mill and joining an old secondary route on the east side of the river near Marietta, Pennsylvania. This line in turn led to several other low-grade freight bypass routes, one of which was formed out of the old Columbia & Port Deposit Railroad, familiarly known as the "Port Road." The "Port Road" followed the Susquehanna to Perryville, Maryland, where it met the PRR's Philadelphia-Baltimore-Washington main line. In essence, any freight moving between Enola and Baltimore or Washington could follow the easy grades of the Susquehanna and the Coastal Plain the entire distance. While it was a more roundabout route, it was considerably cheaper to operate. Eventually most through freight trains between Enola/Harrisburg and Baltimore were diverted from the curving, hilly Northern Central main line to the low-grade "Port Road" route.

(As an aside, Enola's name created a railroad legend which still persists in history books and articles. According to this story, "Enola" is "alone" spelled backwards, and was given to the remote location by a lonely railroad telegraph operator stationed there. The truth is probably more prosaic: according to local sources, the station was named for the daughter of the man who owned the surrounding land and who used the point as his private station.)

Enola yard was built with funds provided by the Pennsylvania and three of its subsidiaries — the Northern Central, Cumberland Valley, and Philadelphia & Erie — with each paying one-quarter of the cost. The yard was completed and placed in service during 1905, and immediately relieved the growing freight congestion at Harrisburg, Baltimore, York, and to some extent, Sunbury.

The economic and social impact of the Enola Yard to the surrounding area was staggering then and remains large now. For many years it held the title of the world's largest freight yard. Still highly active, it offers employment to hundreds of area residents and scores of businesses depend on trade from the facility. As early as 1908 it was estimated that the local economic stimulus from the rail yard was $12 million annually. In 1980 Enola still employed over 500 people, and the local economies of Harrisburg, Lemoyne, and Rockville are still linked to the massive rail yard.

Another Cassatt project involving the Northern Central never went beyond the planning stage. In 1903 the Northern Central Connecting Railway was created to build 32 miles of new railroad on the west bank of the Susquehanna River from Selinsgrove Junction, five miles south of Sunbury, to Aqueduct Station, a point on the PRR main line west of Duncannon, Pennsylvania. This would have formed a cut-off route between Sunbury and the Pennsylvania's main line to Pittsburgh, avoiding the detour through Enola or Harrisburg and backhaul mileage. Cassatt's plan, apparently, was to use the route to move bituminous coal from central and western Pennsylvania to northeastern points via Sunbury.

To cross the Susquehanna, NC trains used the PRR's famous Rockville bridge, located between Enola Yard and Marysville. In this 1902 scene (which looks eastward from the Marysville side) the old double-track iron truss bridge has just been replaced by the presently used four-track stone viaduct. The PRR-NC connections are in the foreground. Smithsonian Institution Collection.

Later Improvements

Some of Cassatt's most monumental projects planned for Northern Central territory had not yet been started when he suddenly died in 1906, another victim of the brutal demands of the Pennsylvania's presidency. These included the Union Station in Baltimore and the Northumberland classification yard just north of Sunbury, Pennsylvania. Both were completed by Cassatt's successor, James McCrea, who became president of the Pennsylvania and Northern Central on January 2, 1907. The conservative and somewhat imperious McCrea continued the policies of his predecessor to the extent that he finished what had previously been started, but he did not break any new ground.

In less than twenty years Baltimore's 1886 passenger station had become inadequate, and its replacement had been the subject of executive meetings since early in 1905. Corporate approval for a new station was quickly granted, and by 1907 New York architect Kenneth M. Murchison had designed the building, an impressive Beaux-Arts structure clad in pink granite. Unlike its predecessor, which had been built below the street at track level, the new Union Station opened directly onto a high-level driveway between Charles and St. Paul Streets. Construction started in 1908. When the station finally opened in 1911 the city held a gala celebration, and the attendant publicity praised the railroads for "monumental accomplishments." Although the bulk of the new Union Station's business consisted of travel along the New York-Philadelphia-Washington corridor, all Northern Central trains passed through it, as well as the Western Maryland's passenger runs. As before, however, many Northern Central local trains continued to terminate at the more centrally located Calvert Station.

In 1906 the Pennsylvania Railroad had begun planning a new freight classification facility at Northumberland, Pennsylvania, immediately north of Sunbury. The existing yards at both Sunbury and Williamsport were overcrowded, and a large yard close to the coal fields was drastically needed. In 1908 the Northern Central and Pennsylvania together purchased 700 acres of land in Northumberland adjacent to their main line, equally sharing the cost of property and construction. The facility became operational on August 6, 1911, primarily handling the makeup of coal trains for Baltimore, Sodus Point, and other destinations, and dispatching runs to the various mines in the area. A new Northumberland passenger station was built in 1910 at the south end of the yard. (As evidence of increasing Pennsylvania Railroad influence, the design of the Northumberland station was duplicated at Perryville, Maryland, on the PRR's New York-Washington line.) To accommodate the ever-increasing traffic the Northern Central also had to double-track the line between Sunbury and Williamsport, and completed that project by 1913.

Baltimore's new "Union Station" (later called Pennsylvania Station, a name it still carries under Amtrak ownership) opened in 1911 on the site of two earlier stations. Both views look northwest; in the lower photograph, St. Paul Street is in the foreground.

Northumberland itself had been one of the early railroad junction towns along the Northern Central line. Located at the confluence of the North and West Branch canal system, it had grown steadily throughout the post-Civil War period. However, the new rail yard created an economic boom for the town. During the 1920s and 1930s more than 1000 people were employed in either direct or secondary railroad jobs, and Northumberland soon became a city of over 3000 inhabitants. Today, although the yard is overgrown with weeds, the roundhouse is gone, and the station is leased as a restaurant, the influence of the railroad on the town can still be observed.

Perfection of the Physical Plant

This frame building at New Freedom, Pennsylvania typified the NC's standardized design used for many stations in the late 19th Century. It survived in 1991. New Freedom Library Collection.

During its "glory years," the Northern Central had become world famous for its immaculately-maintained main line, the beauty of the landscape along its route, and its distinctively designed trackside structures.

Like many large railroads the Northern Central developed a standardized plan for a single-story wood frame station which could be built cheaply at many locations of lesser importance along the line. During the 1870s, 1880s, and even 1890s this rather ordinary design was duplicated in varying sizes at such points as White Hall and Freeland (both in Maryland), and in Pennsylvania at New Freedom (still standing), Emigsville, Mt. Wolf, Goldsboro, York Haven, and Cly. But beginning in the mid-1880s increasing attention was given to creating unique buildings which would give distinct personalities to both the railroad and its communities. Many were the work of commercial architects rather than railroad draftsmen. The stations at York, Ruxton, Millersburg, Monkton, and Northumberland have been mentioned earlier in this chapter. In 1903 the famous Philadelphia architect Frank Furness was hired to build new suburban stations at Sherwood (later Riderwood) and Parkton, Maryland. By this time in his career Furness was less eccentric and whimsical than at his peak in the 1880s, but the two Northern Central stations clearly show his unique creativity. Fortunately, Riderwood still stands in 1991.

Also in the early 1900s the Northern Central constructed several charming stations along its Green Spring Branch. As noted earlier, this line had been reacquired in 1874 after the Western Maryland built a new route into Baltimore. While the branch remained a rustic low-density railroad, the Green Spring Valley had developed as an area of summer resorts and extensive estates. To fit into the rarified status of the line's communities and clientele, the company built several substantial domestic-style stations at locations such as Brooklandville, Stevenson, and Rogers, each a one-of-a-kind design. Brooklandville, for example, was built in a half-timbered Tudor style; Rogers had a distinctive barnlike gambrel roof, seldom seen on railroad stations. The attention given to stations of this type not

The suburban station at Mt. Washington, outside Baltimore, was a two-story board-and-batten design typical of the 1870s, which provided living space for the agent. A. A. Bodine photograph.

The !ittle Chattolanee station (shown in 1886) served summer resort passengers on the Green Spring Branch. Baltimore Public Library Collection; A. H. Brinkemann photograph.

only showed the Northern Central's pride in its facility, but reflected the close association of the company's officers with the suburban communities. It was, perhaps, not coincidental that the Green Spring branch stations were built at about the same time that A. J. Cassatt built a mansion in the area for his daughter, who had just married a man prominent in Baltimore society.

The New York State section of the line also received many new stations during the period, although most were the familiar standardized one-story, board-and-batten style depot. But they were well kept, neat, and clean. Many of the stationmasters, along with numerous town residents who lived near the depots, sculptured the adjacent lawns, planted trees and shrubs, and generally made the station a village showplace.

The Northern Central's unique "pagoda" towers became its unofficial trademark. At a time when railroad traffic was dense and complex, and automation unknown, these structures were essential to maintaining fluid operations. They controlled switches and signals for crossovers,

More memorable and distinctive was the 1892 suburban station at Ruxton, Maryland. S. W. Wiley, Jr. Estate Collection.

Stevenson station on the Green Spring Branch in Maryland, shortly after it was built in the early 1900s. It was later expanded, and, privately owned, exists in 1991. Now largely an upper-income residential area, Stevenson was once a source of iron ore shipped to the furnace at Ashland, Maryland, near Cockeysville. R. Mellinger Collection.

sidings, and junctions; their operators reported train passings to the dispatchers, relayed orders to the train crews, and generally acted as go-betweens for any operating problems. The towers were two-story wooden structures, square on the bottom half and octagonal on top. Capped with a peaked roof and painted ivory white, they presented a striking appearance. There were a total of 46 such towers spread out along the main line from Baltimore to Sunbury, and they were manned by operators from the local towns. The last one, now long gone, was believed to be at White Hall, Maryland.

Although coal revenues provided the capital for the track and buildings, it was nature that created the scenery. Some of it was exquisite. The curving, wooded route along the Gunpowder River in Maryland, hemmed in by hills, the wide Susquehanna River, the mountainous Lycoming Valley, and the lakes and farms of central New York, individually as well as collectively, made the Northern Central a breathtakingly scenic railroad. The company's traffic officers did their best to exploit its attractions.

During the 1880s and 1890s frequent Northern Central promotional campaigns extolled Niagara Falls (reached through New York Central connections), the Finger Lakes, the valleys of the Susquehanna, and resorts and picnic areas in Baltimore County. Tourist traffic grew accordingly. Passenger income on the line north of Elmira continuously

This example of the NC's octagonal tower design stood at Summit Grove, just south of New Freedom, Pennsylvania. New Freedom Library Collection.

increased over the two decades. In addition, railroad handbills published after 1881 list an ever-growing number of passenger trains into Elmira, Watkins, and Canandaigua. For example, as early as 1873 *Lyles Railroad Manual* listed two trains from Elmira to Niagara Falls each day. *Coulton's Manual* for 1885 listed four trains each day and two on Saturdays and Sundays.

The Northern Central itself published a variety of material advertising its scenic route through New York State, often quoting Louis Philippe's famous 1797 description of Havanna (Montour Falls): "the loveliest spot God ever made." (Louis Phillipe, who became king of France in 1830, had painted the Chequagah Falls at Havanna while in exile.) The railroad published pamphlets in 1886, 1889, 1893, and 1896 advertising "the most scenic route between Baltimore and the Great Lakes." The Susquehanna River Valley was sometimes described as "one of the loveliest valleys in the world." In 1900 a handbill published by the Bath and Hammondsport Railroad entitled *How to Reach the Beautiful Lake Keuka* gave Northern Central timetables and lake steamer schedules for tourist travel throughout the Finger Lake region, characterizing the Northern Central as "most elegant."

The Guilford Avenue roundhouse stood just east of the Baltimore Union Station and serviced passenger power. In this 1902 scene, NC No. 3146, a D13 class 4-4-0 built to a standard PRR design by the Altoona Machine Shop, rides the hand-powered turntable. Smithsonian Institution Collection.

The NC maintained a waterfront terminal in Baltimore's inner harbor (then called the "Basin") which was reached through a water transfer. The terminal, labeled "O'Donnell's Wharf," appears in the right center of this 1903 photograph, adjacent to the still-existing power house. Library of Congress Collection.

A standard PRR passenger design, NC No. 53 (renumbered 3053 in 1897 and 4053 in 1903) was an 1892 Altoona product. Smithsonian Institution Collection; C. B. Chaney drawing.

To a lesser extent, the Green Spring Valley outside Baltimore and the Lycoming Valley north of Williamsport also were advertised as resort areas. The Baltimore's sultry summers, for example, sent many people to the nearby resort hotel at Chattolanee on the Green Spring Branch, to Bentley Springs, or to summer homes at places like Ruxton and Lutherville. Day excursions were run to railroad-maintained picnic grounds at Riders, Glencoe, and Walkers Switch in Baltimore County. In 1904 the Northern Central, along with the Susquehanna & New York Railroad, promoted the Lycoming Creek Valley as a sportsman's paradise. Together, both railroads advertised the area's hunting

NC No. 3005, an F1a-class freight 2-6-0, was built by the PRR's Juniata (Altoona) shop in 1899 to the standard Pennsylvania design. It became the 4005 in 1903 and was scrapped in 1922. The location is Mt. Vernon yard in Baltimore. Railroad Museum of Pennsylvania Collection.

A modern heavy freight engine of the turn of the century, NC No. 3011 was a PRR standard H6 class built by Baldwin in 1902. Railroad Museum of Pennsylvania Collection.

and fishing season, the different species of game and fish, and the hotels and boarding houses where individuals could stay.

Overall, the railroad's passenger business boomed. In June 1893 the Northern Central scheduled no less than 32 weekday trains out of Baltimore: seven through runs to Harrisburg, one York local, five Parkton locals, eleven Cockeysville locals, and eight Greenspring Branch trains. The fastest time between Baltimore and Harrisburg was two hours 37 minutes, made by the Washington connection to the PRR's premier New York-Chicago *Pennsylvania Limited.* On the northern end of the line three trains operated each way between Harrisburg and Canandaigua, plus two more between Harrisburg and Williamsport. Through

D16 class No. 4131 poses at the Guilford Avenue (Baltimore) engine terminal in 1912. These heavy, fast 4-4-0s represented the pinnacle of this wheel arrangement on the Pennsylvania system. Smithsonian Institution Collection; C. B. Chaney photograph.

This gingerbready little suburban shelter station stood just north of Lake Roland at what is now Bellona Avenue in Baltimore County. Named Brightside, it served several large nearby estates. A. H. Brinkemann photograph.

sleeping cars were run between Washington and Pittsburgh, Chicago, Buffalo, and Elmira; north of Harrisburg, Northern Central trains also carried a Philadelphia-Williamsport sleeper.

The Northern Central entered the new century busier and in better physical condition than ever, and both its traffic and plant would continue to improve in the years ahead. But some ominous signs began to appear. Soon they would lead to the railroad's loss of identity and, eventually, its decay and dismemberment.

An 1898 scene at Cockeysville, Maryland, the camera looks north a short distance south of the passenger station at York Road. Suburban trains terminated here. Behind the coach is another NC octagonal tower, and behind it is a southbound passenger train stopped at the station. Smithsonian Institution Collection.

CHAPTER 10

Northern Central Communities in the "Glory Years"

Coal, industry, and scenery all combined to make the Northern Central a notable railroad. And as the railroad was growing and prospering so were the towns it served. These were their "glory years" too.

Along the railroad's route were communities of almost every type: large urban manufacturing centers, residential suburbs, smaller milling and manufacturing towns, transshipping or junction points with canals or other railroads, resorts, and agricultural villages. Many, of course, combined several of these functions. While each specific community had its own characteristics, together they shared an environment unique to the 19th Century "railroad town." They also shared a heavy dependence on the railroad for both their commerce and everyday travel. Before World War I, for example, rural children traveled to school by train, as did people making shopping trips to the city or visiting.

Typically, the towns along the line were seldom larger than one-half a mile wide or long, with their center at the railroad station. The station not only was at the physical center, but was the community's commercial and social focus. By the 1890s the Northern Central had constructed some sort of depot at each town along the line. Many of these (notably those in Maryland at Brooklandville, Rogers, Ruxton, Riderwood, Lutherville, Timonium, and Parkton) were substantial masonry buildings, and were significant examples of American railroad architecture. Most, however, were of the familiar standardized one-story, wood frame board-and-batten design and combined both freight and passenger facilities. The station agent usually combined the jobs of telegraph operator, ticket seller, freight and express agent, and mail handler. He was the railroad's primary representative in the area, and in addition to his routine work, he usually acted as the middleman between the railroad organization and the local freight customers in solving a multitude of transportation problems. These individuals became substantial members of the community, and their expertise and advice on business affairs was frequently sought.

Unlike many railroads, the Northern Central generally did not provide living quarters in the station for the agent and his family. The most notable exceptions were located in the Baltimore suburban territory. Stations such as those at Mount Washington, Hollins, Ruxton, Riderwood, Lutherville, Brooklandville, Stevenson, Rogers, Cockeysville, Glencoe, and Parkton (all in Maryland) all were one and one-half- or two-story buildings with living space, and were maintained like the homes they were.

The station was usually located near the main street, and was considered so important that the street leading to it often was called "Railroad Avenue," or sometimes "Depot Street" or "Station Street." Some particularly enthusiastic towns combined them. For example, Bromley's *Atlas of Baltimore County for 1915* shows that the planned Lake Roland community of Sorrento was to be laid out with both a "Station Street" and a "Railroad Avenue." (A station was built for Sorrento, but the planned community never materialized.) Most of these street names may still be found in towns all along the line, although in many cases the railroad itself has disappeared. One southern York County town was (and still is) officially named "Railroad"; the railroad itself, however, identified the station as Shrewsbury, an older settlement located about a mile to the east on the old York Road.

The railroad station was usually open from 6:00 a.m. until 9:00 p.m., and functioned as the town's commercial

Through much of the 19th and early 20th Centuries, the railroad station was a focus of community activities. Such was certainly so at Ruxton, Maryland, although the reason for the gathering here is lost to the past. S. W. Wiley, Jr. Collection.

nerve center. Merchants, shop owners, and farmers were there regularly, picking up consignments or delivering freight for shipment. Travelers were coming and going with the arrival of passenger trains, and children often used local train service to get to school in some nearby town. Train and track crews reported to the station agent for daily assignments or special instructions. Finally, customers using the mail and telegraph facilities kept the town depot a socially active location. The newsstand and telegraph office became standard station fixtures after 1870, and town inhabitants depended on the facility for their general news or their own urgent communications needs. It was the place to dispatch or pick up telegraphic messages or, in some cases, expedite mail. Stations such as Mt. Washington, Riderwood, York, Millersburg, and Sunbury incorporated post offices and residents depended on the fact that mail could be delivered, dispatched, and picked up on a continuous basis.

During their non-working hours residents gathered at the depot for news about the world, local business information, and schedules of social functions along the line. The depot became an informal meeting place where people could pause, exchange information, and discuss community affairs. Frequently, a billboard was established on the wall of the station for the posting of handbills and news items. The experience of one former resident at the Hollins station recalled how important the depot was as a communications center:

> *"Our family lived in the station... My father, Joseph H. Shamberger, was station agent and Postmaster. [An important community event] was the assassination of President Garfield. Father was a telegraph operator and he was the first in the neighborhood to learn the news. There was a great deal of excitement...for several weeks people gathered at the station to hear the news about the critically wounded President."*

In many of the rural towns the location of the rail line actually defined social strata among the residents. Although largely a matter of perception, one side of the tracks was considered the "good" side of town, while the opposite side was the "bad" side of town. Distance from the tracks (with their smoke, dust, and noise) also sometimes determined one's status.

While the station handled express and small freight shipments (generally called "less than carload lots" by the railroad), full carloads of freight often were loaded and unloaded at nearby open "public delivery tracks," or "team tracks." These tracks were located next to a driveway or street so that wagon teams could be positioned next to the car door — thus the term "team track." The town's manufacturing industries usually had their own private freight sidings.

Besides the station itself, there was often a "tower" located in the town — a two-story frame building from which signals and switches were controlled. Before the general installation of automatic signals in the 1920s, these were placed every few miles along the line and usually were manned 24 hours a day.

At many stations, a water or fueling station was located close by. The constant parade of steam locomotives required readily available water and coal. Water was particularly critical; under normal circumstances trains needed to take water at least every 30 miles, and most railroads established water stations about every ten miles. (For a steam locomotive, running out of water was not merely inconvenient; it could be catastrophic. A boiler explosion was likely to result.) Some locations — Parkton, Hanover Junction, Millersburg, Marsh Hill, and Watkins for example — had small engine terminals which combined coaling facilities, water tanks, and turntables or turning "wyes." Generally, six to ten local residents were employed at these service yards and they operated the facility until midnight.

Maintenance of the track, particularly on a heavily trafficked main line like that of the Northern Central, was a never-ending job which required a large amount of manual labor. Typically, the railroad line was divided into "sections," with a resident maintenance crew assigned full-time to each section (called, of course, a "section gang"). During the "glory years" section crews were assigned to most major towns, and many of the workers either came from those towns or settled there. For example, Parkton's crews serviced from the Maryland line south to Glencoe, Maryland; the Hanover Junction section serviced the area between the Maryland line and Glen Rock, Pennsylvania. During later years crews were also maintained at New Freedom, Millersburg, Roaring Branch, Canton (all in Pennsylvania), and Stanley, New York. Each crew had a foreman and six to ten laborers. They were responsible for all aspects of maintenance throughout their section, and usually rode in tiny four-wheeled "track cars," or walked the line conducting inspections. (Often they were called "track-walkers" or "gandy-dancers." The origin of the latter term is obscure, but is thought to derive from the odd gait necessary when walking on railroad ties, which are not spaced for a normal human stride.) The crews became the object of management's wrath when, during inspection tours, any weeds, trash, discarded track materials, or general debris were observed on the right of way. During the summer months a local youngster was usually hired by the track workers as "waterboy" and the crew collectively paid him 50 cents a day. Many rural town youths began their railroad careers in such menial positions.

Thus the railroad itself often provided the town with a significant amount of employment. In addition, some of these "tank towns," as they were frequently called, depended on railroad traffic for their subsistence. Train arrival brought a rush of activity to the rural town. In earlier days, for example, the conductor would call a "30 minute water stop at Hanover Junction," and the pause gave passengers time to detrain. They purchased food and drink, sent telegrams, or purchased sundry articles at the newsstand or general store.

Some type of manufacturing industry was established at virtually every one of the towns along the railroad, and even the smaller communities often had at least two or three small mills or factories. Along the Northern Central between Baltimore and Sodus Point was a wide variety of such businesses, ranging from large cotton duck (sailcloth) mills outside Baltimore to heavy machinery in York. Elsewhere were canneries, furniture factories, saw mills, shoe factories, wire cloth factories, feed mills, stone quarries, and so on.

Typically, these industries had been built to take advantage of rail service, or had grown from primitive, localized businesses which now were able to reach wider markets and obtain raw materials from greater distances. The Jones Falls and Gunpowder Falls in Maryland and the Codorus Creek in Pennsylvania were lined with large and small industries which received raw materials and shipped finished goods by rail. During the 1880s and 1890s some form of freight yard designed to serve local industry had been constructed at every town along the line. The mills and factories located their plants adjacent to the rail line, and as their output escalated, the railroad expanded its yard to accommodate the increasing number of cars. Thus the growth process fed on itself: Cheap, high-capacity rail service created expanded markets, which stimulated more output. As output rose, more workers moved into the communities. And as factory shipments grew, the railroad responded by enlarging its rail yard, thus employing even more residents. Each became dependent on the other, and by the end of the 1890s a symbiotic relationship between the towns, the industries, and the railroad had become firmly established.

Less visible but just as strongly present was the social environment of these railroad towns. Their inhabitants developed a social fabric interdependent with the railroad and the services it provided. Life in the 19th Century small railroad town was limited to a small radius extending outward from the station. Because daily activity was so interconnected with the railroad or with the industries adjacent to it, residents did not live or work further than walking distance from the depot. This area generally expanded no further than one-quarter mile from the rail depot, and within it most social and commercial activity was conducted. Here, typically, the elementary 19th Century services were provided: a blacksmith shop, one or two general stores, a hotel, a saw mill or lumberyard, an ice house, a coal or wood dealership, and a mill or manufacturing plant. From 50 to 200 inhabitants lived in the area, usually in two-story wood frame houses clustered around the rail depot.

Although there were people who lived beyond this tight zone, they were generally large landholders or farmers and employed the familiar horse and buggy to travel into town. Most residents, however, lived, worked, shopped, and socialized within walking distance of the rail

This excursion to the Centennial Exposition in Philadelphia pauses along the Susquehanna at York Haven, Pennsylvania. At the right is one of the NC's ubiquitous octagonal towers. Author's collection.

depot; other than the railroad, they seldom needed transportation. Many never traveled away from "their" town.

The rural town residents also depended on the railroad employees for numerous informal social services. Such services generally evolved out of a long-nurtured friendship between company employees and the townspeople and covered a wide spectrum. For example, conductors frequently supervised the children who rode the trains each day to school. They knew their charges on a first name basis and frequently tolerated pranks, while serious problems were reported to parents upon return to the station.

In addition, many residents and railroad employees participated in what was actually an "underground freight service." This pick-up and delivery service was unreported and free of tariff charges. Station agents and train crews frequently took orders for merchandise from residents they knew and, often for a tip, had them filled at a terminal city such as Baltimore, York, Harrisburg, or Sunbury. Interestingly, big city newspapers were one such item that was continuously placed on the "shopping list."

Moreover, railroad employees frequently would reciprocate favors from the townspeople. Train crews would frequently present a "gift" of a turkey or seafood to a

Passenger traffic also was heavy to parks, picnic grounds, camp meetings, and the like. This crowd waits for a train at a religious meeting ground at Summit Grove, Pennsylvania, near New Freedom, in the early 1900s. New Freedom Public Library Collection.

resident who, over the years, became friends with them. This particular practice lasted well into the 1960s.

Frequently the Northern Central sponsored some major social event for the towns along the line. The "Christmas Train," for example, was dispatched along the line on Christmas Eve to take employees, family, and friends to a nearby city for holiday celebrations. Santa Claus would entertain the children while railroad executives would meet with town officials and employees. In July or August the annual "picnic train" took residents to a scenic spot along the line for a day of festivities. This event, open to all, was considered the highlight of the summer social calendar. Large on-line industries, such as the Baltimore-area cotton mills, sometimes chartered trains for employee excursions, including trips to such attractions as the 1876 Centennial Exposition at Philadelphia.

Finally, the railroad also provided a form of social welfare to the towns along the line. One such service was the "Community Fund." The Northern Central executives either established or contributed to a community fund in many of the rural towns for the use of indigent residents, needy families, or injured employees. The fund was known to exist in York, Sunbury, and Ralston. Its administration and exact funding, however, remain a mystery. Another service that the railroad sometimes provided to the rural town resident was a form of emergency ambulance service. When inhabitants were either injured or critically ill and in need of hospital care, a request at the depot for special transportation brought results. The railroad managers might provide a special car or, if need be, a special train to take patient and doctor to a city hospital.

These were some of the common characteristics of the Northern Central's on-line communities during the late 19th Century. Each one, however, had its own particular personality, industrial complexion, and set of railroad facilities. While a complete description of all Northern Central towns is beyond the scope of this work, what follows is a major cross section of the railroad's territory, its industries, and its human environment. For the most part, the communities are covered in geographic order, working north from Baltimore.

Cockeysville, Maryland (15 miles from Baltimore)

Cockeysville, a town on the York Turnpike, rapidly developed into a manufacturing center under the influence of the Northern Central, and by the late 19th Century was also the line's principal suburban service terminal. A large wood frame two-story station had been constructed there in 1866, and by the 1880s a substantial rail yard was in operation. The station served as rail depot, post office, communication center, and track crew headquarters. Various spurs serviced lumber mills, a rye whiskey distillery, quarries, and furniture manufacturers in and near the town.

Just south of Cockeysville was the oddly named community of Texas. By 1886 some 50 lime kilns at Texas employed 250 workers, and the Beaver Dam marble quarries immediately northwest required a work force of another 100 people. The railroad constructed sidings and

Cockeysville's rail operations revolved around its 1866 frame station and octagonal tower. This view from the 1920s looks northeast; York Road crosses the tracks in the foreground. A few years later an elaborate underpass was built for the increasingly busy highway — a portent for the future. F. A. Wrabel Collection; J. W. Wolf photograph.

A 1931 view of the Cockeysville station, after the underpass was completed. With the rail line long abandoned, the underpass finally was eliminated in 1991. Smithsonian Institution Collection; C. B. Chaney photograph.

freight loading facilities at both industries to accommodate the ever-increasing level of business. The vast quantities of stone and lime, plus agricultural products from nearby farms, kept the railroad facility busy throughout the year. During the 1880s and 1890s a total of 270 residents, most of whom worked in local industry, lived within a mile radius of the station. (In 1991 the greatly expanded stone quarries at Texas remained as the major active freight customer on the one-time Northern Central route between Baltimore and York.)

Cockeysville's railroad facilities also included a "wye" track for turning trains, and for many years the town served as the northern terminal for an extensive suburban service out of Baltimore. In 1893, for example, a total of eleven weekday locals operated each way between Baltimore and Cockeysville. Four additional suburban trains each way continued through to Parkton, and several through Harrisburg trains stopped at Cockeysville.

Ashland, Maryland (16 miles from Baltimore)

Located a mile north of Cockeysville, Ashland Furnace was a classic small "company town," first established in 1844 around an iron works. By 1860 Ashland was producing 8,000 tons of iron a year. After 1864 the Ashland iron furnaces became substantial consumers of Pennsylvania anthracite from the Dauphin and Lykens Valley fields, brought in over the Northern Central.

Its iron ore, on the other hand, originated from pits along the south end of the railroad. During the 1860s and 1870s, ore was dug extensively at Hanover Junction, Pennsylvania and to a lesser extent in Maryland at Phoenix, Glencoe, Lutherville, and Timonium. Farmers frequently supplemented their income by digging ore during the winter months. The ore openings located at the "Caves," situated near the Green Spring Branch, produced such a large tonnage of iron ore that by 1884 the Northern Central actually planned a "loop" rail route off the Green Spring line to allow direct rail access to the mines. The line was never constructed, partly because of Ashland's rapid decline in the 1880s.

Ashland's pig-iron products were loaded onto freight cars at the furnaces and shipped directly to Baltimore, York, and other markets. Numerous sidings into the furnace were constructed during 1860-1863, and a coal trestle and water tank were added in 1875. The improvements made to Ashland's rail facility allowed the plant to consistently increase production and provided the town with a "means for growth."

The "company town" around Ashland grew in proportion to the output. The 30- to 40-person work force of 1850 had grown to 200 in 1860. By 1865 there were 250 workers employed at the site.

Workers lived in duplex company houses with common kitchens and shopped at the company store. The mostly Irish and German immigrant work force labored seven days a week in twelve-hour shifts and were paid \$1-\$1.50 per day. Rent for company dwellings varied between \$1.50 and \$2.50 a month.

By the late 1870s, however, the new Bessemer process began to spell the doom of small local ironmaking plants like Ashland. Iron and steel production became concentrated in large plants, particularly in the Pittsburgh area, and Ashland quickly declined. The firm's president, George Small, announced closure in 1884 and sold the business in 1885. The furnaces were briefly reopened by the Pennsylvania Steel Company in 1887, but by 1889 Pennsylvania Steel had opened its more efficient and better-located Sparrows Point plant. The old furnace and its town was sold in 1892; the iron works were scrapped, but most of the town survived, now unrecognizably prettified and engulfed by new condominiums.

Corbett, Maryland (22 miles from Baltimore)

Corbett, mostly farm land until the 1880s, grew progressively as a small railroad-oriented industrial settlement. By the 1890s the town represented one of the finest examples of a Victorian village that existed along the rail line.

In 1885 Robert Merryman constructed a steam saw mill in Corbett along with numerous houses for the mill workers. The railroad gave Merryman access to outside markets, and as demand escalated, the mill's production increased. Isaac Corbitt (so spelled), for whom the town was named, donated land adjacent to the right of way for the town's depot and by 1887 a general store, post office, and blacksmith shop were all conducting business in Corbett.

The Northern Central erected a station at the town in 1885, and by 1889 rail sidings were installed to service the saw mill, coal bins, and the lumberyard. That year several Victorian-style homes were constructed by the resident business owners and merchants. The town continued to grow throughout the 1890s and by 1896 the following businesses were functioning in Corbett.

Business	Operator
Blacksmith and Wheelwright	R. M. Jones and Co.
Telegraph Agent	Harry C. Merryman
Lumber and Planing Mill	Marion Merryman
Shoemaker	John Miller
Railroad Express Agency Post Office and General Store	J. V. Slade

Pleasant Valley, Maryland (23.5 miles from Baltimore)

Pleasant Valley, roughly half a mile north of Monkton, exemplifies a more ephemeral type of 19th Century railroad settlement, a long-vanished "ghost town" built around short-lived mining operations. Today little is known about the site and even less has been written about it.

Development of Pleasant Valley began in the early 1860s, just before the Civil War. It does not appear on the 1850 *Sidney Map of Baltimore County*, but is shown in the 1877 Hopkins atlas, which indicates buildings, a bridge over Gunpowder Falls, and a road leading west to Hereford. Some Civil War records of 1864 mention the town.

Pleasant Valley was apparently established to mine iron ore and soapstone. The iron ore deposits — like others along the railroad at such points as Glencoe, Padonia, and Lutherville — were worked in the early 1860s because of their proximity to the Ashland Iron Furnace. By 1864 this furnace had changed over to anthracite fuel and could produce more pig iron, requiring new sources of ore. Pleasant Valley soapstone was used in minor quantities by the mills, foundries, and other industries along the railroad.

By the late 1870s Pleasant Valley had become a compact village containing a railroad station, small houses, a tavern, and a hotel — which was unkindly known as the "Rat Trap."

The town declined rapidly between the late 1890s and 1900; by the early 1900s Pleasant Valley, the bridge, and Hereford road had disappeared from official maps. It was dropped from train schedules in the 1890s. The iron ore and soapstone veins had been depleted, and their markets also had disappeared. The site remained derelict for many years. At one time during the 1930s and 1940s the railroad used the old miller's house (the remains of which exist today), and the "Rat Trap" became a meeting place for unemployed workmen during the Depression.

Today Pleasant Valley exists only as a few mysterious crumbling remains which can be seen from the hiking trail built along the old railroad bed. The foundation of the "Rat Trap" hotel, along with a few iron headboards, other stone foundations, and a spring head are all that exist.

White Hall, Maryland (26 miles from Baltimore)

White Hall, located on Gunpowder Falls, was an early and locally important water-powered milling location. (Its name derived from a large white house west of the railroad tracks, which variously served as a post office, station, livery stable, and boarding house.) With the introduction of rail service, the town quickly expanded into a multi-faceted manufacturing center. John Weise operated a paper mill at the site as early as 1832, and he expanded operations there consistently throughout the 1850s. The mill changed from water power to coal-fired steam power about 1863, and the Northern Central mines in Pennsylvania supplied the anthracite.

A second paper mill, owned by George L. Kroh (purchased from Levi Rutledge in 1855), also produced paper at White Hall and took advantage of the clear water and strong current of the town's river. This mill also made the transition to coal during the 1860s.

By 1880 the Weise paper mill provided two hundred individuals with employment and by the early 1900s another one hundred people were employed in other industries such as the Kroh mill, the cannery, and the creamery. Most of these individuals lived in the town.

During its heyday in 1910 White Hall had a post office, a railroad station, a boarding house, a savings bank, two general stores, several mills, and a farm produce and supply center. The Northern Central did a substantial business from not only the paper mills, but also from the numerous other businesses at White Hall. In addition, the railroad progressively upgraded its facility at the town during the 1880s and 1890s to accommodate this expansion. In 1884 rail sidings were constructed to all the industries of White Hall and by 1890 the town had a small rail yard. A new water tower was added in 1891, followed by a coaling facility in 1896. The railroad agent and town resident, E. K. Wright, donated land and erected a Sunday School in 1885.

A new station, one of the railroad's standardized frame structures, was built in 1883, and by 1900 the Northern Central had assigned a track crew to the town. In all, the railroad employed twelve townspeople.

New Freedom, Pennsylvania (37 miles from Baltimore)

Situated just north of the Mason-Dixon Line, the town of New Freedom was probably the quintessential small railroad town on the Northern Central. It was a little bit of everything: a manufacturing and distribution center, a junction point with a rural feeder railroad, and a major main line operating point.

For the Northern Central itself, New Freedom marked the summit of the railroad's ruling grades between Baltimore and Harrisburg. The town was situated on a ridge which divides the watersheds of the Gunpowder on the south (which flows into the Chesapeake Bay) and Codorus Creek to the north (which empties into the Susquehanna). Thus the railroad had to climb over the hill from both directions, and heavy trains invariably required helper engines, which usually were taken off at New Freedom and made ready for the next train to assist. Four train crews resided in the town and two hostlers kept the locomotives ready for service. Also, from 1882 until the late 1900s a track crew was headquartered at New Freedom, and employed eight local men. A small rail yard was constructed near the station in 1881, and a new station — another example of the standardized frame design — came in 1885.

A southbound local stops at New Freedom in the early 1900s. Fast and handsome E3a Atlantic No. 4095 is at the head end. Behind the train is the wire cloth manufacturing plant.

The little Stewartstown Railroad provided the NC line with a regular, if not high volume, interchange of freight and passengers. The railroad's No. 5, a light 2-6-0, gets up steam at Stewartstown in the late 1930s. H. H. Harwood, Jr. Collection; R. P. Wallis photograph.

Also in 1885 the yard was expanded to accommodate the newly-arrived Stewartstown Railroad, an independently built short line typical of the late 19th Century "farmers' railroads." As agricultural output rose in the late 1800s many small farming communities promoted their own lightly built short lines to connect themselves with some large railroad. By doing so, they hoped to avoid the heavy expense of carrying their goods over rural wagon roads or turnpikes, widen their markets, and bring in their supplies more cheaply. In most cases, the large railroads had deemed these rural towns as marginal or uneconomical to serve themselves.

The Stewartstown Railroad was chartered in 1884 to connect the Northern Central at New Freedom with the farming village of Stewartstown, seven miles to the east. Built to minimal standards, it used secondhand materials from the Northern Central, and its right of way rose and fell with the rolling countryside. While the line mostly followed the natural contours of the land with as little grading as possible, it included a large wood trestle and a unique secondhand iron truss bridge originally built in 1870. (The bridge still exists.) Construction proceeded quickly, and the Stewartstown opened for business September 10, 1885. Afterwards, New Freedom took on the added role of a railroad junction town. In addition to freight interchange, the Stewartstown operated a modest passenger service to connect with Northern Central trains to Baltimore and York. In 1892 it scheduled three trains each way; in true "farmer" tradition, the first left Stewartstown at 5:25 a.m. and met Northern Central locals passing through New Freedom in both directions shortly after 6:00 a.m. Also typical of a rural railroad, the Stewartstown often hauled freight cars on its passenger runs. Its loads always were rather modest, and beginning in 1923 a gasoline-powered railbus carried most passengers.

In 1906 an independently financed extension of the Stewartstown, the New Park & Fawn Grove Railroad, was built to connect Stewartstown with Fawn Grove, another farming community nine miles farther east. Even more lightly built and utilized, it lasted only until 1935.

Amazingly, however, the little Stewartstown Railroad survived the Depression, the decline and abandonment of the Northern Central itself, and, in an ironic twist, currently operates a long section of the one-time Northern Central main line.

Manufacturing plants and agricultural service businesses such as canneries and creameries were located and prospered at New Freedom. By 1885 the following establishments were operating in the town:

1 brick yard	2 cigar factories
1 grist mill	1 lumber yard
3 shoemakers	2 wheelwrights
1 cabinet maker	3 dry goods stores
1 ice cream factory	2 physicians
1 tin shop	

The New Freedom Wire Cloth Company constructed a steam-powered factory along the rail line, and by 1910 it employed over 150 workers.

The railroad's influence on New Freedom was impressive. In the words of one town historian, "the railroad was the prime mover in both economy...and population; quicker access to markets allowed businesses to expand, employment to escalate, and the town to grow."

Glen Rock, Pennsylvania (42 miles from Baltimore)

In 1832 Simon Koller erected a water-powered sawmill on the Codorus Creek at the location later called Glen Rock. But in 1837 Koller became distressed when he discovered that the projected line of the Baltimore & Susquehanna Railroad would pass beside his mill, and he sold out to William Heathcote. With the arrival of the railroad, the hamlet became known as Heathcote Station. From 1839 to 1843 William Heathcote sold off building lots from his property near the mill for the mill workers. The town began to grow. In 1843 the establishment of a post office at the town precipitated a name change, and Heathcote himself recommended the name Glen Rock, for the rock outcropping which had been exposed by the railroad construction crew in a glen near the town.

In 1848 more English immigrants arrived. The town also grew as more industries were built along the rail line. By 1852 the original sawmill was converted to a grist mill, and by 1880 the town had a sash factory, a rope and twine mill, and a carriage works. The decade of the 1880s witnessed the introduction of numerous new production techniques. For example, in 1885 Israel Gladfelter installed new devices in the Glen Rock Flour Mill which allowed an output of 75 barrels a day. This, as well as the output from other mills, each with its individual siding, kept the rail yard at Glen Rock busy.

In 1918 J. Frank Owings purchased the original mill and began production of the locally famous June Bug Poultry and Livestock Feed. The firm continued production until the 1960s.

Gradually, however, the town's rail business diminished, and by 1971 almost none remained.

Hanover Junction, Pennsylvania (46 miles from Baltimore)

Hanover Junction got its name in 1852, when the Hanover Branch Railroad opened its 13-mile line from this point west to the manufacturing town of Hanover, Pennsylvania. Independently built, it was operated by the Northern Central from its opening until 1855, when its own organization took over. Still another company, the Gettysburg Railroad, opened a further extension from Hanover to Gettysburg in December 1858. The two companies were merged as the Hanover Junction, Hanover and Gettysburg Railroad in 1874; until it was absorbed by the Western Maryland Railway in 1886, this railroad effectively acted as the Northern Central's connection to the Hanover-Gettysburg territory, and interchanged passenger and freight traffic at Hanover Junction.

A southbound passenger train storms into Glen Rock shortly after 1900. As seen earlier, the NC station was housed in the old commercial building at the right. C. G. Ehrman Collection.

Glen Rock's industry included a carriage factory supplied by this lumber yard, which in turn was supplied by the railroad. The date is 1902. C. G. Ehrman Collection; W. H. Ehrman photograph.

Hanover Junction was an important iron center during the 1870s and 1880s and became a substantial shipping point in its own right. Iron ore had been discovered near Hanover Junction in 1854 and, for over 30 years, was mined at fourteen different locations throughout the area. The ore became a rich source of traffic for the Northern Central, moving primarily to three destinations. Large amounts went to the Ashland furnaces, and served as that industry's primary supply of raw material. In addition, some ore went out the Wrightsville line to the furnaces along the Susquehanna River, and another movement went south for export at Baltimore.

The low-cost railroad transportation created the economic impetus for the mines and furnaces to increase production. Miners gravitated to Hanover Junction, and the little town around the railroad junction boomed. The hundreds of immigrant miners severely taxed the hotel, restaurant, and mercantile establishments. David Henry's "National Hotel" and John Scott's "Farmers Hotel" served the miners, travelers, and railroad employees. Numerous mills, manufacturing establishments, distilleries, and cigar factories grew prosperous with the mining and railroad activity. The large wood railroad depot, built between 1852 and 1854, became the social center of town activity. In the words of one local author,

> *The station area was the focal point of the village...many hours were spent by local residents sitting on the porch, gossiping, whittling and chewing tobacco...the station received mail, newspapers, freight, passengers and telegraphic messages...advertisements and notices were frequently posted on the building...it was the town's connection to the nation and to the world...*

The station was used as a telegraph school for many years after the Civil War and many local residents, upon completion of their training, were assigned as telegraph operators at towers along the Northern Central line.

Substantial freight facilities were constructed at Hanover Junction to accommodate the mines' output. A turntable and small rail yard were built behind the station, and a coaling facility was also installed late that year. In addition, loading facilities were erected a mile north at Seven Valleys (called Smyser's by the railroad), at Gladfelters, three miles north (the Springfield bank at Gladfelters was opened in 1870), and on the Hanover Branch line at Strickhouser's. All locations were adjacent to mine entrances and had individual sidings. In all, the mines provided several train loads of ore each day to the Northern Central.

York, Pennsylvania (57 miles from Baltimore)

The city of York was probably the most important intermediate traffic and operating point on the Northern Central's main line. By the 1880s it not only was a major manufacturing center, but was a busy focal point for branch lines and independent rail feeders.

York was a county seat and an important turnpike crossroads point when the Baltimore & Susquehanna entered in 1838, the first line to provide rail service to the community. Although other railroads later entered York, the Northern Central was always the dominant carrier, reaching all parts of the city and virtually all of the major industries. By the 1880s the economic foundations of York had become dependent on the railroad. The numerous flour mills, the iron companies, and the manufacturing plants all depended on the Northern Central for raw material and market access. Anthracite, grain, and iron ore were shipped to York's industries, and finished products were sent to the seaport and many inland markets — particularly on the wide Pennsylvania Railroad system.

The expansion had been dramatic. In 1860, for example, York had a population of about 8,000, with an economic output of nearly $2 million per year. By 1900 population had increased to 20,000, and its output was estimated at $130 million.

The Northern Central progressively developed its facilities at York throughout the period. In the 1890s freight interchange connections were established with the Western Maryland's new York branch (in 1893), and the York Southern (later Maryland & Pennsylvania) in 1895. Although both of these lines maintained their own passenger terminals, they added considerable through freight to the Northern Central.

By 1903 the Northern Central's operating facilities consisted of three rail yards, a large new brick passenger station (built in 1890), and various freight loading docks and warehouses. One rail yard, along the main line near North and George Streets, served the company car shops. A larger yard was located at the North Street passenger station and occupied two city blocks. This yard served as the connecting point for all rail lines in York and eventually extensive freight facilities and warehouses were located adjacent to the station. The third and largest yard was located in north York along the Codorus Creek, and included a twelve-track freight classification yard, a turning "wye," coaling and water facilities, and an engine house. The facility employed over 130 local residents.

Beginning June 1, 1902 the Northern Central again assumed operation of the York-Wrightsville line, the one-time branch it had effectively given up in 1870 when the Pennsylvania Railroad took direct control of it. At the same time the Pennsylvania transferred its York-Frederick branch to the Northern Central. The York-Wrightsville line had been originally sponsored by the Baltimore & Susquehanna as its first main line to the Susquehanna River. The Pennsylvania had assumed responsibility for it after the Northern Central refused to repair the damage inflicted during the Civil War.

The York-Frederick line had been built independently in piecemeal fashion beginning in 1858 with the Littlestown Railroad's seven-mile-long stretch between Hanover and Littlestown, Pennsylvania. Later the York & Hanover Railroad and the Frederick & Pennsylvania Railroad built the remainder of the route. By 1873 only 17 miles were in operation, but by 1875 the entire York-Frederick line had been completed. The Pennsylvania Railroad assumed operation on January 1, 1875, and leased the Hanover & York Railroad on July 5, 1875. Under the old Pennsylvania control, these lines had been collectively designated as the "Frederick Division." In effect, they gave the Northern Central an east-west line from the Susquehanna River at Wrightsville/Columbia to a junction with the Baltimore & Ohio at Frederick, Maryland. And, combined with the Northern Central's own main line through York, they gave the company direct access to industries on all four sides of the city.

Indeed, the Northern Central clearly dominated York's extensive industry. The list below is representative of the Northern Central's major industrial sidings at York in 1900.

Main Line

Bromell, Schmidt & Steacy Boiler Makers
Keystone Farm Machinery
Pennsylvania Agricultural Works

This large brick station at York was at least the third which served the thriving manufacturing city. Well preserved, it still stood in 1991. Author's collection.

A PRR Frederick branch local poses at Hanover, Pennsylvania about 1885, before the NC was assigned to operate the line. Hanover Public Library Collection.

Susquehanna Iron and Steel Company
Variety Iron Works
York Paper Company
York Safe and Lock Company

Frederick Line

Steam Stone Works
York Brewing Company
York Manufacturing Company
Wrightsville Line
Diamond Silk Mill
Standard Chain Company

The York-Frederick and York-Wrightsville Branches

On the "Frederick Division" were the important mill towns of Wrightsville and Spring Grove, Pennsylvania, along with the larger manufacturing city of Hanover. During the 1880s the Northern Central did a substantial iron ore and lumber business into Wrightsville from both York and Adams County, and the town had grown into a substantial manufacturing site. The Wrightsville Silk Mill, the Kerr Brothers Lime Kilns, and various lumber mills employed over 200 residents. The Susquehanna Casting Company and the Riverside Foundry, ancestors of the early iron furnaces along the Susquehanna, kept the single-track branch busy. Here too, the branch crossed the Susquehanna to connect with two Pennsylvania Railroad lines at Columbia.

Aside from Hanover, the line to Frederick, also single-track, served the giant Gladfelter Paper Mill at Spring Grove, Pennsylvania, 10 miles west of York. With its nine industrial sidings, Gladfelter became the line's largest customer. The other mill towns along the line, Menges Mill, Littlestown, and Taneytown, became important agricultural shipping points, especially after farm yields began to spiral upward during the early 1880s.

Passenger services on the Frederick Division primarily served several short-haul local markets. In 1904, for example, three all-stops locals were scheduled each way for the entire distance between Columbia, Wrightsville, and Frederick, although it seems doubtful that many people rode all the way between the terminals. Added to these three trains were two daily round trips between Columbia and Hanover and one between Columbia and Littlestown. All of these added up to a comparatively dense traffic of six trains each way over the Columbia-York-Hanover portion of the line. Superficially, the strangest services were the three daily round trips that ran over the western end of the line between Bruceville, Maryland (later called Keymar) and Frederick. Their real purpose was to provide Frederick with a connection at Bruceville for Western Maryland passenger trains to and from Baltimore.

Dauphin, Pennsylvania (93 miles from Baltimore)

Dauphin's role as the Northern Central's junction with the coal hauling Schuylkill & Susquehanna Railroad already has been mentioned. Also, from 1908 until 1917 a 42-inch narrow gauge logging railroad operated by the Zartman Lumber Company had a junction at Dauphin with the Northern Central's main line. That firm's prop timber was shipped on the Schuylkill & Susquehanna line, while finished lumber was transported over the Northern Central to Baltimore. The Zartman company constructed its sawmill at Dauphin between the Susquehanna River and the Northern Central tracks in early 1909 and its twin boiler saw mill, "one of the most modern of the era, produced 40-50 thousand feet of cut lumber each day" to the railhead.

Williamsport, Pennsylvania (178 miles from Baltimore)

Williamsport, the giant lumber center on the Susquehanna River, was another major Northern Central junction town and industrial center. Peter Herdic, an enterprising businessman who owned several of the more than 60 lumber mills in the town, is credited with "building" Williamsport with profits earned from his lumber trade into Baltimore's seaport. The mills supplied not only lumber for the railroads, but also wood for bridges, timber for the coal mines, and charcoal wood for the tannery industry.

During the 1870s Herdic paved the streets, erected buildings, and constructed street railways. In the late 1890s, when Williamsport reached a peak of affluence, the city housed eighteen millionaires; the famous Fourth Street "Millionaires Row" was paved with board planks and was home to such notable personalities as Diamond Jim Brady.

Herdic also constructed the large "Herdic House Hotel" which was located adjacent to the railroad. The structure served as the Northern Central's depot and became known as the Park Hotel Station. In 1872 the Philadelphia and Erie Railroad (which also served Williamsport

William McKinley's funeral train passes through Williamsport, Pennsylvania in September 1901. The station was used jointly by the NC and Philadelphia & Erie, and housed the P & E offices. Brown Library (Williamsport) Collection.

and by then was a Pennsylvania Railroad subsidiary) erected a new combination station and office building in Williamsport, which the Northern Central eventually also used. In 1902 the building was enlarged.

In addition, the Northern Central maintained two coal yards and one service facility at Williamsport which employed over 50 people. Coal from the McIntyre mine at Ralston was used by numerous local industries, supplied through these Northern Central coal yards. Collectively, the lumber industry and railroad business at Williamsport was responsible for the city's spectacular growth. Together, they created a pool of over 20,000 employment positions.

Gray's Run, Pennsylvania (196 miles from Baltimore)

Gray's Run was not a typical permanently settled railroad town in the traditional sense. Rather, it was a classic example of the short-lived 19th Century Pennsylvania lumbering settlement, in this case surviving slightly more than twenty years. Located about six miles southwest of Ralston, Pennsylvania, it developed into an important center for processing and shipping lumber from a wide surrounding area. The town itself was located on Gray's Run, a Lycoming Creek tributary, about four and one-half miles upstream from the Northern Central main line. Thomas E. Proctor Lumber Company constructed a sawmill and supporting town at this location during what is believed to have been the late 1880s. Proctor also built a connecting railroad between his mill and the Northern Central, establishing a junction at a point called "Gray's" on the main line. The exact date of construction of the mill is unknown, but one early record reports that it burned down in 1890. Once rebuilt, the new mill at Gray's Run began to produce what Thomas T. Taber III in his *Ghost Towns of Central Pennsylvania* reports to be in excess of over 90,000 feet of hemlock lumber per day. By-products such as bark went over the Northern Central to tanneries in Ralston and Roaring Branch.

When Proctor died in 1894 the mill was transferred to the Keystone Lumber Company. By this time the town of Gray's Run had grown to a population base of 500 workers, and the mill supported another group of business owners and workers, including real estate speculators, blacksmiths, mechanics, and day laborers. Eventually, the logging railroad was extended all over Laurel Mountain.

In 1902 the Gray's Run logging line was incorporated as the Gray's Run Railroad, and in 1903 it was consolidated with the recently formed Susquehanna & New York Railroad. The Susquehanna & New York, a subsidiary of the United States Leather Company, extended about 45 miles northeast from Ralston to Towanda, Pennsylvania, and had been put together as a combination coal and lumber hauler. The Gray's Run line was extended parallel to the Northern Central from Gray's Station to Ralston to connect directly with the Susquehanna & New York. The S & NY also bought two large three-truck geared Shay locomotives to operate the line.

Beginning in the late 1880s and continuing until 1910 the lumber town of Gray's Run, one of the last known operating mill towns of Pennsylvania, delivered huge amounts of lumber and wood products to not only the Northern Central Railway at Gray's but also to the towns of Trout Run, Marsh Hill, and Ralston. Exact statistics on output are not available; however, employment data for 1900 records 700 employees either at the mill, on the railroad, or in local businesses. Considering that size of work force, and the twenty years of operation, the mill's output must have been massive. Many local newspapers commented on the economic benefit that the previously mentioned towns derived from the industry.

While it was functioning, Gray's Station had a small depot and railroad service outbuildings. Documentation of the location is sparse, which has obscured much information about the facility. The Northern Central and the Susquehanna & New York used the interchange as a stop for both freight and passenger trains. In addition, some local residents and farmers used Gray's as a shipping and receiving point. But when the sawmill closed in 1911 the logging railroad network and the Susquehanna & New York connection between Gray's and Ralston were dismantled.

Ralston, Pennsylvania (202 miles from Baltimore)

As mentioned in Chapter 8, Ralston became a coal mining center in 1870 and was one of the major shipping points on the Northern Central's Williamsport-Elmira line. With the arrival of the Susquehanna & New York Railroad in 1903, it also developed as a major junction point. The Susquehanna & New York, which reached neither the Susquehanna nor New York, tapped several large central Pennsylvania lumbering operations, including the C. W. Sones mill at Masten and the enormous sawmill and wood-based chemical manufacturing complex at Laquin, about midway between its terminals at Towanda and Ralston. The people of Ralston were quick to understand the ramifications of the anticipated junction. One reporter commented, "already Ralston has felt the benefits of the new traffic, and people here believe that it will result in considerable commercial and industrial good to the town." It did.

Ralston's station was another variation of the NC's standard wood design. Author's collection.

Area businessmen established the Green Lumber Company, the Ralston Brick Company, and the Elk Tanning Company around the junction. The town grew to absorb 2,000 workers who found employment with either the railroad, coal mines, or industries located adjacent to the rail line.

In 1907 the Susquehanna & New York moved its Northern Central junction point three miles south to a spot called Marsh Hill, where larger plots of property had been purchased for an expanded rail yard. An eight-track interchange yard and coal and water facilities were erected along the valley floor for the joint use of the Northern Central and S & NY. The relationship between the two railroads was consistently cooperative and the town reaped the economic benefits of every-increasing traffic levels. Coal and lumber kept the interchange busy.

By 1910 there were, in total, over 1,000 lumbermen, coal miners, railroad workers, merchants, and day-laborers living in and around Ralston. The railroad hired the Susquehanna Real Estate Company to build ten houses at the junction for railroad workers and the firm independently constructed many additional residences.

On April 4, 1909 the Northern Central and Susquehanna & New York signed an agreement allowing the S & NY trackage rights over the Northern Central line south from the Marsh Hill junction to Williamsport, 21 miles. The Susquehanna & New York began passenger service from the Park Hotel Station in Williamsport to Towanda, and made passenger stops at both Gray's and Marsh Hill. The S & NY also built a new interchange yard at West Williamsport (known as Newberry), where it connected not only with the Northern Central, but with the Reading and the New York Central. The yard employed several hundred men. Although the lumber traffic vaporized quickly (the Laquin mill closed in 1925, and the Masten operation ended in 1930), the Susquehanna & New York limped on until it was finally abandoned in 1942.

A later view of the McIntyre inclined plane from that shown in Chapter 8. At the base of the plane are the railroad loading facilities. Author's collection.

Canton, Pennsylvania (217 miles from Baltimore)

Not all of the Northern Central's communities could boast continuing success and expansion. Canton, Pennsylvania had hoped to become a major junction town, but in this case the projected railroad was stillborn, and the town lapsed into doldrums.

In 1904 ambitious plans designed to "exploit the coal resource of Lycoming, Bradford, and Sullivan counties" resulted in the incorporation of the Pittsburgh, Binghamton & Eastern Railroad Company. The line was planned to extend from Powell, Pennsylvania, east along Towanda Creek into Canton, where it would establish a junction with the Northern Central. It would then continue farther east into the Oregon Hill and English Centre coal fields.

The initial plan was to deliver coal to the Northern Central at Canton for forwarding either south to the seaports or north to the Great Lakes.

The people of Canton supported the project from its inception and provided some financial backing. The Canton First National Bank invested heavily in the line and the bank's president, Daniel Innes, was one of the railroad's directors. A local entrepreneur, F. A. Sawyer, was elected president.

Construction began on a somewhat financially tenuous foundation in 1906. However, on September 15, 1906 a thousand construction workers arrived at Canton with steam shovels and railroad construction equipment. Supplies and equipment inundated the town. Overnight Canton became a boom town; local merchants, restaurant operators, and hotel owners did a thriving business supporting the construction crews.

This continued for two years. Then suddenly in 1908, after seven miles of the line and numerous bridges had been built, the owners filed for bankruptcy. Construction costs had produced debts that the firm could not pay. By 1910 the equipment, supplies, and right of way had been sold at auction.

The town of Canton went into an economic decline. Many workers who had settled in the area moved away. Merchants who had overextended their inventory either cut back, sold out, or closed shop. Many hotels and inns shut their doors forever. The dream of becoming an important junction also faded forever.

Montour Falls, New York (275 miles from Baltimore)

Located south of Watkins, Montour Falls was settled in 1788 and originally called Havanna. (It was renamed Montour Falls at the turn of the century to honor the locally famous Indian "Queen," Catherine Montour.) Senator Charles Cook constructed, more than a hundred years ago, most of the structures which still remain in the town. The Chemung Canal, connecting Elmira with Seneca Lake, was built through the town in the 1840s, and the "Chequagah Falls," then as now, became a popular tourist attraction. In 1849 the Chemung Railroad completed its line, which roughly followed the canal's route between Elmira and Lake Seneca, and for many years afterwards the two modes of transportation coexisted in the town.

Havanna's real industrial growth began in 1880 when James A. Shepard, who at the age of 16 was considered a mechanical genius, started a foundry in the town. Along with his father and brother, Shepard built the family busi-

Canton as it looked in 1905 as a southbound train approached. Author's collection.

North of Canton the railroad passed the front doors of the Minnequa House at Minnequa Springs, seen here in the 1880s. The hotel was typical of many sprawling 19th Century wooden mountain resorts. R. Bosley Collection.

ness into one of the largest manufacturers of mechanical equipment in the area. Today the Shepard-Niles Crane company, although reduced in operations, still employs many people.

Thanks partly to the heavy foundry freight business, Montour Falls was one of the few towns along the New York section of the Northern Central which had dual stations. Both a passenger station and a freight depot were constructed at the town during the late 1880s. Today, although the passenger station is gone, the freight station, after years of neglect, has been restored and is used as a doctor's office.

Located just south of Seneca Lake, Montour Falls boasted separate passenger and freight stations, both of them standardized NC designs. Montour Falls Memorial Library Collection.

Watkins, New York (278 miles from Baltimore)

The town of Watkins (originally Jefferson) serves as an excellent example of a 19th Century commerce center that benefited from the symbiotic relationship between the canal, the railroad, and industry. Independent of the salt industry, Watkins grew and prospered as a trade center because of its strategic location at the south end of Lake Seneca. The lake provided a water route north to the Erie Canal. So at Watkins, canal boats, lake steamers, and railroad interchanged both commerce and passengers. The town of Watkins derived economic vitality from the limited "port" facilities.

The Chemung Canal from Elmira to Seneca Lake, advocated as early as 1790 by the Revolutionary War hero General Sullivan, opened in 1834 as part of a projected water route to the Susquehanna River. It brought a substantial level of trade to Watkins, fostering industries supplying service to the canal trade. Blacksmiths, mechanics, and liverymen settled while inn and tavern keepers provided accommodations for the travelers.

Then in 1849 salt was discovered at Watkins, bringing additional prosperity along with pressures for rail service. In 1850 the Chemung Railroad was constructed into town as part of a planned route between Elmira and Canandaigua. With the advent of rail service markets expanded; during the 1870s, while both the canal and railroad co-existed, the town of Watkins continued to grow in commercial importance.

In the 1870s, after the discovery of coal at Ralston, Watkins became an important transshipping center for coal arriving by rail and destined to points on the waterways. Some coal was distributed to local markets by lake steamers, but most went to towns and industries located along the Erie Canal.

During the 1880s the Northern Central aggressively advertised the Watkins area as a vacation resort. The resulting tourist trade had a staggering effect on the town's economic vitality. During this period, tourist trade con tinued to increase to a point where, by 1895, it amounted to an annual total of approximately $10 million.

Canandaigua, New York (325 miles from Baltimore)

While Newark became an important freight center, Canandaigua, one of the largest junction towns in New York State, became an important tourist center. The Northern Central's line was one of the major passenger routes from southern points to Niagara Falls, Lake Ontario, and the Finger Lakes. For example, by 1880 the line had five passenger trains a day from Elmira into Canandaigua. In addition, during July 1887 the Northern Central constructed a short branch line from the depot in Canandaigua to the lake's shore and erected a station at the water's edge.

The entire town of Penn Yan, New York turns out to see the local troops leaving for World War I. Penn Yan, located between Watkins and Canandaigua, also had both freight and passenger stations of the standard type. Yates County (New York) Genealogical and Historical Society Collection.

The high level of rail traffic through the town required an expansion of facilities. In 1886 both the Northern Central and the New York Central Railroads enlarged the rail yard at the Canandaigua station complex with eight sidings, a coaling tower, and several water tanks. The facility employed 27 local residents.

Numerous businesses in Canandaigua also prospered because of their association with the rail line. The "Railroad Hotel" opened in 1884 adjacent to the New York Central's ornate station, and the basement floor of the hotel served as the Northern Central depot. In addition, several feed mills and agricultural supply firms constructed plants at the rail yard and used the facility extensively.

Newark, New York (331 miles from Baltimore)

The town of Newark was an important agricultural center located on the Erie Canal. A predecessor of the New York Central Railroad began serving the community in 1840, and rapidly captured a large segment of interstate canal traffic during the 1850s. The town grew quickly as a freight interchange point between the railroad and canal, although the canal retained a large segment of local freight. The railroad, on the other hand, took the interstate traffic and the business which required faster handling.

In 1873 the Sodus Bay & Southern completed its north-south line from Stanley, New York to Sodus Point, passing through Newark en route. About ten years later, the New York, West Shore & Buffalo also entered the town with an east-west line closely paralleling the New York Central; the Central absorbed it in 1885.

After the Northern Central bought the anemic Sodus Bay & Southern in 1884 traffic through the town became substantial as coal shipments were sent north to Sodus Point. The agricultural and lumber trade, however, generally went east or west from Newark over the New York Central's main line. But Newark also maintained its role as a rail-canal interchange point, and during the 1890s most residents in the town either worked for or were dependent on the canal, the railroad, or a combination of the two for their livelihoods.

Development of the Northern Central's "Junction Towns"

Many of the communities described above, and several others noted earlier, combined industry with transportation interchanges — that is, junctions with other railroads, canals, or both. The combination of industrial or mining expansion and transportation activity steadily created new employment opportunities. In search of these jobs, arriving immigrants journeyed to the area, often aided

At Newark, the NC's Sodus Point branch crossed the Erie Canal on the truss bridge at the far right of this postcard view, then passed over the New York Central's West Shore line. Passenger traffic on this branch was always relatively light, but the station was quite substantial. Wayne County Historical Society Collection.

by the railroad. Irish, Italian, Welsh, English, Polish, and German families emigrated to what they hoped was their "land of promise." Many settled in the mining towns of Shamokin, McIntyre, or Lykens and found work in the coal fields. However, large numbers of arriving immigrants settled in the junction towns such as Millersburg, Sunbury, Northumberland, and Williamsport. The influx of new families to the area taxed the ability of local governments to house and feed them. The increasing population brought about the construction of many hotels and restaurants near the railroad stations specifically to accommodate the new arrivals. Then enterprising speculators quickly planned and erected residential neighborhoods which fanned outward from the central city.

The scope and degree of development was enormous. The chart below summarizes the extent of population growth during the period for many of the junction towns.

Population % Increase Between 1870 and 1890

Town	1870	1880	1890	1870-90
York	11,000	13,940	20,793	49%
Millersburg	1,371	1,440	1,527	6%
Shamokin	—	8,184	14,403	75%
Sunbury	1,127	—	5,930	—
Northumberland	735	—	3,297	—
Williamsport	16,030	18,934	27,132	43%
Canton	—	—	1,393	—
Elmira	15,900	20,541	29,708	43%
Canandaigua	—	—	5,868	—

Horse-drawn streetcar lines, and later electric street railways, were rapidly constructed outward from the railroad station at the center of town, and in many cases used the stations as the center for radiating lines. The "streetcar suburbs" which resulted from this development allowed residents to work in the central city and to commute to homes away from the industrial heart of town. By the turn of the century, electric streetcars were operating in York, Harrisburg, Sunbury, Williamsport, Elmira, and several smaller towns.

Suburban Development

Beginning as early as 1850, the American railroads began to create a new social phenomenon: the suburb. Traditionally, workers lived close to their jobs, a necessity since they either had to walk to work or ride in a slow, horse-powered streetcar or omnibus. Indeed, through much of the 19th Century, the growth of cities was limited

Despite the marginal (or perhaps even negative) financial return, the NC invested heavily in its Baltimore suburban services. This 1904 scene at Ruxton typifies the attractive stations, immaculately kept grounds, and frequent trains. A D16 class 4-4-0 heads a Baltimore-bound local. H. H. Harwood, Jr. Collection; E. G. Hooper photograph.

by the speed and hauling capabilities of a horse. The railroad, however, permitted those who could afford it to live some distance from the city and still travel to work quickly, comfortably, and relatively cheaply.

The concept of living in a rural area and "commuting" to work on the railroad started slowly, but accelerated dramatically during the 1880s and 1890s. The reasons were complex; some suburban residents commuted because of necessity, and many by preference.

One factor was the shift from small-scale local manufacturing to large industrial plants, usually located in some urban area. By the 1890s large factories in the big cities had put the rural mills and manufacturers out of business, and their workers out of jobs. Some former workers moved from the rural towns to new jobs in the city; many remained, however. They owned their homes, had a vested interest in their community, and liked living in the country. But if they were lucky enough to live on a railroad line which reached some nearby industrial center, they could continue living in their old communities and still work.

More commonly, city dwellers could escape to the "rural ideal," away from city pestilence, crime, filth, and disease. The physical deterioration of the old neighborhoods, the crowded factories, shops, and tenements, were all powerful motivators pushing people to "the country."

The economics for doing so also became more favorable. Rural land prices were affordable. In the late 1800s real estate speculators and land developers began purchasing large tracts of rural land, and laid out impressive communities within the price range of aspiring homeowners. The railroads often involved themselves, both directly and indirectly. In an effort to stimulate traffic, many railroads adopted sharply discounted fare structures for frequent short-distance travel; some bought and sold suburban land, or otherwise encouraged the formation of suburban communities through various incentives. Railroad officers themselves often would settle in suburban towns, and would take a personal interest in creating attractive stations and convenient train services.

Because of both its geography and its corporate outlook, the Northern Central became a modest suburban carrier, and was particularly instrumental in developing several of Baltimore's most prestigious northern suburbs. Indeed, two of the country's earliest specifically-planned railroad-oriented suburban communities were located on the Northern Central outside Baltimore. Not only did the company accommodate such developments, but it encouraged the process by building beautifully designed suburban stations and operating extensive local train services over both its main line and Green Spring Branch. To a lesser extent the railroad also handled suburban traffic to York and Harrisburg.

The Suburban Towns

Not surprisingly, the Northern Central's territory north of Baltimore was the earliest to develop, and became one of the region's most notable suburban areas. The topography of the Jones Falls Valley and its tributaries provided pleasant rolling hills, cool air, woods, and streams, all of which were only a few miles from the city's center. While small milling, quarrying, and agricultural communities had been established along the railroad line, the early 1850s saw the appearance of a new type of settlement: the planned residential community, specifically created as both a summer retreat and year-round home for the city's merchants and professionals. And, of course, an integral feature of these new communities was the railroad link to the city. The town of Lutherville, created in 1852, was the first of these and, in fact, was one of the country's earliest railroad-served, purely residential suburban communities outside a large city. Mount Washington, another Northern Central suburb first developed in 1854, was a close runner-up.

In 1851 two Lutheran clergymen, Dr. John Morris and Dr. Benjamin Kurtz, purchased a large tract of rural land four miles north of the Relay station that was bisected by the Baltimore & Susquehanna rail line. Their original purpose was to found a women's seminary, and to sell residential lots to help finance the school. The plot, mostly woods, was purchased from John and Rachael Burton and cost the new owners $7,051.

The two ministers rapidly partitioned the property and sold building lots to prospective suburban residents. They erected both the Lutherville Female Seminary and residences for their families. In 1853 the Baltimore & Susquehanna constructed its first Lutherville station, which was replaced in 1876 by a large and unusually-designed stone structure. By 1890 over 300 residents were using the railroad's local trains into Baltimore. Like several of Baltimore's early suburbs, Lutherville developed partly as a summer resort for affluent professional people, and partly as a year-round residential suburb.

Ruxton, located about two miles south of Lutherville, typified the later Victorian-era suburban development. The Northern Central built a rather primitive station at Ruxton in 1883. The following year William and Charles Fisher purchased farmland north of Lake Roland that would eventually be sub-divided into building lots. Development proceeded slowly until 1887, when a local paper reported that "architects were busy laying out the plans for Ruxton," and lots were surveyed and actual construction began.

By 1892 the Fisher property had been partitioned and the real estate firm of Wood, Harm and Company had sold over 200 building lots ranging in price from $200 to $500.

A cluster of Baltimore commuters climbs onto a Parkton Local at Lutherville on a winter morning in 1955. According to the best evidence, the large, unusually designed stone station dates to 1876. According to some sources it also served as a hotel for the community. In 1991, it was a private home. R. Mellinger Collection.

That same year, the Northern Central constructed its elegant new depot at Ruxton, which served as the community's social center for many decades. The experiences of one particular person who lived in the building serves as an illustration.

Ruxton's one-time station agent, Mrs. Elsie T. Potts, reported that the depot "was home to me and the informal group of commuters who rode the Parkton Local." Passengers "would gather at the station to exchange information" while civic groups "memorialized soldiers with the planting of an oak tree" and would "decorate a fir tree" for the Christmas holidays.

Ruxton, Lutherville, and other Northern Central suburban communities such as Mount Washington, Riderwood (originally Sherwood), Timonium, and Cockeysville were served by a dense array of local trains. In 1904, for example, a total of eighteen trains a day each way stopped at most of these stations. Eleven of them operated between Baltimore and the terminal at Cockeysville; seven other trains continued up the line as far as Parkton, York, or Harrisburg. A train rider could leave Calvert Station in Baltimore for one of these suburban points as early as 4:40 a.m. or as late as 11:40 p.m. Stations closer to Baltimore, such as Mount Washington, were served by no less than 27 trains each way, since the nine Green Spring Branch locals also stopped along the section between Baltimore and Hollins.

Parkton station and town, about 1910. The view is northeast. R. Mellinger Collection.

Parkton, 29 miles north of Baltimore, was an established rural town on the York Turnpike. In 1861, however, the Northern Central chose it as the northern terminal point for a local passenger service to Baltimore. (It is likely that Parkton was picked because it was one of the few spots along the hilly, curving line where open space was available for terminal facilities.) As a result Parkton became an outer suburb by 1890, and serves as an excellent example of the transformation that some rural towns experienced. Census data for that year reported 137 inhabitants living within a mile radius of the rail depot and that over 50 percent of them commuted to Baltimore for their work. By 1900 the town's population had grown to 200.

In 1903 an elaborate new station, designed by the Philadelphia architectural firm of Furness and Evans, was erected at Parkton and the rail yard was enlarged to handle additional "Parkton Local" trains. In 1904 two Baltimore local trains terminated at Parkton, and seven other trains in each direction stopped there. Most of these trains also served the other small rural and milling towns south of Parkton such as White Hall, Monkton, Sparks, and Phoenix; those towns, too, developed a suburban flavor.

To a lesser extent other cities along the Northern Central in Pennsylvania and New York transformed nearby rural towns into suburban communities. During the 1890s, as more and more rural industries closed, the Northern Central provided a means of access to the locations where manufacturing jobs were becoming increasingly available. In particular, the cities of York, Harrisburg, Sunbury, and Williamsport provided jobs for the rural town residents who found themselves out of work.

For example, such rural towns as Glen Rock, Brilhart, Hanover Junction, Campbell, and Emigsville, Pennsylvania became, in part, suburban satellites of York and Harrisburg. Although the local train services did not approach those of the Baltimore suburbs, it was generally possible to take an early morning train into the city and return in late afternoon. Such schedules were operated between York and Harrisburg, and between Millersburg and Harrisburg. The suburban traffic was merely one specialized aspect of a highly varied and diffuse short-haul passenger traffic which developed during the 19th Century. As noted in the beginning of this chapter, virtually everyone along the railroad line, or near it, used the trains for all types of trips beyond their towns. Beginning about 1880 the Northern Central's short-haul passenger traffic rose steeply and local train services were regularly expanded. Although electric streetcars captured most of the short-distance travel close by cities like York, Harrisburg, Sunbury, Williamsport, and Elmira, other local passenger business remained high well into the early 1900s, when automobiles began to appear in quantity.

Parkton was still an active spot in September 1949 as train No. 505, a mid-day, all-stops Baltimore-Harrisburg local stops at the 1903 station. The power on this trip was a pair of the PRR's unique Baldwin "Centipede" passenger diesels. C. T. Mahan, Jr. photograph.

The chart below summarizes the increase in suburban service trains arriving and departing at the various industrial cities served by the Northern Central over the three decades between 1880 and 1910:

City	Number of local trains per day by year			
	1880	1890	1900	1910
Baltimore	5 (10)	12 (24)	28 (30)	22
York	5 (9)	10 (15)	12 (19)	16
Sunbury/ Northumberland	6 (12)	9 (14)	12 (20)	10 (16)
Williamsport	4 (9)	12 (20)	8 (14)	9 (14)
Elmira	4 (10)	10 (18)	8 (14)	8 (12)

Sources: *Lyles Official Railway Manual*
Coultons Railway Guide
Travelers Official Guide of the Steam Railways and Navigation Lines

**Note: The numbers shown in parentheses includes the number of local trains of other railroads which used the Northern Central's right of way into the cities shown. The statistic eliminates the long distance passenger trains.*

For the communities and the railroad alike, it was a prosperous and interdependent world. But it was all about to change.

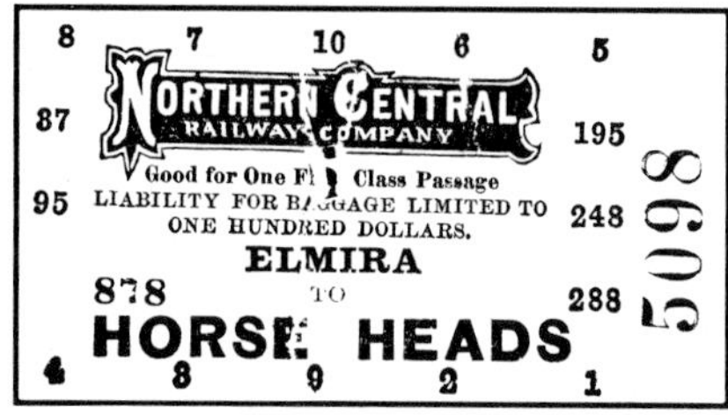

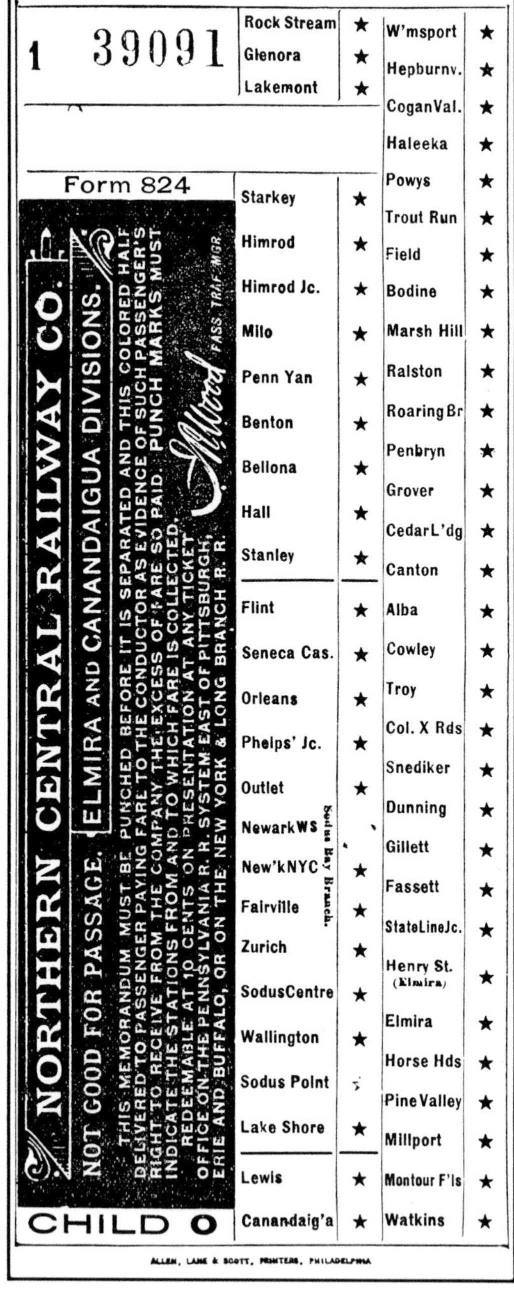

These tickets, from the early 1900s, illustrate the extent of the Northern Central's influence on the upstate portions of the line. Note the numerous towns on the larger ticket; many are now gone. William R. Gordon Collection.

CHAPTER 11

The Pennsylvania Railroad Era...and After

The Seeds of Decline

By the early 1900s, even as the Northern Central was establishing itself as a world class railroad, the elements of its demise began to appear.

Some of the reasons, of course, were common to all railroads: the beginnings of government regulation in 1887 and, later, increasingly tighter federal and state control over rates, joint traffic agreements, and services. The net effect was a gradual lessening of pricing freedom and greater problems in covering operating costs and capital obligations.

Particularly hurtful to the Northern Central, however, was the so-called "commodities clause" of the 1906 Hepburn Act. This provision prohibited railroads from having any ownership interest in the commodities they hauled; it specifically applied to coal-hauling railroads, such as the Northern Central and Pennsylvania, which also owned mining companies. The prohibition, in effect, denied them the revenues obtained from mining and marketing coal. The new mining syndicates which evolved began "shopping" for the lowest freight rate available, and as railroads reduced rates to retain tonnage, profits further eroded.

As a result of the divestiture ruling the Pennsylvania Railroad announced on September 26, 1913 that it had decided to dispose of all security holdings it held in the anthracite coal companies. Stock in the Mineral Railroad and Mining Company and the Summit Branch Mining Company was transferred to the Susquehanna Coal Company and that firm was offered for sale. The Northern Central quickly followed suit. (The Northern Central retained the Shamokin Valley & Pottsville's rail line between Sunbury and Mount Carmel, but the company's coal properties were sold.)

Several other events occurred which had a detrimental effect upon the Northern Central's earning power. First, the canal system which helped to feed it disappeared. The famous flood of 1889 had destroyed a large section of the Susquehanna Canal; in 1901 the last open segment, 180 miles between Columbia and Northumberland, was abandoned, removing the remaining canal transfer trade. The Susquehanna & Tidewater Canal between Wrightsville and

This steel railroad bridge connected the York-Wrightsville branch with PRR lines at Columbia, Pennsylvania. Built in 1897, it was the fourth bridge on this site, and until 1930 it also carried automobile and truck traffic. It was dismantled in 1964 after the rail connection was abandoned. Author's collection.

the Chesapeake Bay at Havre de Grace had been abandoned in 1894, and Wrightsville itself suffered an economic decline.

Second, and more important to the Northern Central, in 1894 long-haul anthracite shipments to Baltimore began a decline which financially hurt the company. The Annual Report for that year noted that the decrease resulted from a "lack of export," but the railroad was optimistic about the "increase in petroleum" traffic. Believed to be only a temporary economic fluctuation at the time, oil began to replace coal as an energy source and the Northern Central's operating revenue rapidly declined. The following year, as "coal to Sodus Point outweighed the tonnage being delivered to Baltimore," a long-term pattern had begun. The anthracite market especially weakened. Bituminous traffic from other territories was somewhat healthier, and anthracite sporadically revived. The overall trend, however, continued down-ward as the internal combustion engine was perfected, automobiles and trucks were mass produced, and petroleum from the Southwest became cheap and plentiful. Revenues never recovered.

Finally, a severe industrial depression which followed the Panic of 1907 forced a large number of furnaces, mills, and other industrial establishments in the rural towns along the line to close. Although a few later reopened, many did not. The Northern Central, always dependent on the rural mills and manufacturers to supplement coal revenues, began to suffer revenue declines.

Lease to the Pennsylvania Railroad

This cloudy outlook revived feelings of financial apprehension among the Northern Central's "outside" stockholders. The dormant "lease faction" resurrected its idea and in 1910 a special committee of stockholders was formed to explore the option of a permanent lease to the Pennsylvania Railroad. In 1911, after diligent and lengthy analysis, the special committee, along with the Board of Directors, recommended a permanent operating arrangement, or lease of the firm, to the Pennsylvania. The recommendation contained a clause favoring not only the lease of the railroad, but also of the equipment, the franchises, and all other property belonging to the Northern Central Railway. The proposed lease would become retroactive to January 1, 1911 and remain in effect for 999 years. The conditions were as follows:

a. An 8 percent dividend payment on the outstanding capital stock after it had been increased 40 percent.*
b. A payment of a 10 percent cash dividend on the stock outstanding before the 40 percent increase.

The NC/PRR facilities at Canton in Baltimore, as they appeared in the World War I period. Author's collection.

c. A sum sufficient to preserve and maintain the company's corporate existence and organization.
d. A payment by the lessee of all fixed charges and taxes.

(*The stock dividend payment represented part of the capital expenditures for physical improvements previously made by the Northern Central.)

Dividends of 8 percent had generally been paid on the old Northern Central stock and earnings had been averaging 12 percent. The 8 percent dividend on the increased shares equated to 11.2 percent payment on the old stock. By the standards of the day, the proposed terms were financially fair and equitable.

The terms of the lease were approved by an overwhelming majority of the stockholders, including 85 percent of the shareholders other than the Pennsylvania Railroad. The lease and stock increases were submitted to the newly created Public Service Commission of Maryland for its approval. However, before a hearing could be arranged a small group of dissatisfied minority stockholders filed two suits to block the lease, one in the United States District Court for the District of Maryland and one in the Eastern District of the State of Pennsylvania. As a result of the litigation, the Pennsylvania Railroad's management decided to postpone the execution of the lease until each suit was settled or until its law department advised that it was proper to go ahead.

The legal struggle may have gone on for several years except for the intervention of a dramatic decline in the NC's coal business which occurred during 1912. Revenues plunged, hundreds of employees were furloughed, and only financial assistance from the Pennsylvania Railroad managed to keep the Northern Central running. It was enough, apparently, to convince the recalcitrant stockholders to abstain from further legal proceedings.

Finally, in 1914 the joint president of the Pennsylvania and Northern Central railroads, Samuel Rea, announced that he "personally favored the lease" and in the Annual Report for that year he stressed the unsettled business outlook, the sale of the Shamokin Valley & Pottsville Railroad's coal properties to the Susquehanna Coal Company, and the European war. That year company records assigned a net worth of $30 million to the Northern Central. Net income was listed as $1.85 million which was "lower than expected." The lease was executed on July 29, 1914. The railroad continued to run and the corporation itself remained alive, but the real Northern Central's life was over as it became an integral part of the vast PRR system.

In 1914 the people along the line were not particularly dissatisfied with the loss of an independent Northern Central. Many were stockholders and approved of the takeover. As the country's largest and most powerful railroad system, the Pennsylvania offered stability and what was thought to be an assured future. This was the Golden Age of railroading, and few people realized what would later happen. But as time went on, service reductions and streamlining of operations began having economic and social effects on the railroad's territory. In some cases final abandonment of major sections of the line was a tragedy from which the railroad towns and their citizens never recovered.

A fully detailed account of the line's life as a unit of the Pennsylvania Railroad is beyond the scope of this study; much of it, in fact, has been covered in other publications. But this chapter will attempt to chronicle the major events affecting the one-time Northern Central system over this period, with particular emphasis on the final years and the present remains.

The Pennsylvania Assumes Operation

After the 1914 lease the Northern Central continued as a corporate entity with its own stockholders and its own skeletal organization, but the Pennsylvania now directly managed all aspects of the company's physical properties. To a large extent it was a case of merely formalizing and cementing a relationship which had begun in 1861 and had become progressively closer afterwards. The new Baltimore tunnels and terminals of the early 1870s had been a joint project of the two companies. By the early 1900s there were many more: notably the Pennsylvania anthracite coal properties, the Rockville bridge route, Baltimore Union Station, Enola Yard, and Northumberland Yard.

More importantly, the traffic flows of the two railroads had become intimately intertwined. By the 1912-1913 period approximately 85 percent of the Northern Central's freight traffic was handled in connection with the Pennsylvania. For the PRR the Northern Central lines were key links in reaching many major traffic generating areas: Baltimore, Washington, the South, upstate New York, the western portion of the anthracite region, and northwestern Pennsylvania. Similarly, the Pennsylvania had provided the Northern Central penetration of a vast array of markets in the east and midwest.

Equipment policies had become common for the two companies, too. Beginning as early as 1875 the PRR's famous Altoona (Pennsylvania) Machine Shops built a large number of the Northern Central's locomotives following the standardized PRR designs. Although the Northern Central ceased to be a separate operating company, the lease proved to be a major benefit to the company as well as to the Pennsylvania. For one, the Northern Central lines needed further upgrading, which the NC was increasingly less able to afford on its own. Heavy traffic demanded heavier rail and new handling facilities, particularly at major terminals. Equipment had to be replaced. By 1910 steel passenger cars and freight equipment (particularly coal cars) were becoming standard in the railroad industry; not only was it necessary to replace the old wood cars, but heavier and more powerful locomotives were needed to haul the new equipment. In 1911 the Northern Central estimated its immediate rehabilitation cost at over $3 million, a sum it felt it could not afford. The cash-heavy Pennsylvania was able to provide the large amounts of capital needed, and after the lease the improvements were started. Ironically, renovations and improvements of this type were exactly what the stockholders' committee had proposed in 1874 when President J. Donald Cameron resigned in disgust.

Following the lease the Pennsylvania moved to integrate the Northern Central system more closely with its own. All former Northern Central lines and branches became PRR operating divisions in 1914. The Pennsylvania also assumed the Northern Central's leases of such lines as the Elmira & Williamsport, the Elmira & Lake Ontario, the Lykens Valley Railroad & Coal Company, and the Shamokin Valley & Pottsville. Further corporate streamlining took place during World War I. On January 1, 1918 the Pennsylvania leased the Philadelphia, Baltimore and Washington Railroad, a previous consolidation of the old Baltimore & Potomac and the Philadelphia, Wilmington & Baltimore, for 999 years. Effective April 1, 1918 it also leased the Union Railroad for 999 years, putting all PRR operations in the Baltimore area under a single corporate umbrella.

Physically, and from a traffic viewpoint, the early PRR years probably marked the Northern Central's high point. Even then, however, clouds were beginning to build. In 1913 Henry Ford's mass-produced and affordable automobile entered the market. And, more worrisome, the railroad's primary support — coal — began showing signs of weakness. In 1911 coal business for both the Northern Central and Pennsylvania Railroad again had dropped sharply. By 1912 the Susquehanna Coal Company could not pay the sublet on the Shamokin Valley & Pottsville coal properties, and by 1916 the coal market had become so depressed that the Susquehanna Coal Company discontinued mining and selling coal. (The 1917 divestiture order forced the Pennsylvania to dispose of its coal properties anyway; the company received $9.3 million in five percent bonds for them.) The annual reports from 1914 to 1920 for the Northern Central and the Pennsylvania Railroads note a yearly decline in anthracite traffic to Baltimore and the increased use and traffic in petroleum products. However, two wars and a strong demand for anthracite at Sodus Point helped prolong the railroad's anthracite traffic, and continued to help support the towns whose existence depended on high volume rail traffic. Bituminous traffic from other Pennsylvania Railroad points also continued to be relatively healthy.

The PRR completed this picturesque coal loading pier at Canton in 1917 to replace earlier NC facilities. Hopper cars were unloaded by a rotary car dumper; the coal dropped by gravity into the tiny cars which may be seen on top of the trestle. These cars operated back and forth on the trestle powered by a continuous cable, and dumped their contents into the movable coal loading chute at the right center of the photograph. H. H. Harwood, Jr. photograph.

With the automobile still only a speck on the horizon, passenger services on the former Northern Central lines reached an all-time peak. Although some short-haul local trains already had been eliminated, in 1916 the Pennsylvania Railroad scheduled 34 passenger trains each way in and out of Baltimore over the Northern Central lines: eight Harrisburg expresses, five Harrisburg or York locals, four Parkton locals, seven Cockeysville locals, eight Green Spring Branch trains, and nine Sparrows Point runs. (Residents of such close-in suburban points as Lutherville had roughly an hourly train service during weekdays.) Nine trains each way operated over various sections of the Columbia-Wrightsville-York-Frederick branch, including three Keymar-Frederick connecting services. North of Harrisburg, nine passenger trains ran each way between Harrisburg and Sunbury, three between Williamsport and Elmira, four between Elmira and Canandaigua, and two on the branch from Stanley, New York to Sodus Point. The anthracite branches were served by four Sunbury-Shamokin/Mt. Carmel round trips, and an equal number operating between Millersburg and Lykens.

Not only was the basic passenger service extensive, but parlor cars, sleepers, and dining cars were available on all but the branch lines, often in an impressive variety. Separate sleeping cars, for example, were operated between Washington/Baltimore and Chicago, Pittsburgh, Detroit, Harrisburg, Cleveland, Cincinnati, St. Louis, Buffalo, Williamsport, Oil City, Canandaigua, and Rochester (the last was routed via Canandaigua). In addition sleepers between Philadelphia and Williamsport, Philadelphia and Rochester, and Pittsburgh and Wilkes-Barre were routed over Northern Central lines for portions of their runs. Daytime parlor car services followed similar patterns.

The Northern Central was barely under the Pennsylvania's wing, and its modernization program had just begun, when World War I put an enormous load on the system. Moving equipment, troops, and supplies south into Baltimore required trains only minutes apart. Residents along the line complained that the traffic kept them up at night. Overuse began wearing out the track. In 1917 both the Northern Central and Pennsylvania reported that the increase in traffic had "seriously impaired operating efficiency." The most critical problems occurred at the ports. Thousands of freight cars sat immobilized waiting for cargo to be unloaded for passage to Europe. The port facility at Baltimore did a record business. By 1917 the situation was so acute that the newly formed United States Railroad Administration took over operations of the nation's railroads. In order to guarantee delivery of war material and manpower, the railroad agency severely restricted civilian passenger access to rail transport. The agency developed a system of priorities for critically needed shipments, and rushed those trains into port. It restricted the railroads' use of steel, which delayed the construction of new equipment and roadbed.

Property and Equipment Improvements

Shortly after the lease a Pennsylvania Railroad-financed improvement and modernization program began that was unprecedented for the Northern Central line. Although interrupted by the war it resumed immediately afterwards and produced a property that was equal to the best of the Pennsylvania's high standards.

In 1920 the government returned the railroads to their private owners and began compensating them for wartime usage. That compensation, some $50 million, allowed the Pennsylvania to make improvements in the Northern Central division it would not have normally made. That year the new 130-pound rail became the standard for renewal work and many sections of the Northern Central received the new rail.

Some new stations were built, usually rather austere structures which followed standardized Pennsylvania Railroad designs of the period. (By this time not only had the elaborate Victorian styles passed from fashion, but the railroads were more concerned with functionalism than ostentation.) In most cases the new stations combined both freight and passenger facilities, were more efficiently designed, and less expensive to maintain. The towns of Marsh Hill, Southport, Benton, Trout Run, and Columbia Crossroads all received the familiar Pennsylvania-type small town depot. Gone forever were the individualistic architectural styles of such elegant structures as the Ruxton, Riderwood, Parkton, and Millersburg stations.

Unhappily, the program also spelled the beginning of the end for the unique pagoda-style towers. Improvements in signaling and communications, and changes in traffic patterns and operations, eliminated the need for many of these facilities as well as the people who operated them. Once the characteristic mark of the Northern Central's pride in its main line, they gradually fell victim to more modern structures or were simply closed. At the more important points, such as York and Cly, Pennsylvania, they were replaced with contemporary rectangular brick towers of no distinction. Although both were closed in the 1980s, the York and Cly towers stand today as examples of the functional modernization conducted throughout the system.

Direct Pennsylvania Railroad management brought another significant (and, ultimately, fatal) change to the Northern Central's Baltimore-Harrisburg line. As described in Chapter 9, in 1906 the Pennsylvania Railroad completed its new low-grade "Port Road" line, which connected Harrisburg and Enola Yard with Baltimore and Washington via Perryville, Maryland. Although this route was longer in mileage, it had far milder grades and less curves than the NC route. The result was that most heavy freight trains between Enola/Harrisburg and Baltimore/Washington were rerouted to the low-grade route. This process began in the early 1920s and was a gradual one, but it marked the beginning of the end for this section of the railroad. By 1930 the Baltimore-Harrisburg main line was handling primarily passenger trains, local freights, and freight traffic to and from York. While this type of business remained heavy in the earlier years, it diminished quite rapidly later; as it did, so did the railroad. More immediately, however, the reduction in freight traffic volume began to affect railroad employment along the line, which

830

PENNSYLVANIA SYSTEM

The Route of the Broadway Limited

Eastern Standard time.

Table 90—BALTIMORE DIVISION.—Trains between Baltimore and Harrisburg. **Eastern Region**

January, 1922.	Ms.	541	991	971	8021	527	505	8033	8005	993	529	8007	8036	8009	553	995	975	507	8037	979	8041	503	535	8039
[LEAVE	...	.....	A M	A M	A M	A M	A M	A M	P M	P M	P M	P M	.....	P M	P M	P M	P M	P M	P M	P M	P M	P M	P M	P M
Washington..	...	.....	†5 10	*7 45	*9 00	*1050	*1145	*1145	†1 05	*1 55	*3 30	†3 03	.....	†4 30	*4 50	†5 00	*6 20	*6 50	*7.00	*7 25	*7 30	*9 40	*1030	*1030
Baltimore.lve.	...	.....	A M	.....	A M	.....	.....	P M	P M	P M	.....	P M	P M	P M	.....	P M	.....	.....	P M	.....	P M	.....	.....	P M
Calvert Sta..	0	A M	*7 20	A M	*1030	Noon	P M	*1 30	†2 30	*3 00	P M	†4 30	†5 15	†5 30	P M	*6 15	P M	P M	*7 55	P M	*1020	P M	P M	*1135
Union Sta...	1.0	*4 05	7 25	*8 55	10 34	*1200	*1 00	1 34	2 34	3 04	*4 27	4 34	5 20	5 34	*5 53	6 19	*7 26	*7 53	7 59	*8 30	10 25	*1055	*1132	11 40
Woodberry	3.3	4 11	7 33	— —	10 40	— —	— —	1 40	2 40	3 10	— —	4 40	— —	5 40	— —	6 27	— —	— —	8 05	— —	10 30	— —	— —	11 45
Melvale........	4.3	4 13	7 36	— —	10 42	— —	— —	1 42	2 42	3 13	— —	4 42	— —	5 43	— —	6 29	— —	— —	8 08	— —	10 32	— —	— —	11 47
Mt. Washington	6.0	4 16	7 41	— —	10 46	— —	— —	1 46	2 46	3 17	Sleeping Car. Broiler-Buffet Parlor Car.	4 46	5 29	5 46	— —	6 33	— —	— —	8 11	— —	10 34	— —	— —	11 51
Hollins+ ...♁	7.1	4 19	7 45	— —	10 50	— —	— —	1 49	2 49	3 20		4 49	— —	5 49	— —	6 36	— —	— —	8 14	— —	10 36	— —	— —	11 54
Brightside	7.4	— —	7 46	— —	10 52	Parlor Car. Dining Car.	— —	1 50	2 51	3 21		4 50	— —	5 50	— —	6 37	— —	— —	8 15	— —	— —	— —	— —	11 55
Lake	7.8	— —	7 48	— —	10 53		— —	1 51	2 52	3 22		4 51	5 33	5 51	— —	6 38	— —	— —	8 16	— —	10 38	— —	— —	11 56
Ruxton+	8.4	4 22	7 50	— —	10 55		— —	1 53	2 54	3 24		4 53	5 34	5 53	— —	6 40	Sleeping Car. Parlor Car. Dining Car.	Sleeping Car. Dining Car. No Coaches.	8 18	— —	10 40	— —	— —	11 58
Riderwood+...	9.2	4 24	7 52	— —	10 57		— —	1 55	2 55	3 27		4 55	5 36	5 55	— —	6 42			8 20	— —	10 42	— —	— —	12 00
Lutherville+ ..	10.5	4 27	7 55	— —	11 01		— —	1 59	3 00	3 30		4 59	5 39	5 59	— —	6 45			8 24	— —	10 46	— —	— —	12 04
Timonium	11.7	4 30	7 58	Parlor Car. Dining Car.	11 04		Sleeping Car. Dining Car.	2 02	3 04	3 33		5 03	5 42	6 02	Sleeping Car. Dining Car.	6 48			8 27	— —	10 49	— —	— —	12 07
Texas+	13.5	4 34	8 02		11 10			2 06	3 10	3 37		5 09	5 47	6 06		6 52			8 31	— —	10 53	— —	— —	12 11
Cockeysville+♁	14.9	4 37	8 08		11 15			2 10	3 14	3 42		5 13	5 50	6 10		6 56			8 36	— —	10 56	— —	— —	12 15
Ashland+	15.8	4 39	8 10		11 17			2 12	P M	3 44		P M	5 52	P M		6 58			8 37	— —	10 59	— —	— —	12 17
Phœnix+.......	17.7	4 43	8 15		11 22			2 17	.....	3 49		.....	5 57	.....		7 02			8 41	Sleeping Car.	11 04	— —	Sleeping Car.	12 21
Sparks+.......	19.6	4 47	8 19		11 27			2 22	.....	3 53		.....	6 02	.....		7 07			8 45		11 09	— —		12 25
Glencoe+.......	20.5	4 49	8 21		11 29			2 24	.....	3 56		.....	6 06	.....		7 09			8 47		11 11	— —		12 27
Corbett	22.3	4 53	8 26		11 34			2 29	.....	4 00		.....	6 11	.....		7 14			8 51		11 16	— —		12 31
Monkton+	23.0	4 55	8 28		11 37	— —		2 31	.....	4 03		.....	6 14	+ Coupon stations; ♁ Telegraph stations. STANDARD—*Eastern time.*		7 16			8 52		11 18	— —		12 32
Blue Mount....	25.0	4 59	8 33		11 41	— —		2 35	.....	4 08		.....	6 19			7 20			8 56		11 22	— —		12 36
White Hall+ ..	26.5	5 02	8 37		11 47	— —		2 39	.....	4 12		.....	6 24			7 23			8 59		11 25	— —		12 39
Parkton+ ...♁	28.8	5 07	8 42		11 55	12 47		2 45	.....	4 18		.....	6 30			7 30			9 05		11 30	11 41		12 45
Walker	30.1	5 10	8 45		11 58	— —		P M	.....	4 21		.....	P M			7 33			P M	— —	P M	— —	— —	A M
Bentley Spgs.+	31.5	5 14	8 48	— —	12 02	— —	— —	.....	.....	4 25	— —	.....	.....		— —	7 36	— —		.....	— —	.....	11 46	— —	.....
Freeland+.....	34.3	5 22	8 55	— —	12 09	— —	— —	.....	.....	4 31	— —	.....	.....		— —	7 42	— —		.....	— —	.....	11 52	— —	.....
New Freedom +.♁	37.1	5 31	9 05	— —	12 17	1 05	— —	.....	.....	4 40	5 28	.....	.....		— —	7 48	— —		.....	— —	.....	12 00	— —	**For Index of Stations, see pages 289-295.**
Shrewsbury+..	38.6	5 34	9 08	— —	12 20	— —	— —	.....	.....	4 43	— —	.....	.....		— —	7 51	— —		.....	— —	.....	12 03	— —	
Seitzland+	41.0	5 40	9 14	— —	12 24	— —	— —	.....	.....	4 47	— —	.....	.....		— —	7 56	— —		.....	— —	.....	— —	— —	
Glenrock+ ..♁	41.8	5 42	9 18	— —	12 26	— —	— —	.....	.....	4 50	— —	.....	.....		— —	7 59	— —	— —	.....	— —	.....	12 10	— —	
Hanover Jn+ .♁	46.3	5 53	9 27	— —	12 35	— —	— —	.....	.....	4 58	— —	.....	.....		— —	8 07	— —	— —	.....	— —	.....	— —	— —	
Smyser+	47.1	5 56	9 29	— —	12 38	— —	— —	.....	.....	5 01	— —	.....	.....		— —	8 10	— —	— —	.....	— —	.....	— —	— —	
Glatfelter+.....	49.0	6 01	9 32	— —	12 43	— —	— —	.....	.....	5 05	— —	.....	.....		— —	8 14	— —	— —	.....	— —	.....	— —	— —	
Brilhart+......	52.4	6 07	9 38	— —	12 49	— —	— —	8023	.....	5 11	— —	.....	.....		— —	8 20	— —	— —	.....	— —	.....	— —	— —	
Grantley.......	55.7	6 14	9 44	— —	12 55	— —	— —	A M	.....	5 17	— —	.....	.....		— —	8 25	— —	— —	.....	— —	.....	— —	— —	
York+ ......♁	57.2	6 28	9 57	10 35	1 00	1 40	2 38	†8 00	.....	5 31	6 05	.....	.....		7 26	8 37	9 05	9 30	.....	10 06	.....	12 40	1 06	
Emigsville+...	61.6	6 37	10 07	— —	P M	— —	— —	8 09	.....	5 39	— —	.....	.....		— —	8 45	— —	— —	.....	— —	.....	— —	— —	
Mount Wolf+..	65.0	6 44	10 14	— —	.....	1 53	— —	8 15	.....	5 45	— —	.....	.....		— —	8 51	— —	— —	.....	— —	.....	12 53	— —	
York Haven+..	68.5	6 50	10 22	— —	.....	2 00	2 55	8 21	.....	5 52	— —	.....	.....		— —	8 57	— —	— —	.....	— —	.....	1 01	— —	
Goldsboro+ .♁	72.4	6 58	10 31	— —	.....	2 08	3 03	8 29	.....	6 00	— —	.....	.....		— —	9 05	— —	— —	.....	— —	.....	1 10	— —	
New Cumberland+.	81.2	7 20	10 49	— —	.....	2 25	— —	8 41	.....	6 18	— —	.....	.....	.....	— —	9 21	— —	— —	.....	— —	.....	— —	— —	.....
Harrisburg+..♁	84.3	7 30	11 00	11 15	.....	2 35	3 22	8 50	.....	6 28	6 45	.....	.....	.....	8 05	9 30	9 45	10 10	.....	10 47	.....	1 30	1 45	.....
[ARRIVE	....	A M	A M	A M	.....	P M	P M	A M	.....	P M	P M	.....	.....	.....	P M	P M	P M	P M	.....	P M	.....	A M	A M	.....

STATIONS.	8030	50	990	574	8034	976	992	8024	530	8036	500	502	8006	8038	8008	544	994	970	8010	524	8040	998	518	996	8130	8132
[LEAVE	.....	A M	A M	A M	....	A M	A M	A M	A M	.....	P M	P M	.....	.....	.....	P M	P M	P M	....	P M	.....	P M	P M	A M	.....	.....
Harrisburg ...	.....	*4 40	*4 50	*5 25	....	*6 55	†7 55	†9 20	*9 50	.....	†12 01	*1 00	.....	.....	.....	*3 50	*4 10	*5 30	....	*7 00	.....	*8 20	*11 54	§7 30	.....	.....
New Cumberland...	.....	— —	4 59	— —	....	— —	8 04	9 29	— —	.....	12 10	— —	.....	.....	.....	— —	4 19	— —	....	— —	.....	8 29	12 03	7 39	.....	.....
Goldsboro......	.....	— —	5 14	— —	....	7 13	8 19	9 46	*s* —	.....	12 27	*s* —	.....	.....	.....	— —	4 34	— —	....	— —	.....	8 45	12 20	7 57	.....	.....
York Haven ...	.....	— —	5 21	— —	....	*t*7 19	8 28	9 53	— —	.....	12 34	— —	.....	.....	.....	— —	4 43	— —	....	— —	.....	8 53	12 28	8 04	.....	.....
Mount Wolf ...	.....	— —	5 28	— —	....	— —	8 36	10 00	— —	.....	12 41	— —	.....	.....	.....	— —	4 51	— —	....	— —	.....	9 01	12 36	8 11	.....	.....
Emigsville	.....	— —	5 34	— —	....	— —	8 42	10 06	— —	.....	12 47	— —	.....	.....	.....	— —	4 57	— —	....	— —	.....	9 07	12 43	8 17	.....	.....
York	.....	5 25	5 47	6 15	....	7 43	8 58	10 15	10 35	.....	1 02	1 45	.....	.....	.....	4 35	5 13	6 13	....	7 43	.....	9 22	12 57	8 32	.....	.....
Grantley.......	.....	— —	5 52	— —	....	— —	9 04	A M	— —	.....	1 08	— —	.....	.....	.....	— —	5 19	— —	....	— —	.....	9 28	1 03	8 38	.....	.....
Brilhart.......	.....	— —	5 57	— —	....	— —	9 11	....	— —	.....	1 15	— —	.....	.....	.....	— —	5 25	— —	....	— —	.....	9 32	1 09	8 44	.....	.....
Glatfelter......	.....	— —	6 03	— —	....	— —	9 17	....	— —	.....	1 21	— —	.....	.....	.....	— —	5 31	— —	....	— —	.....	9 38	1 16	8 50	.....	.....
Smyser	.....	— —	6 06	— —	....	— —	9 21	....	— —	.....	1 25	— —	.....	.....	.....	— —	5 35	— —	....	— —	.....	9 42	1 20	8 53	.....	.....
Hanover Jn...	.....	— —	6 09	— —	....	— —	9 23	....	— —	.....	1 28	— —	.....	.....	.....	— —	5 38	— —	....	— —	.....	9 45	1 23	8 56	.....	.....
Glenrock	.....	— —	6 16	— —	....	— —	9 32	....	— —	.....	1 36	— —	.....	.....	.....	5 01	5 48	— —	....	— —	.....	9 53	1 32	9 04	.....	.....
Seitzland	.....	— —	6 18	— —	....	— —	9 34	....	— —	.....	1 38	Sleeping Car. Parlor Car. Dining Car.	.....	.....	.....	— —	5 50	— —	....	— —	.....	9 56	1 34	9 06	.....	.....
Shrewsbury....	.....	— —	6 24	— —	....	— —	9 40	....	— —	.....	1 44		.....	.....	.....	— —	5 56	— —	....	— —	.....	10 01	1 40	9 12	.....	.....
New Freedom	.....	— —	6 28	— —	....	8 17	9 46	....	*s* —	.....	1 48		.....	.....	.....	5 11	6 00	— —	....	— —	.....	10 05	1 45	9 17	.....	.....
Freeland.......	.....	— —	6 34	Sleeping Car. Dining Car.	....	— —	9 52	....	— —	.....	1 55		.....	.....	.....	— —	6 06	— —	....	— —	.....	10 11	— —	9 23	.....	.....
BentleySprings.	.....	— —	6 39		....	— —	9 59	....	Sleeping Car. Broiler-Buffet Parlor Car.	.....	2 00		.....	.....	.....	— —	6 12	Parlor Car. Dining Car.	....	— —	.....	10 16	— —	9 29	.....	.....
Walker	A M	— —	6 41		A M	Sleeping Car. Parlor Car. Dining Car.	10 01	....		Noon	2 03		.....	P M	.....	— —	6 14		....	— —	P M	10 18	— —	9 32	P M	P M
Parkton........	†5 30	— —	6 46		*7 32		10 07	....		†12 00	2 07		.....	†4 00	.....	— —	6 20		....	— —	*9 20	10 22	— —	9 35	§2 03	§7 20
White Hall	5 33	Sleeping Car.	6 51		7 35		10 12	....		12 05	2 12		.....	4 05	.....	— —	6 25		....	Parlor Car.	9 25	10 28	— —	9 40	2 07	7 25
Blue Mount....	5 36		6 54		7 38		10 16	....		12 08	2 15		.....	4 08	.....	— —	6 28		....		9 28	10 31	— —	9 43	2 10	7 28
Monkton.......	5 41		6 58		7 43		10 21	....		12 12	2 19		.....	4 12	.....	— —	6 32		....		9 32	10 35	— —	9 47	2 14	7 32
Corbett	5 43		7 00		7 45		10 23	....		12 14	2 21		.....	4 14	.....	— —	6 34		....		9 34	10 37	— —	9 49	2 16	7 34
Glencoe........	5 47		7 04		7 49		10 28	....		12 19	2 25		.....	4 19	.....	— —	6 39		....		9 39	10 41	— —	9 53	2 21	7 38
Sparks.........	5 49		7 06		7 51		10 30	....		12 21	2 27		.....	4 21	.....	Parlor Car.	6 41		....		9 41	10 43	— —	9 55	2 23	7 41
Phœnix........	5 53		7 10		7 55		10 35	8002		12 25	2 31		.....	4 25	.....		6 46		....		9 45	10 47	— —	9 59	2 28	7 45
Ashland	5 57		7 13		7 59		10 39	A M		12 29	2 36		P M	4 29	P M		6 50		P M	— —	9 49	10 51	— —	10 03	2 33	7 48
Cockeysville ...	6 00	— —	7 18		8 02		10 45	†9 00		12 32	2 38		†3 50	4 32	†5 23		6 56		†7 27	— —	9 52	10 53	— —	10 05	2 35	7 54
Texas..........	6 03	— —	7 23		8 05		10 49	9 03		12 35	2 41		3 53	4 35	5 26		6 59		7 30	— —	9 55	10 56	— —	10 08	2 38	7 58
Timonium	6 08	— —	7 29		8 10		10 54	9 07		12 40	2 46		3 58	4 40	5 31		7 04		7 34	— —	10 00	11 01	— —	10 13	2 43	8 05
Lutherville	6 11	— —	7 32	— —	8 12		10 57	9 10		12 43	2 49		4 01	4 43	5 34	— —	7 07	— —	7 37	— —	10 03	11 04	— —	10 16	2 46	8 07
Riderwood.....	6 15	— —	7 35	— —	8 15		11 01	9 12		12 46	2 52		4 04	4 46	5 37	— —	7 10	— —	7 40	— —	10 06	11 07	— —	10 19	2 49	8 10
Ruxton	6 17	— —	7 37	— —	8 17		11 03	9 14		12 48	2 54		4 06	4 48	5 39	— —	7 12	— —	7 42	— —	10 08	11 09	— —	10 21	2 51	8 12
Lake...........	6 19	— —	7 39	— —	8 19		11 05	9 16		12 50	2 56	— —	4 08	4 50	5 41	— —	7 14	— —	7 44	— —	10 10	11 11	— —	10 23	2 53	8 14
Brightside	6 20	— —	7 41	— —	8 20		11 06	9 17		12 51	2 57	— —	4 09	4 51	5 42	— —	7 16	— —	7 45	— —	10 11	11 12	— —	10 24	2 54	8 15
Hollins	6 22	— —	7 43	— —	8 22		11 07	9 19		12 53	2 58	— —	4 10	4 53	5 43	— —	7 18	—	7 46	— —	10 13	11 14	— —	10 25	2 55	8 17
Mt. Washington	6 25	— —	7 47	— —	8 26		11 10	9 22		12 57	3 02	— —	4 13	4 57	5 47	— —	7 21	— —	7 49	— —	10 17	11 18	— —	10 28	2 58	8 22
Melvale........	6 30	— —	7 51	— —	8 30		11 15	9 27		1 02	3 06	— —	4 17	5 02	5 51	— —	7 25	— —	7 52	— —	10 22	11 22	— —	10 32	3 02	8 27
Woodberry	6 33	— —	7 54	— —	8 33	— —	11 18	9 30	— —	1 05	3 10	— —	4 20	5 05	5 54	— —	7 28	— —	7 55	— —	10 25	11 25	— —	10 35	3 05	8 30
Union Sta ...	6 40	7 00	8 00	8 05	8 40	9 15	11 26	9 36	12 10	1 11	3 16	3 20	4 26	5 11	6 00	6 10	7 36	7 45	8 00	9 15	10 31	11 30	2 45	10 41	3 11	8 36
Calvert Sta..	6 45	.....	8 05	.....	8 45	....	11 30	9 40	.....	1 15	3 20	....	4 30	5 15	6 05	.....	7 40	.....	8 05	....	10 35	P M	A M	10 45	3 15	8 40
Baltimore.arr.	A M	A M	A M	A M	A M	A M	A M	A M	P M	P M	P M	P M	P M	P M	P M	P M	P M	P M	P M	P M	P M	.....	.....	A M	P M	P M
Washington..	8 05	8 05	9 10	9 10	10 20	10 20	1 15	10 40	1 15	3 25	4 20	4 20	....	6 25	7 15	7 15	8 45	8 50	9 10	10 13	....	1 10	.....	.....	4 20	.....
[ARRIVE	A M	A M	A M	A M	A M	A M	P M	A M	P M	P M	P M	P M	....	P M	P M	P M	P M	P M	P M	P M	....	A M	.....	.....	P M	.....

Additional Trains—Leave Baltimore for Cockeysville †6 00, §9 00 a.m., §12 30 p.m. Returning, leave Cockeysville §12 25, §4 35 p.m.

* Daily; † daily, except Sunday; § Sunday only; *s* stops Sunday only; *t* does not stop Sunday.

Table 91—Sparrow's Point Branch.—Leave Baltimore, Union Station, for Biddle Street (1.5 miles), Orangeville (3.0 miles), Highlandtown (3.9 miles), Fifth Avenue (5.0 miles), Colgate Creek (6.0 miles) (B. & S. P. R.R.), Sutton (6.3 miles), St. Helena (6.8 miles), Dundalk (7.5 miles), Turner (8.6 miles), Sollers (9.2 miles), Chesapeake Mills (10.4 miles) and Sparrow's Point (10.9 miles) *6 00, †7 20, †8 10, §8 20, *10 50 a.m., §1 30, †2 00, †4 05, *5 05, §7 55, §10 05, †11 10 p.m. Returning, leave Sparrow's Point *7 12, †8 08, §9 25, †9 45 a.m., *1 00, *3 45, †5 15, †6 08, §6 15, §8 45, §10 45, †11 59 p.m. Running time, about 30 minutes.

September 25, 1921.

Northern Central passenger train services in January, 1922.

PENNSYLVANIA SYSTEM

The Route of the Broadway Limited

Table 155—WILLIAMSPORT AND ELMIRA DIVISIONS.—For Through Car Service, see pages 351 and 352. **Eastern Region**

561	575	631	571	541	37-557	503-8403	579-8409	501-8401	515-8405	35-577	Mls.	*October* 24, 1921. Eastern time.	500	8412-578	8418-568	8414-570	580	8420-574	8402-578	506	576	630	560	554	562
A M	P M	P M	....	A M	P M	P M	P M	A M	.....	P M	.....		P M	P M	A M	P M	A M	A M	P M	A M	Noon	P M	A M	P M	A M
2 00	5 00	2 00	....	2 00	11 30	9 00	6 00	10 05	.....	8 40	.....	lve... **New York**...arr.	6 00	8 20	4 55	10 10	9 30	10 00	8 20	6 20	12 00	2 00	2 30	5 55	12 10
....	5 00	2 00	A M	....	11 30	9 00	6 00	10 00	A M	8 40	.....	..**Pennsylvania Station**..	6 00	8 20	....	10 10	9 35	10 00	8 20	6 20	12 00	2 00	.....	5 55	12 23
												Hud. Ter.(H.& M.R.R.)													
5 15	7 30	a4 50	8 20	5 15	.....	11 45	8 10	12 25	8 20	11 10	.....	lve..**Philadelphia**..arr.	2 45	6 50	2 15	7 56	7 48	7 48	6 25	4 25	9 22	12 02	11 55	a3 54	9 36
....	c7 35	c4 55	c8 25	....	.....	c11 50	c8 16	c12 30	c8 25	c11 15	.....	lve.. **West Phila**...arr.	d2 40	d6 45	d2 10	d7 50	d7 43	d7 43	d6 20	d4 20	d9 17	d11 57	d11 60	.....	d9 30
....	6 20	3 30	7 45	....	.....	10 30	7 25	11 45	7 45	10 30	.....	lve.. **Washington**..arr.	4 20	7 15	.....	8 50	9 10	9 10	7 15	.....	10 20	1 15	1 10	4 20	10 15
4 05	7 25	4 27	8 55	4 05	.....	11 32	8 30	1 00	8 55	11 32	.....	lve...**Baltimore**....arr.	3 16	6 10	2 45	7 45	8 05	8 05	6 10	.....	9 15	12 10	11 30	3 20	8 15
A M	P M	P M	A M	A M	*A M	A M	P M	P M	A M	A M	.....	LEAVE] [ARRIVE	A M	P M	P M	P M	A M	A M	P M	A M	A M	A M	P M	A M	P M
												Williamsport Division													
§8 10	*10 25	*7 40	*11 35	†7 50	§4 25	*3 29	*11 02	*3 40	†11 45	*2 45	0	+... **Harrisburg**.. ♁	11 45	3 20	10 45	5 18	4 40	5 00	3 20	1 35	6 30	9 15	7 10	11 45	6 50
8 15	– –	– –	– –	7 55	– –	– –	– –	– –	11 50	– –	1.5	....Maclay Street....	11 40	– –	10 39	– –	– –	– –	– –	– –	– –	– –	7 04	11 40	6 44
8 22	– –	– –	– –	8 02	– –	– –	– –	3 52	11 57	– –	5.3	+.....Rockville...♁	11 33	– –	10 30	– –	– –	– –	– –	– –	– –	– –	– –	11 30	– –
8 27	– –	7 56	– –	8 07	– –	3 45	11 20	3 56	12 02	– –	8.0	+......**Dauphin**....♁	11 28	3 04	10 22	– –	– –	– –	3 04	– –	6 12	– –	6 51	11 24	6 31
8 33	– –	– –	– –	8 15	– –	– –	– –	4 03	– –	– –	11.9	.......Speeceville......	11 20	– –	10 15	– –	– –	– –	– –	– –	– –	– –	6 42	11 14	6 23
8 38	– –	– –	– –	8 19	– –	– –	– –	4 08	12 11	– –	14.2	+...Clark's Ferry..♁	11 15	– –	10 10	– –	– –	– –	– –	– –	– –	– –	6 37	11 08	6 17
8 41	– –	– –	– –	8 22	– –	– –	– –	4 12	12 14	– –	16.1	.......Inglenook......	11 11	– –	10 05	– –	– –	– –	– –	– –	– –	– –	6 33	11 04	6 14
8 52	– –	8 16	– –	8 32	– –	– –	11 40	4 21	12 22	– –	21.2	+......Halifax....♁	11 02	2 44	9 57	– –	– –	– –	2 44	1 01	– –	– –	6 23	10 55	6 06
8 58	– –	– –	– –	8 38	– –	– –	– –	4 27	– –	– –	24.8	......McClellan......	10 55	– –	9 49	– –	– –	– –	– –	– –	– –	– –	6 16	10 48	6 00
9 03	– –	8 26	s12 13	8 43	g5 03	4 15	11 50	4 33	12 32	– –	27.0	+... **Millersburg**. ♁	10 50	2 35	9 44	– –	– –	– –	2 35	12 52	b5 38	8 31	6 11	10 44	5 55
9 07	– –	– –	– –	8 48	– –	– –	– –	4 38	12 36	– –	29.3	.........Liverpool......	10 45	– –	9 39	– –	– –	– –	– –	– –	– –	o8 29	6 04	10 40	5 49
9 15	– –	– –	– –	8 54	– –	– –	– –	4 44	– –	– –	32.0	.....Mahantongo......	10 40	– –	9 33	– –	– –	– –	– –	– –	– –	– –	5 59	10 35	5 45
9 22	– –	8 42	– –	9 02	– –	4 30	12 07	4 54	12 49	– –	37.0	+.......Dalmatia....♁	10 31	2 20	9 24	– –	– –	– –	2 20	12 37	– –	m –	5 49	10 24	5 36
9 31	– –	8 50	– –	9 11	– –	4 40	12 16	5 03	12 58	– –	41.9	+......**Herndon**....♁	10 21	2 12	9 16	– –	– –	– –	2 12	12 30	– –	8 12	5 39	10 14	5 27
9 39	– –	– –	– –	9 19	– –	– –	– –	5 12	– –	– –	46.0	.......Fisher's Ferry......	10 12	– –	9 08	– –	– –	– –	– –	– –	– –	– –	5 31	10 05	5 20
9 46	– –	– –	– –	9 25	– –	– –	– –	5 18	1 07	– –	48.5	+ **Selinsgrove Jn**.♁	10 07	– –	9 03	– –	– –	– –	– –	– –	– –	– –	5 26	10 00	5 15
9 56	11 42	9 08	12 47	9 35	g5 37	4 58	12 36	5 27	1 15	4 04	53.4	arr.+ **Sunbury** ♁.lve.	†9 57	†1 54	*8 55	*4 08	*3 16	*3 36	§1 54	*12 11	*4 55	†7 54	†5 15	§9 50	§5 04
10 01	11 47	9 12	12 52	9 43	g5 47	5 10	12 41	5 37	1 20	4 14	53.4	lve.... **Sunbury** ♁.arr.	9 46	1 47	8 45	4 08	3 08	3 31	1 47	12 07	4 55	7 54	5 06	9 45	5 04
10 29	12 06	9 38	e1 10	10 20	g6 18	5 47	1 06	6 13	1 49	4 40	65.9	...........**Milton**.......	9 08	1 21	8 18	z3 45	2 40	z3 07	1 21	11 37	h4 30	7 28	4 33	9 18	4 30
11 25	12 50	10 30	1 51	11 25	g7 10	‖6 56	2 00	‖7 10	‖2 43	5 28	93.1	ar.+**Williamsport** ♁lv.	†8 10	†12 35	*7 25	*3 05	*1 47	*2 25	§12 35	*10 45	*3 48	†6 40	†3 35	§8 30	§3 37
A M	A M	P M	P M	A M																P M	A M	A M	A M	P M	A M	P M

37-557	503-8403	579-8409	501-8401	515-8405	35-577	Mls.	Station	500	8412-578	8418-568	8414-570	580	8420-574	8402-578
7 25	7 25	2 15	7 22	†3 05	A M	93.1	lve....**Williamsport**.arr.	A M	12 27	7 10	†10 10	A M	1 56	12 20
7 40	7 40	– –	7 35	– –	.....	98.9	.....Hepburnville....	....	– –	6 54	9 57	....	– –	12 03
7 45	7 45	– –	7 39	3 19	.....	100.3	+...Cogan Valley....	....	– –	6 50	9 54	....	– –	11 59
7 47	7 47	– –	7 42	– –	.....	101.3	........Haleeka.......	....	– –	6 46	9 50	....	– –	11 56
7 51	7 51	– –	7 45	– –	.....	103.0	..........Powys.......	....	– –	6 43	9 46	....	– –	11 53
7 59	7 59	– –	7 53	3 32	.....	106.3	+.....Trout Run...♁	....	12 00	6 36	9 38	....	1 26	11 47
8 06	8 06	– –	8 00	– –	.....	110.2	............Field.......	....	– –	6 27	9 29	....	– –	11 38
8 11	8 11	– –	8 04	3 42	.....	112.1	+.........Bodine....♁	....	– –	6 23	9 24	....	v1 14	11 33
8 18	8 18	– –	8 10	3 48	.....	113.9	.:**Marsh Hill Junc**.	....	– –	6 18	9 19	....	– –	11 29
8 26	8 26	3 04	8 18	3 56	.....	116.8	+.........Ralston....♁	....	11 43	6 11	9 10	....	1 04	11 22
8 36	8 36	– –	8 27	4 05	.....	120.9	+..Roaring Branch♁	....	11 34	6 01	8 59	....	12 54	11 12
8 48	8 48	– –	8 38	– –	.....	125.7	+..........Penbryn....♁	....	– –	5 52	8 48	....	– –	11 02
8 53	8 53	– –	8 42	– –	.....	127.7	+..........Grover........	....	– –	5 48	8 40	....	– –	10 58
– –	– –	– –	8 45	– –	.....	129.2	+....Cedar Ledge......	....	– –		8 34	....	– –	10 54
9 02	9 02	3 38	8 50	4 27	.....	131.1	+..........Canton.....♁	....	11 16	5 40	8 31	....	12 35	10 50
9 10	9 10	– –	8 58	– –	.....	135.0	+...........Alba.........	....	– –	5 29	8 22	....	– –	10 41
9 17	9 17	– –	9 04	– –	.....	138.0	+........Cowley.....♁	....	– –	5 23	8 15	....	– –	10 34
9 28	9 28	4 04	9 15	4 50	.....	143.3	+...........Troy......♁	....	10 51	5 09	8 01	....	11 57	10 21
9 37	9 37	– –	9 23	4 57	.....	147.9	+Columbia X Roads♁	....	10 42	4 57	7 51	....	11 46	10 11
9 46	9 46	– –	9 31	– –	.....	152.1	+........Snediker.......	....	– –	4 41	7 43	....	– –	10 04
– –	– –	– –	9 35	– –	.....	154.9	..........Dunning.......	....	– –	– –	7 36	....	– –	– –
9 53	9 53	– –	9 39	5 12	8415	156.0	+..........Gillett.....♁	....	– –	4 30	7 34	8416	11 31	9 53
10 01	10 01	– –	9 47	– –	P M	159.8	+..........Fassett........	....	– –	4 21	7 26	P M	– –	9 44
10 24	10 24	4 52	10 06	5 34	†12 58	167.5	+....Henry Street......	....	10 04	3 58	7 08	9 17	– –	9 28
10 27	10 27	4 55	10 10	5 37	1 01	168.3	arr....+**Elmira**..lve.	....	10 01	3 55	†7 05	9 15	10 52	§9 25
10 35	10 35	5 04	P M	5 41	1 05	168.3	lve........**Elmira**♁.arr.	....	9 57	3 45	A M	9 15	10 45	A M
10 47	10 47	5 15	.....	5 52	1 15	173.6	+...**Horseheads**..♁	....	9 47	3 35	....	8 59	10 34	....
10 55	10 55	– –	.....	– –	1 23	178.0	+.....Pine Valley..♁	....	– –	3 26	....	8 48	– –	....
11 01	11 01	5 26	.....	– –	1 28	180.6	+.........Millport....♁	....	– –	3 19	....	8 40	– –	....
11 12	11 12	5 37	.....	6 12	1 39	186.6	+...Montour Falls.♁	....	9 23	3 06	....	8 27	10 02	
11 21	11 21	5 45	.....	6 20	1 47	189.9	+........**Watkins**....♁	....	9 16	2 58	....	8 17	9 55	
11 34	11 34	5 58	.....	6 32	1 59	196.2	+....Rock Stream.....	....	9 04	2 45	....	7 59	s9 43	
11 40	11 40	– –		6 36	2 04	198.3	+.........Glenora........	....	8 59	2 40	....	7 52	s9 39	
11 43	11 43	– –		i –	2 07	199.4	+.......Lakemont.......	....	8 56	2 37	....	7 47	– –	
11 47	11 47	6 11		6 43	2 11	200.9	+.......Starkey.....♁	....	8 54	2 33	....	7 44	9 35	
11 55	11 55	6 18		6 50	2 18	204.8	+........**Himrod**.....♁	....	8 47	2 24	....	7 34	s9 27	
12 02	12 02	6 26		– –	2 32	208.4	+............Milo..........	....	– –	2 16	....	7 24	s9 21	
12 13	12 13	6 36		7 07	2 42	212.4	+......**Penn Yan**...♁	....	8 32	2 08	....	7 12	9 13	
12 21	12 21	– –		– –	2 50	216.4	+..........Benton.......	....	8 24	1 55	....	6 59	– –	
12 26	12 26	6 50		7 20	2 55	218.3	+..........Bellona........	....	8 20	1 51	....	6 55	s9 02	
12 34	12 34	6 59		7 26	3 04	222.2	+............Hall..........	....	8 14	1 44	....	6 48	8 55	
12 44	12 44	7 09		7 34	3 14	224.9	+.........**Stanley**...♁	....	8 08	1 37	....	6 40	8 49	
12 52	12 52	7 17		– –	3 22	228.6	+.........Aloquin........	....	– –	1 26	....	6 30	s8 41	
1 10	1 10	‖7 35		7 55	3 40	236.6	+..**Canandaigua**.♁	....	†7 45	*1 08	....	†6 15	*8 25	
P M	P M	A M	.....	P M	P M	.....	ARRIVE] [LEAVE	....	A M	P M	....	P M	P M	
†2 38	†2 38	‡9 10	.....	9 30	6 49	.....	......**Rochester**........	....	6 30	11 15	....	2 40	6 50	
†5 10	†5 10	‡11 45	.....	11 45	8 45	.....	........**Buffalo**........	....	†4 35	9 30	....	1 00	4 50	
†6 55	†6 55	†2 05	.....	P M	9 38	.....	.... **Niagara Falls**.....	....	A M	†8 30	....	11 50	*3 47	....
P M	P M	P M	.....	.....	P M	.....	ARRIVE] [LEAVE	....	....	A M	....	†A M	P M	....

Elmira Division

For Index of Stations, see pages 289-295.

+ Coupon stations. ♁ Telegraph stations.

z Stops to leave passengers from the Buffalo and Elmira divisions.

* Daily; † daily, except Sunday; § Sunday only; a time is for North Philadelphia; b stops week-days to take for Harrisburg and beyond and to leave from Williamsport and beyond, signal stop on Sunday; c regular stop to take; d regular stop to leave; e stops week-days to take for Williamsport and beyond and to leave from Harrisburg and points beyond, signal stop Sunday; g stops to leave Pullman passengers; h stops to take passengers for Nescopeck or beyond and for Harrisburg and beyond or to leave from Williamsport and beyond; i stops to leave from Williamsport and beyond; k Saturday only; m stops to leave passengers from Sunbury and points west and to receive for Harrisburg and beyond; n train from New York and Newark arrives Harrisburg 2 35 p.m.; o stops to take for Harrisburg and beyond or to leave from north of Emporium Junc.; s stops Sunday only; t stops to take for Harrisburg and beyond or to leave from Williamsport and beyond; v stops Monday morning.

Additional Trains—Leave Harrisburg †10 00 a.m., †5 45 p.m., arrive Millersburg 10 59 a.m., 6 45 p.m. Lv. Millersburg †7 52 a.m., †3 56 p.m., arr. Harrisburg 8 55 a.m., 4 55 p.m.

Table 156—SODUS BAY BRANCH.

8445	8429	8425	8429	Ms	*September* 25, 1921.	8428	8426	8428	8446
P M	A M	P M	A M	....	LEAVE] [ARRIVE	A M	P M	A M	P M
§8 05	§8 25	†3 40	†8 25	0	..... **Stanley**	8 00	1 15	8 00	7 40
8 14	8 35	3 50	8 35	4.9	...Seneca Castle...	7 49	1 04	7 49	7 29
8 18	8 39	[illegible]	8 39	6.6	+.... Orleans....♁	7 45	12 59	7 45	7 25
8 28	8 50	4 04	8 50	10.5	+Phelps Junction♁	7 36	12 50	7 36	7 16
8 39	9 03	4 17	9 03	16.8	+.... **Newark**...♁	7 24	12 38	7 24	7 05
– –	9 11	4 24	9 11	18.0	.**Newark** (*N.Y.C.*).	7 18	12 30	7 18	6 58
9 02	9 37	4 50	9 37	28.6	+. Sodus Centre.♁	6 55	12 05	6 55	6 33
9 05	9 41	4 54	9 41	29.8	+.. Wallington ..♁	6 52	12 02	6 52	6 30
9 12	9 49	5 02	9 49	33.4	+.**Sodus Point**.♁	6 44	11 54	6 44	6 23
9 15	9 52	5 05	9 52	34.0	... **Lake Shore** ...	†6 40	†11 50	§6 40	§6 20
P M	A M	P M	A M	....	ARRIVE] [LEAVE	A M	A M	A M	P M

‡On Sunday leaves Philadelphia 3 35 p.m., West Philadelphia c3 40 p.m. ‡On Sunday arrives Rochester 11 10 a.m., Buffalo 12 55 p.m.

● Electric trains between Montandon and Mifflinburg.

‖ Meals.

STANDARD—*Eastern time.*

Table 157—BERWICK BRANCH.

8603	9601	Mls	*September* 25, 1921.	9602	9604
P M	....	....	LEAVE] [ARRIVE	P M	....
†1 35	....	0	...... **Berwick**	1 10	....
2 05	....	10.8	.....Light Street	12 38	....
2 09	....	11.8	......**Paper Mill**.....	12 35	....
2 22	A M	17.1	.....Mordansville.....	12 20	P M
2 41	†7 45	21.4	........**Millville**........	12 05	5 45
2 48	7 52	19.2	.....**Eyersgrove**.....	11 56	5 38
2 59	8 02	22.3	......Jerseytown....♁	11 44	5 25
3 11	8 13	26.5	...Strawberry Ridge.♁	11 34	5 12
3 19	8 22	29.3	........Ottawa......♁	11 26	5 02
3 24	8 27	31.1	.......Schuyler.......	11 21	4 56
3 30	8 35	33.1	.....Turbotville....♁	11 17	4 50
3 40	8 44	36.7	.... McEwensville	11 08	4 39
3 50	8 53	39.1	arr...**Watsontown**♁lve.	†11 00	†4 30
P M	A M	....	(*Eastern time.*)	A M	P M

158—LEWISBURG & TYRONE AND BALD EAGLE VALLEY BRANCHES.

8587	8585	8565	8557	8535	8533	Mls	*September* 25, 1921.	8530	8532	8560	8568	8588
●	●A M	●P M	●A M	P M	A M	....	(*Eastern time.*)	A M	P M	●P M	●P M	●P M
P M	§10 01	*5 37	†9 43	†1 20	†5 58	....	lve....**Sunbury**...arr.	9 30	4 55	1 47	8 45	5 04
§1 30	10 23	6 05	10 12	1 43	6 18	0	+...**Montandon**...♁	9 07	4 33	1 12	8 10	4 29
3 00	10 35	6 12	10 19	1 49	6 24	1.6	+....**Lewisburg**....♁	9 01	4 25	1 05	8 05	4 21
3 20	10 55	6 33	10 39	1 59	6 36	7.1	+.... Vicksburg	8 48	4 10	12 41	7 11	4 01
3 31	11 06	6 44	10 50	2 06	6 44	10.9	+....Mifflinburg....♁	8 42	4 03	*12 30	*7 00	§3 50
P M	A M	P M	A M	2 19	6 57	16.3	+.....Millmont.....♁	8 28	3 51	P M	P M	P M
.....	.....	.....	.....	2 26	7 05	19.7	+.... Glen Iron ....♁	8 22	3 44	.....	.....	.....
.....	.....	.....	.....	3 06	7 50	36.7	+......Coburn.......♁	7 50	3 06	.....	.....	.....
.....	.....	.....	.....	3 21	8 05	43.5	+.. Rising Spring ..♁	7 31	2 43	.....	.....	.....
.....	.....	.....	.....	3 36	8 18	49.4	+... Centre Hall ...♁	7 18	2 30	.....	.....	.....
.....	.....	.....	.....	3 47	8 29	54.8	+... Linden Hall ...♁	7 06	2 14	.....	.....	.....
.....	.....	.....	.....	3 52	8 34	56.8	+.....Oak Hall.......	7 01	2 08	.....	.....	.....
.....	.....	.....	.....	3 58	8 41	58.4	+Lemont (State College)♁	6 56	2 04	.....	.....	.....
.....	.....	.....	.....	4 25	9 05	67.6	+... **Bellefonte** ...♁	†6 30	†1 35	.....	.....	.....
.....	.....	.....	.....	P M	A M	....	ARRIVE] [LEAVE	A M	P M	.....	.....	.....

Additional Electric Trains—Lve. Lewisburg for Montandon †9 52, §10 03 a.m., *5 40, *9 14 p.m., for Sunbury †7 15, †9 07, §9 12 a.m., †4 41 p.m.; Sunbury for Lewisburg *9 12 p.m.; Montandon for Lewisburg †7 37, †9 24, §9 28 a.m., †1 13, §4 42, †4 48, *8 26 p.m.

The horses which had powered the NC's Baltimore street switching operations since the 1830s were finally replaced by these peculiar rubber-tired gas-electric tractors in 1917. In one form or another, this unique tractor operation survived into the 1980s. Smithsonian Institution Collection.

in turn sapped economic vitality from the intermediate communities. As operating employees were furloughed, businesses that derived income from them began to close, and the hotel and restaurant business began to evaporate.

In Baltimore the Canton property received a new coal pier in 1917 and merchandise piers in 1923. (The coal pier, a picturesque structure consisting of a steel trestle pier and tiny coal-carrying cars operating in a continuous loop,

Typical of NC local passenger services between the 1920s and the 1940s was this Parkton Local, powered by a PRR E-5 class Atlantic. It is June 12, 1947, and the outbound commuter train is braking to a stop at Lutherville, Maryland. C. T. Mahan, Jr. photograph.

Another Atlantic-powered local stops at Hollins station at Lake Roland in the early 1930s. The track out of the picture at the left is the Green Spring Branch. Baltimore Chapter N. R. H. S. Collection; R. K. Henry photograph.

survived until 1989.) Following them in 1924 a new and modern grain elevator was erected to serve the expanding grain export business. As of 1990 it still operates, although not under railroad management. A new rail yard and coal-loading pier were put into operation at Sodus Point during 1927.

Similarly, renovation work on the New York portion of the line began soon after the lease. For example, during the 1920s both the single-tracked Elmira and Williamsport section and the Canandaigua division received new 130-pound rail and heavy ballast. In addition, the old iron girder bridges either were replaced with steel or bypassed with realignments.

After 1914, the locomotives and cars of the Northern Central were slowly relettered "Pennsylvania." (Most originally had been built to standard Pennsylvania designs.) Heavier cars and trains brought either the retirement or downgrading of lighter locomotives such as the classic American-type 4-4-0s, once the backbone of Northern Central passenger service, and the older 2-6-0s and 2-8-0s extensively used for freight. As a heavy freight and passenger carrying component of the Pennsylvania, the one-time Northern Central lines were assigned some of the PRR's newest and largest steam power.

Most notable were the hulking I-1 class 2-10-0 Decapods, appropriately nicknamed "hippos" by railroaders and rail enthusiasts. Between 1916 and 1923 the Pennsylvania ordered or built an astounding total of 598 of these slow, ponderous but powerful machines for use on the heavy-tonnage and heavily graded parts of its sys-

A pair of PRR I-1 class Decapods wheels a train of mixed freight on the Shamokin branch in 1956. H. H. Harwood, Jr. Collection.

tem. The I-1s became the primary freight power on the Northern Central lines north of Harrisburg. Many of the engines were put on the Elmira Division where they remained until the end of steam in 1957-1958.

The Baltimore-Harrisburg line, on the other hand, had a heavy passenger traffic including many trains which carried through coaches, sleepers, and parlor cars handled by main line PRR trains west of Harrisburg. The most characteristic locomotive on this section became the famous K-4 class Pacific, the Pennsylvania's standard heavy passenger locomotive. (The system owned no less than 425 of these.) To cope with the combination of heavy trains and the Northern Central's curves and grades, the K-4s often were doubleheaded over the line. After 1938 the line also played host to the Pennsylvania's two huge experimental K-5 Pacifics, originally built in 1929 as prototypes for a never-produced fleet of successors to the K-4.

In 1928 the Pennsylvania Railroad began planning a rebuilding of its route through Baltimore, including some Northern Central facilities. The system of tunnels, an operating headache from its opening, was becoming an increasingly intolerable problem as traffic grew. Both the Union and the Baltimore & Potomac tunnels were double-track bores and, as mentioned earlier, both had severe grades; they had become smoky bottlenecks, and were maintenance problems to boot.

On November 1, 1928 Pennsylvania president W. W. Atterbury announced the planned electrification of the PRR's New York-Washington main line between New York and Wilmington, Delaware. While nothing specific was said about the remainder of the route from Wilmington to Baltimore and Washington, it was a foregone conclusion that it would follow soon afterward. Along with the electrification would come additional multiple trackage. The brutal effects of the depression postponed the project several years, but by 1932 loans from the government-sponsored Reconstruction Finance Corporation and Public Works Administration, amounting to $77 million, allowed work on the Washington section to begin.

As a part of the Washington electrification program, it was planned to rebuild both sets of Baltimore tunnels to accommodate extra tracks. A new double-track Union Tunnel was to be built parallel to the old one, which was to be converted to single track to allow greater clearances. In 1932 the Arundel Corporation was awarded a $2.7 million contract for the new Union Tunnel, to be constructed 51 feet south of the 1873 structure. Work began July 17, 1933. Over 700 men labored on the project, using the familiar cut-and-cover method. However, a large boring machine was actually lowered underground to complete a portion of the tunnel. The project was finished on September 27, 1934 and opened for rail traffic on November 12th. The Washington electrification project itself was completed in 1935.

The Baltimore & Potomac tunnel, the worst of the two sets, also was projected to receive a new bore, but interference from city officials reduced that project to a partial renovation of the original structure. The walls were enlarged and cement guns waterproofed the interior. In addition, the track line was reset to allow higher and wider equipment clearance. This was only partially helpful; eventually additional gauntlet tracks also were required to clear certain types of freight cars.

The Pennsylvania also planned to build a direct head-on connection between the east end of the Baltimore & Potomac Tunnel and the Northern Central main line to Harrisburg. The original junction layout in Baltimore was awkward for handling the through passenger trains which operated between Washington, Harrisburg, and western points. These trains had to reverse direction in Baltimore. Trains originating in Washington, for example, were hauled backwards to Baltimore, then a steam locomotive was attached to the opposite end and the train was taken forward up the Northern Central line. An elaborate plan was drawn up to build a new station on the west side of Baltimore, a "wye" connection within the Baltimore & Potomac tunnel to join the Northern Central. This would permit a direct through operation between Washington and Harrisburg, bypassing the Union Station. Needless to say, the project was never completed, although some preliminary work was done. Until the end of the through passenger services, trains continued to be hauled backwards between Baltimore and Washington.

As part of a later project to electrify the PRR main lines to Harrisburg, the Northern Central line between Wago Junction (York Haven) and Enola Yard, as well as the entire "Port Road" route, was electrified in 1938. This section, as noted in Chapter 9, formed part of the Pennsylvania's system of bypass freight routes east of Harrisburg. But steam continued to power all trains on the Northern Central's old Baltimore-Harrisburg main line.

During this period parts of the Northern Central main line were relaid with the Pennsylvania's new standard 152-pound rail, some of the heaviest rail on any American railroad. Money was also appropriated to improve the piers along Baltimore's waterfront. In September 1934 another modern pier was added to the Canton facility. The new fireproof structure, 930 feet long, could accommodate four ocean class craft at one time. It cost $14 million and once completed was used to capacity.

Passenger Problems and Progress

Although the 1920s generally are considered to be a peak period for railroad traffic, weaknesses in the passenger business had begun to become clear and worrisome. Thanks to Henry Ford's Model T and its imitators, automo-

Unlovely but economical, gas-electric cars such as this took over many Parkton Local runs in later years. Car No. 4666 works an afternoon northbound trip past Bellona Avenue in Ruxton in June 1947. No. 4666 has been preserved and restored. C. T. Mahan, Jr. photograph.

bile use began a spectacular growth. With it came pressure for better roads, which in turn encouraged more automobile use. In 1916 there were 3.3 million motor vehicles registered in the United States; by 1921 the figure had almost tripled, to 9.5 million. In 1926 it reached 19.2 million.

Few people drove their cars from Baltimore to Chicago, of course, but those living in small towns and rural areas quickly adopted the automobile for their short trips to the city or to nearby towns. Motor buses had also developed into reliable, practical vehicles and often offered cheaper and more frequent services than the railroad. Inevitably, the extensive local passenger train services of the early 1900s were regularly reduced or eliminated entirely. The process began in earnest in the early 1920s, and by 1925 the Pennsylvania had developed a multi-pronged strategy to deal with the problems. Said PRR president Samuel Rea that year:

> *Like other railroads, the Pennsylvania has felt, for several years, serious inroads upon its traffic, particularly in passenger business...resulting from the general use of bus, motor trucks, and private automobiles... It is deemed wise to abandon service...certain branch lines...and substitute motor service for rail transport... It is also deemed advisable...to enter the business of motor bus and truck transport...to protect investors and dividends.*

Northern Central timetables showed the results. In 1928, for example, only four locals operated on the Green Spring Branch, half the 1916 service. The seven locals operated each way in 1916 between Baltimore and Cockeysville had now been reduced to three. On the Columbia-Wrightsville-York-Frederick line overall service had been cut from six trains each way to five, but service on the York-Hanover section was substantially reduced and the Frederick-Keymar trains completely eliminated. North of Harrisburg the main line services to Sunbury and Williamsport remained healthy, and the number of trains on the Shamokin/Mt. Carmel branch actually increased from four to five round trips. But the Lykens Branch had been cut in half, from four trips to two, and only three round trips (out of four in 1916) were scheduled between Elmira and Canandaigua.

Not only did the local trains disappear outright, but increasingly, the survivors were handled by "motor cars" — self-powered gas-electric cars commonly called "doodlebugs." These vehicles were unglamorous and sometimes unreliable, but considerably cheaper to operate than a steam locomotive hauling two or three conventional passenger cars. Sometimes towing a trailer car, the gas-electrics usually provided sufficient accommodations for the dwindling patronage. Buses of the PRR-controlled Pennsylvania General Transit Company (later a Greyhound affiliate) supplemented or substituted for trains in some areas. By early 1930 gas-electric cars operated the single remaining round trips on the Lykens and the Sodus Point branches and a Harrisburg-Millersburg commuter run. Buses handled half of the Shamokin/Mt. Carmel trips and a single daily bus also operated between Baltimore and Harrisburg, using the York Road and Susquehanna Trail.

The disaster of the Depression meant more than merely a temporary drop in business for the railroad; it accelerated and intensified the move to motor vehicles. Public works programs produced more improved roads; former train riders also took the cheaper buses, or calculated that it was more economical to drive their cars. At the

While short-haul passenger business diminished during the Depression, the long-distance trains connecting Washington and Baltimore with western points remained heavy and impressive. Here a pair of K4 Pacifics pound through Timonium in 1945. Bob's Photos Collection.

same time trucks took more of the merchandise freight. Manufacturers not only were producing less, but their customers were buying hand-to-mouth, resulting in smaller shipments which had to be delivered quickly — shipments that ideally fitted truck service. And there were many hungry truckers waiting, unemployed people who had bought secondhand trucks and were willing to quote low rates to generate some kind of income. They went after the traffic which the railroads could least afford to lose, the high-value, high-rated shipments.

Two years later the Washington-Chicago Liberty Limited heads upgrade past the Ruxton suburban station. C. T. Mahan, Jr. photograph.

By mid-1939, Northern Central local passenger services had shrunk dramatically. There were no passenger trains whatever on the Green Spring Branch, the Sparrows Point Branch, or the Sodus Point Branch. Buses handled all runs to Lykens and the Shamokin-Mt. Carmel area, as well as the Millersburg-Harrisburg commuter service. All Cockeysville locals were gone; the remaining suburban service operations consisted of only five Baltimore-Parkton locals each way. A single local passenger train serviced Frederick, although travelers in the area between York and Columbia still had a relatively wide choice of five trains each way, which now ran as far east as Lancaster, Pennsylvania. Casual business trav-

Heavy snow always cursed the NC's upstate New York section. Here a 1946 blizzard has marooned a snow-clearing crew. Montour Falls Memorial Library Collection.

elers in the area between York and Harrisburg also could ride an early morning train into Harrisburg and return at 4:13 in the afternoon. Service to Canandaigua was cut to two round trips and no sleepers, diners, or parlor cars operated north of Williamsport.

But if the local services were withering, the Pennsylvania continued to be optimistic about the long distance passenger runs. Automobiles and buses still were less appealing for extended trips, and air travel was expensive, often uncomfortable and uncertain, and (it was thought) dangerous. Sleeping car service, although reduced, still operated over a surprisingly wide variety of routes. In addition to the usual sleepers between Washington, Baltimore, and PRR western terminals, one could still ride in a Pullman between Washington and Buffalo or between Washington and Erie, Pennsylvania. Sleepers also still ran between Philadelphia and Williamsport, Philadelphia and Buffalo, New York and Oil City, Pennsylvania, and between Pittsburgh and Scranton. One author reported that the combination of first class trains and the scenery made the Northern Central line one of the "most picturesque" rides "in the Nation."

And in 1938 the Pennsylvania reequipped its Washington-Baltimore-Chicago *Liberty Limited*, for many years the finest, fastest, and most prestigious train on the Northern Central line. Designed to compete directly with the Baltimore & Ohio's *Capitol Limited* for the first-class Washington-Chicago trade, the *Liberty Limited* was an overnight train running on a schedule similar to the Pennsylvania's famous *Broadway Limited* from New York. The 1938 *Liberty Limited* received many new streamlined, lightweight cars built specifically for the train, including private-room sleepers and a round-end bedroom-lounge-observation car.

Added to the Northern Central route's regular passenger services were the occasional VIP special movements. As a link between Washington and various western and northern points, the line was intermittently used by American presidents and other dignitaries. (And it handled at least four presidential funeral trains — that of William Henry Harrison in 1841, Zachary Taylor in 1850, Lincoln in 1865, and Warren G. Harding in 1923.) Among the last and most memorable of such trips over the line was the "Royal Train" of Britain's King George VI en route to Washington the evening of June 8, 1939. The Royal Train was followed by another special carrying that inveterate train rider Franklin D. Roosevelt.

Despite renovations and modernization, train wrecks still inevitably occurred. In the 1930s there were two which many people remember even today. In July 1930 a passenger train southbound from York derailed and wrecked at Mt. Washington. Although no fatalities resulted, many people were injured. Juveniles placing steel spikes on the track was the official cause. On June 7, 1934 a steam engine plunged off a Gunpowder Falls bridge near Parkton. One passenger, Margaret Frederick, engineer T. F. Bossom, and fireman J. O. Blather were killed in the accident.

World War II Brings Indian Summer

In 1939 another war in Europe began affecting the operations of the Northern Central Division. As in World War I the conflict would provide a temporary traffic stimulus and, in this case, would postpone the inevitable inroads of motor vehicles and air transportation. The Second World War would, for the time being, delay the days of reckoning.

Efforts to supply the Allies again strained the railroad. Supply demands created the most urgent burden on the lines which had modern, efficient east coast port facilities. As the major eastern carrier, the Pennsylvania Railroad

Two scenes at Parkton, Maryland during the transition from steam to diesel. In this early-morning scene in December 1949, K-4 Pacific No. 830 is pulling out of the layover yard with a commuter train for Baltimore, while at the right a gas-electric car has just arrived from the city. C. T. Mahan, Jr. photograph.

In September of the same year a pair of Baldwin "Centipede" passenger diesels roared past the north end of Parkton yard with the Baltimore-bound combined Gotham Limited and St. Louisan. The first-class condition of the main line gives no clue to its fast-approaching disintegration. C. T. Mahan, Jr. photograph.

shouldered a heavy responsibility in getting supplies on their way to the war zone. The modern Canton marine terminal in Baltimore became a primary export point. Although the railroads remained under private ownership during this conflict, they were regulated by the Office of Defense Transportation, an agency created to avoid the problems of congestion created during World War I.

Overall, between 1939 and 1944 freight traffic more than doubled and passenger traffic more than quadrupled. Supply trains were given highest priority. Trains from the steel mills and coal mines were sent south on the Northern Central only minutes apart. At one point the bucolic Greenspring Branch handled 22 military trains each day. Army troops were assigned to the sidings to prevent sabotage. And as a major passenger link to Washington, the Northern Central's through passenger trains were filled to capacity.

The Days of Reckoning

Once World War II was over, however, the downturn resumed and both the Northern Central and the rural towns that had flourished along the line began their trips into oblivion. During the first decade after the war the process was slow but relentless; afterwards it accelerated. By the end of the 1970s little was left of the original Northern Central system, and much of what survived had severely deteriorated. Many of its on-line towns, too, had declined or had radically changed their complexions.

Many of the causes already have been mentioned in one way or another. Consumption of the railroad's principal freight commodity, anthracite, virtually evaporated after the war. Petroleum and natural gas had proved cheaper, cleaner, and far more convenient for home heating and cooking; many industries also converted to oil, gas, or cheaper bituminous coal. By this time, too, many of the major anthracite seams had been extensively worked, making the remaining coal more costly to mine. Instead of a universal fuel, anthracite became an expensive specialty.

Bituminous traffic also declined, except for certain markets such as steelmaking and, to some extent, electric utilities. Both domestic and imported petroleum proved to be cheaper to extract and cheaper to transport — and supplies were then abundant. Many industries, including a large number of utilities, switched to oil. The postwar dieselization of the railroads removed another major coal market.

The decline in coal traffic created serious problems for eastern railroads such as the Pennsylvania, since it was generally a very profitable type of business to handle: it moved in solid, heavy trainloads, did not demand extra services, and claims for loss and damage were relatively low.

Increasingly, trucks took much of the general merchandise freight business. Although often more expensive than comparable rail shipments, truck service offered many advantages which substantially reduced the shipper's total costs. It was usually much faster, less susceptible to loss and damage, and the job of loading and unloading was quicker and cheaper. Trucks were enormously flexible, too; they could pick up or deliver split shipments at several different locations and, of course, could reach off-track customers without the need to transfer goods between a rail car and a truck. The Interstate Highway system, begun in the 1950s, vastly improved trucking economics, speed, and service quality.

Many railroad-oriented industries also developed problems, particularly in the eastern territory served by the Pennsylvania. High labor costs and obsolete plants forced many of them either to relocate to a cheaper site (often in the South), retrench, or close completely.

Former railroad passengers, of course, deserted the trains for their automobiles and, for the longer trips, airplanes. For them too, the Interstate Highway system was a boon, as was the jet revolution in the 1960s.

The once-mighty Pennsylvania Railroad found itself as one of the worst victims of these trends. Its eastern territory was generally "mature," meaning that industrial plants were old and costs were high. It was also most susceptible to motor competition. On the other hand its elaborate, costly, high-capacity physical plant was increasingly underutilized, resulting in higher costs for the remaining business. The once omnipotent company slipped into an irreversible decline, desperately attempting to reduce its expenses by cutting services and abandoning unprofitable lines. As it did so, an endless cycle started: more business went onto the highways, producing more rail cutbacks and rate increases, which put even more on the highways....

Gradually, the Pennsylvania and most other railroads gave up entire segments of their business. Branch line and local passenger services became hopeless and were completely abandoned. In the early 1950s the Post Office made wholesale diversions of mail from rail to truck, effectively removing the economic support of many short-haul passenger trains. The practice of handling small-lot freight shipments (usually called "less-than-carload" or "l.c.l.") also was wholly discontinued, along with the freight stations which handled them.

The process was both painfully slow and unpleasant. Communities became alarmed at the reductions, or the loss of their last train, and protested to the various regulatory agencies. So, of course, did the railroad labor unions and their supporters. It was a difficult situation for both the communities and the railroads. Many people and businesses still depended on rail service to one degree or another, but the nature of the rail traffic was changing rapidly and, for the railroads, the economics were worsening. At the time, unfortunately, the general public and the political bodies still viewed the privately-funded railroads as "rich," and able (indeed, obligated) to support unprofitable services. Direct government aid to the railroads was an anathema. This attitude changed dramatically in the 1970s, but before that time the shrinking process was drawn out and controversial, creating antagonisms between the railroads and the communities and resulting in visibly decaying services and facilities.

This grim process was reflected everywhere on the Northern Central lines. By the 1940s the Baltimore-Sodus Point system really consisted of three separate parts, each with its own traffic and economic characteristics. The Baltimore-Harrisburg section was the weakest of the three. With virtually all through freight moving over the low-grade line through Perryville, it carried primarily passenger trains and local freights serving the 19th Century industries along the line and its branches. York, Hanover, and Spring Grove were still healthy freight traffic producers, but at many other points business was disappearing to the trucks, or the plants themselves were closing.

Between Harrisburg and Sunbury it was a mixed picture: the once-vital anthracite business was rapidly drying up, but the main line itself was a key link in the Pennsylvania system and carried large amounts of bituminous coal and general freight which originated and terminated in other territories. (This section, in fact, remains healthy today.)

Finally, the Williamsport-Elmira-Sodus Point segment had its own pluses and minuses. Essentially, the line was still supported by coal moving to Sodus Point. During the post-World War II decade coal shipments from central Pennsylvania to Sodus Point averaged over five million tons per year, much of it Pennsylvania bituminous. Even as late as 1955 the line was still handling 28 million tons of freight per year. Several other points along the line also generated healthy freight revenues. Salt from Watkins and stone from Wallington amounted to one train per day for many years. Finally, agricultural products from the Finger Lakes region of New York added 30 cars a day. But otherwise, it was a dark picture; at many local points in New York State shippers had switched to truck.

Abandonments Begin

The fate of each of these three sections was different. Not surprisingly, the Baltimore-Harrisburg line suffered the worst, and the process began earliest.

The Green Spring Branch, which had been embargoed west of Rockland on December 15, 1959, was gradually removed during the summer of 1960. The old Green Spring Valley summer resorts had long since closed, and the on-line territory was virtually devoid of freight business. In its later years the branch had been maintained primarily for emergency use as a connection between the Western Maryland Railway's main line at Garrison and the Northern Central route into Baltimore. Slowly the salvage crews removed what had been the original main line of the Baltimore & Susquehanna Railroad. Most remaining structures were razed, although the picturesque stations at Brooklandville and Stevenson were saved and stand in 1991, both still with their brick platforms intact.

The main line between Baltimore and York was withering at the same time. By the late 1950s the only train service on this part of the railroad was an occasional through freight, a local freight, three Parkton locals each way, and three through passenger trains each way. The Washington/Baltimore section of the *Spirit of St. Louis* had been dropped in 1956, and in 1958 the premier *Liberty Limited* made its last run as a separate train. Afterwards the remaining through cars between Washington and Chicago were carried on the *General* west of Harrisburg. By this time all passenger services on the line were showing large deficits, and the remaining freight traffic was not enough to support the elaborate physical plant. In 1956 the Pennsylvania's division managers began planning for the elimination of passenger service on the line, and for reducing trackage and facilities.

Beginning in 1957 the double-track main line was reduced to single track between Baltimore and York. That year one track was taken up between York and New Freedom; shortly thereafter it was reduced to one line as far south as Glencoe. By late 1960 most of the Northern Central had been reduced to a single-track operation.

Passenger train cutbacks continued. On June 27, 1959, after ICC approval, the locally famous "Parkton Local" made its last trip, ending all suburban service. Government agencies and the communities served by the trains protested the action. However, the Public Service Commission ruled two to one in favor of the railroad. The dissenting commissioner, Albert L. Sklar, noted that the line had potential because it was "in a region expecting rapid growth." He pointed out, incorrectly, that patronage had not declined and that the railroad should economize operations. In addition, both Baltimore city and county governments had opposed the Pennsylvania's discontinuance petition, but, significantly, neither were willing to subsidize the operation. As noted earlier the abandonment came at a time before it was realized that services such as this had to be publicly financed. The McMahon bus company took over service to many of the "Parkton Local" communities; somewhat ironically, McMahon was later absorbed by the state-operated Mass Transit Administration. The handsome stations at Ruxton and Parkton were demolished, but,

The Parkton Local in its last, dreary years. In this bleak 1954 scene, the diesel-powered morning run picks up a few hardy commuters at Ruxton. Enoch Pratt Library Collection; R. F. Kniesche photograph.

happily, Riderwood and Lutherville were converted to homes.

The three through passenger trains each way between Baltimore and Harrisburg continued into the 1960s, and sleepers were still carried between both Washington and Chicago, and Washington and Buffalo. By 1968 the overnight Washington-Buffalo train, the *Northern Express/Southern Express*, was gone. On the eve of Amtrak's

It is now 1963; the Parkton Local has been gone for four years and the handsome Ruxton station is following it. Sunpapers photograph.

In the waning days of passenger operations in 1964, train No. 548, carrying through cars from Chicago to Baltimore and Washington, rolls past the former suburban station at Riderwood, Maryland. The station, designed by Philadelphia architect Frank Furness, has become a private home. H. H. Harwood, Jr. photograph.

takeover of all long distance rail passenger service in 1971, a single daily Baltimore-Harrisburg train remained, reduced to one coach. North of Harrisburg, passenger service consisted of one train operating every other day between Harrisburg and Buffalo. Employees on the line correctly called them "the ghost trains." Amtrak took over neither service, and the last tattered survivors of Northern Central passenger service died on May 1, 1971.

The end of the line, or close to it. A skeletal version of the Buffalo Day Express passes the weed-grown station at Milton, Pennsylvania in August 1969. Railroad Avenue Enterprises Collection.

Surprisingly, through freight operations reappeared on the Baltimore-Harrisburg line in the mid-1960s. At the time, the Pennsylvania had enthusiastically entered the new business of hauling highway trailers on flatcars — nicknamed "piggyback" or "TOFC" by railroaders. As part of its program it inaugurated an all-piggyback train between Baltimore and western points. But clearances on the low-grade freight route between Harrisburg and Baltimore did not permit the high trailers, so the new train was routed over the Northern Central until the low-grade route was modified.

Inevitably, branch line service was pruned back in the area. The line from York to Wrightsville and Columbia, which had been the Baltimore & Susquehanna's original main line to the Susquehanna canal trade, steadily declined.

Following World War II the mills, factories, and industries along the line either closed or turned to trucks operating on the nearby Lincoln Highway. Buses had been substituted for passenger trains in the early 1950s, and by the 1960s freight had largely vanished. The bridge over the Susquehanna between Wrightsville and Columbia was dismantled in 1964, severing the rail connection at that end; the Wrightsville branch itself was embargoed in late 1969 and later taken up east of an industrial park in York.

While the Harrisburg-Sunbury segment remained viable and comparatively busy, the anthracite branches were not. From 1950 to 1960 these lines suffered the most extensive freight traffic loss of the entire Northern Central system. The accompanying economic deprivation that settled over the supporting mining towns drove many of them into oblivion.

First, the Lykens Valley line, which coexisted with the Reading Company after the latter had constructed a branch line into Wiconisco during the early 1870s, began freight service reductions in 1946. Passenger service, which long before had been reduced to a single round trip made by an over-the-road bus, ended in 1956. Regular coal trains came off the line in 1960. Employees were furloughed, and operations were carried on an as-needed basis. Unemployment during the late 1960s and the 1970s devastated the entire area. Many residents moved away, miners changed occupations, and numerous businesses closed.

The line remained in place, but dormant, during the Penn Central period. It was purchased in 1975 by attorney Donald Meyer, supposedly for use in the planned revival of coal resources resulting from the national energy crisis. He operated the line on an as-needed basis for five years under the name of the Lykens Valley Railroad, apparently without success, and in 1981 it was scrapped. The next year the old Reading line, which entered the Lykens coal fields from the opposite direction, was also removed.

The same process occurred on the Sunbury-Shamokin-Mount Carmel branch. After World War II its traffic declined as the anthracite market evaporated. For a period in the mid-1950s, however, the Shamokin/Mt. Carmel branch revived with iron ore traffic moving eastward from Northumberland to Mt. Carmel, where it was turned over to the Lehigh Valley Railroad. These trains originated at the Lake Erie transshipping dock at Erie, Pennsylvania and were destined for the Bethlehem Steel complex at Bethlehem, Pennsylvania. During the last days of the steam era four of the hefty I-1 Decapods — two at the head end and two pushing — were needed to wrestle each of the heavy ore trains up the 1.31 percent grade to Shamokin.

A pair of ponderous but powerful I-1 class "hippos" work an iron ore train upgrade on the Shamokin Branch in 1956. G. C. Corey photograph.

But beginning in 1958, the Pennsylvania began to reduce operations and defer maintenance along the Shamokin line. Following the 1976 creation of Conrail, which absorbed all the once-competitive railroads in this area, most of the remaining coal traffic was taken completely off the branch and rerouted over former Reading routes. Finally in 1983 Conrail embargoed the section of the line between Sunbury and Shamokin and scheduled it for scrapping; however, in 1987 it was sold to a local public rail authority for operation by an independent short line railroad. There were further delays, but finally a contract was made with Richard Robey, the owner of several other short lines in the area (including a portion of the old Lackawanna & Bloomsburg). Robey formed the Shamokin Valley Railroad to operate the line, and the first Shamokin Valley train ran on December 12, 1988. As of early 1991, traffic on this line was quite light, with train service only once or twice a week.

The Williamsport-Sodus Point portion of the Northern Central suffered from some of the same problems that plagued both the Baltimore and York County sections of the main line. But because Sodus Point coal facility was used until 1967, the process of decline there occurred much later than on the south end of the line.

By the late 1950s and 1960s most of the local freight sources along this section had shifted to truck. Passenger traffic after World War II was virtually nonexistent. Consequently, most of the trains left on the line by the 1960s were through freights bound for either Elmira or Sodus Point. From 1959 until 1967, although the coal trade declined almost every year, the coal docks were loading over a million tons per year.

In 1957 steam operations were replaced by diesels, affecting such "tank towns" as Marsh Hill, Columbia Crossroads, Gillet, Starkey, Millport, and Stanley. Many of the local residents who worked on the railroad lost their jobs. Businesses that depended on rail traffic suddenly lost a substantial amount of income.

In 1959 the coal customers supplied by the Sodus Point dock also began to dwindle rapidly. The Pennsylvania retrenched along the entire line from Williamsport to Sodus Point. Division managers deferred maintenance to an "as needed" basis. Numerous stations, rail yards, and support facilities were either closed or reduced. Stanley, Flint, Orleans, Starkey, and Himrod, New York, along with Ralston, Troy, and Canton, Pennsylvania had their stations closed. Sidings were torn up on a wholesale basis. The Williamsport, Southport, Elmira, and Canandaigua yards began to scale back operations. Hundreds of employees were furloughed, trains were eliminated, and service was reduced.

Sodus Point continued active, however. Its 1927 coal pier could load lake freighters in two hours. Both anthracite and bituminous coal were shipped from there across Lake Ontario to markets in Toronto, Hamilton, and Prescott, Ontario. The facility was so busy during the 1940s and 1950s that a Sodus newspaper, *The Record*, reported on residents complaining of excessive noise from the loading dock. This business (and the noise) had remained consistently high and, in fact, even in the early 1960s, remained at high levels as this historical record shows:

Year	Total Tonnage
1872	32,174
1900	1,376,243
1925	1,024,967
1956	2,401,676
1960	1,217,993
1963	2,267,893
1965	1,137,673
1967	102,066

The Sodus Point facility employed, exclusive of train crews, 39 gangmen and four shakers. But this too changed. Coal exports to Canada dropped abruptly for a variety of reasons — the increased use of oil and gas, hydroelectric power, the opening of the St. Lawrence Seaway, the enlargement of the Welland Canal, and increasing environmental restrictions on coal-burning. In late 1967 it was decided to close the Sodus Point pier and rail yard. All 43 workmen lost their jobs. The loading pier remained dormant until 1970 when Arthur Reed, a local businessman, purchased the pier for conversion to a marine facility. However, on November 5, 1971 workmen using acetylene torches for the renovations started an accidental fire which consumed the structure. In the late 1980s only the concrete pier abutment, a derelict custom house (itself scheduled to be razed), and an overgrown single-track rail line (which once served the now defunct Genesee Brewery adjacent to the extinct rail yard) remained to mark the spot that was once world famous for its coal commerce.

The Northern Central Disappears

The decades of the 1950s and 1960s had mostly marked a slow process of retrenchment and disintegration, but by and large the Northern Central's basic system was still intact. Several closely-spaced events in the 1970s, however, brought on a rapid collapse, wiping large portions of the railroad completely off the map.

In 1968 the weakening Pennsylvania had merged with the equally shaky New York Central to form the infamous Penn Central system. Historically the two companies had been arch-competitors in much the same territories, and in many areas they had overlapping lines and services. Merger eliminated the need for many of these lines. In the northern portion of the old NC territory, for example, a New York Central line also extended from Williamsport north to Watkins Glen and other upstate New York points; it roughly covered the same area as the Northern Central's Canandaigua route, but followed easier grades. Although Penn Central was slow to abandon redundant lines outright, it began to reroute traffic. Since upstate New York was heavily "New York Central territory," with extensive main line trackage and services, much of the PRR/NC business was fed through former New York Central lines in the area.

Then on June 21, 1970 Penn Central collapsed into what turned out to be a hopeless bankruptcy. With no funds to sustain marginal operations, it simply let them disintegrate in place, discouraging what business remained. The Baltimore-York section of the Northern Central became a prime example. By 1971 freight traffic on the line had dropped significantly. Penn Central operated a freight train from Baltimore to Parkton only on Wednesdays. Another switcher worked south from York into New Freedom on Tuesdays, Fridays, and occasionally on Saturday. That year only 498 carloads were handled along the south end and over half of those, 263 cars, came from or went to the Stewartstown Railroad at New Freedom. Only one passenger train was left on the line at that time, but it was taken off May 1, 1971. Managers quietly planned to "embargo and abandon" the Cockeysville-New Freedom section. The line was clearly dying.

The next blow came from nature. On June 23, 1972 Tropical Storm Agnes inundated Maryland and Pennsylvania with one of the century's worst rainstorms. Severe flooding destroyed several major bridges and large sections of track and roadbed. In both states the damage was significant.

The trackbed and many bridges along Gunpowder Falls in Baltimore County were severely damaged. In York County major bridges spanning the Codorus Creek at Reynolds Mill (the "twin arch") and Hanover Junction were totally destroyed. Smaller structures all along the line between Cockeysville and York were severely damaged by the flood. The west end of the York-Frederick branch also was severed by the destruction of the Monocacy River bridge outside Frederick.

Along the Williamsport-Elmira section similar damage occurred. A major bridge crossing Lycoming Creek at Hepburnville, 12 miles north of Williamsport, was destroyed. In addition, the storm caused extensive damage to major sections of the trackbed and destroyed numerous small bridges.

The cost estimates to repair the damage climbed into the millions of dollars, money that Penn Central could not and would not appropriate.

The widespread destruction made any abandonment legalities academic. Service simply was not resumed between York and Cockeysville, Maryland (outside Baltimore), nor on the section between Williamsport and Elmira.

Soon after the disaster the merchants and businessmen who had a vested interest in the line began pressuring political leaders, government agencies, and railroad executives, demanding rebuilding. They argued that without rail service, the remaining industries would either be forced to depend entirely on higher-cost motor carriers or perish. In Maryland the Campbell quarry at Texas, the Baker Quarry at Blue Mount, and the Federal Paper Company at White Hall all joined the struggle to get the line open. Both the Summers Canning Factory and the Weyerhaeuser Lumber Company at New Freedom switched to truck, but lobbied legislators to get the rail line restored. A determined effort by the owners of the now-isolated Stewartstown Railroad was met with continued resistance from Penn Central executives. The little "farmers railroad," dependent on the Northern Central connection at New Freedom, also had to suspend service. Penn Central, however, adamantly refused to repair anything but the Baltimore to Cockeysville segment, which had suffered only minor damage and served the only significantly large customers. The Maryland Public Service Commission ordered Penn Central to restore the line into York, but the railroad appealed the order.

On the northern section of the old NC, the owners of both the Troy Machine Works and the Canton Wood Mill pressed for the rebuilding of the line north of Williamsport.

Although the fate of the Maryland section of the Cockeysville-York line seemed sealed, the portion in Pennsylvania turned into a long-running political struggle which, ultimately, was successful. On September 25, 1972 the United States District Court at Lewisburg, Pennsylvania heard Penn Central's appeal of the Public Utilities Commission order. Judge Malcolm Muir refused to halt Penn Central's abandonment plans. The ruling, in effect, gave the railroad the right to ask the Interstate Commerce Commission (ICC) to allow for total abandonment. Penn Central immediately filed for ICC approval.

The first ICC abandonment hearing was held March 19-22, 1973, presided over by Administrative Law Judge Robert M. Glennon. To the chagrin of the railroad and the delight of its customers, he recommended against abandoning the line. Baltimore County officials had been conspicuously absent from the hearing. As a result, the owners of the Stewartstown Railroad implied that Penn Central restored the Baltimore-Cockeysville segment in exchange for an agreement that Baltimore County would not oppose abandonment of the balance of the line. Frederick L. Dewberry, the chairman of the Baltimore County Industrial Development Commission, determined that the line was neither essential for the economic development of Baltimore County nor was it needed as a mass transit route. Pennsylvania, on the other hand, wanted the line opened for both industrial development and for possible commuter service.

Without support from Maryland, the Pennsylvania Department of Transportation acted on its own, and on June 27, 1973 quietly purchased the York to New Freedom section of the line for $85,000. It had been a courageous act. The line was destroyed at several locations, spiraling inflation was dramatically increasing the repair costs, and any industrial or passenger use remained questionable. However, the Stewartstown Railroad, which was not damaged by the storm, along with several industries in New Freedom, needed rail service.

After the second ICC hearing on July 16, 1973 the examiners still refused to allow the Penn Central to abandon the line from Cockeysville to the Maryland line. But the question now had become even more academic.

By that year, the next traumatic event had occurred — virtually every major northeastern railroad had followed Penn Central into bankruptcy. The victims included the Reading, the Erie Lackawanna (a previous merger of the Erie and the Delaware, Lackawanna & Western), the Lehigh Valley, and the Jersey Central. The Penn Central disaster already had begun a significant shift in political thinking on public railroad policy; the demise of the other railroads intensified the crisis. Belatedly, it was finally realized that radical surgery and government support both were needed to preserve some semblance of a strong eastern rail system.

A complex set of federal laws emerged which had the effect of simultaneously consolidating all the bankrupt railroads into one entity — most familiarly known as Conrail — and also permitting the abandonment or subsidy of low-density lines. Extensive studies were made to determine which lines would be absorbed by the future Conrail and which would be excluded. Any lines excluded could be automatically abandoned outright or, if state or local governments wished, could be subsidized and operated independently. Of the Northern Central lines, Conrail would assume operation only of the short Baltimore-Cockeysville branch, the still-viable main line trackage from York to Harrisburg and Harrisburg to Williamsport, and the section in New York State between Elmira and Sodus Point. Conrail had no responsibility for the Cockeysville-York and Williamsport-Elmira portions.

During the pre-Conrail planning process efforts had been made to preserve the Cockeysville-York line in its entirety. But at a June 3, 1975 meeting the United States Railway Administration (USRA) admitted to all parties that the prospects for renewal looked grave. The federal rail planning agency implied that because the Pennsylvania Department of Transportation owned the section between New Freedom and York, and the line north of Cockeysville had no viable source of revenue, it could no longer support keeping the Maryland portion. Then, later in June 1975, the Pennsylvania Department of Transportation sent a final letter to the USRA urging reestablishment of the line from Cockeysville to York. It argued that a through route was vital to economic growth of southern York County. It was the final effort to save the line as a through route to Baltimore.

However, the people and businesses along the line continued to fight for the reestablishment of rail service. Old-fashioned boosterism was used to gain political support. In the summer of 1975 Maryland Congressman Clarence Long supported the project and attempted to get the rail line rebuilt. It, too, was a futile effort. The ICC approved abandonment of the line between Cockeysville and the Pennsylvania state line in 1975, and the rail was removed late in 1975 and early 1976.

Conrail officially came into being April 1, 1976, absorbing Penn Central and the other bankrupt lines. As planned, it purchased the Northern Central's lines between Baltimore and Cockeysville, York and Williamsport, and Elmira and Sodus Point. At the same time, the Maryland & Pennsylvania Railroad (which by then had abandoned most of its own lines) took over operation of the York-Frederick branch and the Northern Central main line through the center of York. The York-Frederick line later was partly dismembered; the M & P retained the York-Hanover section, the line between Hanover and Taneytown, Maryland was abandoned, and the newly formed Maryland Midland Railway assumed operation of the west end between Taneytown and Walkersville, Maryland. As of 1991 the entry to Frederick has not been restored.

As an odd by-product of Conrail's creation, the medium-sized Delaware & Hudson Railway was doubled in size in order to provide railroad competition in some territories where Conrail otherwise would have a monopoly. As part of this expansion the D & H extended its operations southeast from Wilkes-Barre, Pennsylvania to Potomac Yard, outside Washington, D. C. To accomplish this it bought the former PRR line between Wilkes-Barre and Sunbury, once a major Northern Central connection, and used trackage rights over the old Northern Central main line between Sunbury and Harrisburg/Enola. This operation also started April 1, 1976. The D & H's 1988 bankruptcy caused a major rerouting and the Enola service subsequently became erratic, but it may revive with the D & H now owned by the Canadian Pacific Railway.

The tiny Stewartstown Railroad inherited operation of the NC's main line between York and New Freedom, Pennsylvania. The once-bustling facilities at New Freedom looked like this in 1990 as a Stewartstown excursion train stands by the old NC station and the remnants of a pair of PRR-style position-light signals. H. H. Harwood, Jr. photograph.

The York-New Freedom Line Revives

The Cockeysville-New Freedom and the Williamsport-Elmira lines were gone forever, but controversy continued over the fate of the York-New Freedom section. The previous purchase of this line by the Pennsylvania Department of Transportation at least had preserved the property for future restoration. But the damage from Tropical Storm Agnes was severe, and the traffic prospects still uncertain. It remained intact but dormant for twelve years, while the ties deteriorated from non-use and vegetation grew unchecked. Basically, however, the heavy rail and ballast installed by the Pennsylvania many years earlier were in relatively good condition.

In 1975 the Stewartstown Railroad proposed the formation of the York County Southern Railroad, a private enterprise which would restore and operate the line from York to New Freedom. When that phase of the plan was completed the Stewartstown Railroad would again have a rail outlet at New Freedom. The state of Pennsylvania was receptive to the idea, but would only allow a non-profit corporation to conduct business along the route. As a result, the formation of a non-profit association, the South-

Farther north, a typically short southbound Stewartstown freight train passes the ancient frame station at Hanover Junction in 1986. The diesel is leased from the Maryland & Pennsylvania Railroad. Compare this scene with that shown in Chapter 6 on page 60.

ern York County Corporation, began immediately. Throughout the long struggle which followed, the owners of the Stewartstown Railroad remained the primary boosters of the project, and were instrumental in finally bringing the railroad back to New Freedom and Stewartstown.

Afterward the Pennsylvania Department of Transportation's state-wide rail plan was completed. It estimated that restoration of the Northern Central line would eventually bring 106 primary jobs, 58 secondary jobs, and over a million dollars in wages each year to the area. Indeed, during 1978-1979 southern York County had rapidly expanded in both industry and population. The report documented increasing business in the "lumber, building material, merchandising, grain and fruit and vegetable markets." It concluded that rail service to the area would be an economic impetus.

Eventually the non-profit corporation was formed and the Stewartstown Railroad was named as the designated operator to run the line under contract. The Southern York County Corporation applied to the York County Planning Commission for community development grants to finance the renewal. The applications were approved in 1982, the state appropriated reconstruction money, and the construction contracts were signed in 1983. The Bear Creek Construction Company did the rebuilding and the cost was tentatively set at $1.36 million. The work was done during 1983 and 1984, replacing the damaged stone arch bridges with utilitarian steel girder spans. The first revenue trip, a single car of lumber, was made from York to New Freedom on January 14, 1985. The Stewartstown Railroad also rehabilitated its own "original" line from New Freedom to Stewartstown, and reopened that in May 1985.

The revived York-New Freedom operation actually started at Hydes, just outside the south side of York in Spring Garden Township, where it interchanged with the Maryland & Pennsylvania. When Conrail started up on April 1, 1976 the "Ma & Pa" had taken over the old Northern Central main line through York, beginning at its original junction east of the passenger station and ending at Hydes, where some industry was located. Thus it acted as an intermediate carrier between the Stewartstown and Conrail or Chessie System (now CSX) at York.

As of 1991, the little Stewartstown Railroad continues to operate the York (Hydes)-New Freedom line under contract, as well as its own line between New Freedom and Stewartstown. Its future, however, is uncertain. Freight traffic has been very thin, and virtually all of it is concentrated at New Freedom. The town of Stewartstown has generated only nominal freight, although regular passenger excursions along this picturesque route have proved popular. The intermediate territory between York and New Freedom, including the once-active shipping points of Glen Rock and Hanover Junction, is essentially now barren of rail-oriented industry.

Suburban Service Reborn

The energy crisis of the 1970s stimulated thinking about alternatives to the Baltimore area's overdependence on automobiles. Particularly following the gasoline shortages in the winter of 1973, "light rail" proposals sprang up like spring crocus. ("Light rail" essentially is an updated version of the old electric trolley, less elaborate and costly than subway lines but nonetheless clean, fast, and efficient.)

The Northern Central main line paralleled Interstate 83 through Baltimore's northern suburbs, and the highway had stimulated intense development along its route. The Baltimore-Cockeysville section of the railroad was still active, albeit on a limited basis, as a Conrail branch serving the quarry at Texas and several lumber dealers. Mass transit proponents viewed the right of way as a readily available corridor through a rapidly growing area.

In March 1974 a report entitled *Initial Feasibility Investigation of Commuter Rail Transit in the Northern Central Right-of-Way* was released. It stated that commuter trains running to Cockeysville were possible in two years at a cost of $40 million. The then-Secretary of Transportation for the State of Maryland, Harry R. Hughes (later governor), turned down the proposal, feeling that buses operating on the highways were cheaper and more practical.

The idea never died, however. Over the next several years, numerous studies were made — so many, in fact, that one reporter was prompted to write "use the (Northern Central) tracks for commuter trains so that we can stop spending money on studies."

But in 1987 Governor William Donald Shaefer became enthusiastic over the idea of a "central light rail" corridor extending south from Cockeysville, passing through downtown Baltimore, and continuing to Glen Burnie in Anne Arundel County. With Shaefer's backing, the project came quickly to life. In early 1990 the state purchased the former Northern Central right of way from Conrail, and work on the project actively started. (Conrail was to continue operating freight service over the line.) Electric train service was scheduled to begin in 1992. Ironically, a new generation of residents along the one-time Northern Central main line protested the planned suburban service as disruptive to the local environment. By then few people were left who remembered the days of dense, steam-powered passenger train operations, coal trains, and through merchandise freights pounding over the line. Few, too, knew or cared that it was the railroad which had created these suburbs.

The old coexists with the new along the Jones Falls valley in Baltimore, the earliest portion of the Northern Central. In April 1990 a Conrail stone train passes the one-time Melvale Mill, still active as a vinegar plant. This line will carry "light rail" electric trains starting in 1992. H. H. Harwood, Jr. photograph.

The Northern Central in 1991

Today, the Northern Central line is barely recognizable as the immaculate two-port railroad that was once instrumental in delivering the vast tonnages of Pennsylvania coal to the export piers at Baltimore. The old main line has been severed in several areas and scrapped; other portions have been reduced to Conrail industrial branches or taken over by independent short lines. Conrail's retrenchments and reroutings have resulted in downgrading other sections of main line, and now only the Harrisburg-Williamsport section retains any semblance of true main line stature.

The 13-mile line between Baltimore and Cockeysville, Maryland, the earliest section of the Baltimore & Susquehanna's route north, currently is a Conrail industrial spur operating primarily for the Genstar Corporation's quarry at Texas, Maryland. The Cockeysville branch (which also technically serves the large Hunt Valley industrial and office park, but handles no business there) was allowed to deteriorate significantly. But as noted earlier, this section currently is being rebuilt as a "light rail" commuter line, with much of the old double track restored.

Between Ashland, Maryland (north of Cockeysville) and the Maryland-Pennsylvania state line, the right of way is now a scenic hiking trail operated as a state park. The beautifully restored Northern Central station at Monkton serves as the park's visitor center. Legally, however, rail service on this section could be restored if ever needed.

From New Freedom to Hydes station on the south side of York, the Stewartstown operates a lightly-used freight service and occasional passenger excursions. The Maryland & Pennsylvania Railroad maintains service from Hydes into York, passing the still-preserved passenger and freight stations and long-closed interlocking tower. Conrail also retains an active presence in York, connecting with the "Ma & Pa" and serving industries on the east side of the city, including the remaining stub of the old Wrightsville branch.

From York to Harrisburg and Enola the old NC main line is an active Conrail branch, although traffic has considerably diminished. Conrail recently downgraded or closed sections of the old Pennsylvania Railroad's system of low-grade freight lines east of Enola, removing most of the trains from the once-busy section between Wago Junction (York Haven) and Enola. North of Harrisburg/Enola, however, the main line still thrives. Also Conrail-owned, this line is single-tracked between Dauphin and Williamsport, but nonetheless is busy and well-maintained, laid with heavy welded rail and well ballasted.

The Williamsport-Elmira section was never repaired after the Agnes floods, and was removed in 1976. North of Elmira the line between Horseheads and Watkins Glen slowly deteriorated from 1974 until 1983 when it was embargoed; it was removed in 1985. From Penn Yan to both Canandaigua and Newark the railroad also has been removed. The roadbed was salvaged over a long period beginning in 1976 and ending in 1980.

The 22 miles between Watkins Glen and Penn Yan, New York remains active as another Conrail industrial branch serving the International Salt Company adjacent to Lake Seneca at Watkins Glen. The Watkins segment is viable and Conrail has assured the industry owners of its continued operation.

A final segment in upstate New York, the Northern Central line between Newark and Sodus Point, was scheduled for abandonment in early 1978 when Conrail was disposing of unprofitable sections all over its system. In an effort to preserve rail service the state of New York and Wayne County governments purchased the line and leased operations to the Ontario Midland Railroad, another short line operator which also had taken over segments of the former New York Central in the Sodus area. The Ontario Midland assumed operations on October 1, 1979.

Originally the Ontario Midland had government subsidies to cushion the erratic business; these ended September 30, 1981. The line's primary customer, the Genesee Brewery at Sodus Point, later closed, making continued viability of the Sodus Point end of the line questionable. But the bulk of the route, the 12.5 miles between Newark and Wallington, New York seems relatively secure, since it forms the only outlet for the Ontario Midland's other lines.

The Fate of the Northern Central Towns

Both the Northern Central and its on-line communities were essentially 19th Century creations and flourished in the period before and immediately after the turn of the century. During this time, the prosperity of one fed the other; local industry, commercial and social activity, and the railroad were intertwined and interdependent. Afterwards many of the towns faced economic reverses and readjustments in varying ways, and with different degrees of severity. Some, dependent on railroad employment for a major part of their livelihood, were directly and irreversibly damaged as the railroad shrank. Some even disappeared. Others were victims of the obsolescence of their industries, depletion of their resources, or loss of markets — all of which, in turn, affected the railroad too. (The most devastating, of course, was the collapse of the anthracite market.) And, almost without exception, both the towns and the railroad were twin victims of the overwhelming shift to motor vehicles. For the railroads it meant severe losses of business and eventual disappearance or, at best, merely a token presence in the community. For the towns it meant both a physical and a social dispersion, a movement away from the community's old focus — the railroad station — to a more scattered collection of shopping centers and industrial parks along the highway.

The process was spread out over many decades (some railroad towns even disappeared in the 19th Century), but began in earnest during the Depression and accelerated in the post-World War II period. When it was over, whether the tracks were still there or not, the towns had irrevocably changed.

A tour of the old Northern Central territory today reveals many different kinds of examples, from towns which have disappeared with barely a trace, to those still healthy but considerably altered in makeup. Happily, there are even a few cases where rail traffic still thrives, although in a far different environment from earlier times.

Any description of the present-day Northern Central communities must begin at the old breadbasket of the railroad: the anthracite country. Many of the more than 100 mines which once made the Shamokin-Mt. Carmel area the "heart of anthracite" for the Northern Central have closed. Some of the largest mines, the Diminick and Glen Burn Colliery (Cameron mine) for example, have been dismantled. Some mines remain open, however, and still ship anthracite east for export to foreign markets in France, Norway, Korea, and Canada.

The economy of Shamokin continues to live on the coal business, although obviously far reduced from its thriving "glory years." And, to a modest extent, there is still a railroad presence in the area. But with the consolidation of the various independent anthracite-hauling railroads into a single Conrail, the number of routes and facilities has been greatly reduced. The remaining coal business moves out of the area over the former Reading lines, and little or none uses the Northern Central branch from Sunbury. As described earlier in this chapter, the branch is now operated as an independent short line.

If Shamokin is still relatively healthy, much less can be said of the rural railroad towns along the old Northern Central Shamokin branch line. The villages began to decline when the mines began reducing output. When dieselization removed the steam facilities, that employment disappeared too. Many of the rural towns along the line — such as Keefer, Deibier, and Reeds — suffered economic isolation and began to deteriorate.

Snydertown is another example. Once a passenger stop midway between Sunbury and Shamokin, it served as a satellite town where both miners and railroad employees lived. In 1892 it was an energetic town of 242 residents, numerous businesses, a railroad station, post office, and several general stores. The majority of the residents were miners and each day they took the trains to their jobs at the Shamokin mines. Today the rail line through Snydertown is lightly used, and had been overgrown with brush during several years of inactivity. The infrastructure of the town has disappeared. There are four residences within a half mile of the railroad, and the highway through town resembles a country road rather than main street. The railroad station is gone, the miners are gone, and for all intents and purposes the town has vanished.

The Lykens area presents somewhat the same mixed picture. As of 1987 Lykens thrives, albeit with fewer operational mines, fewer miners, and no rail facility. The transition that the town of Lykens accomplished is a bright chapter in an otherwise bleak story. Four of the once two dozen mines currently operate at Lykens. Two, the Wilmot Heavy Media and the Meadowbrook Coal companies, actively mine in Lykens and provide economic stimulus for the area. However, dump trucks haul the coal to specialty markets. The railroad depot, now exquisitely restored, stands on the southwest side of town, a stark reminder of the once prosperous "glory years."

The rural towns along the old Lykens line, once completely dependent on rail traffic, failed to make the transition. As examples, both Woodside and Oakdale, once compact "walking towns" where numerous miners lived, have for all intents and purposes ceased to exist. Today they resemble suburban cul-de-sacs rather than the bustling rural railroad towns of the 19th Century.

Along the Baltimore-York portion of the main line are many examples of small manufacturing, rural, or suburban towns; some of them have survived well, some marginally, and some are almost entirely gone. Many of them still have the outward appearance of a 19th Century community, with factory and mill buildings, houses, and commercial structures clearly recollecting a now-vanished way of life.

Parkton, Maryland is one example of a rural town that managed, somewhat painfully, to survive. Located where the railroad crossed the old York Turnpike, its transition from rail to highway orientation had begun years before the railroad's abandonment. The hotel adjacent to the railroad and the former York Turnpike closed some time between 1911 and 1918. (It survives in 1991 as a residence.) When Parkton Local service ceased in 1959, service businesses began to decline. By the time the rail line perished the general stores, the bank, and several mercantile establishments had closed. The off-track Roser feed mill lingered on, but went out of business in 1974. Today one business remains, now dependent on truck service. Many residents remain, commuters who travel to work in Baltimore via the increasingly congested Interstate 83 expressway. But there is virtually no visible clue that Parkton was once a busy railroad terminal with a large passenger station, freight station, tower, yard, turning "wye," and locomotive servicing facilities.

Similarly, White Hall made a partial transition. Beginning with the railroad's retrenchment and continuing through the end of service, businesses, one by one, began to close. Over a period of years the White Hall Bank, general stores, and mercantile establishments all ceased operation. Residents and mill workers moved on. The Federal Paper Company remained, the single survivor of the numerous paper mills located in northern Baltimore County; it used truck service until it too closed. The former White Hall railroad station served a feed supply firm until 1986, when it was destroyed by fire. It was the last vestige of White Hall's connection to the railroad era.

Glen Rock and New Freedom, Pennsylvania are two additional towns that switched to truck as the rail line declined and died. However, numerous firms found the cost of business too excessive and closed. Glen Manufacturing, Coleman Enterprises, and American Machine located in Glen Rock all went out of business. At New Freedom a veneer manufacturer, the Summers Canning Factory, and a large lumber company changed to motor transport. When the Stewartstown Railroad resumed rail operations two of these companies returned to carload shipments for some of their business.

Others were less lucky. For example, Sparks, Maryland, once a vibrant little "tank town" of the early 1900s, no longer exists. The general store, post office, and bank have all closed. The railroad station and most residences are gone. Only the one-time bank building and another stone structure — both of them converted to other uses — remain to mark the location of the former railroad town. Its once proud heritage is now only revealed in faded photographic images. (Today Sparks remains as a community and post office name, but it is not the same Sparks which once clustered around the railroad line. The name migrated a short distance west to York Road, where it was applied to the old town of Philopolis.)

In addition, the towns of Corbett and Bee Tree suffered similar social and physical deterioration. Both towns lost their once thriving businesses, railroad stations, and merchants. People moved away and the towns declined into suburban alcoves. Corbett remains a charming, somewhat isolated pocket of 19th Century rural architecture, but has no economic support of its own.

The list goes on. Many other railroad towns have either perished completely or deteriorated to such a degree that they no longer resemble towns. In Maryland, Hollins (at Lake Roland in Baltimore), Blue Mount, and Graystone (north of White Hall) are gone with little trace of a distinct community. In Pennsylvania some typical brick 19th Century buildings stand around one-time railroad stops at such points as Seitzville, Hanover Junction, Glatfelters, and Brilhart; these, too, however, no longer function as self-sustaining settlements.

York, like the larger cities along the railroad (Sunbury, Williamsport, and Elmira are others), not only has survived the transition from the railroad era, but grows. It also still supplies a relatively impressive amount of railroad traffic. But the nature of the industries and the railroad are substantially different. Many of the older in-town industrial buildings are now vacant or used for other purposes; most of the rail traffic comes from outlying industrial parks or from rail-truck intermodal facilities. York's railroads are also different. Conrail, the Northern Central's direct descendent, still does a fair business on the east side of the city, but otherwise the area is the domain of short lines — the Maryland & Pennsylvania, Yorkrail, and the Stewartstown.

At the northerly end of the Northern Central the story is similar.

Millersburg and Canton, Pennsylvania, as well as Montour Falls, New York, offer more examples of communities that managed the transition from railroad to highway. Currently each town is centered along a major highway which provides both freight and passenger service to the area. Along the railroad line at Millersburg, wood mills, the Millersburg Milling Company, coal yards, and two manufacturing businesses closed. At Canton, Belmar Manufacturing, the Preston Mill, a box company, and numerous other small businesses, one by one, closed their doors. At Montour Falls the production of two specialty steel firms, the Montour Steel Company and the Shepard-Niles Crane and Hoist Corporation, steadily declined. In 1985 the rail line into the town was embargoed; by 1988 it had been removed.

Marsh Hill, Pennsylvania, north of Williamsport, was an example of a pure railroad town which died with the railroad. Originally established in the early 1900s as the junction between the Northern Central and the lumber-carrying Susquehanna & New York, the community lost much of its purpose in 1942 when the S & NY was finally abandoned. Dieselization of the main line came in the 1950s, ending the need for steam locomotive facilities. In 1972 the main line itself was washed out by floods and never reopened. Today the town is virtually unrecognizable as such. The Northern Central-S & NY junction yard is a campground, and none of the ten railroad buildings survive. The twelve houses constructed by the Northern Central for its workers were torn down, burned down, or collapsed. The railroad station, hotels, general stores, and milling industries have long since disappeared. The streets have returned to field. Only a handful of residences remain.

McIntyre, Pennsylvania, located on top of the mountain adjacent to Ralston, declined with even more devastating results. The demise of this coal town is probably one of the most tragic stories of any town along the line. The village was constructed in the 1870s and rapidly became a boom town of 1500 miners. For many years bituminous coal was sent down the mountain to the railroad at Ralston. In the 1890s the town declined as its limited coal resources were depleted; today it does not exist on area maps. The entire infrastructure, rail line, roads, houses, and businesses are gone. One can walk through a densely wooded area and discover an overgrown graveyard, the last remnant of McIntyre. It had taken nature only a few years to reclaim what was once exclusively hers.

Other settlements along the line north of Williamsport have disappeared. In Pennsylvania such stations as Grays (near Ralston), Tin Bridge (near Troy), Ceder Ledge (near Canton), and Fields (near Bodine) no longer exist. Along the New York section towns that have disappeared include Calcianna, Maple Lane, Aloquin, and Kershong.

"Them Days are Gone"

Today the railroad, where it exists at all, is lean and austere. Lineside structures — stations, towers, roundhouses, water facilities, section houses, and the like — are largely unneeded; they have been sold for other uses, allowed to decay, or, usually, have simply disappeared. Gone too are the railroad people. Except at terminals and major operating points, and except for the train crews themselves, few railroaders are to be found along the lines. The section gangs are gone, replaced by mechanized equipment operated by crews who roam systemwide. Diesel locomotives need no intermediate fueling or servicing. Computers, microwave communications, radio, and centralized traffic control have eliminated railroad agents, operators, and clerks. The towns along the line may see trains go by, but the railroad really is not a part of the community any more. Even the locally operated short lines which now serve some sections of line are minimally staffed, and are seldom significant local employers. They have, however, returned local control and local interest to areas which had long ago lost them as railroads such as the Northern Central grew larger, and were in turn taken over by progressively bigger entities.

At present the future of the railroads is ambiguous. A change in public and political attitudes has helped the

railroads to operate more efficiently and compete more effectively. Improving technology has helped to control costs, as have different labor-management relationships. Regular programs of transferring marginal rail lines to low-cost independent short lines (such as was done with several former NC lines) have preserved service where it might otherwise be lost. And often the short lines have recovered business lost to trucks, and stimulated new traffic. But the trucks remain strong competitors and, barring a major petroleum shortage, always will be. The worst declines in rail traffic seem to be over, but significant growth, particularly in the East, is questionable.

In any event, for many of the small towns along the line, the book is closed. And this is where the story ends. It ends with a melancholy sense of loss: the loss of once-stable and thriving communities, and the loss of the transportation line that created, supported, and stimulated those communities. Finally, the story ends poignantly because the demise of the rural railroad towns destroyed a portion of our link with the past. Their failure has denied future generations a legacy of tradition; a tradition of craftsmanship, work ethic, patriotism, and sense of town pride has been lost in the transition to cosmopolitanism. They remain today only as photographic images of obscure places — remnants of the 19th Century which long ago were denied a place in the world of modern existence.

Steam power is long gone and much of the Northern Central is also a memory. But on August 27, 1988, the past miraculously reappeared as PRR K4 Pacific No. 1361 burst out of the south portal of the NC's Howard Tunnel with an excursion train from York, Pennsylvania. The next day, like Brigadoon, it was gone. H. H. Harwood, Jr. photograph.

Appendix 1

LOCOMOTIVE ROSTER AS OF DECEMBER 1858

(From Northern Central Railway 1858 Annual Report with additional data from William D. Edson)

Loco No.	Loco Name *	Type	Builder/C.N./ Date	Cylinders (inches)	Driver Diameter	Weight (pounds)	Comments
1	Herald	0-6-0	R. Stephenson, #7, 9/32	11 x 16	40	26,000	Orig. 0-4-0; RB to 4-2-0; RB to geared 0-6-0; sold '59
2	R. M. Magraw	0-8-0	R. Winans, 4/51	19 x 22	42	57,300	"Camel"; dr. 1880
3	Daniel Webster	0-8-0	R. Winans, 7/51	19 x 22	42	57,300	"Camel"; sold '78 to B & P
4	John S. Gittings	0-8-0	R. Winans, 12/51	19 x 22	42	57,300	"Camel"; sold '78 to B & P
5		0-8-0	R. Winans, 1/52	19 x 22	42	57,300	"Camel"; dr. 1875
6		0-8-0	R. Winans, 8/52	19 x 22	42	57,300	"Camel"; sold '78 to B & P
(2nd) 7	Niagara	4-4-0 (?)	Norris, 7/58	11 x 22	60	36,000	Exploded 1861
8		0-8-0	R. Winans, 11/52	19 x 22	42	57,300	"Camel"; dr. 1880
9	Wrightsville	4-4-0	R. Stephenson, #147, 1836	12 x 18	48	34,500	Orig. WY & G; blt. as 2-2-2, sold '59
10		0-8-0	R. Winans, 2/53	19 x 22	42	57,500	"Camel"; dr. 1875
11		0-8-0	R. Winans, 3/53	19 x 22	42	57,500	"Camel"; dr. 1875
12	Major Whistler	4-4-0	R. Winans, 10/49	14¼ x 18	60	39,100	Dr. 1875
13	General Taylor	4-4-0	B & S Shop, 10/46	18 x 18	48	53,100	Scrapped 1863
14	J. Edgar Thomson	0-8-0	R. Winans, 3/51	19 x 22	42	57,300	"Camel"
15	Samson	4-4-0	R. Stephenson, #152, 8/38	15 x 18	48	43,300	Orig. 2-4-0; cyls. 15 x 16
16	Pennsylvania	4-2-0	Locks & Canals, #40, 1838	11 x 16	48	16,000	Sold 1859; orig. 2-2-0
17	York	4-4-0	Locks & Canals, #48, 3/39	13 x 18	60	41,200	Orig. 0-4-0; Re# 73
18	Wm. H. Watson	4-4-0 (?)	B & S Shop, 3/47	18 x 18	48	53,100	RB to 0-6-0, 8/63
19	Howard	4-2-0	Locks & Canals, #28, 1839	12 x 18	48	36,000	Sold 1859
20	George Winchester	4-4-0	New Castle Mfg., 1846	16 x 20	54	46,500	Dr. 1872
21	Robert S. Hollins	4-4-0 (?)	B & S Shop, 1851	15 x 18	60	43,300	Dr. 1867
22	Baltimore	4-2-0	Locks & Canals, #31, 1837	13 x 18	54	36,500	Orig. 0-4-0 or 2-2-0
23	Chieftan	4-4-0	R. Stephenson, #151, 8/38	15 x 18	60	43,300	Orig. 2-4-0; cyls. 15 x 16
24	Susquehanna	4-4-0	Locks & Canals, #27, 3/39	12 x 18	48	32,000	Orig. 0-4-0; Re# 74
25	R. Clinton Wright	4-4-0 (?)	B & S Shop, 11/52	15 x 22	60	45,000	Scrapped 1870
26	John P. Kennedy	4-4-0	B & S Shop, 11/55	16 x 22	66	58,000	RB to 4-6-0, 1865
27		0-8-0	R. Winans, 1/56	19 x 22	42	60,000	Dr. 1875
28		0-8-0	R. Winans, 1/56	19 x 22	42	60,000	RB 1857; dr. 1876
29		0-8-0	R. Winans, 10/56	19 x 22	42	60,000	Dr. 1876
30		0-8-0	R. Winans, 10/56	19 x 22	42	60,000	Dr. 1876
31		0-8-0	R. Winans, 10/56	19 x 22	42	60,000	Scrapped 12/63
32		0-8-0	R. Winans, 10/56	19 x 22	42	60,000	Dr. 1878
33	John H. Doane	4-4-0	Lancaster, 12/56	16¼ x 22	66	58,000	Re# 59, 7/72; dr. 1878
34	Zenus Barnum	4-4-0	Lancaster, 2/57	16¼ x 22	66	58,000	Re# 60, 7/72; dr. 1881
35	Lancaster	4-4-0	Lancaster, 7/58	16 x 22	60	58,000	Blt. for Sunbury & Erie
36	Gov. Pollock	4-4-0	Lancaster, 7/58	15½ x 22	60	46,000	Blt. for Sunbury & Erie
37	Green Ridge	4-4-0	Wm. Swinburne, 7/58	15 x 22	60	45,000	Blt. for Sunbury & Erie
38	Carbon Run	4-4-0	Wm. Swinburne, 7/58	16 x 22	60	54,000	Blt. for Sunbury & Erie
39		0-8-0	R. Winans, 10/58	19 x 22	42	60,000	Dr. 1874
40		0-8-0	R. Winans, 10/58	19 x 22	42	60,000	Dr. 1877
41		0-8-0	R. Winans, 10/58	19 x 22	42	60,000	Dr. 1877
42		0-8-0	R. Winans, 12/58	19 x 22	42	60,000	Dr. 1879

ABBREVIATIONS: B & S = Baltimore & Susquehanna RR   Dr. = Dropped from roster   RB = Rebuilt   Re# = Renumbered
WY & G = Wrightsville, York & Gettysburg RR

* ***NOTE:*** *After approximately January 1852, the B & S and NC ceased naming locomotives and assigned numbers.*

Appendix 2

LOCOMOTIVE ROSTER AS OF 1873

(From Northern Central Railway 1873 Annual Report with additional data from William D. Edson)

The year 1873 marked the end of "independent" locomotive design and purchasing by the Northern Central. After this date, all new Northern Central locomotives were built to Pennsylvania Railroad standard designs, and the major portion of them were built by the Pennsylvania Railroad's own shops in Altoona, Pennsylvania.

Loco No.	Type	Builder/C.N. Date	Cylinders (inches)	Driver Diameter	Weight (pounds)	Assignment	Comments
1	4-6-0	A. & W. Denmead, 5/59	19 x 22	48	60,000	Balt.	"Camel"; dr. 1875
2	0-8-0	R. Winans, 4/51	19 x 22	42	57,300	Balt.	"Camel"; dr. 1880
3	0-8-0	R. Winans, 7/51	19 x 22	42	57,300	Balt.	"Camel" sold '78 to B & P
4	0-8-0	R. Winans, 12/51	19 x 22	42	57,300	Susq.	"Camel" sold '78 to B & P
5	0-8-0	R. Winans, 1/52	19 x 22	42	57,300	Balt.	"Camel"; dr. 1875
6	0-8-0	R. Winans, 8/52	19 x 22	42	57,300	Balt.	"Camel"; sold '78 to B & P
(3rd) 7	4-6-0	Baldwin, #1038, 2/62	18½ x 22	48	63,000	E-C	Dr. 1880
8	0-8-0	R. Winans, 11/52	19 x 22	42	57,300	Susq.	"Camel"; dr. 1880
(2nd) 9	4-4-0	Lancaster, 10/61	16¼ x 22	60	54,200	E-C	Scrapped 7/85 as #79
10	0-8-0	R. Winans, 2/53	19 x 22	42	57,500	Sham.	"Camel"; dr. 1875
11	0-8-0	R. Winans, 3/53	19 x 22	42	57,500	Sham.	"Camel"; dr. 1875
12	4-4-0	R. Winans, 10/49	14¼ x 18	60	39,100	Balt.	Dr. 1875
(2nd) 13	4-4-0	Baldwin, #1192, 1/64	16 x 24	60	58,100	Balt.	Dr. 1875
14	0-8-0	R. Winans, 3/51	19 x 22	42	57,300	Balt.	"Camel"
(2nd) 15	4-4-0	Wm. Mason, #88, 8/59	16 x 22	60	58,000	E-C	Scrapped 7/88
(2nd) 16	4-4-0	Wm. Mason, #89, 8/59	16 x 22	60	58,000	E-C	Sold 7/88 to A. H. King
(2nd) 17	4-4-0	N. C. Bolton Shop, 12/66	16 x 24	60	59,000	Balt.	Sold 10/88 to E. H. Wilson
(2nd) 18	0-6-0	N. C. Bolton Shop, 8/63	16 x 22	43	54,000	Balt.	RB 12/76; Scrapped 3/93
(2nd) 19	4-6-0	Baldwin, #1033, 2/62	18½ x 22	48	63,000	Susq.	Dr. 1875
(2nd) 20	0-6-0	Bolton Shop, 11/72	16 x 22	43	55,400	Balt.	Re# 3020 '97, scrapped 5/98
(2nd) 21	4-6-0	Bolton Shop, 11/67	17 x 24	54	63,000	Susq.	Dr. 1882
(2nd) 22	4-6-0	Bolton Shop, 12/67	17 x 24	54	63,000	Sham.	Dr. 1886
(2nd) 23	4-6-0	Bolton Shop, 6/66	17 x 24	54	63,000	Balt.	Dr. 1882
(2nd) 24	0-6-0	Bolton Shop, 2/72	16 x 22	43	55,400	Balt.	Scrapped 9/93
(2nd) 25	0-6-0	Bolton Shop, 5/70	16 x 22	43	55,400	Balt.	Scrapped 3/92
(2nd) 26	4-6-0	Bolton Shop, 12/65	17 x 24	54	63,000	Sham.	Dr. 1882
27	0-8-0	R. Winans, 1/56	19 x 22	42	60,000	Susq.	Dr. 1875
28	0-8-0	R. Winans, 1/56	19 x 22	42	60,000	Balt.	RB 1857; dr. 1876
29	0-8-0	R. Winans, 10/56	19 x 22	42	60,000	Balt.	Dr. 1876
30	0-8-0	R. Winans, 10/56	19 x 22	42	60,000	Balt.	Dr. 1876
(2nd) 31	4-4-0	Baldwin, #1218, 3/64	16 x 24	60	58,100	Balt.	Re# '73; re# 129, 1884; sold 5/88 to A. H. King
32	0-8-0	R. Winans, 10/56	19 x 22	42	60,000	Balt.	Dr. 1878
(2nd) 33	4-6-0	Baldwin, #3128, 2/73	18 x 24	54	68,000	Balt.	Re# 1859; scrapped 10/89
(2nd) 34	4-6-0	Baldwin, #3129, 2/73	18 x 24	54	68,000	Balt.	Re# 166; scrapped 9/91
35	4-4-0	Lancaster, 7/58	16 x 22	60	58,000	E-C	Blt. for Sunbury & Erie
36	4-4-0	Lancaster, 7/58	15½ x 22	60	46,000	Balt.	Blt. for Sunbury & Erie

ABBREVIATIONS:

Balt. = Baltimore Division Assignment
B & P = Baltimore & Potomac Railroad — lease
B & S = Baltimore & Susquehanna Railroad
Dr. = Dropped from roster
E-C = Elmira and Canandaigua Division Assignment
E & W = Elmira & Williamsport Railroad
JM & I = Jeffersonville, Madison & Indianapolis Railroad
RB = Rebuilt
Re# = Renumbered
Sham. = Shamokin Division Assignment
Susq. = Susquehanna Division Assignment
SV & P = Shamokin Valley & Pottsville Railroad
URR = Union Railroad (Baltimore) — lease

Loco No.	Type	Builder/C.N. Date	Cylinders (inches)	Driver Diameter	Weight (pounds)	Assignment	Comments
37	4-4-0	Wm. Swinburne, 7/58	15 x 22	60	45,000	Balt.	Blt. for Sunbury & Erie
38	4-4-0	Wm. Swinburne, 7/58	16 x 22	60	54,000	Balt.	Blt. for Sunbury & Erie
39	0-8-0	R. Winans, 10/58	19 x 22	42	60,000	Susq.	Dr. 1874
40	0-8-0	R. Winans, 10/58	19 x 22	42	60,000	Sham.	Dr. 1877
41	0-8-0	R. Winans, 10/58	19 x 22	42	60,000	Sham.	Dr. 1877
42	0-8-0	R. Winans, 12/58	19 x 22	42	60,000	Susq.	Dr. 1879
43	4-6-0	Bolton Shop, 9/72	18 x 24	54	68,150	Balt.	Scrapped 4/86
44	4-6-0	Baldwin, #1035, 2/62	18½ x 22	48	63,000	Balt.	Dr. 1880
45	4-6-0	Baldwin, #1037, 2/62	18½ x 22	48	63,000	Susq.	Dr. 1878
46	4-6-0	Baldwin, #1040, 3/62	18½ x 22	48	63,000	E-C	Scrapped 9/85
47	4-6-0	Baldwin, #1042, 3/62	18½ x 22	48	63,000	Sham.	Scrapped 1878
48	4-6-0	Baldwin, #1043, 3/62	18½ x 22	48	63,000	E-C	Scrapped 5/87
49	4-6-0	Baldwin, #1057, 5/62	18½ x 22	48	63,000	Susq.	Dr. 1875
50	4-6-0	Baldwin, #1059, 5/62	18½ x 22	48	63,000	E-C	Scrapped 8/85
51	4-6-0	Baldwin, #1116, 3/63	18½ x 22	48	63,000	Susq.	Scrapped 1878
52	4-6-0	Baldwin, #1117, 3/63	18½ x 22	48	63,000	Susq.	Dr. 1881
53	0-4-0T	Baldwin, #1075, 8/62	11 x 16	48	36,950	Balt.	Ex-PRR 251; acq. 1863; dr. 1879
54	4-6-0 (?)	N. J. Loco. & Mach., 6/55	16 x 22	48	63,000	Sham.	Ex-SV & P #1; dr. by 187
55	4-6-0 (?)	N. J. Loco. & Mach., 7/55	16 x 22	48	63,000	Sham	Ex-SV & P #2; dr. by 188
56	4-6-0 (?)	N. J. Loco. & Mach., 8/55	16 x 22	48	63,000	Sham.	Ex-SV & P #3; dr. by 188
57	0-8-0	R. Winans, 7/58	19 x 22	43	57,300	Sham.	Ex-SV & P #4, "Camel"; dr. 1880
58	4-6-0	Baldwin, #1067, 8/62	18½ x 22	50	65,000	Susq.	Ex-SV & P #5
59	4-4-0	Lancaster, 12/56	16¼ x 22	66	58,000	E-C	Ex-NC #33; Re# 7/72; dr. 1878
60	4-4-0	Lancaster, 2/57	16¼ x 22	66	58,000	E-C	Ex-NC #34; Re# 7/72; dr. 1881
61	4-4-0	Rogers, #511, 7/54	15 x 20	66	51,400	E-C	Ex-E & W #3; dr. 1882
62	4-4-0	Rogers, #514, 8/54	15 x 20	66	51,400	E-C	Ex-E & W #4; dr. 1882
63	4-4-0	Rogers, #521, 8/54	15 x 20	66	51,400	E-C	Ex-E & W #5; dr. 1881
64	4-4-0	Rogers, #531, 9/54	15 x 20	66	51,400	E-C	Ex-E & W #6; dr. 1882
65	4-4-0	Norris, 6/56	17 x 22	60	54,500	E-C	Ex-E & W #7; dr. 1881
66	4-4-0	Norris, 6/56	17 x 22	60	54,500	E-C	Ex-E & W #8; dr. 1872
67	4-4-0	Lancaster, 6/56	16½ x 22	60	55,100	E-C	Ex-E & W #9; dr. 1882
68	4-6-0	Rogers, #672, 6/56	16 x 22	52	48,700	E-C	Ex-E & W #10; dr. 1881
69	4-6-0	Rogers, #680, 6/56	16 x 22	52	48,700	E-C	Ex-E & W #11; dr. 1884
70	4-6-0	Rogers, #686, 6/56	16 x 22	52	48,700	E-C	Ex-E & W #12; dr. 1884
71	4-4-0	Lancaster, 6/56	16½ x 22	60	55,100	E-C	Ex-E & W #13; dr. 1881
72	4-4-0	Lancaster, 6/56	16½ x 22	60	55,100	E-C	Ex-E & W #14; dr. 1881
73	4-4-0	Locks & Canals, #48, 3/39	13 x 18	60	41,200	E-C	Ex-B & S "York", NC #17
74	4-4-0	Locks & Canals, #27, 3/39	12 x 18	48	32,000	E-C	Ex-B & S "Susq.", NC #2
75	4-4-0	Baldwin, 4/64	15 x 20	60	40,500	E-C	
76	4-6-0	N. J. Loco. & Mach., 6/64	18½ x 22	48	63,400	Balt.	Dr. 1878

ABBREVIATIONS:

Balt.	=	Baltimore Division Assignment
B & P	=	Baltimore & Potomac Railroad — lease
B & S	=	Baltimore & Susquehanna Railroad
Dr.	=	Dropped from roster
E-C	=	Elmira and Canandaigua Division Assignment
E & W	=	Elmira & Williamsport Railroad
JM & I	=	Jeffersonville, Madison & Indianapolis Railroad
RB	=	Rebuilt
Re#	=	Renumbered
Sham.	=	Shamokin Division Assignment
Susq.	=	Susquehanna Division Assignment
SV & P	=	Shamokin Valley & Pottsville Railroad
URR	=	Union Railroad (Baltimore) — lease

Loco No.	Type	Builder/C.N. Date	Cylinders (inches)	Driver Diameter	Weight (pounds)	Assignment	Comments
77	4-6-0	N. J. Loco. & Mach., 7/64	18½ x 22	48	63,400	Balt.	Dr. 1882
78	4-6-0	N. J. Loco. & Mach., 7/64	18½ x 22	48	63,400	E-C	Dr. 1883
79	4-6-0	N. J. Loco. & Mach., 7/64	18½ x 22	48	63,400	Balt.	
80	4-6-0	N. J. Loco. & Mach., 9/64	18½ x 22	48	63,400	Susq.	Scrapped 4/83
81	4-6-0	N. J. Loco. & Mach., 9/64	18½ x 22	48	63,400	Balt.	Dr. 1882
82	4-6-0	N. J. Loco. & Mach., 10/64	18½ x 22	48	63,400	Balt.	Scrapped 12/82
83	4-6-0	N. J. Loco. & Mach., 11/64	18½ x 22	48	63,400	Balt.	Scrapped 1/84
84	4-6-0	N. J. Loco. & Mach., 12/64	18½ x 22	48	63,400	URR	Scrapped 1/84
85	4-6-0	N. J. Loco. & Mach., 12/64	18½ x 22	48	63,400	Balt.	Dr. 1870
86	4-4-0	Baldwin, 11/65	16 x 24	60	58,000	E-C	Dr. 1881
87	4-4-0	Taunton, #361, 8/65	16 x 24	60	58,000	E-C	Sold 1/86; Wilcox RR #1
88	4-4-0	N. J. Loco. & Mach., 4/66	16 x 24	60	58,000	Susq.	Scrapped 3/83
89	4-4-0	N. J. Loco. & Mach., 4/66	16 x 24	60	58,000	Susq.	Scrapped 8/87
90	4-4-0	N. J. Loco. & Mach., 7/66	16 x 24	60	58,000	Sham.	Dr. 1879
91	4-6-0	N. J. Loco. & Mach., 7/66	18½ x 22	48	63,400	Balt.	Scrapped 2/85
92	4-6-0	N. J. Loco. & Mach., 8/66	18½ x 22	48	63,400	Balt.	Dr. 1875
93	4-4-0	Bolton Shop, 3/67	16 x 24	60	59,000	Balt.	To B & P #7, 6/78
94	4-4-0	Baldwin, #1569, 2/67	16 x 24	60	58,000	Balt.	Scrapped 9/89
95	4-4-0	Baldwin, #1571, 2/67	16 x 24	60	58,000	Balt.	Scrapped 12/88
96	4-4-0	Baldwin, #1572, 2/67	16 x 24	60	58,000	Balt.	Scrapped 6/91
nd) 97	4-4-0	Grant, 12/70	16 x 24	60	58,300	E-C	Dr. 1875
98	0-8-0	R. Winans	19 x 22	43	58,000	Balt.	Secondhand; acq. 12/67; sold '69 to C & P 23
99	?-4-?	S. Wilmarth	12½ x 16	43	?	B & P	Secondhand; acq. 12/67; Dr. 1875
100	4-4-0	Bolton Shop, 6/68	16 x 24	60	59,000	Balt.	Re# A & F 51
101	4-4-0	Bolton Shop, 8/68	16 x 24	60	59,000	Balt.	Sold 10/88 to E. H. Wilson
102	4-4-0	Pittsburgh, #18, 5/68	17 x 24	60	62,750	E-C	Scrapped 12/88
103	4-4-0	Pittsburgh, #19, 5/68	17 x 24	60	62,750	E-C	Scrapped 3/89
104	4-4-0	Pittsburgh, #20, 5/68	17 x 24	60	62,750	E-C	To B & P 18 in 1880
105	4-4-0	Pittsburgh, #21, 6/68	17 x 24	60	62,750	E-C	To B & P 8 in 1878
106	4-4-0	Pittsburgh, #22, 6/68	17 x 24	60	62,750	E-C	To JM & I 636 in 1881
107	4-4-0	Pittsburgh, #23, 7/68	17 x 24	60	62,750	E-C	Dr. 1881
108	4-4-0	Pittsburgh, #24, 7/68	17 x 24	60	62,750	E-C	Scrapped 12/89
109	4-4-0	Pittsburgh, #25, 8/68	17 x 24	60	62,750	E-C	Scrapped 9/91
110	4-4-0	Pittsburgh, #26, 8/68	17 x 24	60	62,750	E-C	Dr. 1881
111	4-4-0	Pittsburgh, #27, 9/68	17 x 24	60	62,750	E-C	To JM & I 615 in 1882
112	4-4-0	Pittsburgh, #35, 1/69	17 x 24	60	62,750	E-C	Scrapped 4/92
113	4-4-0	Pittsburgh, #36, 1/69	17 x 24	60	62,750	E-C	Scrapped 1/89
114	4-4-0	Pittsburgh, #37, 2/69	17 x 24	60	62,750	E-C	Scrapped 4/92
115	4-4-0	Pittsburgh, #38, 2/69	17 x 24	60	62,750	E-C	Scrapped 4/90
116	4-4-0	Pittsburgh, #39, 3/69	17 x 24	60	62,750	E-C	Scrapped 5/87
117	4-6-0	Pittsburgh, #40, 5/69	18 x 24	54	69,000	E-C	Dr. 1886

ABBREVIATIONS:

Balt. = Baltimore Division Assignment
B & P = Baltimore & Potomac Railroad — lease
B & S = Baltimore & Susquehanna Railroad
Dr. = Dropped from roster
E-C = Elmira and Canandaigua Division Assignment
E & W = Elmira & Williamsport Railroad
JM & I = Jeffersonville, Madison & Indianapolis Railroad
RB = Rebuilt
Re# = Renumbered
Sham. = Shamokin Division Assignment
Susq. = Susquehanna Division Assignment
SV & P = Shamokin Valley & Pottsville Railroad
URR = Union Railroad (Baltimore) — lease

Loco No.	Type	Builder/C.N. Date	Cylinders (inches)	Driver Diameter	Weight (pounds)	Assignment	Comments
118	4-6-0	Pittsburgh, #41, 5/69	18 x 24	54	69,000	E-C	Scrapped 12/91
119	4-6-0	Pittsburgh, #42, 5/69	18 x 24	54	69,000	E-C	Scrapped 7/91
120	4-6-0	Pittsburgh, #43, 10/69	18 x 24	54	69,000	E-C	Scrapped 1/89
121	4-6-0	Pittsburgh, #44, 10/69	18 x 24	54	69,000	E-C	Scrapped 6/90
122	4-4-0	Bolton Shop, 7/69	16 x 20	60	59,000	Balt.	Sold 7/88 to A. H. King
123	4-4-0	Bolton Shop, 9/69	16 x 20	60	59,000	Balt.	Sold 12/90 to E. H. Wils
124	4-4-0	Baldwin, #1837, 2/69	17 x 24	60	62,750	Susq.	Sold 10/81
125	4-4-0	Baldwin, #1838, 2/69	17 x 24	60	62,750	Susq.	Scrapped 6/87
126	4-4-0	Baldwin, #1848, 3/69	17 x 24	60	62,750	Susq.	Scrapped 12/91
127	4-4-0	Baldwin, #1849, 3/69	17 x 24	60	62,750	Susq.	Dr. 1882
128	4-4-0	Baldwin, #1856, 4/69	17 x 24	60	62,750	Susq.	Dr. 1882
129	4-4-0	Baldwin, #1858, 4/69	17 x 24	60	62,750	Susq.	Scrapped 8/84
130	4-4-0	Baldwin, #1860, 4/69	17 x 24	60	62,750	Susq.	Dr. 1874
131	4-4-0	Baldwin, #1862, 4/69	17 x 24	60	62,750	Balt.	Scrapped 3/90
132	4-4-0	Baldwin, #1871, 5/69	17 x 24	60	62,750	Susq.	Scrapped 1/83
133	4-4-0	Baldwin, #1872, 5/69	17 x 24	60	62,750	Balt.	Scrapped 3/90
134	4-6-0	Baldwin, #2979, 11/72	18 x 24	54	68,150	Balt.	Scrapped 8/95
135	4-6-0	Baldwin, #2980, 11/72	18 x 24	54	68,150	E-C	Scrapped 9/90
136	4-6-0	Baldwin, #2986, 11/72	18 x 24	54	68,150	E-C	Scrapped 12/92
137	4-6-0	Baldwin, #2992, 11/72	18 x 24	54	68,150	E-C	Scrapped 1/94
138	4-6-0	Baldwin, #2987, 11/72	18 x 24	54	68,150	Balt.	Scrapped 5/91
139	4-6-0	Baldwin, #3006, 12/72	18 x 24	54	68,150	Balt.	Scrapped 5/92
140	4-6-0	Baldwin, #3008, 12/72	18 x 24	54	68,150	Balt.	Scrapped 5/93
141	4-6-0	Baldwin, #3022, 12/72	18 x 24	54	68,150	Balt.	Scrapped 4/94
142	4-6-0	Baldwin, #3030, 12/72	18 x 24	54	68,150	Balt.	Scrapped 6/92
143	4-6-0	Baldwin, #3032, 12/72	18 x 24	54	68,150	Balt.	Re# 140 12/92; scrapped 12/94
144	4-6-0	Baldwin, #3196, 4/73	18½ x 22	54	68,150	Balt.	Scrapped 6/92
145	4-6-0	Baldwin, #3199, 4/73	18½ x 22	54	68,150	Balt.	Scrapped 12/94
146	4-6-0	Baldwin, #3203, 4/73	18½ x 22	54	68,150	Balt.	Scrapped 12/92
147	4-6-0	Baldwin, #3205, 4/73	18½ x 22	54	68,150	Balt.	Scrapped 1/94
148	4-6-0	Baldwin, #3220, 5/73	18½ x 22	54	68,150	Balt.	Scrapped 7/94
149	4-6-0	Baldwin, #3248, 5/73	18½ x 24	54	68,150	Balt.	Scrapped 2/88
150	4-6-0	Baldwin, #3249, 5/73	18½ x 24	54	68,150	Balt.	Dr. 1890
151	4-6-0	Baldwin, #3256, 5/73	18½ x 24	54	68,150	Balt.	Scrapped 4/92
152	4-6-0	Baldwin, #3259, 5/73	18½ x 24	54	68,150	Balt.	Scrapped 12/91

By 1873, Northern Central's heavy freight power consisted largely of 4-6-0s such as No. 47, an 1862 Baldwin product. Railroad Museum of Pennsylvania Collection.

Appendix 3

BRIDGES OF THE NORTHERN CENTRAL RAILWAY as of December 31, 1861

This appendix lists all bridges on the NC between Baltimore, Sunbury, and Shamokin, shown in geographical order, beginning at Baltimore. It is included partly to emphasize the unusually large number of bridges which the NC and its predecessors were forced to build, and partly to illustrate the bridge types being used on major American railroads in the Civil War period.

Bridge No.	Name	Type	When Built	Total Length (ft.)	No. of Spans
1	Clipper	Girder	1859	21	1
2	Woodberry	Girder	1854	61	1
3	Jones' Falls	Girder	1856	117	2
4	Melvale	Trestle	1861	161	2
5	Mahogany Mills	Girder	1859	22	1
6	Mt. Washington	Girder	1859	41	1
7	Relay House	Iron	1860	91	1
8	Robinson's	Girder	1859	23	1
9	Lutherville	Girder	1857	15	1
10	Farley's	Girder	1859	16	1
11	Owings'	Girder	1859	16	1
12	Bonn's	Girder	1860	20	1
13	Cooper's	Girder	1851	25	1
14	Cockeysville	Girder	1860	23	1
15	Beaver Dam	Trestle	1861	89	1
16	Western Run	Howe	1861	109	1
17	Jessop's	Girder	1859	20	1
18	Gunpowder	Howe	1845	333	3
19	Ryson's	Girder	1859	20	1
20	Phoenix	Girder	1859	28	1
21	Phoenix Race	Girder	1854	25	1
22	Phoenix Head Race	Girder	1854	30	1
23	St. James'	Iron	1851	55	1
24	Sparks'	Girder	1859	16	1
25	Metcalf's	Girder	1859	20	1
26	Glencoe	Girder	1859	20	1
27	Faunce's	Howe	1845	122	1
28	Clemens'	Howe	1845	152	1
29	Pleasant Valley	Girder	1859	23	1
30	Light's	Girder	1852	93	1
31	Row's Race	Girder	1860	25	1
32	Row's Dam	Howe	1852	72	1
33	Ritze's	Howe	1852	95	1
34	McComas'	Howe	1852	73	1
35	Hunter's	Girder	1851	35	1
36	Whitehall	Girder	1860	22	1
37	Pierce's Mill	Girder	1861	106	2
38	Pierce's Race	Girder	1859	24	1
39	Burns'	Iron	1861	87	1
40	No name	Girder	1855	62	2
41	No name	Girder	1859	62	2

Bridge No.	Name	Type	When Built	Total Length (ft.)	No. of Spans
42	No name	Girder	1855	94	2
43	Parkton	Girder	1853	61	1
44	Parkton	Girder	1853	26	1
45	Turner's	Girder	1853	25	1
46	Walker's	Girder	1860	40	1
47	No name	Girder	1859	21	1
48	No name	Girder	1860	48	1
49	No name	Girder	1860	21	1
50	No name	Girder	1860	55	1
51	E. Walker's	Girder	1856	45	1
52	E. Walker's	Girder	1854	34	1
53	No name	Girder	1854	34	1
54	Bee Tree	Girder	1854	44	1
(55)	(omitted from original document)				
56	No name	Girder	1855	44	1
57	No name	Girder	1853	86	2
58	No name	Girder	1859	32	1
59	Eatons	Girder	1859	25	1
60	Eatons	Girder	1859	26	1
61	Eatons	Girder	1859	35	1
62	Baileys Dam	Girder	1860	40	1
63	Baileys Race	Girder	1860	39	1
64	No name	Girder	1860	24	1
65	No name	Girder	1860	33	1
66	County	Girder	1850	36	1
67	Millers	Girder	1859	21	1
68	Henry Dam	Girder	1855	24	1
69	Henry Race	Girder	1855	24	1
70	Strausburg	Girder	1856	28	1
71	Klienfelter	Girder	1859	22	1
72	Shaffers	Girder	1860	24	1
73	Glen Rock	Girder	1860	51	1
74	Groves	Girder	1855	70	2
75	Groves	Girder	1855	68	2
76	Henrys	Girder	1855	28	1
77	Feltys	Howe	1850	107	1
78	Caslows	Girder	1859	20	1
79	Deals	Howe	1850	110	1
80	Butts	Girder	1859	19	1
81	Rileys	Girder	1855	132	2
82	Smysers	Girder	1859	21	1
83	Gisselmans	Girder	1856	36	1
84	Gladfelter	Howe	1850	199	2
85	Dipyers	Girder	1859	24	1
86	Fissells	Girder	1854	241	1
87	County	Girder	1854	24	1
88	Brillharts	Howe	1850	202	2

Bridge No.	Name	Type	When Built	Total Length (ft.)	No. of Spans
89	Minicks	Howe	1850	212	2
90	Hydes	Girder	1856	40	1
91	Minick Branch	Girder	1859	18	1
92	County	Girder	1854	70	1
93	No name	Girder	1859	20	1
94	Poor House	Girder	1859	27	1
95	Loucks	Girder	1859	77	2
96	No name	Girder	1853	15	1
97	No name	Girder	1848	18	1
98	Cadoras	Howe	1848	336	2
99	No name	Girder	1859	28	1
100	Rutters	Girder	1857	26	1
101	Myers	Girder	1859	27	1
102	Emigs	Girder	1857	26	1
103	Coves	Girder	1856	81	3
104	County	Girder	1861	97	3
105	Pikes	Girder	1856	24	1
106	County	Girder	1848	68	1
107	County	Girder	1848	73	1
108	No name	Girder	1860	23	1
109	No name	Girder	1860	23	1
110	No name	Girder	1859	16	1
111	No name	Girder	1856	40	1
112	No name	Girder	1856	30	1
113	No name	Girder	1855	86	2
114	No name	Girder	1855	61	1
115	No name	Girder	1855	55	1
116	Rhodes	Girder	1855	60	1
117	Hough	Girder	1855	60	1
118	Gut	Howe	1848	274	2
119	Conewago	Howe	1848	326	2
120	York Haven	Girder	1860	25	1
121	York Haven	Girder	1860	26	1
122	York Haven	Girder	1860	31	1
123	Goldsboro	Girder	1855	109	2
124	No name	Girder	1859	14	1
125	No name	Girder	1859	25	1
126	No name	Girder	1860	16	1
127	No name	Girder	1859	16	1
128	No name	Girder	1860	20	1
129	No name	Girder	1859	27	1
130	No name	Girder	1854	24	1
131	No name	Girder	1859	40	1
132	No name	Girder	1859	21	1
133	No name	Girder	1859	39	1
134	No name	Girder	1859	39	1
135	No name	Girder	1859	29	1

Bridge No.	Name	Type	When Built	Total Length (ft.)	No. of Spans
136	Yellow Breech	Girder	1859	37	1
137	Yellow Breech	Howe	1848	168	1
138	No name	Girder	1859	39	1
139	No name	Girder	1859	28	1
140	No name	Girder	1860	24	1
141	No name	Howe	1856	32	1
142	No name	Girder	1856	19	1
143	Conodoquinet Creek	Howe	1856	266	2
144	County	Girder	1856	61	1
145	No name	Girder	1856	20	1
146	No name	Howe	1856	62	1
147	Dauphin (Susquehanna)	McCollum	1857	3846	18
148	Stony Creek	Howe	1857	131	2
149	No name	Howe	1857	18	1
150	No name	Howe	1857	139	1
151	No name	Girder	1857	18	1
152	Clarks Creek	Howe	1857	86	1
153	No name	Girder	1857	14	1
154	No name	Girder	1857	26	1
155	No name	Girder	1857	18	1
156	Halifax	Howe	1857	136	1
157	Halifax	Howe	1857	49	1
158	Halifax	Girder	1857	18	1
159	Millersburg	Howe	1857	614	10
160	Shippes	Howe	1857	34	1
161	No name	Girder	1857	18	1
162	Mahantongo	Howe	1857	263	2
163	No name	Howe	1857	31	1
164	Almers	Howe	1857	27	1
165	Logans Run	Girder	1856	17	1
166	Bordners	Girder	1856	19	1
167	Steepers Run	Girder	1856	21	1
168	Steepers Run	Girder	1856	24	1
169	Fidlers Run	Howe	1856	54	1
170	Sucker Run	Howe	1856	28	1
171	Mahonoy	Howe	1856	218	1
172	Wetsels Run	Howe	1856	18	1
173	Boyles Run	Howe	1856	61	1
174	Hollands Run	Howe	1856	60	1
175	No name	Girder	1856	21	1
176	No name	Girder	1856	18	1
177	No name	Girder	1856	21	1
178	No name	Girder	1856	24	1
179	Shamokin	Howe	1856	309	2

Taken from the Eighth Annual Report of the Northern Central Railway.

BRIDGES OF THE WRIGHTSVILLE LINE
as of December 31, 1861

Bridge No.	Name	Type	When Built	Total Length (ft.)	No. of Spans
1	—	Girder	1857	49	1
2	Bears	Girder	1855	20	1
3	Wademans	Girder	1860	23	1
4	County	Girder	1859	34	1
5	Housers	Girder	1855	24	1
6	Sticklers	Girder	1859	73	1
7	Stoners	Girder	1848	38	1
8	Duncans	Girder	1860	57	4
9	Heistands	Girder	1860	33	1
10	Wilsons	Howe	1845	64	1
11	Deitzs	Girder	1860	55	1
12	Hoovers	Girder	1855	57	1
13	Spotted House	Girder	1857	19	1
14	Garvers	Girder	1861	63	1
15	Beidlers	Girder	1860	71	1
16	Beidlers	Howe	1850	79	1
17	Sticklers	Girder	1854	35	1
18	Sticklers	Girder	1861	76	1
19	Log House	Howe	1850	101	1
20	Mifflins	Girder	1853	93	1
21	Mifflins	Girder	1860	34	1
22	Detwilers	Girder	1861	22	1
23	Detwilers	Girder	1851	162	3
24	Wrightsville	Girder	1861	105	3

Taken from the Eighth Annual Report of the Northern Central Railway.

SELECTED BIBLIOGRAPHY

1. Books, articles and dissertations

Baer, Christopher T., *Canals and Railroads of the Mid-Atlantic States, 1800-1860* (Wilmington, Delaware: Eleutherian Mills-Hagley Foundation, Inc., 1981).

Bogen, Jules I., *The Anthracite Railroads* (New York: Ronald Press Co., 1927).

Burgess, George H., and Miles C. Kennedy, *Centennial History of the Pennsylvania Railroad Company* (Philadelphia, Pennsylvania: Pennsylvania Railroad Co., 1949).

Carter, W. C., and A. J. Glossbrenner, *History of York County* (Harrisburg, Pennsylvania: The Award Press, 1930).

Chalfant, Randolph W., *Calvert Station: Its Structure and Significance*, in *Maryland Historical Magazine*, March, 1979.

Egle, William Henry, *Illustrated History of the Commonwealth of Pennsylvania* (Harrisburg, Pennsylvania, 1876).

Fernon, Thomas S. (ed.), *United States Railroad and Mining Register* (Philadelphia, Pennsylvania, 1867).

Frey, Richard B., *Conrail's Anthracite Lines*, in *Railpace Newsmagazine*, July 1986.

Gilchrist, David T., *The Growth of the Seaport Cities: 1790-1825* (Charlottesville, Virginia: University of Virginia Press, 1967).

Gladfelter, Armand, *Das Siebenthal Revisited: The People of Seven Valleys, Pennsylvania* (York, Pennsylvania: Mehl-Ad Associates, 1981).

Grant, J. Lewis, *The Early Modes of Travel and Transportation* (Auburn, New York: 1889).

Guernsey, A. H., and H. M. Alden, *Harper's Pictorial History of the Civil War* (New York: The Fairfax Press, 1866).

Haupt, Herman, *Reminiscences of General Herman Haupt* (Milwaukee, Wisconsin: Wright and Joys Co., 1901).

Heydinger, Earl J., *Railroads of the First and Second Anthracite Coal Fields of Pennsylvania*, in *Railway & Locomotive Historical Society Bulletin 105* and *107*, October 1961 and October 1962.

Hilton, George W., *The Ma & Pa: A History of the Maryland & Pennsylvania Railroad* (Berkeley, California: Howell-North Books, 1963).

Jones, Chester L., *Economic History of the Anthracite-Tidewater Canals* (Philadelphia, Pennsylvania: John C. Winston Co., 1908).

Kaseman, E. L., *Story of the Susquehanna & New York* (Williamsport, Pennsylvania: Lycoming Printing Co., 1979).

Kelker, Luther R., *History of Dauphin County, Pennsylvania* (Lewis Publishing Co., 1907).

Livingood, James W., *The Philadelphia-Baltimore Trade Rivalry* (Harrisburg, Pennsylvania: Pennsylvania Historical and Museum Commission, 1947).

Lloyd, Col. T. W., *History of Lycoming County* (Topeka, Kansas: Historical Publishing Co., 1929).

Lyle's Official Railway Manual (New York: Linday Walton & Co., 1870).

Meginness, J. F., *Otzinachson: A History of the West Branch Valley of the Susquehanna* (Williamsport, Pennsylvania: Gazette & Bulletin Printing House, 1889).

Meyers, Frank, *The Comanches* (Baltimore, Maryland: Kelly, Piet & Co., 1871).

Moedinger, William, Jr., *From Baltimore to Harrisburg on the PRR*, in *Trains*, August 1944.

Official Guide of the Railways and Steam Navigation Lines of the United States (title varies, including *Traveler's Official Guide...*), various monthly issues, 1880-1971. (New York: National Railway Publishing Co.).

On the Elmira Branch: Single Track Railroading, in *Pennsy Magazine*, 1955.

Pennsylvania R. R. Co., *List of Stations and Sidings, 1900* (Philadelphia, Pennsylvania: Pennsylvania R. R. Co.).

Poor, Henry V., *History of the Railroads and Canals of the U. S. of America* (John H. Schulty and Co., 1860).

Roe, Frederick (ed.), *Roe's Atlas of the City of York* (Philadelphia, Pennsylvania, 1903).

Rosenberger, Homer Tope, *The Philadelphia and Erie Railroad: Its Place in American Economic History* (Potomac, Maryland: Fox Hills Press, 1975).

Rubin, Julius, *Canal or Railroad: Imitation and Innovation in Response to the Erie Canal in Philadelphia, Baltimore and Boston* (Philadelphia: American Philosophical Society, 1961).

Scharf, J. Thomas, *History of Baltimore City and County* (Philadelphia, Pennsylvania: Louis H. Everts, 1881).

Schotter, H. W., *The Growth and Development of the Pennsylvania Railroad Company* (Philadelphia, Pennsylvania: Allen, Lane & Scott, 1927).

Stover, John F. *The Life and Decline of the American Railroad* (New York: Oxford Univ. Press, 1970).

Taber, Thomas T. III, *Ghost Lumber Towns of Central Pennsylvania: Laquin-Masten-Ricketts-Grays Run* (Muncy, Pennsylvania: Thomas T. Taber III, 1970).

Taber, Thomas T. III, *Railroads of Pennsylvania Encyclopedia and Atlas* (Muncy, Pa.: Thomas T. Taber III, 1987).

Taylor, George R., *The Transportation Revolution*, contained in *The Economic History of the United States* (New York: Holt Rinehart, 1951).

Van Horn, Martin K., *The Green Spring Branch — Site of the Lake Roland Electric Railway*, in *The Headway Recorder*, October 1962.

Virtue, G. O., *The Anthracite Combinations*, in *Quarterly Journal of Economics*, April 1896.

Vernon, Edward, *American Railroad Manual* (Philadelphia, Pennsylvania: J. B. Lippencott and Co., 1873).

Walton, Al, *Bottleneck in Baltimore: A History and Operations of the Baltimore & Potomac and Union Tunnels*, in *Rails Northeast*, August 1978.

Ward, James A., *J. Edgar Thomson: Master of the Pennsylvania* (Westport, Connecticut: Greenwood Press, 1980).

Wearmouth, John M., *Baltimore and Potomac Railroad* (Baltimore and Washington Chapters, N. R. H. S., 1986).

Whiteford, Noble E., *History of the Canal System of the State of New York* (Albany, New York, 1906)

Wilson, William B., *History of the Pennsylvania Railroad Company* (Philadelphia, Pennsylvania: Henry T. Coats & Co., 1899).

2. Corporate annual reports

Baltimore and Susquehanna Railroad, 1828-1854.

Dauphin & Susquehanna Railroad & Mining Co., 1848.

Northern Central Railway, 1855-1926.

Pennsylvania Railroad Co., 1861-1967.

Shamokin Valley & Pottsville Railroad, 1859

Susquehanna & New York Railroad, 1904.

Susquehanna Railroad Co., 1854.

Williamsport & Elmira Railroad, 1835.

3. Newspapers

Baltimore American

Baltimore Clipper

Baltimore County Advocate

Baltimore News American

Baltimore Republican

Baltimore Sun

Maryland Journal

Sullivan Review

Susquehanna Press

Williamsport Daily Gazette and Bulletin

Williamsport Sun

York Dispatch

4. Official documents (Federal, State, etc.)

Maryland: *Laws of Maryland*, Chapter 49, 1830, "An Act to Authorize the Baltimore and Susquehanna Railroad to Construct a Lateral Railroad to Westminster..."

Maryland: *Laws of Maryland*, Chapter 72, 1828, "An Act to Incorporate the Baltimore and Susquehanna Railroad Company."

New York State: *Analysis of Port Development at Great Sodus Bay, A Special Studies Series Report* (Rochester, New York, 1971).

New York State: *Laws of New York*, Chapter 4, Sect. 6 (May 14, 1845).

Pennsylvania: *Mine Survey of York County* (Harrisburg, Pennsylvania, 1875).

Pennsylvania: *Pennsylvania Dept. of Transportation, Light Density Line Studies — Final Report*, Feb. 22, 1980.

Pennsylvania: *Pennsylvania Law*, "An Act to Incorporate the York and Maryland Line Railroad," March 14, 1832.

U. S. Interstate Commerce Commission: *Valuation Reports* (Washington, D. C., 1921).

5. Manuscript collections

Civil War Papers, Maryland Historical Society, Baltimore, Maryland.

Confederate Records, Orders and Circulars Issued by the Army of the Potomac and Army and Department of Northern Virginia, C. S. A., 1861-1865, Record Group 109, M921. National Archives, Washington, D. C.

Creamer, David, Diary (1861). Maryland Historical Society, Baltimore, Maryland.

Luetscher, George D., *The Struggle Between Philadelphia and Baltimore for the Trade of the Susquehanna* (MSS, Wisconsin State Historical Library).

McCallum, Brvt. General D. C., *Report*, Record Group 92 — Quartermaster Generals, U. S. Military Railroads. National Archives, Washington, D. C.

Telegrams Collected by the Office of Secretary of War, 1861-1862, Record Group 107, M473. National Archives, Washington, D. C.

INDEX